The Land of the Moors

THE LAND OF THE MOORS

A COMPREHENSIVE DESCRIPTION

BY

BUDGETT MEAKIN

FOR SOME YEARS EDITOR OF "THE TIMES OF MOROCCO"
AUTHOR OF "AN INTRODUCTION TO THE ARABIC OF MOROCCO,"
"THE MOORISH EMPIRE, A HISTORICAL EPITOME,"
"THE MOORS," "SONS OF ISHMAEL," ETC.

WITH 83 ILLUSTRATIONS AND A MAP

LONDON
SWAN SONNENSCHEIN & CO., LIM.
NEW YORK: THE MACMILLAN COMPANY
1901

To

The Prince of African Explorers,

Sir Henry Moreton Stanley,

and to

All Travellers and Students,

who have in the past contributed,

or in the future may contribute

to our knowledge of North Western Africa,

this work is dedicated

by a grateful and expectant

comrade.

PREFACE

OF the shortcomings of neither of my volumes on Morocco am I more painfully aware than of those of the present one, the more so since it will lie within the power of any casual reader on each spot described to find faults which it has been impossible to avoid in a first edition, the correction of which can only be effected by much kind co-operation on their part. My only consolation is that those who know the most will be the least exacting, and I am content to leave my work in their hands.

The mass of material here collected for the first time can be but imperfect, in spite of every care, and its crudity of form could only be removed by re-writing the whole, a task which I would willingly have undertaken could I have added sufficient time to the years which it has already occupied. Another year at least could profitably have been spent in further travel and investigation of native sources, to say nothing of a closer attention to the natural and physical description of the country. I can only hope that by the time an increased interest in the subject calls for a second edition the unavoidable gaps may have been filled by the collaboration of my readers.

It had formed part of my original programme, drawn up twelve years ago, to include in this volume lists of Moorish flora, fauna, minerals, etc., collected from the various writers on these subjects, supplemented by personal observation, but in the absence of popular interest to warrant the additional labour which this would entail, I have reluctantly abandoned the idea, though for the guidance of those who may follow I have appended indications where to seek this special information. All that I have attempted in this section is to bring together some of the most interesting statements of previous writers, corrected as far as possible by my own enquiries, but relying chiefly on the authorities quoted.* This will explain the comparative incompleteness of my treatment of the natural and physical features of Morocco, the drier text-book facts regarding which are easily obtainable. It had also been my intention to give some account of the native tribes and their distribution, but limits of both time and space entirely preclude the attempt in this volume.

It is therefore with some misgivings, and with much regret, that I consign this volume to the printer as it is, satisfied that though my ideal has not been achieved, I have succeeded in preparing for others a work which would have been invaluable to me throughout my Moroccan studies. But the thanks of my readers are due to the numerous foreign residents who have so kindly revised each chapter, some of them too modest to permit my naming them, though without their aid even the

* As every detail will be found in the *Bibliography of Morocco* by Playfair and Brown, I have abstained from giving the titles of works referred to. Most of those to which reference is made will be found critically reviewed in Part III of my volume on *The Moorish Empire.*

I must, however, mention the names of the late Miss Herdman, of Misses Bolton, Jennings and Perston Taylor (Mrs. Rudduck): and of Messrs. F. G. Aflalo, W. H. C. Andrews. Bewicke, Leon Corcos, G. H. Fernau, Lewis Forde, Geddes, Grieve, W. B. Harris, R. L. N. Johnston, Kerr, Daniel Madden, W. Miller, J. M. McLeod, Muir, C. Nairn, C. Payton, C. Reed, R. Spinney, W. Summers, and H. E. White.

attempt I have made at completeness would have been impossible. Similarly I have once more to thank those previously named who placed their libraries at my disposal, as also the several artists whose names are appended to the reproductions of the photographs which they have been good enough to permit me to copy.

On this occasion I avail myself with pleasure of permission to express my thanks by name to Miss Kate A. Helliwell, the gifted and generous friend to whom again I have been indebted for invaluable assistance in revising my work for press.

And in conclusion I would repeat the request that those of my readers in a position to detect any of the defects of this volume would oblige me, and ultimately the public, with their criticisms and suggestions. Letters may be addressed to the care of the London publishers.

HAMPSTEAD, 1900.

NOTES OMITTED FROM CHAPTER V., p. 119, AND CHAPTER XVI., p. 298.

An account of the "Rebellion of Tangier" in 1643, extracted from the Spanish Archives, is given by Primandaie in the *Rev. Africaine*, No. 94, July 1872, p. 313. The ḳaṣbah was seized by night by a wide-spread conspiracy, without blood-shed, the governor and his wife being seized in bed by the archdeacon.

For the Spanish overtures to regain Tangier from the English, see *Life of Lord Clarendon*, vol. iii.

Since Chapter XVI. was printed I learn that the view of a Marrákesh Street, represented on p. 298, was photographed by Mr. A. Lennox.

THE SPELLING OF ARABIC WORDS

IN such a work as this the question of transliteration calls for remark, and its importance has secured its most careful consideration. The system followed is that adopted by the Beïrût missionaries in 1838 and confirmed in 1860, modified to suit the singularly pure and classical Maghribin pronunciation under the advice of several well-known Arabic scholars, and as the outcome of many years of experiment. Since each Arabic letter is distinguished by a dot or other sign, the original form of a word can be at once reproduced; and since Arabic is written phonetically, the correct pronunciation can be arrived at by anyone acquainted with the values of the original characters. In my Morocco-Arabic Vocabulary this system was strictly adhered to—printer's errors excepted,—but in a work intended to present native words in a form for popular use, it has been deemed essential to make certain modifications for the sake of simplicity.*

These modifications have, however, involved me in a maze of difficulties, and have failed to satisfy either party, the pedantic or the slovenly, so critics attack them from either side. I am nevertheless convinced that no other course than a via media would have suited my purpose, and since the publication of *The Moorish Empire* further modifications with this view have been introduced. These I trust will meet some objectors, but I see that the correction of the proofs having taken place partly while travelling in Morocco and America, several discrepancies and variations have been overlooked, for which I must ask my readers' indulgence.

* This does not of course apply to Arabic names of objects, phrases, etc., which are transliterated strictly.

In this volume 'aïn is represented throughout by 'a instead of â, and I have discarded "ee" and "oo" almost altogether, in favour of î, ï, or û, retaining the former only in words of one and two syllables when the accent falls upon it, for the convenience of ordinary English readers; the final yá (î) of adjectives derived from names is also modified to i. The final h is usually omitted from feminine proper names (students will remember that it always follows an unaccented a, becoming t for euphony when the following word begins with a vowel). The accent ´ denoting the initial álîf or "vowel prop" is omitted when the initial vowel is a capital. The dots which distinguish consonants unknown in English (ḍ, ḥ, ḳ, ṣ, and ṭ), the tie-dash beneath letters which can only be approximately rendered by two characters in English (d̲h̲, g̲h̲, k̲h̲); and the sign ' (representing the hamzah), necessary to enable students to identify the words, can always be omitted in popular use; but it is strongly recommended that, with the exception mentioned, the accent be always retained, as on it so much depends. The standard for the names of places is throughout the local spelling (and therefore pronunciation) of the educated classes, to obtain which special pains have been taken.

It is the hope, therefore, of the writer, who has made large concessions in this matter to the views of others, that he has not expended this labour for his own works alone, but that he has provided a standard of spelling which will be adopted by future writers. It may be added that these renderings are in accordance with the principles adopted by the Royal Geographical Society, the Foreign, India, Colonial, and War Offices, the Admiralty, and the Government of the United States, all of which will here find their authority for Moorish names.

(A glossary of common words will be appended to *The Moors*, and a list of place-names to the present volume.)

SYSTEM OF TRANSLITERATION.

Every letter is pronounced: Consonants as in English, and single vowels as in Italian.

a	َ	nisbah, short open sound, as "a" in "can," sometimes "ŭ" as in "but."
á,	ا	álif with nisbah, longer open sound, as "a" in "far."
à,	ى	limálah, or álif maksoorah, as final "a" in "papa" (always final).
b,	ب	bá, as in English.
d,	د	dál, " "
dh,	ذ	dhál, " "
ḍ,*	ض	ḍád, strongly articulated palatal "d."
d̲h̲,*	ظ	d̲h̲á, thick "dh," something like "th" in "thee."
e,	َ or ِ	nisbah or k̲h̲afḍah, short English "e."
ee,	ـِي	yá with k̲h̲afḍah, as in English.
f,	ف	fá, as in English.
g,	ڨ	gáf, " " hard.
g,	ج	jeem, " " " (g).
g̲h̲,*	غ	g̲h̲aïn, deep guttural.
h,	ه	há, as in English.
ḥá,	ح	ḥá, " " like "hh."
i,	ِ	k̲h̲afḍah, as in English.
í,	إ	álif with k̲h̲afḍah, like the first "i" in "India."
î or ī,	ي	yá, as in English.
j,	ج	jeem, " "
k,	ك	káf, " "
ḳ,	ق	ḳáf, peculiar hard "k" low in the throat, as "ck" in "kick."
k̲h̲,*	خ	k̲h̲á, rough guttural sound as in Scotch "loch."

l,	ل	lám, as in English.
m,	م	meem, " "
n,	ن	noon, " "
ṇ,	ً ٍ ٌ or * (doubled final short vowels)	" "
o,	ُ	rofâh, " "
ô,	و	waû, " "
oo,	وُ	" with rofâh, as in English.
r,	ر	rá, as in English.
s,	س	seen, " "
ṣ,*	ص	ṣád, " " hard, like ss.
s̲h̲,	ش	sheen, " "
t,	ت	tá, " "
ṭ,*	ط	ṭá, short palatal "t."
t̲h̲,	ث	t̲h̲á, as in English "three," but rather more of the "t" sound.
u,	ُ	rofâh, as in English.
ú,	أ	álif with rofâh, as in English "up."
û,	و	waû, Continental "u" sound, as in "pull."
w,	و	waû, as in English.
y,	ي	yá, " "
z,	ز	zaïn, " "
',*	ع	'aïn, guttural, far back in the mouth, as in the "baa" of a sheep.

' = ء hamzah, showing that the preceding vowel is cut off short, and a slight pause made.

' shows that a letter is elided in the pronunciation, generally "a" in ordinary conversation. In past participles it is generally "u" which is elided.

· is placed between two letters which *might* be sounded as one, to separate them.

* The correct pronunciation of these letters is only to be acquired from a native; the nearest possible English rendering being given, no difficulty will be experienced in connecting them with their Arabic equivalents.

MODIFICATIONS IN COMMON WORDS

For A'l or él . . .	El.
„ A'llah . . .	Allah.
„ A'meer . . .	Ameer.
„ 'Aráb . . .	Arab.
„ Banî . . .	Beni.
„ Ḳaïd . . .	Kaid.
„ Moḥammed (or more strictly Muḥammad) . . .	Mohammed.
„ Mûlâï . . .	Mulai.
„ Seedî (more correctly Seyyidî)	Sidi.
„ Sulṭán . . .	Sultan.

MODIFICATIONS IN NAMES OF PLACES

For A'sfî . . .	Saffi.
„ E'l Jazaïr . . .	Algiers.
„ E'l Jazîrah . . .	Algeciras.
„ Fás . . .	Fez.
„ Ḥajrat N'kûr . . .	Alhucemas.
„ Jazaïr Zafrán . . .	Zaffarines.
„ Melilîyah . . .	Melilla.
„ Miknás . . .	Mequinez.
„ Rîbaṭ . . .	Rabat.
„ Sibtá . . .	Ceuta.
„ Slá . . .	Salli.
„ Talimsán . . .	Tlemçen.
„ Ṭanjah . . .	Tangier.
„ Tettáwan . . .	Tetuan.
„ Tûnis . . .	Tunis.

THE LAND OF THE MOORS

CONTENTS

PART I.—NATURAL AND PHYSICAL

PART II.—POLITICAL

PART III.—EXPERIMENTAL

APPENDIX

LIST OF ILLUSTRATIONS

A NEW MAP OF MOROCCO

Showing only what has actually been surveyed, with the routes of the travellers to whom we are indebted for the information.

THE LAND OF THE MOORS

PART I—NATURAL

CHAPTER THE FIRST

PHYSICAL FEATURES

"Quantus erat, mons factus Atlas. Nam barba comæque
In silvas abeunt, juga sunt umerique manusque:
Quod caput ante fuit, summo est in monte cacumen;
Ossa lapis fiunt, tum partes auctus in omnes
Crevit in inmensum—sic, di, statuistis—et omne
Cum tot sideribus cælum requievit in illo."

OVID, *Metam* : IV. 657.

The Mighty Atlas.

PHYSICALLY considered, Morocco is marked by few prominent features, but it is rich in the classic Atlas. The possession of this range distinguishes it from the other countries of North Africa, affecting its climate, its productiveness and its natural resources; while the influence upon its people is almost as great. The height to which the Atlas rises in Morocco is sufficient to protect the central and northern portions from the furnace blasts which render summer in Algeria unbearable, and although at certain periods in southern and trans-Atlantic* Morocco, hot winds blow which render life intolerable, in the sheltered northern districts there is only the locally heated air of the cis-Atlantic plains to be agitated.

* Morocco is the poorer for the incorrect application of this epithet to the New World, which is "trans-Atlantican,"—*i.e.* beyond the Atlantic Ocean—not "trans-Atlantic"—*i.e.* beyond the Atlas Mountains.

MT. AFARAZ, CENTRAL ATLAS.

Photograph by the Hon. E. W. Loch.

The snow-caps of the Greater Atlas, melting slowly in summer, feed rivers which, though short and insignificant as rivers go, are plentiful and well distributed. All through the year its narrow valleys and rounded slopes are green with verdure in successive zones, and wherever steps can be built on the hill-sides cultivation is achieved by hardy Berbers. Its rugged peaks among the clouds are traversed only by the goat-herds and their flocks, disputing the scant herbage and the thorny scrub with the Moroccan wild sheep—the 'aôdád,—covered by the eagle, and in some parts yet from time to time the prey of lion or panther.*

Water System.

Although by reason of the unsettled and warlike state of the people, and their constant rebellion against outside influence—including that of the Moors—the Atlantic district of Morocco still remains unmapped and unexplored, certain general state-

Unexplored Region.

* The Greek legend that on the shoulder of Atlas was borne the extended heaven has been explained by the suggestion that the name recalls that of some primitive astronomer: it was a favourite subject for works of art.[1] According to popular mythology, Atlas was a son either of Japetus (Japhet) and the nymph Asia, or of Uranus and Gaia; he was the father of the Pleiades and Hyades His abode on the verge of the unexplored ocean, where all manner of conjecture was possible, and probably also the sight from the sea of snowy peaks, led to the supposition that here was one of the supports of the firmament. The Moors still believe that the flat earth—500 years' journey across—is surrounded first by such a range, Jebel Ḳáf, and then by the encircling ocean, Baḥr el Mohît. According to the ancients, Hercules relieved the weary Atlas of his burden —presumably substituting his own pillars near by,—but afterwards replaced it; a poetical way of saying that he made known two rival "sky-supporting" mountains in the west, but that afterwards the honour was restored to its rightful possessor.

It is related by Ovid[2] that Atlas was a King of Africa who had expelled all strangers from his territory, surrounding his orchard with solid walls and setting a huge dragon to guard it, but that when he opposed the landing of Perseus, he was shown the horrible face of Medusa, whereupon he was transformed into a mountain, as described in the lines quoted.

[1] PAUSANIAS, iii. 18, 7 and v. 18, 1.

[2] *Metamorphoses*, bk. iv., fable ix.

ments may be ventured, subject to correction. The well-defined chain of the maps is the peculiar property of the geographers, although undoubtedly there does run a continuous back-bone, called the Idráren Dráren —"mountains of mountains,"—from Cape Geer ("Strong Wind") on the Atlantic (about 1000 ft. in height) to the Algerian frontier and far beyond. Very little is known of its configuration, except just south of Marrákesh, and at the three points where it is crossed by passes. These are the Bîbáwán, which leads to Sûs, the Gláwi on the route from Marrákesh to Tafîlált and Timbuctoo, and the Ḳ'ṣábî es-Shorfà on the way from Fez to Tafîlált.*

Moroccan Explorers.

De Foucauld, who alone has explored the Atlas generally, has left records of his travels which secure to him the foremost place among Moroccan explorers, and which furnish the only reliable data concerning those parts. Between the points he visited and has so carefully mapped, all detail is mere conjecture, excepting where Thomson worked, † and where several other Europeans have preceded or followed him, myself among the number. Even the famous Miltsin,

* Although several Europeans have crossed by the first-named pass—notably Höst, Lemprière, Jackson, Lenz and Thomson—De Foucauld, Maclean and Harris are the only ones who have followed the second beyond the Kaïd's fortress, while with Caillé, Rohlfs and De Foucauld remain the honours of the third. Lenz calculated the Bîbáwan Pass as about 4250 ft. (1300 m.) above the sea; Hooker made that of Tagharat at the head of the Gheghháya valley, 11,400 ft. (3500 m.); De Foucauld reckoned the Gláwi or Teluet Pass at 8640 ft. (2634 m.) and that of the Ḳ'ṣábî es-Shorfà, 7160 ft. (2182 m.). By way of comparison it is of interest to notice the heights of the Mont Cenis Pass—the highest in Switzerland—over 10,000 ft. (3000 m.), and that of St. Bernard over 8000 ft. (2500 m.). In height and form the Atlas mountains strongly resemble the Alps, but when viewed from the plains, (1000 to 1500 ft.) so much lower a standpoint than is to be found in Switzerland—the lowest parts of which are already high above the sea,—they are far more majestic.

† Unfortunately Thomson's instruments for taking altitudes were found on his return to be inaccurate, so that his figures cannot be relied upon.

pointed out by Washington,[1] is not to be identified by that name, and it was only by investigation on the spot that I ascertained the monarch of the range to be Mṭ.-Tag͟harat, the highest peak of which is called Tûbkál.[2] This has not as yet been scaled by Europeans, though I have been some way up it; and Thomson, standing on the neighbouring height of Likimt,—which he found to rise 13,150 feet,—estimated this "magnificently rugged peak" to reach at least 15,000 feet, possibly more.*

The Highest Peak.

Gradually dropping off in height to the south, the line of peaks divides Morocco proper from the fertile but undeveloped province of Sûs, inhabited almost entirely by Berbers, the ports of which, Agadîr, Massa, A'rkshîsh and Assáka, are closed to trade. Its rivers, the Sûs, the Massa, the Nûn and the Drâa, are slightly known at their mouths, but Gatell, Lenz and De Foucauld alone have told us somewhat of its inland mountains and plains, the value of which has without doubt been much exaggerated.[3] Of its towns, only Tarudant, the capital, is known, and that but slightly. Ilîgh and Talent, the native head-quarters, are familiar to us merely by name, their exact position being undetermined. To the south an unknown course is followed by the Drâa, which rises somewhere south of the Central Atlas, and, except along the coast, marks the southern limit of all Moorish claims of suzerainty, though the actual rule of the Sultan hardly reaches the Nûn.

Sûs.

* Thomson, however, makes the mistake of calling it by the name of a lower mountain which from his point of view lay beyond, Tamjurt. De Foucauld thinks that perhaps the Jebel 'Ayáshî, half way between Fez and Tafîlált, may ultimately prove the highest of the whole range, but certainly Mt. Tag͟harat crowns the Great Atlas, as this lofty section is justly styled.

[1] R. G. S. Journal, vol. 1., 1831, p. 123.

[2] See chapter xxiv.

[3] See chapter xix.

Beyond the Central Atlas to the southward there would appear to run an irregular lower range, which has been called the Lesser Atlas, following to some extent the same direction, often indistinguishable from the more important range, which maintains its character, although diminishing in height towards the Algerian frontier. To the south of this again, already on the borders of the desert, lies the date-growing district of Tafîlált, the centre of commerce in those parts, and the home of the reigning dynasty. Further off, away to the south-east, many days' journey across the desert, lies the dependent oasis of Tûát, coveted by France as lying between possessions to the North and West, but with this exception Moorish allegiance on that side grows indefinite, being chiefly religious, for the people are self-governing, mutually destructive Arabs and Berbers.

Tafîlált.

To the North of the principal chain, Central Morocco is defined by a series of transverse spurs running out to the coast towards Rabat, dividing the northern portion of the Empire into what were once the kingdoms of Marrákesh (Morocco) and Fez. Here, as elsewhere throughout the mountainous districts, the Berbers hold sway, and even an imperial army can only pass through by fighting. This part is therefore almost entirely unknown; only De Foucauld and some of the European drill-instructors of the native army having traversed it from Tádla to Mequinez. This district has been described as that of the Medium Atlas, and it is to the south of it that De Foucauld thinks the highest peaks will one day be discovered.

Central Morocco.

To the west of these spurs, stretching along the Atlantic coast till they reach the ridge which runs out to Cape Geer, lie the extensive series of plains and uplands known as the Ḥaûz, or Central Provinces. Their distinctive names are—as one travels from north to

CROSSING A MOORISH RIVER (LEKKÛS) WITH GRAIN.

Photograph by R. J. Moss, Esq.

south—Támsna, Sháweea, Dukálla, 'Abda, Shiádhma, and Ḥáḥá, with Shrágna and Raḥámna lying inland from the last three. From these three the northern third, Sháweea and Támsna, are divided by the principal Moorish river, clear and deep, the Um er-Rabî'a, ("Mother of Grass"), which debouches by Azammûr; a river which has often been the boundary between contending dynasties and rival sovereigns. To the early Arabs the whole of Morocco was known as Sûs, the Um er-Rabî'a forming the division between Sûs el Adná or "Hither Sûs" to the north, and Sûs el Aḳṣà or "Further Sûs" to the south. The Melwîya was the frontier to the east.[1] Further north, the Bû Ragrág* ("Father of Glittering"),—which once offered shelter to the Salli rovers, and had been the southern limit of the ancient Mauretania—forms a boundary to Támsna, and bears off the waters of the central ranges on their western side. The red-streamed Tansîft, which, with its tributary the N'fees, drains the Great Atlas north and south of Marrákesh, portions off the southern third of these central plains, dividing 'Abda from Shiádhma. These three are the only rivers of note in this section. The red colour of the Tansîft is due to the admixture of ferruginous ochre[2] in the argillaceous soil of the district through which its middle third flows. In this province, consequently known as Blád el Ḥamrá or "the Red Country",† even the houses, built of the soil, are red, and the women dress by contrast in dark blue, their forefathers having been transplanted from Sûs.‡

Plains and Rivers.

* Literally Raḳráḳ, otherwise translated "Ravines." Formerly Wád Asmîr.

† Similar to the soil around Granáda, of which the Moorish palace is built, in consequence known as "El Ḥamrá," "the Red"—(Alhambra). The same soil may be seen between Gloucester and Malvern.

‡ The usual clothing of Central Morocco is white; blue is favoured towards the desert.

[1] Raôḍ el Ḳarṭás, p. 12. [2] Schousboe, p. 7.

These are rich and fertile districts, peopled chiefly by Arabs—though with a Berber admixture along the foot of the Atlas,—in which Europeans may travel with safety in time of peace; but unless one is bound from the coast to Marrákesh,—situated in Raḥámna, on a great plain of the Blád el Ḥamrá,—or to the mountains beyond, there is not much in them to attract the traveller. The only other inland town of importance in Central Morocco is Tádla, lying among the hills to the east, on the Um er-Rabî'a, beyond the reach of Europeans. The remaining towns, like El Ḳalâ and Zettát, are but insignificant half-ruined clusters of houses, under the protection of ḳaṣbahs, like feudal castles, dotted throughout the land, within which the villagers can crowd for protection. The condition of their settlements, the frequent ruins, the scattered villages, the nomad encampments and the vast uncultivated areas, oppress the thinker with a sense of desolation as these roadless provinces are crossed, hour after hour, day after day, on horse or mule.

Central Provinces.

At intervals, between the plains, rise groups of hills, like those of Jabilát ("Mountlets") parallel to the Great Atlas, which cut off the Marrákesh plain or the Jebel Akhdár ("Green Mountains") of Dukálla and the Jebel Ḥadeed ("Iron Mountain") in 'Abda, so-called from the ore it contains, once rudely worked.* A peculiarity of the plains near Marrákesh is the presence of "camel-back" flat-topped hills of limestone and marls, with tabular masses of chalcedony, rising to some 1850 ft., or about 200 ft. above the general level. Then through Sháweea,† generally following the coast, is a long line of bold escarpments, evidently once the limit of the ocean, whose up-raised bed, of the

Physical Features.

* 2470 feet (Thomson). See illustration, p. 29.

† Anglicé "abounding in sheep."

later tertiary period, may yet be studied in its nakedness along the road from Mogador to Mazagan. Salt lakes exist between Marrakesh and Saffi, in 'Abda, fed by saliferous springs in the surrounding red shales, while many of the smaller streams from the Atlas are salt.

THE MOROCCO COAST NEAR SAFFI.
(Province of Abda.)
Photograph by Edward Lee, Esq.

Fertile Strip.

For some distance back from the coast runs a specially fertile strip, chiefly confined to this old sea bed, beyond which the all but treeless land is sadly denuded and barren, though rich when worked. In addition to occasional wells and springs, these provinces are here and there provided with cisterns (mitfeeahs), either built of masonry or excavated in the solid rock, but too often they are in a crumbling or neglected condition. The lack of trees is one of the most regrettable features of the Moroccan plains, but trees to the mind of the natives mean shelter for robbers, and the Arab is only brave when the coast is clear. Nevertheless these plains afford good sport with greyhounds and barbs, jackal, wild boar, gazelle, and fox being easily found, with partridges and hares in abundance, not to speak of the greater and lesser bustard, the golden grouse, the quail, and plovers of many sorts, for which some of the kaïds keep hawks.

Sport.

Another local interest in the southern portions of these Central Provinces, and in the Lower Atlas, is the presence of remains of pre-historic man, whose caves, stone implements and other relics are awaiting systematic investigation. Some few have been visited, as by the side of the Tansîft and above Marrákesh, but this is a field as yet almost untouched.*

Of modern man the most important settlements are on the coast, attracted by foreign trade; Rabat and Salli on the North, then Dár al Baïḍa ("White House")—or, as it is also known, Casablanca, —Azammûr, Mazagan, Saffi and Mogador. All of these, save Salli and Azammûr, exist as outlets mainly for the farm or agricultural produce of the central plains, and, with the same exceptions, each contains a European colony. Of them all Mogador alone has a passable harbour, sheltered by an island, that of Mazagan ranking next, though at several unoccupied points exist magnificent natural harbours, notably at Waladîya, between Mazagan and Saffi. Saffi, Mazagan and Casablanca are open roadsteads, sheltered only from certain winds, that of Saffi being very treacherous. The bar between Salli and Rabat has closed the Bû Ragrág to all but the smallest of local craft, and is often impassable even to lighters. Such is also very much the case with the Um er-Rabî'a,

Ports.

* The only serious effort in this direction has been made by Dr. Talcott Williams of Philadelphia, the results of whose researches and collections he is embodying in reports to scientific institutions in America.

and though probably under a European government all three of these rivers would be utilized for navigation, at least with barges, no use is now made of them, and the lack of bridges renders them a serious obstacle, instead of an aid, to internal communication.

Northern Morocco.

Although that portion of Morocco just described is at present of the greatest commercial importance, and under an enlightened rule would in all probability rank first in most respects, it is the northern section, stretching from Salli to the south of Oojda on the Algerian frontier, which politically takes the foremost place. Close to its southern border, which follows the foot of the Atlas, is the metropolis, Fez, with, at a short distance, Mequinez, third among the Moorish cities: on its northern shore is Tangier, the diplomatic capital, and on its Mediterranean coast are the Spanish Possessions, Ceuta, Velez, Alhucemas, Melilla and the Zaffarines.

The Rîf.

The greater part of Northern Morocco, the mountainous district known as Er-Rîf, stretching from the south side of the straits of Gibraltar—Baḥr ez-Zoḳáḳ ("the Narrow Sea")*—to the frontier of

* Idreesî says the Mediterranean was at first but an inland lake, and that the people of Morocco and Spain were constantly at war till Alexander caused a canal to be dug, twelve miles long and six wide, the rush of the sea through which has widened it to the adjoining hill-sides.[1] More modern theorists have pointed to the grave-like pits on the right of the lane to the Marshán at Tangier as part of a pre-historic cemetery, the remainder of which is to be sought for on the opposite shore, but they are evidently no more than tan-pits. 'Abd el Wáhid[2] tells us that the chronicles available in his day—the time of William Rufus—reported a bridge thrown across the straits by the Romans, of which the people of Tarifa could see the remains in calm weather.[3] But what is most remarkable in this author's statements is that from the Straits "the country turns towards the south, to arrive at Abyssinia and India," he being apparently aware of the Cape route long before it was dreamed of in Europe.

[1] p. 198. [2] p. 258.

[3] See also EL MAS'ÛDI *tr.* BARBIER DE MEYNARD, vol. ii., p. 373.

Algeria, is inhabited by untamed Berbers, and is no better known than any other mountain region of Morocco,* very few Europeans having even ventured to make the journey from Fez, viâ Táza, to Tlemçen, along the valley to the south of it but the province of El Ghárb ("the West") to the west and north of Mequinez, once traversed by Roman roads, is the only well-known part of Morocco.

NORTH MOROCCO COUNTRY.
(Environs of Tangier.)
Photograph by Dr. Robert Brown.

This district has an open port of its own, Laraiche, built at the mouth of a considerable stream, the Lekkûs; but the ports of Azîla, between it and Tangier, and of Mehdîya, between it and Salli, are *El Ghárb.*

* A most useful summary of all available information with regard to "*La dernière partie inconnue du Littoral de la Méditerranée, le Rîf,*" was published in 1888 by Henri Duveyrier, who always took great interest in things Moroccan.

closed. At the latter point there flows into the sea one of the most important rivers of Morocco, the Sebû, which drains the Atlas south of Fez, and the south of Er-Rîf. *

Another noteworthy physical feature is the presence along the coast, between Laraiche and Mehdîya, of two long, shallow fresh-water lakes, divided from the sea by sand-banks. These are fed by no important river, though the Sebû runs not far from the greater of the two, called Merja' Rás ed-Dûra, some twenty miles in length, but only one and a half in width; the smaller, Merja' Mulai Buselham, is only about five miles long. On the other side of the Sebû, to the south of its estuary, is the so-called Forest of Ma'môra, which, from what I have seen in skirting it, would appear to contain scrub and brushwood rather than trees.

Coast of the Straits.

The small towns of El Ḳaṣar and Wazzán are the only centres of importance inland, but to the north, beyond the Gh̲árb proper, is Tetuan, the only Moorish port on the Mediterranean.† On the same neck of land stand Jebel Mûsà, about 2800 ft. (856 m.),‡ the southern Pillar of Hercules,—though Ceuta has an equal claim to this distinction—and Cape Spartel, § the north-west point of Africa, on which rises the only light-house in Morocco (312 ft.), with Tangier "in the streights' mouth" between

* Reckoned by Campouspas 550 kilometres in length (330 from the mouth to near Fez), with a fall up there of 1 in 1000, reduced to half that near its mouth, where he gives the width in flood time at 300 metres, at the ford near Ḳarîat el Habásî, 135 metres, and near Fez 30 metres, with a depth of from 6 to 8 metres at the mouth.

† The country round Tangier and Tetuan used to be called Bl‌ád el Habaṭ.

‡ The height of the neighbouring round summit has been estimated at 1560 ft.

§ The height of Gibraltar signal station is 1255 ft., and of O'Hara's Tower, 1408 ft.: that of the hill behind Spartel is 1066 ft.

them. At the foot of Jebel Mûsà lies the little "Parsley Island"—Perejil in Spanish—which has from time to time been coveted by various nations as a coaling station.* Somewhere on the coast which sweeps away to the south from Spartel, must have been the Garden of the Hesperides, identified by many with Laraiche.

This brief outline of the most important physical features will serve as a setting for subsequent detailed pictures. The extent of Morocco is calculated by geographers at 220,000 square miles, more or less, against 184,000 square miles in Algeria, and 45,000 in Tunis.

Climate.

The climate of Morocco must, upon the whole, be considered good, and there is no occasion to challenge the verdict of Jackson[1] that it is "healthy and invigorating; from March to September the atmosphere is scarcely ever charged with clouds, and even in the rainy season, from September till March, there is seldom a day wherein the sun is not seen at some intervals. The inhabitants are robust, and some live to a great age." The mountainous districts, if developed according to European ideas, would undoubtedly become great summer resorts, and though on the plains the heat does grow intense from June to August, as judged by English standards, it is a dry and not unhealthy heat. There are few parts in which English families could not spend the whole twelve months with comfort if surrounded by the conveniences to which they have become accustomed. As it is, in Tangier and Mogador frequent sea-breezes rendert he climate bearable, with

* It was occupied by England during the American War of Independence, and in 1808 a garrison was sent over from Gibraltar. An ineffectual attempt to secure it surreptitiously by quietly hoisting the Spanish flag was made in 1887, since which time the Moors have kept a guard there. (See *The Moorish Empire*, pp. 188, 351.) It has an anchorage with a depth of 20 fathoms close in, and it rises to about 243 ft. above sea-level.

[1] p. 10.

due precautions, throughout the summer, warm though it may seem to those who have not lived in the tropics.

As winter health-resorts, Tangier and several other parts would soon spring into favour if developed, and already the first-named has an established reputation for those who suffer from chest complaints.* The best times for travelling are spring and autumn, summer being too hot, and the rains in winter rendering the tracks in many parts impassable in the absence of roads, to say nothing of bridges. The districts along the coast, known as Sáhel, flat and sandy, and the stony parts called "blád ḥarsh," are traversable at all times, but the loamy agricultural districts, "blád teersh," and the slopes of the hill-sides, soon become impassable when wet, while swollen rivers sometimes keep one waiting for days. Winter travellers must therefore be prepared to put up with a good deal, as I know to my cost,[1] for travel of any description in Morocco is rough, though safe enough on the plains. The mountains still invite explorers rather than tourists.

Seasons.

Reference has already been made to the pre-eminent position of De Foucauld among those who have attempted to explore Morocco. Entering the country at Tangier in 1883, he was one of the first Europeans to visit Sheshávan, and from Fez made an excursion to Táza. Then from Mequinez he found his way by a record journey through the mountains viâ Tádla to the plain of Marrákesh, whence, without approaching the capital, he turned south over the Gláwî Pass to the Dra'a, and crossed Sûs to

De Foucauld's Exploration.

* According to Rohlfs,[2] from October to February the N. W. wind predominates; February, all points at once; March, north; April to September, east, S. E. and south; on coast, sea breeze 9 a.m. to afternoon, then S. E., also cool.

[1] See chapter xxi. [2] p. 33.

Agadîr, arriving at Mogador in a condition which made it hard to recognise him as a European. From Mogador, undaunted, he turned back in 1884, through Sûs to the Dra'a by another route, following the southern side of the Atlas till, north of Tafîlált, he struck the road thence to Fez, by which he recrossed the range, immediately turning eastward from Ḳ'ṣábi es-Shurfà to Dibdû, Oojda and Tlemçen.

*Other Authorities.**

Though Caillé (1828) and Rohlfs (1862) made the journey, one from, and the other to, Tafîlalt viâ Fez, and Harris and Maclean (1894) did so from Marrákesh; and though others passed through Sûs to Timbuctoo, the magnificent achievement of De Foucauld remains unapproached.† Erckmann (cir. 1880) and Le Vallois skirted the Central Morocco mountains, while Hooker (1871) and Thomson (1889) confined themselves to the Great Atlas. Disguised as "Kaïd Ismaïl" Joaquin Gatell had, in 1865, accomplished a journey in Sûs, and still remains our best authority for that region, giving both maps and plans.

* The works of all these travellers are dealt with in Part III. of *The Moorish Empire*.

Timbuctoo Expeditions.

† The first European known to have reached Timbuctoo was a French sailor, Paul Imbert, who, having fallen into the hands of the Moors when shipwrecked on their coast in 1630, found his way there as a slave, and as he died in slavery his story has never been told. In 1781 two Frenchmen reached Morocco from the Senegal and Guinea, being escorted from place to place.[1] Major Laing made the attempt in 1826, from Tripoli, and successfully reached his destination, but was murdered on his way back. Caillé was the first to return. In 1850 Panet made the journey from the Senegal to Mogador, and in 1854 Dr. Barth was also successful by Major Laing's route. The Rabbi Mardokhaï Abi Sarûr made the journey in 1857, the results of his observations being published by M. Beaumier, then French Consul at Mogador. Lenz followed in 1881, and he again was successful. "Robert Adams," who first laid claim to this honour, in 1816, turned out to be one Benjamin Rose, who had never been there![2] In 1823 Belzoni attempted to reach Timbuctoo from Morocco, but was turned back from Fez, and died while making another attempt from Benin.

[1] LEMPRIÈRE, p. 347. [2] See *The Moorish Empire*, pp. 462 and 531.

2

No other modern travellers in Morocco have deserved the name of explorers, although Capt. Colville and his wife made a plucky trip from Fez to Tlemçen (1880), and several have imagined they were breaking new ground. Nor are the results of any other journeys of equal value in proportion, except those of Hooker and Thomson, most travellers having been unprovided with instruments and taking few observations, their notes having often been, as in the case of Rohlfs, extremely meagre. Dr. Lemprière, who, in 1791, went to attend the Sultan's son at Tarudant, added not a little to our knowledge of that part; and so did Dr. Buffa, sent on a like errand to Fez in 1806; and Capt. Beauclerk, who accompanied another doctor, summoned to the Court at Marrákesh in 1826. Several have lost their lives in attempting to enter the Berber strongholds, such as Davidson, who was murdered after having penetrated as far as Wád Nûn in 1836, leaving a fair itinerary, but no map; and Douls, who barely escaped the same fate in Sûs in 1887, and finally perished two years later on his way to Tafîlált.

Early Travellers.

The most important contributions of previous travellers come from the Redemptionist Fathers, especially Nolasquez and Busnot, 1704—1712. Their journeys were almost invariably over the routes from the ports to the royal cities, afterwards traversed so often by foreign embassies, the early recorders of which, as Windus in 1721 and Braithwaite in 1728, added not a little to our knowledge of the country. The Christian slaves, with the exception of Mouëtte (1681) and Pellow (1735), did little to improve our notions of Moroccan geography, but the latter left itineraries to distant parts, which, though not always accurate, at least attest the genuineness of his narrative. Most authors of this class were concerned more deeply with the hardships of their lot than with the collection of information. Wrecked seamen, such as Adams (1810), Riley (1815), Puddock (1818) Cochelet (1819) and Jannasch (1886) have done better.

The early maps are chiefly from the descriptions of Leo Africanus and Marmol, and up to the beginning of the present century the majority of the names on the North African maps were from these sources, with a few from Idreesî, while their lists of towns

Maps.

AN ATLAS VALLEY.
(The Ghegháya.)

Photograph by Dr. Rudduck.

long since lost sight of were gravely and unsuspectingly quoted by Richardson as late as 1859! Of the many modern maps, that of Beaudoin,—prepared for the French War Office in 1848, on account of the ignorance disclosed by the war of 1844—chiefly compiled from native information and itineraries, though perforce inaccurate, is valuable; but we have yet to see the production of a map which shall only embody what is positively known, or at least distinguish between that and mere borrowed belief.* Even the English War Office maps of 1889 and 1890 are replete with glaring errors.

The most detailed maps of Morocco are Renou's;[1] that of Beaudoin, referred to; Ch. Lasailly's[2] (1888 etc.), a most useful compilation; and Guido Cora's;[3] the last two of which include the work of Tissot and De Foucauld. A more recent French publication is the map by De Flotte de Roquevaire, † well-executed and comprehensive. In addition to the travellers named, the most important contributors of route maps have been Trotter (Tangier to Fez, 1880), Marcet (Mazagan to Marrákesh and Mogador, 1882), and Martinière (Tangier to Wazzan, Mequinez and Fez, 1887). The others have either not covered new ground, or have left data too inaccurate and fragmentary to be of much value. Tissot's archæological map of the Roman province, however, is of the front rank. ‡

Methods of Exploration.

As for the most practical methods of exploring Morocco, all the foremost travellers, "Ali Bey", Caillé, Davidson, Rohlfs, Gatell, Lenz, De Foucauld, Douls and Harris, have declared the disguise of a native indispensable, § a declaration which I mostly heartily endorse from personal experience. The European, as De Foucauld points out,[4] "is not interfered with or killed as an infidel, but as a spy." The

* The map accompanying this volume is an attempt in this direction.

† Pub. by Barrère, Paris, 1897.

‡ A series of important trigonometrical observations on the route from Tangier to Fez and Mequinez was made by MM. Des Portes and François in 1878, and is recorded in the Bul. Soc. Géog. of Paris, Vol. xv., p. 213 etc. (B. Mus., Ac. 6035).

§ "Ali Bey" posed as a Turkish philosopher (see portrait in *The Moorish Empire*, p. 448); Lenz as a Turkish Doctor "'Omar bin 'Ali"; De Foucauld as a Jerusalem Rabbi; the others mentioned as natives of Morocco.

[1] In Vol. viii. of the Exploration Scientifique d'Algérie, 1846.

[2] First issued in "Kerdec-Chény's" Guide, afterwards separately several times.

[3] Cosmos, vol. x., tavola vi., 1890—91.

[4] p. xiv.

few who have attempted exploration as Europeans have been compelled to do so with escorts which have most effectually curtailed their expeditions, rendering them objects of suspicion to the natives, to whom such escorts are foes. The more insignificant the character assumed, the less the attention attracted, the greater the chance of success. "Ali Bey" alone attempted to travel in style, but his departure was at last very like flight. Caillé and Rohlfs became actual beggars, although the latter, as a surgeon, could always subsist, and the lining of his Fez cap concealed a five-pound note. It is of the utmost importance that the traveller should have some ostensible object before him, and some "visible means of subsistence," which the natives can appreciate, wherewith to disarm suspicion and appease the curious. For this purpose medicine or trade is best, but some Europeans have penetrated far as public entertainers, even to the Atlas fastnesses.

Disguise.

If a part is to be played, thorough metamorphosis is needed, rather than disguise. Half measures profit nothing: a man must either without qualms of conscience throw himself into Islám, prepared to go any length, or he had better make no pretence, in which case he will avoid either testifying to a belief in Mohammed, or conforming to Mohammedan rites and ceremonies. Clad as a native, a European acquainted with the people and their language may travel freely and unconstrainedly through all the open parts of the country without attracting attention, yet without concealing either his nationality or his creed from those with whom he converses. This is what I have myself done with the best of results, having often found it difficult to persuade those whom I met that I was in very deed a foreign Christian. The difference this change of habits and costume makes in one's relations with the natives is enormous; a wide and all but impassable gulf disappears, as it does when Orientals, coming to England, lay aside their picturesque garb and, to us, uncouth manners, conforming as best they can to our dress and usages. We then feel that we can meet them socially, whereas otherwise they would move among us only as curiosities.*

But such a course is not to be recommended to those who do not hope to feel at home with the natives, or who are not prepared for real hardship. Two of the entries in Davidson's Journal are here worth quoting:

Hardships.

"To-day I have parted with all my hair, the last remains but one of Christian appearance, and taken up the tasbîḥ (rosary) . . . on Wednesday . . . we are to put on the turban and start . . ." [1]

"I never expect to become white again. My beard is very long, my hair is cut close to the head, leaving one long tuft over the left ear, my bare legs and arms are covered with the bites of vermin; my cheek bones are very prominent, and teeth very sharp from having little or nothing to do." [2]

A knowledge of the language is indispensable, preferably a colloquial knowledge, picked up without effort, but by a determined mind, in residence among the people.† Such a knowledge, with all its errors, goes much farther, and arouses less suspicion than the best of classical styles without the local idioms and expressions. Rohlfs has truly remarked that the first obstacles passed, it is not difficult to converse in Ara-

The Language.

* See chapter xxii.—Some ten years ago, when in Morocco, I offered, with a most capable friend, to undertake at my own expense, the exploration of some of the unknown parts of the Central Atlas, provided that either the English or the Scottish Geographical Societies would lend the necessary instruments for observation, loss or damage to be made good by me, but as they did not see their way to accept the offer, the idea was abandoned. We had planned to travel as natives.

† It was with this conviction, and to meet this need, that I compiled and published my "Introduction to Morocco Arabic," now, to my great satisfaction, the text-book of travellers and missionaries in Morocco.

[1] Oct. 7. [2] Nov. 25.

bic, as "no great vocabulary is required, some four or five hundred words, with practice in their use, that is all." [1]

"The great thing," he shrewdly adds, "is always to have the words 'Allah' and 'Prophet' in one's mouth, to talk of Paradise and Hell, not to forget the Devil; and devoutly to murmur over the rosary as it slips through the fingers. Should it happen that one is doubtful about a sentence, or forgets a word, and says instead of it 'Allah is the greatest,' or 'Mohammed is the favourite of Allah,' or 'Allah confound the Christians,' no Moroccan would notice it, even though the exclamation had no reference at all to what had preceded it, and would finish the sentence or find the word himself."

Intercourse with Natives.

It is also necessary that the traveller, whether in European or native guise, should have some knowledge of Oriental ways, especially of official etiquette and obstruction. Detailed hints on this point for the present day would here be out of place, but it may be worth while to recall the quaint advice given by Mouëtte, quoted by James and others, to show what was considered politic two centuries ago. Those who know Morocco now will observe how much applies still, notwithstanding its antique flavour.

"First visit the Governor," says the ex-slave, "and make a handsome present; afterwards pay him frequent visits, and consult him in cases of the least difference with Moors or Jews, that he may gain by fining them, and that we may not be despised, as no one dares to interfere with the Governor's friends. When summoned by any Governor, not to fail to appear before him and to make friends of his kindred and friends, who may obtain favours: not to revile or give offensive answers to the Moors before witnesses, much less to lift the hand to strike them; not to spit in their faces, nor even in their presence when in a passion—it is much better to complain to the Governor: not to rely too much on Governors, who are all dogs that bite as well as fawn, promising what they do not need to fulfil, eager in receiving, and sure to do no good: never to go from one town to another without the Governor's leave, or he would become an implacable enemy: never to trust goods to Moors or Jews without three or four sureties, as they have no real estate besides houses and gardens of small value. Take no goods on credit, and keep no book accounts, for they always write down a fourth part more than they deliver."

[1] p. 270.

Present Day Hints.

Infinitely more practical and up-to-date are the following hints by an experienced resident, invaluable to the new-comer who contemplates a journey in the Land of the Moors.*

"Bring your own saddle, and don't forget a breast-plate for up-hill work, a bath, a water-proof sheet and a hold-all, in addition to your other luggage, no single item of which should weigh more than 112 lbs. Except in Tangier no tents are to be hired. Bring a letter of credit to any respectable firm in the seaport which is to be the base of your operations, and that firm will give you drafts if required on any inland town you may wish to visit, besides putting you in the way of engaging the best available guides, muleteers etc. But *don't* expect any English resident you may happen to meet to devote more than two hours a day to the delirious joy of interpreting for you. And if a man asks you to lunch, don't fill his hall with a crowd of curio-pedlars. Bargaining with these picturesque ruffians may be interesting to you, but the purest pleasures are apt to pall when indulged in to excess.

"In preparing for the road, inspect every animal that you have hired, and if practicable make a false start, camping only a few miles from the town. This will enable you to test the quality of your mules, and allow of your making good any deficiences. Something is always forgotten; matches, candles, soap, salt, or some other trifle which you may find it almost impossible to replace until you reach a town. Don't overload the animals. Two cwt. with a man on the top are quite enough for the strongest mule to carry on a journey of five or six hours a day, which will satisfy ordinary aspirations.

"Start at daybreak, after a light meal. Beaten up eggs, coffee and dry biscuits, will keep you going until ten o'clock, when, if near to water, a halt should be made. If necessary you can do another two or three hours comfortably before sunset. Unless you are absolutely certain of obtaining barley, it is best to carry enough for each night's fodder. And a single animal breaking down may cause most annoying delay.

"In choosing a mount for yourself, bear in mind that none but the best trained horse is so comfortable for long journeys as a good pacing mule, which will do her average four miles and a half per hour for eight hours a day, without turning a hair or tiring the rider. One pretty good sign of an easy pace (which depends mainly on length of stride) is when the hind hoof overlaps the print left by the fore foot. The longer the overlap the better the pace. No overlap at all is the sure mark of a jolter, from which may Allah defend you."

* Presumably, from internal evidence, by Mr R. L. N. Johnston.

CHAPTER THE SECOND

MINERAL RESOURCES

THE time is yet far distant when it will be possible to sketch the geological formation of Morocco, or to estimate its wealth in minerals or metals, for until the country has been properly explored, we must content ourselves with the sparse notes of travellers in well-known districts, and the indications of a few imperfect native workings. Traditions handed down from ancient times, supported by a striking similarity between the systems separated by the Gate of Hercules, afford sufficient ground, however, for assuming that the subterraneous treasure of the Moorish Empire is not small, and that once opened up by an enlightened ruler, it would rank among its principal resources. But the firm belief of its people that to permit foreign enterprise in this direction would inevitably lead to foreign encroachments, renders its development at present out of the question, for even casual inquiries regarding rocks or metals are sufficient to arouse suspicion, and secure evasive or misleading answers.

Lack of Data.

Efforts are nevertheless made periodically to tempt the Sultan to confer monopolies on speculators, or to lease the mining rights of certain districts. Some years ago, indeed, in 1846,a native of Algeria, Bû Derba, obtained permission to develop certain antimony mines in Anjera, but when it was discovered that they would be worked with foreign skill and capital, the permit was bought back for 40,000 francs. A genera-

Native Prejudice.

tion later a concession of the same mines and of another known as the Zîäïda, between Rabat and Casablanca, was withdrawn from the Dukálli family for a like reason.

Coal. Mulai el Ḥasan III. went so far as to permit a European engineer in his employ* to prospect for coal, which he did with success, but his discoveries —in Anjera, not far from Tangier—were not followed up, and everyone is left to estimate the possibilities himself. That mines of some sort have long been worked by the natives is evident, not only from the traces of their workings in various districts, but also from the references in their histories,† while still in some parts metal ores, where easy of access, continue to be extracted.

Gold is included by some in their list of Moroccan metals, but the evidence of its existence is too slender

Gold. to warrant great expectations, though Gatell testifies to its discovery in Sûs. Ibn Haukal[1] wrote of gold mines near Sajilmása; and Gråberg[2] went so far as to describe it as found in quartz or calcareous spar, chiefly in grains, but sometimes in flakes; and at "Idá-oo-ltilt," in Sûs, in conjunction with copper. That quartz abounds in various regions is certain; Hodgkin[3] describes huge blocks of it south of the Jabîlát range as resembling new white buildings or great blocks of quarried stone, the ground being strewed with fragments. Leared[4] also records a legend with regard to buried gold in a neighbouring district abounding with quartz, near "M'zôdia," off the Mogador Marrákesh road. Three small isolated hills called Kôdîát A'thûs were pointed out as the treasure hoards of the Nazarene after whom they are named, the entrance to

* The late Kaid Silva.

† As the mention in Raôḍ el Ḳarṭás (p. 277) of mines worked in 1154 A.C. on the road from Fez to Marrákesh.

[1] p. 21. [2] p 31. [3] p. 89.

[4] p. 117. See BEAUMIER, in the Bul. Soc. Géog., Paris, 1868, p. 330.

ON THE MARCH.
(Moorish Government Officials.)

Drawn by R. Caton Woodville.

which is open but once a year Jackson,[1] too, had heard of a gold mine on the south side of the Massa in Sûs, the mouth of which was obstructed by immovable stones, of which the natives still speak.[2] Similar traditions lurk around many natural grottos and strange formations, whose awe-inspiring recesses are unfathomed by the credulous natives, in whose minds they are invariably associated with Rûm—foreigners *i.e.*,—treasure and devils. A much more certain source of the gold which was once exported from this Empire was the trade across the Saḥara with Timbuctoo, where gold dust was received for salt and European imports.[3]

Silver.

Silver, also, has been reported by various writers as found in the bluish soil and sand of the Massa; in rich mines at "Elála" and Shtûka; at "Frasegina," near Agadîr;[4] at "Rakendor," six days south of Marrákesh:[5] at "Warkennas," three stages from Mequinez,; in Mounts "Aden" and "Aroukanez," near Wád Nûn; and between Tádla and Tafîlált, near "Rabáṭ ben Tawîla:" but here again the indications are vague, and the evidence only hearsay.

Copper.

Copper, the presence of which has been known since the time of Strabo, is worked in several parts at the present time, although in a most imperfect and primitive manner. The geographer Idreesî mentions "a fine light coloured quality" as procured from near Tádla, but the mountains above Tarudant[6] at "Tasellergt," near the Bîbáwan Pass, have long been the principal source, though the district of Mesfîwa near Marrákesh has also been worked, and Thomassy mentions a mine near Mequinez—probably the Tádla one—as furnishing over 20,000 quintals a year for export to France. In 1741 a French "tartane" was taken by the

[1] p. 73. [2] ANDREWS, *Times of Morocco*, No. 21. [3] See MOUETTE, p. 317.
[4] JACKSON, p. 74. [5] MAS LATRIE, p. 380.
[6] LENZ, vol. i., p. 285, among others.

privateer *Revenge* while conveying copper from Agadîr,[1] but it is a long time since more was produced than was required for native coinage and household utensils. Specimens of copper ore found in Sûs were presented to the Arksîs adventurers in 1883, together with ores of iron, lead, and antimony,[2] and their successors in 1898 picked up copper ore there.[3]

ANCIENT IRON MINE.
(Jebel Ḥadeed, 'Abda.)
Photograph by Joseph Thomson, Esq.

Iron has been extracted in several parts, notably from the extinct volcanic crater of Jebel Ḥadeed (Iron Mountain) in 'Abda, where at a height of 2470 feet the ancient galleries may yet be followed,[4] and at "Ida-oo-ltilt" in Sûs, whence metal is obtained for the gun-smiths who have made that province famous. Urquhart[5] obtained permission in 1848 to search for ore round Rabat, and workmen in iron were brought

Iron.

[1] Wyatt, p. 23.
[2] Andrews, l.c. Cf. Lenz, vol. i., p. 333.
[3] Grey, p. 77.
[4] See Thomson.
[5] vol. ii., p. 120.

from the Rîf. Twenty camel loads were procured, and furnaces, suitable for copper only, erected in the back-yard of the consulate.

Tin, Zinc and Lead.

In the 17th century we read of tin being found on the road from Salli to Tetuan—in Anjera probably—great revenue being derived from the lading therewith of barques for Marseilles, but possibly the worthy friar who records this was mistaken,[1] and should have written antimony, which is really found there. Some tin, however, is believed to exist, and also tutty, an impure protoxide of zinc rarely found in a natural state. Lead is referred to in the Tádla district again, and it is also found in Sûs, where there is a sugar-loaf peak called Bû Na'amán, south of Tiznît, which has been mined for this ore.[2] That it was once extensively worked appears from the possession by the Venetians of a monopoly for its export in the middle ages,[3] though it is possible that the ore exported included also antimony.

Antimony.

This latter metal has been long produced, and is in constant demand for adorning the eyes, which it is said to preserve from disease, though Dr. Ovilo maintains that it is rather a cause of trouble.* Mines exist in Anjera and in the Atlas, and it has been also reported with lead from Tafîllát. Rohlfs, on his journey up country, records having picked up pure antimony in pieces 1½ inch thick, and again speaks of a mine at "Knetsa," between Tafîlált and Fîgîg.[4] In Morocco it is known as el k'ḥôl.

Another mineral largely employed in Morocco for toilet purposes is ghasool, a sort of fullers' earth, of

* Its method of application I have fully described in *The Moors*, ch. iv.

[1] Père Dan, p. 207.

[2] Andrews, *Times of Morocco*, No. 22.

[3] Mas Latrie, *Relations*, p. 162.

[4] p. 366.

excellent quality, used in the baths, and also exported.* Urquhart[1] describes it as containing "silex, alumina, magnesia, and lime," and declares that this particular variety is only to be found in Morocco, from which he infers commerce with Morocco when he traces remains of it beneath the Baalbek temple. Its ashes, called "kissermill," he says, make mortar as hard as stone, one part each of ashes, lime, and sand being used. Jackson mentions ghasool as employed in the preparation of Morocco leather.[2]

Fullers' Earth.

Mineral springs exist in several parts, and their medicinal value is well-known, although attributed to the influence of "saints" interred hard by, as in the best known case of Mulai Ya'kûb, in the mountains between Fez and Mequinez—the Aquæ Dacicæ of the Romans—where some of the most extraordinary scenes in the Empire are to be witnessed, men and women bathing apart in pools *al fresco*, ejaculating, "Cold and hot, my lord Jacob! Cold and hot!" to prevent that worthy supplying the latter alone from his subterraneous cauldrons. Very few Europeans, however, have visited them, but sample bottles have been obtained which show their virtue to consist chiefly in the sulphur they contain. The natives tell of a hole near the top of the peaks, from which the rush of air is so great that sticks cannot be thrown into it. Similar springs exist in the Kabîlah Gla'ïa, in the province of Er-Rîf, and Rohlfs[3] mentions sulphur vapours as rising from a stony field one day out from Wazzán, on the road to Fez, near Manṣûrîya on the Sebû, where the neighbours said that flames were sometimes seen. The same author speaks of a spring so rich in carbonic-acid gas that it resembled champagne, in an oasis called "Tasanakht," near the

Mineral Springs.

* Duty fixed by treaty of 1857, 1s. 9d. per cwt.

[1] *Lebanon*, ed. 1860, vol. ii., p. 385. [2] p. 78. [3] p. 271.

cañon-like pass, five days from Tarudant, on the way to the Dra'a.[1] Sulphur itself has been dug in the Atlas opposite Tarudant, wherewith was manufactured by the Oolád Bû Sbáḥ a gunpowder more highly esteemed than that of Europe.[2]

Salt.

Convenient supplies of saltpetre abound in the vicinity of Tarudant and near Marrákesh, where it is extracted from pits,[3] though one writer describes it as obtained from the street sweepings of that city,[4] but of this I have not heard. Common salt has always proved a source of wealth, and reference is made at an early epoch to large mines near Fez.[5] There is one near the Ḥajar el Wákif, not far from the tomb of Sidi M'ḥammed es-Shilḥ on the Sebu. Lenz[6] tells of another such mine at Wád Telli, 19 days from Tendûf on the Timbuctoo road, where salt begins to grow precious. In some parts not only are the rivers and lakes impregnated therewith, as on the plain of Marrákesh and in 'Abda, but there arer ocks of salt,[7] as at "La'alooah," near Casablanca, where is a huge hill of salt[8] with crystals of all colours, and in the Atlas valleys.[9] An hour and a half from Wazzán, on the road El Ḳaṣar, a large district is made desert by the presence of salt springs,[10] and the Lake of Zîma in the Blád el Ḥamrá, some eight hours' ride from Saffi, is about a mile and a half long and a mile broad. Its red alluvial salt is sold by the Government to the neighbouring tribe for a yearly sum. On the sea-shore, as at Old Tangier, salt is collected in pans, as it is always in demand. In the Atlas passes I have watched the mule-trains carrying great slabs to the saltless desert beyond.

Porphyritic tuffs and coarse-grained diorite are plentiful

[1] p. 340. [2] Jackson, p. 76; Andrews, *Times of Morocco*, No. 24.
[3] Erckmann, p. 36. [4] Leared, p. 101. [5] Raôḍ el Ḳarṭás, p. 39.
[6] p. 377. [7] Jackson, p. 75. [8] Godard, p. 174.
[9] Fritsch, *Bibliog.*, Art. 1109. [10] Spence-Watson, p. 259.

in the Great Atlas, interspersed with eruptive basalts, and in the same region granite abounds. Disused quarries in which pillars remain partially cut may be seen about four days from Mogador towards Marrákesh, but since Roman times much does not seem to have been done in this way, for the Moors use little stone, and import their marble. Little is now quarried beyond mill-stones which are in constant demand. Rock crystals and amethysts are attributed to Er-Rîf,[1] and chalcedony in great quantities has been observed between Marrákesh and Mogador—"some specimens, the size of a child's head, and free from flaws."[2]

Stones.

Lime and gypsum (gibs) are prepared in many parts, and are largely employed in the interior decoration of town houses. One of the most noteworthy geological features of Morocco is the presence in many districts, just below the surface, of a remarkable layer of tufa or travertin, probably formed by the washing in of soluble carbonate of lime from above, or by its being drawn up with the moisture from below by great heat. This forms a sort of impervious covering, underneath which the natives excavate their grain pits.*

The principal contributors to our knowledge of this subject have been Dr. Hodgkin, who in 1866 made careful observations along the Mogador-Marrákesh road; Mourlon, who in 1870 compiled a geological sketch from notes taken round Mazagan, and between Tangier and Fez;[3] George Maw, who contributed a valuable appendix to Hooker and Ball's work; Dr. Bleicher, who in 1874 made notes on the way from Tangier to Mequinez; Lenz, who gathered information along

Authorities.

* See Hodgkin, paper presented to British Association, and the notes by Maw, who holds the latter theory.

[1] GRÅBERG, p. 32. [2] HODGKIN, p. 53.

[3] Bul. Acad. Rle. de Belgique, 2nd série, No. 7, 1870.

his interesting route; and Thomson, whose detailed information under this head concerning the Great Atlas is particularly valuable.* Other travellers have added little that can be relied on, though De Foucauld and several more give cursory observations of interest.

Summary of Thomson's Observations.

* The following is a summary of Mr. Joseph Thomson's observations: "The Lowlands are practically conterminous with the Tertiary deposits, among which apparently Eocene, Miocene, and Pliocene rocks are represented. The latter consist of shelly sands 200 to 300 feet thick, gradually rising to a height of 700 feet south and east of Saffi. Their surface is often covered with the slaggy tufaceous crust described by Maw. The local presence of this crust and the porous character of the deposit elsewhere have preserved it from denudation, and thus (in the opinion of the author) its surface still presents the appearance of the Tertiary sea-bed on which it was formed. Certain quarry-like pits, one of which contains a pillar of white crystalline calcium carbonate, are supposed to be due to the explosion of steam connected with the existence of hot springs.

"The Plateau is underlain by three rock-formations:—(*a*) Metamorphic rocks including clay-slates, which probably underlay the whole Plain of Morocco, and rise into a group of rugged hills called the Jabîlát [Little Hills], in contradistinction to the Jebel or Atlas proper. (*b*) The Lower Cretaceous rocks, consisting of red shales and sandstones, the former frequently giving rise to brine springs and containing salt-deposits at Damnát in the Atlas. (*c*) The Upper Cretaceous rocks, chiefly white and cream-coloured limestones, which attain their greatest development on the Plateau.

"The Atlas itself is made up for the most part of the same rocks.[1] There is a core of metamorphic rocks, which is better developed and wider at the western end of the range, and narrower towards the east. Next comes the great development of the Lower Cretaceous strata, followed by a diminutive representative of the Upper Cretaceous rocks. These rocks are much broken by folding and faulting, and their structure is displayed in several sections taken across the range from Damnát westward. The first signs of glacial action were met with at 'Titula,' consisting of moraine-like heaps of débris; elsewhere scratched stones were found. The boulder-deposits described by Maw were not seen either east or west of the locality described by that author; but Maw's original section was not traversed, and the present author does not offer any opinion as to the origin of the beds. Intrusive basalts penetrate the Cretaceous rocks, while porphyrites, diorites and other igneous rocks pierce the metamorphic rocks of the central core."

[1] But with an entire absence of palæozoic rocks, and probably also of triassic and jurassic.

CHAPTER THE THIRD

VEGETABLE PRODUCTS

ALTHOUGH in certain districts much has been done to contribute to our knowledge of the Moroccan flora, notably by Hooker, Ball and Cosson—the last named of whom has presented us with a compendium of all that his predecessors had accomplished,—it is only possible as yet to guess at the products of the greater part of this Empire.* But there are certain economic plants and prominent species of wide distribution which, as features of the country, call for special notice. In Spring the abundance of flowers on the verdant plains is as remarkable as the absence of trees, and even when the Atlas is reached, with its successive zones of vegetation, shrubs are more

The Moroccan Flora.

* A paper contributed by Ball to the Journal of the Linnæan Society[1] opens with an useful résumé of the work of previous students in this field, and summarises his own results. Of the 1627 species which he tabulated, 165 were peculiar to Morocco, 96 to Spain and Morocco, and 64 to Algeria and Morocco. They consisted of 25 Leguminosæ, 23 Labiatæ, 10 Cruciferæ, 11 Umbelliferæ, 10 Scrophularineæ, 15 Corymbiferæ, 10 Cynaraceæ and 7 Euphorbiaciæ. The proportion of Compositæ Leguminosæ and Giliaceæ he found to be unusually large, that of Gramineæ and Ranunculaceæ exceptionally small.[2] One new species, discovered in the Central Atlas above Arromd, he named Chrysanthemum catananche (Ball). The most singular feature he observed in the Great Atlas flora was the presence of large numbers of the common species of Central Europe, annual and perennial, many not being found nearer than the Spanish mountains, many not so near.[3] Nevertheless he decided that "the Morocco flora is altogether a portion of that great Mediterranean flora which, with local peculiarities, one finds from the Indus to the Atlantic Islands."

Ball's Researches.

[1] Vol. xvi., 93. [2] p. 298. [3] p. 302.

common than larger growths. Only such useful trees as the date and the olive, the walnut, the fig and the árgán are to be frequently met with, and of these the first, at least, does not appear to be indigenous.

NOON BENEATH A LOTUS TREE.
(Province of Raḥamna.)
Photograph by Dr. Rudduck.

The most common wild tree on the plains is the thorny sidr or lotus (*Rhamnus nabeca*, or *Zizyphus Lotus* —sometimes known as the *Mimosa nilotica*) the abundant fruit of which, called nab'k, is so undeservedly famous. High upon the mountain sides it grows in stunted patches, mere thorns on the ground, but on the plains the traveller is often grateful for its shade. In some districts cork oaks are plentiful, and of them many of the so-called forests are composed. At times their bark has formed an article of export—once an important monopoly—but unfortunately their chief use is to feed ovens and furnaces; the acorns (bellooṭ), which are of large size, are often

The Lotus.

Cork Oak.

eaten.* Addison mentions the growth around them of the lentisk (*Pistacia Lentiscus*), the juice of which is used for tinting earthenware.[1] The resin of this shrub is the gum-mastic of commerce. *Shrubs.* Gum-cistus is one of the common flowering shrubs which are a prominent feature in the northern parts, scenting the air for miles. The arbutus often grows beside the cistus on the hills, with its bright red fruit, which among the Moors has the reputation of intoxicating. Down beside the water-courses often flourish the oleanders (*Nerium ol.*), and thousands of acres are covered with the palmetto or dwarf palm (*Chamærops humilis*), the fruit of which is eaten, but chiefly by goats, and the root by the Moors as a vegetable, while the fibrous leaves are used for making baskets, ropes and canvas. On the lower slopes of the Atlas the graceful juniper (*Juniperus phœnicea*) adds beauty to the scene, beside its more pretentious kinsman the 'ar'aár. Fragrant broom adorns the sand dunes of the coast, but except in the hilly districts, one may often travel far without seeing either wild tree or shrub.

The principal substitutes are the sharp-pointed aloe (*Agave Americana*) and the *Opuntia* cactus. Throughout the northern districts aloes are in great request for boundaries, but in the south are less frequently encountered.† *Aloes.* The cactus in question is commonly known as the "prickly pear," or by Americans as the "Barbary fig"—a much more appropriate name—though the natives would appear to trace it to a home still further east, by calling it *Prickly Pears.*

* A mémoire on this subject will be found referred to in the *Bibliography*, art. 447. The *Quercus suber* and *Q. ilex* are both met with.

† Notwithstanding its many valuable properties, the only other use made of the aloe is that of its sharp points for goads.

[1] p. 77.

the "Indian fig," karamoos el Hind, or simply Hindî,* and in the south, karamoos 'Nṣárà, "fig of the Nazarenes." There is no more refreshing or satisfactory fruit than this all-but-tasteless cactus, especially when gathered in the cool of the early dawn and kept damp; covered up till towards noon it is skilfully peeled by the shadeless road-side. Except on an empty stomach, it may be consumed by the dozen without fear, since its action is the reverse of that of most fruits, and to relaxed constitutions it is a grateful restorative. The sweet varieties are seldom met with, and are not to be compared to the plain sort, but purple as well as yellow "hindîs" are grown. Their troublesome, hair-like thorns are removed from the flesh by the natives by dragging over the spot the hind legs of a horse-fly. The eucalyptus also has of late been introduced † with such success that in another century or two it is likely to rank as one of the typical trees of the country.

Eucalyptus.

Palms are not apparently indigenous, and do not flourish in the northern parts of Morocco, where the date-bearing variety (*Phœnix dactylifera*) alone is cultivated, and that only towards the south, beginning with the plain of Marrákesh. The dates of Tafîlált are the best in the world, large, solid and luscious; they are scarcely to be purchased in the country, since the Jews buy them up for export direct.‡ Instead of being known in Morocco by its proper name, the date is here called et-thamr, "the fruit" *par excellence*. Tafîlált alone is

Dates.

* The Berbers of the south, however, know it as takanareet (*i.e.* Canaryite) which also points to a foreign origin, such as must likewise be found for the aloe and orange.

† By the late Sir John D. Hay and the late Col. F. A. Mathews, the latter of whom also planted Californian pines on the Spartel Hill.

‡ Unless content to purchase a whole box, I found it cheaper to obtain supplies in Tangier from London.

said to produce thirty kinds, the rival centre being the Dra'a district, in which also palms constitute the chief wealth. The varieties most highly esteemed by the natives are: the bû eṭ-ṭôb, with its delicate taste and almost imperceptible stone, which keeps well and defies insects; the greenish bû zekri from Akka, very sweet, but good for travelling; and the bû figgoos of Tatta, the Dra'a and Wád Ziz—so called with Oriental exaggeration in implied comparison with the marrow; the jeehal and the tahar mooshat. But these varieties seldom find their way out of the country, a fate also shared by the majḥool of Tiznît and other districts —which, though of large size, and very abundant, has a large stone,—as well as the smaller bû sooáïr of Wád Ziz and the Lesser Atlas, there considered so inferior that it is principally used as food for cattle. In those parts dates are excessively cheap, but transport across the Atlas so greatly enhances their value that only the poorer qualities are to be commonly met with in Moorish towns, and then often in bad condition.

Varieties.

The complement of the date, without which it should never be eaten,* is the walnut, which rich with grateful foliage, abounds beside the irrigation channels of the Atlas. The broken kernels are exposed for sale in Marrákesh in great quantities. Almonds too, are plentiful, especially in Sûs, whence apricot kernels also form a valuable export for the manufacture of "essence of almonds." The wayside fruit-tree found in some parts is the kharrob—"John-Baptist" or "locust bean"—(*Ceratonia Siliqua*), whose long brown pods, full of sweet mealy pulp, are not unpleasant when eaten in small quantities. They

Walnuts.

Almonds.

Locust Beans

* In Persia, where also dates and walnuts are eaten together, I found a most delicious sweat-meat prepared of the two pounded in a mortar, pressed into a mould, and sugared over.

are most in favour at the feast of the 'Aáshoor, but are also used for drenching and fattening horses.

Figs.

Most common and grateful of all the cultivated trees of Morocco are the fig and olive. Both may be seen either in groves or gardens, or out on the plain where once some plot has been tilled. The leafy fig-trees, with their early barren—"unripe"—fruit, and a second crop after they have been fertilized by hanging bunches from the one tree on the other, are often grown also in the court-yards of the poorer classes; vines being trained on trellis-work across the yard or street, so that in very deed they dwell beneath their own vines and fig-trees.

Vines.

Vines are fortunately cultivated almost entirely for grapes to eat, and these are plentiful, though wine and spirits are prepared by the Jews from raisins, grapes, figs, etc.

Olives.

Few sights are more welcome to the traveller than ancient olive-groves with sward beneath, and running water, such as clothe the choicest valleys of the Atlas and many a hill on the plains. Some of the groves, as those round Mequinez, are very extensive. Most of the Moorish olives are black, and are delicious when prepared by being boiled in lemon juice. Their oil is largely exported to France, notwithstanding the primitive means employed in its extraction, and the lack of care, which often leave it rancid or unpleasant to the taste, so that it does not enjoy the best of characters. Wild olive trees (zibbooj), too, are frequently seen, and are easily distinguished from "the good."

The Argán.

But in Morocco the oil of the olive has to give place to that of the thorny árgán (*Eleodendron* or *Sideroxylon argan* *), more highly esteemed in the South, but not by foreigners. This is peculiar in being

* Also, though less correctly, *Sideroxylon spinosum*, *Rhamnus siculus* and *R. pentaphyllus*.

CAMP BENEATH AN ARGÁN TREE.
(Province of Ḥáḥá.)

Photograph by Herbert White, Esq.

not only confined to Morocco, but to one district therein, the provinces of Ḥáḥá and Shiadhma, where one may ride through miles of árgán trees which appear to grow wild. Though at first sight the árgán might be taken to resemble the olive, it does so neither in leaf nor in fruit, the latter being much larger. Many of the trees are of great age, and goats are quite at home in their gnarled, wide-spreading branches, for they, as well as camels, sheep and cows, are very fond of the fleshy pericarp, of which no other use is made. The nuts having been cracked between stones by the natives, the kernels are roasted, pounded and kneaded by hand, first with the addition of a little hot water, then of cold. The oil is then expressed, and the residuary cake is given to cows and goats, as horses and camels refuse it. Argán oil is really good, but suffers, like that of the olive, from the primitive process employed.

Argán Oil.

It is necessary to clarify it and to burn off impurities before use, unless one is hardened to its acrid taste and pungent smoke. This is accomplished by boiling the oil with a sliced onion, and when hot, dropping in a piece of crumb bread, which is allowed to char, and is then thrown away. Both oils are used for burning in native lamps. Belonging to an almost exclusively tropical family, the árgán's nearest kindred are among the genus *Sideroxylon*, which reach their northern limit in the Madeira and Cape Verde Islands, but are unknown in the Canaries. Efforts to introduce it to other countries of similar climate, at first full of promise, have not been successful.* It yields a hard, though fine-grained yellow wood.

* A good deal has from time to time been written on the subject of the árgán tree and its oil; see Bibl. arts. 747, 755, 1109 and 1259; Schusboe's Morocco Botany (art. 480) and the able summary of all that is known about it in an appendix to his work on Morocco by Sir Joseph Hooker.

Another tree for which Morocco has long been famous is the citrus* or thuja, otherwise the 'arár or gum-sandarach tree (*Callitris quadrivalvis* or *Thuja articulata*). This again is chiefly of local growth, but its habitat includes at least the greater part of Barbary, and its next-of-kin hail from South Africa. Pliny says Mount Atlas was its native home.[1] It is of the cypress family, and must not be confounded with the citron. Its peculiarity consists in an enlargement at the ground level of the base of the trunk, which is beautifully marked in the grain, and is of exquisite hardness. It was from this that the Roman patricians cut their precious tables,[2] valued at more than their weight in gold if as much as four feet in width. Beams are still cut, and are believed to be practically indestructible by damp or insects. It was the *arbor vitæ* of Theophrastus, with which the Romans roofed their temples, and of it the Moors hewed beams a thousand years ago which still exist in the Córdova mosque. In Morocco it is similarly used, as also for the manufacture of tables, boxes etc., being especially appreciated for its pleasant cedar-like odour; it is light in colour, and being hard it takes an excellent polish. The gum which it exudes is one of the important exports of Mogador.

Citrus or Gum Sandarach.

The only remaining tree which calls for notice is the ṣanobar (*Abies atlantica*) or scented fir of the Atlas and Er-Rîf, whence its red beams are transported for building. Insects object to its pleasant odour, so it is also in demand for boxes and cupboards. Pitch (ḳiṭrán—*i.e.* "dropping") is prepared from trees of this class in furnaces of clay, being widely used for lining water-vessels, and as a remedy in skin diseases.

Fir.

* The Latin name citrus is supposed to be a corruption of cedrus.

[1] PLINY, *Nat. Hist.*, bk. xiii., ch. 5. 15, 29 and 30. See BOSTOCK'S translation, vol. iii., p. 194; HORACE, *Carm.* bk. iv, Od. i; *Odyssey* ii, 6; and STRABO, xviii., § iv.

[2] PLINY, bk. xii., chs. 3, 7, and xiii., 15.

Morocco Gums.

Two other gums are exported in no small quantities, the red Morocco gum ('alḳ 'amrád) and a lighter variety of the same ('alḳ 'awarwár) commonly known as gum-Arabic, but also as gum-Senegal, and both are comprehended in the name 'alḳ ṭalḥ or gum-acacia *(Acacia* or *Mimosa gummifera).* The best kinds are produced in Sûs, or just north of the Atlas spur which shuts off that province, what is found further north being poorer. The tree producing the 'awarwár is the larger of the two, but botanists do not appear to have distinguished between them, unless one is the *Acacia arabica*, not known in Morocco, the product of which is transported across the Atlas by caravan.

Euphorbium.

The gum-euphorbium, (farbîoon or daghmoos,) which exudes from a cactoid plant with crimson flower, (*Euphorbia resinifera*) once in demand as an emetic and purgative,[1] is now no longer largely exported.* Its growth is confined to southern Morocco, where it affords another instance of a "tropical form advancing far north in the extreme west of the old world," with its nearest ally in the Canaries. The plants are pricked but once in four years, when the juice is left to dry into gum by September, by which time its caustic effects are such that those who gather it have to cover their mouths and nostrils; it is used in tanning, and as a depilatory.[2] †

Ammoniacum.

Gum Ammoniacum or fasookh is the produce of a plant resembling fennel, only larger *(Ferula tingitana* or *Elæselinum humile)*, found on the central plains in waste districts. It is used as

* See Consul's Report for Saffi, 1881, notes by Mr. Hunot, p. 112. It is said not to be found north of Aït 'Amar and Cape Geer.[3]

† Gatell[4] speaks of the daghmoos "or likiout" juice as a kind of mild honey, harmless to the teeth, but causing the mouth to smart.

[1] See PLINY, bk. v., c. 12.
[2] JACKSON, p. 81.
[3] ANDREWS *Times of Morocco*, No. 24.
[4] p. 260.

incense for which purpose and as a depilatory it is sent to the East. The plant is bled by an insect which lives upon it, in its turn to be picked off by the hovering vulture.*

Henná.

Among the minor vegetable products of Morocco is henná or "Egyptian privet" *(Lawsonia inermis)*, cultivated in many parts, as in Dukálla, in the Zaïr country and in Tafîlált, on account of the favourite orange dye which it yields, much used for flesh and hair.

Indian Hemp.

Ḥasheesh *(Cannabis indica)* also holds an important place, though at times its cultivation has been forbidden. Pellow says that in his day more of this was raised than of anything except grains, but the word 'ḥasheesh' (herbage) is applicable also to fodder, the word 'keef' referring only to the leaves as used in smoking, or prepared in the form of a sweetmeat.

Tobacco.

Tobacco also is extensively grown, and I have seen the two side by side on the Atlas near Amzmiz. Wád Nûn, the Dra'a and Tûát are all famous for their tobacco, and in those districts it is much more widely consumed than elsewhere in Morocco, that from the first named source being especially recommended. In 1750 a report on Moorish tobacco stated that of Saffi and Salli to be better than that of Virginia,[1] but the development of this article has not been encouraged, since its use has always been regarded as of doubtful legality, and by Sulaimán II. and El Ḥasan III. it has twice within a century been destroyed throughout the Empire, but in vain.[2] A wild variety is indigenous.

A plant called zurnakh or "Jews' mallows" has the credit of being a substitute for the cravings caused by

* For an epitome of what has been recorded of these several gums see the appendices of Hooker and Ball's work. For special researches on the subject see Bibl. arts. 471 and 2, 480, 1165 and 1512. The last being a report drawn up subsequently to that of Hooker.

[1] Thomassy, p. 231. [2] Ali Bey, p. 173, and *Times of Morocco*, March 10 and 17, 1887.

Medicinal Plants.

the use of hemp, and also of an aphrodisiac. Of other medicinal plants in use may be mentioned colocynth, of which a large variety used to be exported from Mogador with the rind left on for exhibition in druggists' windows; "tserbil," a sort

MOORISH IRRIGATION WHEEL.

Photograph by Herbert White, Esq.

of sage used as cooling for wounds; squills, called "Pharoah's onions" (b'sál Faraôn), abound in the Beni Ḥasan and Zarhôn country, the root is pounded in water and the fibres of the stalk are used to supplement goat-hair in weaving canvas for tents. Mignonette is indigenous to Morocco,* having been transported first to France, —where it obtained its European name—and thence in 1742 to England.[1] Many sweet herbs are cultivated, but there are many districts in which there is so much wild peppermint that the air around is scented as one's horse treads among it.

Sugar.

The sugar-cane, though at one time extensively cultivated, is now practically unknown in Morocco—whence it was formerly exported to Europe[2]—the province of Dukálla being in those days known as Blád es-Sukkár, "the sugar country." Idreesi speaks of the sugar of Sûs, for which the district was famous,[3] as the best in the world. Tarudant owed its early importance to this lucrative trade, and Agadîr was coveted as the port of its shipment. Mills were built by Europeans, and Christian slaves were employed in its manufacture in the sixteenth century. A more recent attempt to revive the business is called to mind by the ruined sugar-mill erected in the fifties for the Sultan by an English engineer, at the extreme point of the Agudál park at Marrákesh.

Cotton, Rice and Dyes.

Another product of bygone days was cotton, of which Idreesi says enough was produced round Tádla to supply all the Maghrib;[4] and indigo was extensively grown in the Dra'a.[5] Rice, too, has been and is still grown in the neighbourhood of Fez, but whatever quantity of these three may now be raised, it is insignificant, as foreign importations have altogether superseded the native articles, except possibly in the far interior. A dye called "takaût", yielding a dark brown, is still exported, and is prepared from the fruit of a tree like the tamarisk, abundant in the oases of the Dra'a and Ziz.[6] Madder also is found, and is sometimes exported.

* As throughout the whole of North Africa and Syria.

[1] Ms. note of Sir JOSEPH BANKS.

[2] See *The Moorish Empire*, pp. 399 and 401.

[3] p. 71.

[4] See MARMOL and TORRES.

[5] p. 85; IBN KHALDUN, vol. 1., p. 195.

[6] DE FOUCAULD, p. 209.

Other roots of which use is made are liquorice, which over-runs the ground beneath the palms in the Dra'a,[1] known as 'arak es-Sûs, Sûs juice; and truffles (tarfás), black and white, found in abundance in sandy districts, where the wild pigs root them up. In time of famine a variety of arum root called yernah (*Arum arisarum*) is much sought for by the poor, and I have seen them hunting for it in the holes the boars had left. From this white flour can be prepared which makes fair bread. As a remedy for "foot and mouth" disease it is applied fresh to the sore with salt and grease on a piece of leather which is sewed on and left for a day or two; it is also used by men for ulcers etc.[2] The violet-scented orris or iris root also figures among exports from Morocco.

Roots.

At the head of the garden fruit of Morocco stands the orange, albeit an importation from the East, as its name, litsheenah or el chin—"the Chinese"—indicates more truly than the name it bears in Eastern Barbary, bortogán—*i.e.* "Portugal." Many fine varieties are grown, especially round Tetuan, Marrákesh, and other towns. One modern introduction, misnamed, is known as the "Tangerine" as well in London as in Tangier, and Laraiche exports large quantities to Seville. Limes and lemons, too, are plentiful and good. Wazzán is famous for its pomegranates, and some of the quinces grown are splendid. Apricots, peaches, plums and damsons follow each other in quick succession in May and June, after which come the water and sugar melons, abundant on the plains, but not to be compared with those of Central Asia, where I found the best in my experience. Apples, pears and cherries do not flourish well, and grapes, like most of the Moorish-grown fruits, are frequently poor from want of attention. All

Fruits.

[1] ROHLFS, p. 34. [2] PELLOW.

sell so cheaply, and the people are so poor, that there is no incentive to improvement, and the European population of Tangier is actually supplied with well-favoured fruits from Spain.

Vegetables.

Of vegetables the same may be said. The most prominent are broad beans, turnips, onions, garlic, capsicums, peas, cucumbers, marrows, pumpkins, artichokes, radishes, carrots, asparagus, and, in some parts, having been introduced from abroad, potatoes, cabbages, cauliflowers, kohl-rabi, French beans, egg-plants, beetroots and tomatoes. Lettuce, marjoram, mint, parsley, celery, sage, thyme, coriander, fenugreek and verbena are also used in large quantities, and other herbs are occasionally met with, many of them wild.

Cereals.

The rich alluvial plains of Morocco produce abundant cereal crops, but the greater portion lies barren because the exportation of those most in demand—wheat and barley—is prohibited. Maize, millet, broad beans, chick-peas, canary-seed, cummin and fenugreek, all find an outlet in spite of an unreasonable tariff, and the events of the year hinge on the rain-fall which determines the harvest. This occurs in May and June, when country labour is for once at a premium, and arms are assumed with reluctance. The primitive methods of agriculture have been treated of elsewhere.*

Flowers.

The cultivated flowers of the country are chiefly rose,s lilies, jessamine, violets, pinks and geraniums, the last named of which may often be seen in the hedge-rows near Tangier. The time to see the flowers is just after the rains have ceased, when the plains are literally carpeted with colour. Some idea of their appearance may be gleaned from the following graphic description of the district round Mogador from the pen of Mr. R. L. N. Johnston.

* See *The Moors*, ch. ix

"With March comes the climax of our Spring, the brief but brilliant 'day of herbage' apostrophised by so many Moorish poets, which carpets the light sandy soil with a wealth of wild flowers. Shaded by gigantic bushes of Spanish broom, from which the perfumed January blossoms have already fallen, we find on every hand ruddy clusters of pimpernel—the poor man's weather-glass—snowy white lady's-smock, deep golden sprigs of sweet musk balsam, and lighter hued 'shoes and stockings' (tufted horse-shoe vetch). Here and there you come upon a drift of queenly asphodel, contrasting bravely with the modest crane's-bill and tiny bird's-eye. Blue and pink immortelles, larkspur, thyme, ox-eye and camomile daisies are all in luxuriant flower; in every bridle-path your horse treads on purple convolvuli, wild, scentless mignonette, pink and white stocks—Venus's looking-glass we called them in Sussex—wild mustard and dainty hare-bells, purple and blue iris, neutral-tinted hyacinths, as well as poppies, lupin and many, to me novel, varieties of vetch."

Wild Flowers.

In addition to these, and others already mentioned, there are several other wild flowers worth notice, as a magnificent butterfly orchis (called by the Arabs Sultánat en-Nooár, "Queen of flowers"); ice-plant, ghasool—the leaves and stalk of which are used in washing; honey-suckles and lavenders (British and Moorish varieties of each); campanulas, marigold, two varieties of narcissus, the sand-hill lily, a small yellow broom, "butcher's broom," scarlet gladiolus, yellow flax, snow-drop, snap-dragon, pansy, wild pea, blue borage, red adonis, wild pink, crysanthemums, yellow ranunculus, a fine black-pointed smilax, jessamine, flowering asparagus, a fine clematis, garlic, white and pink erythrea, myrtle, brambles, laburnum, the poisonous *Datura stramonium*, and a host of others less familiar to us, of which only Latin names would be available. On the central plains near the coast flourish a remarkable variety and number of "everlasting" flowers, pink, blue and white, which long preserve their colours.

Authorities.

Most travellers in Morocco tell us something of its plants, but few have made them a special study, although they have fared better than its minerals. The only separate work on the Moroccan flora is

Schusboe's, adorned with plates, published in Copenhagen in 1800, and in French and Latin in Paris in 1874. Schusboe was Danish consul at Tangier for thirty-two years. * The earliest whose achievements are available is Surgeon Spotswood of the Tangier garrison in 1673, whose collection numbered 600 species, found within the fortifications, but many of these are now almost beyond identification. †

A century later Dr. Broussonnet collected plants for botanists in various countries, including Morocco, as did also his companion, the Abbé Durand: some of their specimens still exist in our National Collection. Salzmann, in 1825, procured two hundred specimens from Tangier, complete sets of which are to be seen at Kew. P. B. Webb, the well-known botanist, spent a few months in Morocco in 1827, during which he discovered the *hemicrambe* near Tetuan, the only locality in which it is known, and where Ball found it again in 1871. Then, in April 1859, the Rev. Thos. Lowe made use of a few days in Mogador to gather 177 species of flowering plants. In the same year, during the Spanish war, Fernando Weyler noted 460 species near Tetuan and Ceuta, though his list is often in error.

Collections.

Balansa made an important botanical expedition from Mogador to the Great Atlas in 1868, as also did Professor von Fritsch in 1872, when he and Professor Rein ascended Tizi-n-Tagharat (Miltsin). Fritsch described especially the argán and other peculiar species. John Ball, who had preceded him, subsequently published notes of importance on several new species and varieties that he had collected, in addition to comparative notes in an appendix to

Botanical Expeditions.

* The seaweeds enumerated by Schusboe are dealt with in a pamphlet published in Paris in 1892, *Les algues récoltés en Maroc*, etc.

† Zanoni, in his *Istoria Botanica*, published in 1675, deals with specimens from Tangier.

Hooker's work. He also catalogued for Miss Drummond Hay 168 species collected in Northern Morocco, which is the most valuable list available. Dr. Robert Brown, too, must be named among the careful observers of natural history who have visited this country and have contributed to our knowledge of this subject. Some botanical data by Professor Graeles were collected on the Spanish expedition to Sûs in search of "Sta. Cruz de Mar Pequeña," and published in 1878. The late 'Abd el Kareem Grant of Rabat made useful collections, used by Cosson, who in 1881 and 1887 issued a compendium of the flora of the Barbary States, *Compendium.* supplemented by illustrations of the new and less known plants enumerated. The only collection of note subsequent to this, is one of 155 species from Laraiche and Casablanca, made by Alphonse Melleris, the catalogue being edited by Edmond Bonnet. Mr. Payton has compiled a valuable list of Mogador flora with illustrations of interesting varieties.

CHAPTER THE FOURTH

ANIMAL LIFE

WILD beasts of large size no longer abound in Morocco, though some still exist in the remoter mountain districts, where they are beyond the ken of Europeans, who may live and travel for years in the country without ever crossing the track of anything more formidable than wild boar or fox or jackal; for they have to venture far before they catch sight of wild sheep, or even gazelle. But time was, and that not so very distant, when in the then much better wooded hills the roar of the king of the forest was heard, and lions were trapped, as they may be yet in some parts.

Wild beasts disappearing.

That they once abounded is beyond all doubt, not only on account of frequent references to them in modern as well as in ancient writers, but also on account of the number sent to Europe by various sultans as presents, many of which found their way to London.[1] * Idreesi, Leo, and other authors are agreed that their favourite haunts in Morocco were in the central mountainous district between Fez and Támsna, and down towards Salli, where, in the Ma'môra forest, Leo says, were "the most cruel and devouring lions in all Africa."[2] Those, however, whose habitat was the district of the Wád Warghá, between Fez and Wazzán,

Lions once plentiful.

* The only Barbary lion I ever saw was in the Zoological Gardens of Berlin, where also I first saw an áûdád.

[1] E.g. OCKLEY, p. 2. [2] Ed. BROWN, p. 410.

although numerous, were reported timid,[1] so much so, adds Gråberg,[2] that they became a byword, a timid man being said to be "brave as the lions of Agla—a calf could eat his tail!"

As this was not the character they usually bore, the anonymous writer "Ro. C." declared in 1609 that "the Country people where the Lyons most breed, when they meet with one looketh sternly and angerly in the Lyon's face, miscalling and rating him: in so doing the Lyon wil run away like a Dog." In recommending which course to foreign travellers, the practical Pellow suggests delivering abuse, for fear he may not understand English, in the language —if they can—of the country. Upon this "hollowing and staring at him," Pellow continues, "he gets him on his legs, and severely lashing his loins with his tail, walks from them, roaring after a terrible manner, and sits himself down again in the road, about the distance of a mile or two, when both traveller and lion behave again in the same manner; and after proving them thus a third time, the lion generally leaves them without interruption."[3] Then, what is more to the point, he adds, though he is no more unimpeachable than other travellers—"This I know to be true, having been obliged several times in my travels through the country to make the experiment." To this Dr. Brown appends in a note the statement concerning the Arabs that this is "an exact description of their present *modus operandi*,"[4] but for my own part I never yet came across a Moor who could record personal experience in this direction. Charant recommended frightening the royal beast by letting fly at him an unwound turban "like snakes,"[5] but Jackson reported the Arabs to have greater confidence in meeting him naked,

How to meet a Lion.

Doubtful evidence.

[1] Ed. Brown, p. 494. [2] p. 46. [3] Ed. Brown, p. 108. [4] Ib., p. 342. [5] p. 82

and Leo said, on the authority of natives, men and women, that if a woman did so, the lion would, "with crying and roaringe, cast his eyes upon the grounde, and so depart!"[1] But he cautiously adds "Beleeue it they that list."

There is a popular idea, too, that lions consider Jews, women, and children beneath their notice, so that a Jew is usually selected as keeper to one in confinement.[2] Buffa confirms" this[3] by the story told him of a Jew whom Mulai el Yazeed had let down to his lions when they had fasted for twenty-four hours; the lions refused to touch the seemingly dead man, though greedily devouring the heifer which followed.

Capture of Lions.

Mouëtte records the capture of lions in underground granaries (maṭmôrahs) baited with sheep,[4] which Jackson endorses,[5] but the introduction of gun-powder sounded their doom. Previous to that they had been so abundant that in 1549 more then fifty were collected by the ameer's order, each from a different ḳäïd, and their heads were fixed over a gate specially made in the ḳaṣbah wall of Marrákesh that he might march thence to the conquest of Fez.[6] Some of these were very large, the hide of one, morethan two *varas* ("yards") in length, being tanned for Torres, who tells the tale,[7] and who saw a stuffed lion in Tarudant more than twelve palms long. Fréjus, in 1670, saw lions roaming in the plains between Alhucemas and Táza,[8] and in 1681 and 5 they were met with both by Brooks and Phelps in their flight to the coast. Busnot described them early in the eighteenth century as growing bold and plentiful during the wars of succession, but they have since greatly diminished in numbers, and are only reported as occasionally seen in their old Central

[1] Ed. Brown, p. 946. [2] Hay's Life. [3] p. 116. [4] p. 79. [5] p. 35.
[6] See *The Moorish Empire*, p. 118. [7] p. 217. [8] p. 116.

Morocco haunts among the Zemmûr and above Tádla.[1] Gråberg says that in his time, 1832, lions and panthers were wont to come down from the Benî Arôs to the gates of Laraiche,[2] and Sir John Hay left on record the killing of a lion on the site of "Ravensrock," on Spartel Hill, near Tangier, about 1846. Gatell says their tracks in the sand were often pointed out to him in Sûs.[3]

Moorish Menageries.

Many of the Moorish sultans have kept native lions, panthers and other wild beasts in menageries at their capitals; to these animals condemned slaves and others were thrown,[4] as in a pit described by St. Olon at the gate of the Agudal of Marrákesh.[5] Sometimes strangely incompatible animals were brought up with young lions, as two gazelles and an eagle,[6] or a dog which had been cast in to them seven years before as food.[7] Mulai el Ḥasan III. kept panthers in this way, so tame that Erckmann saw them jump on the tent of the Council of State without anyone moving, since the beasts belonged to their master.[8] But the most remarkable Moorish lion story is told by Captain John Smith, of a young English watch-maker named Archer, who had found his way in those early days to Marrákesh. He had tamed a young lion which he afterwards gave to a French merchant, who in his turn took it to the King of France, by whom it was presented to King James I. of England. When, some time after, Archer found himself back in England, his servant visited the Tower of London, where the beast was confined, and it greeted him "with such an expression of acquaintance" that he was admitted to the cage for it to fawn upon him, and after his departure it refused to eat or drink for several days.

[1] De Foucauld, pp. 45 and 59. [2] p. 46. [3] p. 262, Oct. 1869.
[4] Puerto, p. 69; Mouette, *Hist.*, p. 317; Seran de la Tour, p. 12; Windus, etc.
[5] p. 263. [6] Davidson, p. 54. [7] Crouzenac, p. 95. [8] p. 222.

This story has its parallel in an experience of the late Sir John Hay. He had bred a Moorish leopard till full grown, when he had sent it to the Zoological Gardens in London, where, after two years, it was quick to recognize him on being addressed in Arabic. The Morocco leopard (namr)—the beast described by some writers on this country as a panther, sometimes also incorrectly as a tiger,—is of the size of a tiger, but spotted; it, too, is caught in maṭmôrahs. Lemprière reports the killing of one close to Tarudant, when he was there a century ago.[1] It is rarely that leopards' skins are exposed for sale, except in Sûs, but while the mountain districts remain closed to travellers these are the only proof of the continued presence of this animal.

Leopards.

Most of the other wild beasts in Morocco are also practically harmless unless attacked. The bear (ḍubb) is *said* to exist high up in the Atlas,[2] but I have never met anyone who had seen one. The hyena (ḍbâ) is found in caverns of the mountains, from which, unless, according to Leo, allured by music,[3] it only emerges at night, when in the dark it grubs up its food in the grave-yards, or attacks domestic animals, cows and donkeys even. So little do the plainsmen know of these creatures, that they get mixed up with the jackal (dheeb), * which is very common.

Other Wild Beasts.

Mouëtte tells of a wolf being slain at mid-night at the entrance to the new palace at Mequinez, by way of inauguration, the head being afterwards burned by the Europeans,[4] but it was probably a jackal to which he referred. This animal has again been confounded by some with the fox (tâleb), from which it may be easily distinguished, as, unlike Reynard, having no smell, and it has also been described as "a sort of wild dog." An-

* A name which properly means wolf.

[1] p. 178. [2] JACKSON, p. 26. [3] Ed. BROWN, p. 947. [4] *Hist.*, p. 243.

other writer says with regard to jackals, "wolf their sire, and fox their dam." * "Ro C." tells of hunting in Morocco "the Stagg, Antelop, Roe-Bucke, Hare, Fox, Debe —halfe a Dog halfe a Fox,—Wilde Hoge, Tiger, Wilde Cat and Leopard," but his list embraces too much. The other (Kelb el má', *i.e.* "water-dog"), is also found.

Elephants.

At one time the elephant might have been included, for it is mentioned by Pliny as belonging to these parts,[1] a statement strangely confirmed by the discovery in a raised sea beach near Tangier, of the jaw and tooth of an elephant (*Elephas antiquus*).[2] But even more remarkable was the discovery in Sûs by the Rabbi Mardokhaï, of ancient sculptures representing the elephant, rhinoceros, giraffe, and other animals long since extinct in that district.[3] The elephants' tusks exported till the beginning of the century were all imported from the western Şûdán and Timbuctoo. An elephant presented by the British Government in 1891 created such consternation in the Berber mind that it always preceded the army to clear the way. The only other mention of elephants occurs when one was brought from the Şûdán in the sixteenth century, and when another was presented by England to Mulai Ismâïl.

Aûdád or Wild sheep.

The áûdád (*Ovis tragelaphus*), a sort of wild sheep, is certainly the most typical of the horned beasts of Morocco.† It inhabits the almost inaccessible heights of the Atlas, where it has the reputation of throwing itself down great distances on to its

* The prevalence of similar ideas concerning the origin of the wolf is shown by an expression in Will Carleton's *Third Settler's Story*, which describes the dread creature as

"Beneath brute level; Half dog, half devil: The Indian animal he!"

† Sometimes confounded by sportsmen with the smaller moufflon (*Ovis musimon*), the wild sheep of Corsica and Sardinia. See illustration, p. 81.

[1] viii., 1. [2] Proc. Roy. Inst., vol. xiii., No. vi., and Quart. Journ. Geol. Soc., vol. xxxiv., "On the Geology of Gibraltar."

[3] Bull. Soc. Geogr., Bordeaux, t. xii., p. 129, with plate from "squeezes."

massive horns, sustained by still more massive shoulders. In appearance it is between a goat and a sheep, of reddish-brown colour and smooth hair, the fore-quarters somewhat resembling those of a horse in shape, but crowned by a pair of very thick, pointed, in-curling horns Extremely shy and keenly observant, it needs most careful stalking, especially on account of the slight cover found near its haunts, but has been hunted with success in mountains near the sea-coast, about 40 miles S. of Mogador.*

Gazelle.

The gazelle (ghazál) is also often met with in the plains, and is highly esteemed for its grace, on which account it is sometimes domesticated. A species of antelope (m'hor) is said never to lie down.[1] From this animal the natives extract the stomachic formation known as the "bezoar stone" (baïḍ el m'hor), † held in eastern lands to be an antidote for poison, especially for that of serpents, but I could not hear of it north of the Atlas. The rock-squirrel (satinjáb er-rûm) is common in some parts, as among the Zemmûr; and the sibsib, a kindred species, is eaten as a delicacy—although not lawful food—its back being first well rubbed with a stone, under the impression that this will make it tender.[2]

Smaller Wild Animals.

The porcupine (ḍurb or ḍurbán) and the hedgehog (ḳanfood) ‡ are both found, as also the caracal lynx (kâb), which has such an unpleasant smell that it is said that even fleas refuse to settle on it! Ichneumons (zardab), genets and weasels are numerous in the South. A tail-less "ape"—*Macacus inuus*—(ḳard) is principally found in Anjera on the Gibraltar Straits, in the neighbourhood of Jebel Mûsà—known therefore to Europeans as Apes' Hill,—the original stock of the Simian family still residing in diminished numbers on

* It breeds very freely in the London Zoological Gardens.

† A calculus found in the bladder, weighing 3 to 4 oz., and selling at about $2½ per oz.

‡ Pron. "ginfood" in the South.

[1] Jackson, p. 29.

[2] Jackson.

the rock of Gibraltar. The natives also know a monkey (ḳimrood) with a tail.

The wild cat (ḳaṭṭ el khlá) is also occasionally met with, and so once were wild cattle (baḳar el khlá), said to have existed in the woods of "Boomar" till the beginning of the century, the last—according to Hay[1]—having been killed about 1835. They were described by this contemporaneous writer as of a dun colour, with long horns, but light of frame; dangerous when wounded. In the western Saḥara cattle of any sort are rare.[2]

Wild Boar.

Wild pigs (ḥalloof) still remain plentiful enough in the marshes and brushwood throughout the country. By natives they are hunted with greyhounds (sloghîs), which take hold by the nape of the neck, but by Europeans they are shot in the south and speared in the north, the latter sport having been introduced by that modern Nimrod, Sir John Drummond Hay.[3]* Notwithstanding the prohibition of the pig (khanzeer) as food, its wild congener is sometimes devoured by the mountaineers, and one sultan is described as having a weakness for pork, fattening pigs for his table; but then he also bred and ate rats![5] These latter creatures

Rats, etc.

are so abundant in some districts that they become a veritable plague to the farmers, and might almost have given rise to Dick Whittington's fortune, but that his venture seems to have succeeded somewhere east of Morocco.[6] The jerboa or "jumping mouse," called here the zarbo'a, is also found. Rabbits (koneeah) are found north of the Bû Ragrag chiefly, and hares (árneb) are common in most parts, but

* A specially fine boar, shot in 1898 near Laraiche by Sr. de Cuevas, measured from snout to end of tail 6 ft. 9. in.; height at shoulders, 3 ft. 4 in.; length of lower tusks, 7¾ in., the skull, after skinning, 16 in. in length.[4]

[1] p. 66. [2] De Foucauld, p. 125. [4] Al-Moghreb Al-Aksa, Ap. 16th.

[3] See Murray's Magazine, vol. iii., Mch. and Apl., for his "Boar-hunting in Morocco."

[5] Braithwaite, p. 320. [6] See *The Moorish Empire*, p. 400.

"PIG-STICKING" IN MOROCCO.

though the former are lawful food, they are seldom eaten, on account of their resemblance to the forbidden hares. Some tell us seriously of strange hybrids (áfghool) in this country, such as the offspring of bull and ass or bull and mare,[1] to say nothing of more fanciful creatures due to distorted descriptions and native imagination.

Camels.

Among the domestic animals it is hard to know whether to give the first place to the camel or the horse, since each in its sphere and use is supreme. But the camel is more typical of its masters, slow-going but plodding; hardy, ill-kempt and grumbling, if not rebellious: even our name for it is borrowed from the Arabic, jemel.[2] In the northern and mountainous parts it is by no means common, for the southern districts bordering the desert are its home, and the mountain routes prove fatal to such large numbers, that mules and donkeys are there employed in preference. The sharp stones cut their feet, and being unprovided with wool like the varieties I encountered in high altitudes in Persia and elsewhere, they suffer much from cold. Barley is then given them once a week, and such importance is attached to their service that when on the march with his army, the late sultan himself would be present to see that they got it.[3]

The Camel as Food.

The pad-like feet of the camel soon slip on moist ground, and if the leg of one with a load slips outwards, as it usually does, the camel cannot rise again, for the muscles are strained, so it is at once despatched with a knife that it may become lawful food. The flesh is not unpleasant—it seemed to me like somewhat tough beef—and the hump, mostly fat, is in great request.* In order to divide the carcass fairly, it is cut up in as many portions as there are

* The hump (drooa) of a young camel, if abnormally fat, is sometimes removed by incision, and the skin replaced. [Andrews.]

[1] Davidson. [2] Pronounced in Egypt gemel. [3] Erckmann, p. 294.

CAMEL CARAVAN OUTSIDE THE WALLS OF MARRAKESH.

Photograph by F. G. Aflalo, Esq.

claimants for shares, and each having been requested to contribute some small article for the purpose, a passer-by or one of their number is deputed to place one article on each share, which is thus allotted to the owner of the article deposited upon it. The flesh that is not immediately eaten is cut into strips and dried in the sun for future consumption. *

Varieties of Camels.

The varieties of camels employed are numerous, the classification chiefly depending on speed, though to the north of the Atlas they are now seldom used except for burdens, which they carry far —five hundredweight a piece—but slowly, seldom covering more than thirty miles a day. I have nevertheless been assured by an otherwise trustworthy native, of a case in which one of the fleetest kind—a dromedary—mahri mahar or haria—performed the journey from Fez to Tangier and back in a day, some 300 miles in all, but then my informant had only the word of the rider. Jackson records a passage from Fort St. Joseph in Senegal to Mogador in seven days,[1] and Leo says that men have travelled on camels from Timbuctoo to Dra'a and Tafîlált in eight days,[2] but many native figures are only figures of speech.

Figures of Speech.

A dromedary reputed to perform three days' journey in one is styled thlataï, and is reckoned worth thirty ordinary camels; a dromedary doing seven days' journey in one is a sebá'í, worth 100; and one of those rare creatures capable of undertaking nine to the every-day one—a ķesá'í—if it is to be found, is estimated as worth 200, while an enthusiastic Moorish friend has written down for me the name of

* On the desert, when all but starving, the party of Arabs who had captured Riley beyond Wád Nûn, not only ate the entrails unwashed and raw, but cooked the blood and consumed it,[3] contrary to one of the most rigidly observed Mosaic laws endorsed by Mohammed.

[1] p. 39. [2] p. 941 (Brown). [3] *Narrative*, p. 120.

the 'ashárî, as good for ten times thirty miles in twenty-four hours, or just the distance of the first record mentioned above. Leo declares that some have gone for fifteen days without water, five or nine days being the regulation intervals between their drinks, adding that to make them go when tired they are sung to by their drivers.[1] The natives say that the number of ordinary day's journeys a camel will accomplish in twenty-four hours is the number of days it "sleeps," *i.e.*, while its eyes remain closed, after birth.[2]

Camels are very seldom ridden in North Morocco except by prisoners, four of whom I once saw chained in pairs, slung on the back of one animal: it was not until a camel-corps was forming in Assuán for the Ṣûdán campaign that I had a chance of riding one myself. Leo also mentions dancing camels, trained on a heated floor, but though I never heard of such, I have seen the she-camels (náḳahs), hobbled with their young in the open, execute a very creditable caper on my approach on a bicycle, their long-legged offspring careering round them in style.

In the far south, camel's milk is the chief article of diet for man and beast,[3] but in Morocco proper it is much less used, only the slender desert-horse (ḥabb er-reeḥ or "gust of wind") being so dieted.*[4] But this is an exceptional breed, seldom met with, and the average Moorish horse—or rather pony, according to our standards—is a wiry little beast, accustomed chiefly to barley and broken straw, with grass in Spring, and beans when in season to fatten him. Geldings are unknown, and stallions are only ridden by the military and official classes; farmers and Arabs prize

Horses.

* The first, and frequently the second, draught is often brought up again, and a laxative is required after dismounting.

[1] p. 942 (Brown). [2] St. Olon, p. 24. [3] See Caillé's *Narrative*. [4] Jackson, p. 42.

more highly their mares, which they commonly ride, very often on top of heavy loads. The 'Abda and M'tûga breeds are celebrated, and at El 'Adeer, adjoining the closed port of Waladîya numbers are bred for the Sultan, who maintains some hundreds in his stables. His Majesty, while prohibiting their exportation otherwise, frequently presents them to foreign governments, or visitors.

Breeds of Horses.

Colonel Trotter remarked that most of the steeds he saw in the imperial stables seemed to have about them somewhat of the dray-horse, which he thought was perhaps accounted for by the fact that George III. made the Sultan of his day a present of some stallions of that breed.[1] Queen Victoria in her jubilee year sent several diminutive Shetland ponies to His Shareefian Majesty; perhaps some future traveller will trace their influence. When, in the fifties, Portugal was threatened by Spain, an Englishman was sent to Morocco to attempt the purchase of 500 horses for the Portuguese, but after consultation with his ministers, 'Abd er-Raḥman replied that it would be contrary to the practice of Islám, and dangerous to his Empire to provide the Nazarenes with so many steeds, which he must decline to do.[2] The efforts of Sir John (then Mr.) Hay in 1837 to secure for the young Queen's riding a barb of pure breed, were also futile. In spite of the fine creatures often raised, especially in the imperial stables, pure breed is rare, and pedigree has been lost sight of.

Characteristics.

The most highly prized beast has a small head, and tremendous shoulders in proportion to his small and rapidly sloping hind-quarters; mane and tail are left long: the shoeing is rough, but light. Many have their hind legs weakened by the sudden drawing up on their haunches in the "powder-play" when young, so that but few have a fair chance.

[1] p. 134. [2] RICHARDSON, vol. i., p. 166.

In documents of sale ('aḳd el bee'a) they are disposed of as "bones in bag" (el a'dhm f'il khanshah), *i.e.*, "for better for worse," and the signatures of notaries are necessary, which can only be obtained on payment of a tax to the appointed officer. Horses being considered noble creatures, are prohibited as mounts to unprotected Jews; formerly they were prohibited to non-official Europeans;* now even Jews evade this restriction, outside towns and in open ports. Horses are never flayed for the worth of their skins, as leather made from "unclean" animals is not used in Morocco. If a soldier's horse dies on the road, he cuts off the right ear to present as a proof that he has not sold it. But when Mulai el Ḥasan heard, on one of his Sûs expeditions, that as they could not support them the men were cutting off the ears of live horses which were then deserted, he made them ride their horses ear-less.[1] The cavalry allowance for steeds is about half a stone of barley a day, but artillery horses, and those for imperial use, get about double, with straw in addition.[2] Wealthy Moors prefer mules for travelling, on account of their pace, and their prices are therefore higher in proportion.

Horse Dealing.

Military Horses.

Of the remaining domestic animals there is but little to say. Mules and donkeys do most of the work in the towns, oxen ploughing in the country, to the detriment of beef. As they and the cows are left to pick up what they can in the open, whatever the weather, the latter give little milk, and that but for a short time in spring, yielding it only while the calf looks on.† Sheep do better, as feeding on

Humble Domestic Animals.

* As late as 1837 the Governor of Tangier allowed the Consuls-General to keep only one horse each, on the understanding that no one else was to ride it.[3]

† A custom common in the East. I have seen stuffed calves exhibited in India to deceive the cows about to be milked.

[1] Erckmann. [2] Ib., p. 248. [3] F. O. Docs, "Morocco," vol. iv.

less and better protected; their wool—of good quality—forms one of the principal exports, but a wool-less, hornless breed (dimán) is found in Dra'a and Tafilált.[1] On the upper part of the back the hair has a tendency to curl, but is otherwise straight; their flesh is excellent.

Sheep are said to be indigenous to the slopes of the Atlas, whence they have spread all over the world,[2] but this would not be easy to substantiate. They yean twice a year, bearing two at a time, but even at that they cannot keep pace with the goats, which abound, and furnish the famous leather; goat-flesh is eaten, but is held in less favour than mutton. The remaining domestic quadrupeds are the familiar cats and dogs, the former not plentiful. The latter abound, being everywhere employed as guards. To escape their attack when approaching a village, Urquhart recommends the plan adopted by Ulysses, of dropping one's stick and sitting down, when the dogs will crouch too. But they will seldom face a volley of stones, or even the motion of throwing, seemingly considering their duties those of warning, not of defence.

Birds of Prey.

Of flying things Morocco has good store,* not a few being birds of prey: the golden and Bonelli's eagles ('oḳáb or nisr), the griffon-vulture, the Egyptian vulture (rukhm), the osprey (bû ḥoot—"father of fish"), the sparrow-hawk (bû 'amṣeerah), the hen-harrier (bû h'seen), the marsh-harrier (hadî), the peregrine falcon (n'bli or ṭaïr el ḥorr—"the free bird"), the kestrel (báz), the kite, the raven (ghuráb) and the carrion-crow (sarroo'). In the South many of the governors hunt with

* For a more complete list with Latin names, see IRBY, *Ornithology of the Straits of Gibraltar*. Mr. C. A. Payton has ready for press a work on *Birds of Southern Morocco*, also with Latin names for 242 varieties. I am indebted to him for a kind revision of this superficial enumeration. The native names here given are chiefly those of Northern Morocco.

[1] ROHLFS, p. 348, and HARRIS. [2] KNIGHT's Encyclopædia.

HAWKING IN MOROCCO.

hawks and falcons, and birds for that purpose are sometimes imported, although at one time counted among Moorish exports.[1] Sir John Hay records that when the east winds commence in March, hundreds of falcons, eagles, hawks, kestrels, kites and buzzards cross the straits from the Marshán near Tangier, flying against the wind.[2]

Storks.

Among less formidable birds, though larger, must be named the stork (bilárj), which holds a special place. On roofs of houses, on cottage thatch, on ruins and mosque-towers, the storks collect the rude assemblage of sticks which form their nest, adding certainly a picturesque effect, though from their noisiness not pleasant neighbours. As a slayer of serpents the stork is held sacred, and if he fails to return any year to his accustomed haunt, some evil is feared. From his coign of vantage he can look down into the women's quarters, so the love-sick trust to him their messages and secrets. Thus an imaginative writer on Morocco hears a lad sing to the stately bird: "O Stork; O thou of the tall figure; thou who dwellest on the top of the tower; go thou and salute for me the scornful coquette who wears anklets on her echoing feet, and who spurns my passion." Another story makes out the stork to have been a ķáḍî, "at the time of the world's transformation" (miskh), when, before Mohammed's time, there occurred sundry changes. Still another account represents these birds as transformed Arabs who have ventured to plunder the Mekka caravans.[3]

Fez Legend.

In Fez there once was money left to provide for the care of sick storks,[4] of which I gleaned the following account in that city, where there is still a "Stork Street" (Zunkat Bilárj) in memory of

[1] See treaty with Pisa in 1358, MAS LATRIE's collection.

[2] *Life*, p. 268. [3] ST. OLON, p. 30. [4] ALI BEY, p. 74.

the affair. The story runs that several hundred years ago a stork came to the ḳáḍî of Fez, and laid at his feet a pearl necklace. The ḳáḍî sent for the muédh-dhins to see if they, who got good views of the town, could say whence this bird came. One of them recognized it as the owner of a nest which a certain man had just cleared away from his roof. The ḳáḍî sent for the man, who confessed to having done so, upon which the ḳáḍî asked him what he would take for the whole house, selling the necklace and paying him out of the funds. The surplus and the rent of the house he handed to Sidî Farj, with instructions to always tend, doctor and feed any sick storks which might be brought to the place, while the dispossessed bird went and rebuilt its nest. The truth of the matter seems to be that a stork let drop a pearl necklace it had stolen, like the jackdaw of Rheims, with the proceeds of which, as the owner could not be found, the ḳáḍî purchased a house still in existence, since called Stork House, the rent of which is collected by the administrator of Sîdî Farj, with the injunction to receive storks as if human beings, since the house came to them through the instrumentality of those birds. There is a similar "Stork Hospital" in Marrákesh.

Ostriches.

Formerly the ostrich (na'ám) was considered one of the birds of Morocco, but if met with at all within the Sultan's dominions, it is to the extreme and practically unknown south that it is now confined. Yet Idreesi speaks of ostriches as existing in Sháwiya in incredible numbers[1] Jackson tells us that the natives of the Saḥara used to catch them by hurling a short stick (zarwátah), cut from the gum-arabic tree, wherewith they broke their legs.[2] He confirms Idreesi's recommendation of the fat for bruises, sprains and external maladies, but not for deafness. The feathers used

[1] p. 82. [2] p. 60

to find an important outlet at Mogador,* but European marts have long been mainly supplied from other countries. Now only their eggs are brought, for hanging in the shrines of saints, or for the European "curio'" trade.

Ornithological Summary.

When one comes to the less common birds, identification by native names is exceedingly doubtful, since the general ignorance is such that any name is given to enquirers at random, and few natives know the names of any but the commonest species. Often the confusion grows almost hopeless, whether with beast, bird or fish, and so it must remain till naturalists themselves have an opportunity of systematically scouring the country.† Most of the native appellations are merely local nick-names. Meanwhile the ornithological list includes the flamingo (bû'l malaf), pelican (ḥaml el baḥri, *i.e.* "sea-burden,") gannet, various gulls and many terns, heron ('onk-hu ma' el wád, *i.e.* "neck-in-river" or 'aïshoosh) said to be deaf, wild goose (burk el khlá), wild duck (wuzz), about fifteen varieties of teal, greater bustard (ḥabás), lesser bustard (ra'áḍ), ruffed bustard (ḥabás es-sulṭán), guinea-fowl (tafarmah), plovers grey—(karzeeṭ), green (bibaṭ) and golden (duráj)—red-legged and three-toed partridge (ḥajlah), francolin (lakut), sand-grouse (kudri), snipe (bû manḳash or bel ower), quail (samánah or rookah), wood-cock (daját el ghábah), rock-pigeon and wood-pigeon (ḥamám),‡ dove (leemám), turtle-dove

* Jackson gives as the average proportion of feathers in 100 lbs., worth $900, about 1800: 75 lbs. small black, 8½ best ("zumar"), 8½ long black, and 8½ lbs. passably fine, including 2 lbs. surplus face, 3 lbs. fine face, 3 lbs. 2nd quality, reckoned as 2 lbs., 4 lbs. face reckoned as 2 lbs.; and 3 lbs. poor face reckoned as 1 lb. Four surplus face were reckoned an ounce, or 54 feathers a pound. Young ostriches are called deelm.

† The valuable contribution by Favier and Irby deals almost exclusively with Tangier and the country round, for which it is fairly exhaustive.

‡ Barbary pigeons have given their name to the variety called "Barbs," for which Mary Queen of Scots pined in captivity. See also *Henry IV.*, Part 2, Act II., Sc. IV., "He will not swagger with a Barbary hen."

(gereega or dhukr Allah, "praise God"), stone-curlew (bû m'khaït), whimbrel, scops owl (ma'roof), white owl (moo-kah), little owl (muïkah), tawny owl (oolwál or hámt el jráf), screech-owl (saher or boomah) and blue roller (shar-raḳráḳ) swarming in the date-palms round Marrákesh.

SPURS, BIT, GLOVE AND HOOD USED IN HAWKING.
Drawn by R. Caton Woodville.

Minor Feathered Creatures.

Among the smaller feathered creatures and songsters are the swift (sooïf or ṭaïr ábábeel), linnet (simrees), lark (zaree'a el baḳurí), crested lark (ḳob'a), nightingale (b'laghlagh, mû'lḥasan or andaleeb), wood-pecker (nakab), red-breast (áḥmar ásdar), gold-finch (makneen), magpie (ben srindi), cuckoo (takkook), swallow (khuṭeefah), sparrow (burṭálah or joosh), buff-backed egret (ṭaïr el baḳar, *i.e.*, "cow-bird")—which frees cattle from parasites,—peewit or lapwing (beebeet)—named by its cry,—said once to have been a Jew, and still to wear the black cap though it has accepted Mohammed; black-bird (khádm el jinán—"garden-slave"), starling (zarzoor), wag-tail (el m'kaḥḥal—"the antimony-holder") and a shrike called el háj—"the pilgrim,"—which has been said to follow the caravans to Mekka and back, when at home residing chiefly on the argán trees, feeding on putrified beetles which it has impaled on thorny bushes till "ripe."[1] The hoopoe and the brilliant bee-eater are also known.

As a domestic bird, the ordinary chicken is found in abundance, but of small size; the duck is common only in certain districts, as round Mazagan; the turkey chiefly in Marrákesh; while pigeons haunt the grain marts if not actually bred there When the Spaniards were besieging Algeciras in 1279 the Moors communicated with the beleaguered town from Gibraltar by carrier-pigeons,[2] but this use for them is now unknown.

Amphibia.

The amphibious creatures of Morocco include the tortoise (fakran), of which Leo says that under seven years old it is "a perfect medicine against the leprosie."[3] The water-tortoise abounds in the rivers, and the land-tortoise, also very numerous, is at times exported to England for hawking about our streets. Frogs and toads are plentiful. Leeches ('alḳ) used to be exported in great numbers when more widely prescribed, the monopoly being sold as late as 1859 for $25,000. They are most troublesome to animals drinking from the streams, so that in travelling one needs to be on the look-out for them.

Reptiles.

Among the reptiles in Morocco, several of the snakes (haïyah) are venomous, the most important being the puff-adder (bû sakka) and the hooded snake, *Cobra capella** (el fáa'), from the bite of which the

* Of this Mr. W. H. C. Andrews writes, that although without the *distinct* design on the hood and back of the Indian cobra, it is sometimes possessed in a modified form.

[1] JACKSON p. 70. [2] RAÔḌ EL ḲARṬÁS, p. 473. [3] Ed. BROWN, p. 950..

victim soon dies, the body gradually turning black. Both of these species are tamed by the 'Aïsáwa charmers. Equally dangerous is the áûsáṭ. Riley tells the story[1] of a contest between a man and a fáa' and a bû sakka. The man was wounded all over, bleeding and swollen; his teeth had to be forced open with a piece of iron, and a blackish liquid poured into his mouth as well as over his wounds, his comrade holding his lips together and breathing into his lungs by his nose till he revived. The effect of music—such as it is—on these serpents may often be seen on the markets; but I have also watched a snake on a house-top mesmerise a bird till it could not fly away.[2] It is said that they fear man, but not woman, and that while the latter pass they will keep quiet. Of the harmless varieties (ḥensh) * some, as the bû marueeh, are allowed to live in the house as good omens, eating the rats etc.

Small Fry.

The chameleon (tátah or booïah), which is common in many parts, is also called "the serpent's foe,"[3] (a'dooh el áḥnish); its dried body is used as an antidote to snake-bite and as an aphrodisiac. Lizards (takleet) are frequently seen, one (ḍabb) which habits the borders of the Saḥara, being, according to Leo, a cubit in length.[4] Scorpions ('aḳrab) are occasionally encountered, of various sorts, brown, black and yellow, of which the black is said never to be fatal, while the last-named is most dangerous. Cauterization is the only remedy, the limb stung being well bound above the bite, but the natives have much faith in the flesh of the creature itself, and often keep a decoction in oil ready for application. There is also a poisonous spider, smaller than the ordinary *tarantula*, (bû siḥa) which, though fatal to

* The Saḥara is said to contain no other, but to include the boâ (to'abán).

[1] p. 551. [2] Cf. IRBY, p. 83. [3] See ed. BROWN, p. 954. [4] Ib., p. 953.

horses and cattle, is not so to man.* Two vipers are found the horned *cerastes* and *V. 'latastii*. Centipedes (shooát el khaïl) are plentiful, and so are minute obnoxious insects which need no enumeration. De Foucauld mentions a peculiar sort of long-haired caterpillar (yakh), which is said to be born of the snow, on the disappearance of which it is discovered on the Ghaïáta mountains in eastern Morocco only, and is greedily eaten by goats.[1] Some few silk-worms are bred in Fez, but most of the silk is imported. Locusts (jerád) periodically swarm up from the desert, and in the grub state are eaten by boars, jackals, foxes etc., while egg-laden females are esteemed a delicacy, boiled in salt and water like prawns, which they resemble. Chickens eat so many that their own flesh tastes of locust. At the same time Morocco is remarkably free from dangerous or really troublesome insects such as often render life unpleasant in southern latitudes, venomous creatures of no sort being common, and pests like white ants are unknown. Mosquitoes are only troublesome in towns or near water.

Ocean Denizens.

The waters of the Morocco coast and interior afford a very interesting study.† To begin with the largest inhabitants of the Ocean, whales are not infrequently observed in the offing, and sometimes found dead on the shore, when diligent search is made for the much coveted ambergris. The grampus is known in the South as tizmikt or asabán. The most numerous shark is the hideous hammer-head (izimmer): the voracious blue shark is common enough, while the

* A hot bath, or intense perspiration induced by placing the patient, rolled in blankets, in a hole in the ground which has been heated by the burning of straw, is the approved native treatment.[2]

† For most of the information given under this head I am indebted to Mr. C. A. Payton, now British Consul at Calais, who has been so kind as to revise the whole section.

[1] p. 28. [2] Kerr, p. 85.

SHABEL FISHING ON THE UM ER-RABÎ'A AT AZAMMÛR.

Photograph by F. E. Aflalo, Esq.

white shark and the thresher or sea-fox are occasionally met with. Sharks do not as a rule come close to the shore, so that sea-bathing is in most parts indulged in fearlessly. The dolphin (*Delphinus delphis*), abundant all along the coast, is often confounded with the porpoise, which is much scarcer.

Food Fish.

Turning to food-fish, we find Southern Morocco visited occasionally by large and valuable shoals of azlimzah, (*Sciæna aquila*), known farther north as the *corbina* or *maigre*, averaging about 30 lbs., but running up to 60 lbs. or over, and the tasargelt (*Temnodon saltator*), identical with the "blue fish" of North America.* The tunny is occasionally caught, also the smaller short-finned tunny, the albacore and the germon. On the north-western coast a considerable fishery for bonito and mackerel is carried on by boats from Spain and Portugal, salting down their takes on the spot.[1] Otherwise, with the exception of quantities of shabel or "shebbel," a very rich flavoured variety of *Clupea alosa*†—which runs in vast numbers up the larger rivers, as the Sebû and Bû Ragrag, in spring, and is roughly salted for the interior and the Saḥára, where it affords a healthful change from a date-diet,—and a good deal of tasargelt and aẓlimzah similarly treated, the fisheries of Morocco are not developed beyond the supply of local demands. Cod is among the fish caught by the Spaniards off the Canaries, and besides being far more plentiful there, its quality is reputed in Spain to be much better than that of either Newfound-

Salted Fish.

* In September 1887 it returned to our shores in a vast shoal after an absence of nearly twenty years.

† Frequently misnamed the "Barbary Salmon," in reality of the shad family.

[1] See Lieut. PEDRO PUENTE, *Informe sobre las Pesquerias de los Canarios en la Costa de Africa*, a report to the Spanish Minister of Marine, Madrid, 1882; and PEREZ DEL TORO, *España en el Noroeste de Africa*, Madrid, 1892.

land or Scotland.[1] A large quantity of this is actually salted on the Morocco coast.[2] *

Flat-fish are represented by excellent and plentiful soles and less common turbot, both known as ḥoot or ḥeut Mûsà ("fish of Moses"), also large and numerous skate (fajar or "fijjer"), not eaten by the natives, thornbacks, eagle and sting-rays, and the electric ray or torpedo. This or a similar "numb-fish" is said to go some distance up some of the rivers, as the sting-ray certainly does. It produces an effect like an electric shock on being touched, an effect attributed also to a sort of sand-eel in the Ṣûdán rivers, by which the whole body may be paralysed for half an hour.[3] Bass are very plentiful, especially in the South, where they are known as bû shaûk or "father of thorns," from the spinous dorsal fin.

Flat-fish.

Grey mullet (boori) are everywhere numerous, and ascend rivers to a great distance from the sea, being even caught near Morocco City. The red mullet or surmullet is known as sulṭán el ḥoot or "king of fish," also as "rûmi" or European, a name flatteringly applied in the South to other estimable fish, such as the John Dory (*Zeus faber*). Conger-eels (asîghagh or asîrar) are plentiful, also pink snapper and red stump-nose (*Pagrus auriga* and *Pagrus unicolor*), interesting from their resemblance to Australian and South African fish. Several varieties of the bream family

Favourite Dainties.

* Mr. Payton tells me he never saw a cod on his part of the coast, where the only representatives of the *Gadidæ* family appeared to be the hake (*Gadus Merlucius*), the "great fork-beard (*G. bifurcatus*), sometimes erroneously termed rock-cod, and the bib or pouting (*G. Luscus*), all three numerous at Mogador, where the two latter are called towilkt, and the hake taghaïud.

[1] Capt. F. Duro, Report in *Annuario de la Comision de Pesca*, Madrid 1868—9, p. 200.

[2] See Herbert Hounsell of Bridport, *Fisheries Exhibition Literature*, vol. v., p. 157.

[3] Davidson.

(*Pagellus Owenii*, *centrodontus*, *mormyrus*, etc.), two or three varieties of *lichia*; garfish, scad, several wrasses, and, of smaller food-fishes, sardines (sardeel) very plentiful in summer, and taken in great quantities in ground sieves at Mogador, the big azlimzah which follow them into shallow water to prey on them being sometimes caught in the same net, also the less-esteemed anchovy (shtoon or sanamoorah) and atherine or sand-smelt (wizeet or hamreeda). Mackerel, variously styled "zerroeg" or "cavalli" is also common. Dog-fish (kelb el b'ḥar) are chiefly represented by the piked, spotted and smooth hound and black-mouthed species. The curious "scabbard-fish" and "silvery hair-tail" are sometimes encountered.

River Fish.

The principal river fish are the barbel varieties, *Barbus camptacanthus*, *B. Fritschii* and *B. Reinii*, which attain a fair size in the larger rivers, and are sometimes salted for sending moderate distances. The trout, (*Salmo fario macrostigma*) which appears similar to the Algerian variety, occurs in streams in the Anjera hills near Tangier, Wád Aguilar, affluents of the Tetuan river, the Beni Hassan mountains and elsewhere. Eels, which sometimes attain a considerable size, abound in rivers and lakes, and are said to be speared and salted in the latter. Between Mehdîya and Laraiche the natives hunt them with poles from a sort of punt-like raft of rushes. Davidson says that fish are caught in the south by putting pieces of a small tree about 5 feet high ("yeghan traino") into the water, which intoxicates and blinds them.

Crustaceans and Molluscs.

Of crustaceans the red-brown crayfish (asfél) is much more common than the lobster (tarooshṭ); the edible crab of Europe does not seem to occur, but there are plenty of spider and soldier-crabs (akreesha), and minor varieties; the prawn (cameroon) is very plentiful, the true shrimp extremely scarce.

Of edible molluscs, small rock-oysters are plentiful in parts, mussels of two varieties immensely abundant in rocky grounds, attaining great size, and much used as bait. Cockles are found in suitable localities. The octopus (azaïs) and squid (amrumd) are plentiful, especially the former, attaining considerable size, and forming the favourite bait for the larger fish.

Authorities.

Quite a number of writers have contributed to the far from perfect list of Moroccan fauna, but there has been no serious attempt at completeness. In addition to the authors quoted, whose remarks are merely casual, a list, not always correct, was completed by Fernand Lataste in 1885, as part of a work on the Barbary States, which is the only thing of the sort in existence. Dr. Bleicher had ten years previously collected a few notes from his own observation, as had also Prof. Graeles on the coast of Sûs, where Duro collected specimens from Ooïna.[1]

Sport.

Sport has received more attention, especially at the hands of Sir John Drummond Hay, and in the valuable reports and articles of Mr. Payton, formerly Consul at Mogador;[2] Messrs. Alvarez and Stutfield having also done something in this way. Pig-sticking in Morocco has been ably dealt with by Captain (now Colonel) Baden-Powell in his work on that subject.*

Ornithology and Icthyology.

The birds of Morocco have been studied by Carstensen, who published an imperfect list of those met with round Tangier in 1852; by Tyrwhitt-Drake, who covered the same ground in 1867; and by Favier, whose list has been incorporated in the ornithology of the Straits of Gibraltar by Lieut.-Col. Irby (1875), and under the nom-de-plume of "Sarcelle,"

* See note at end of chapter. I have also to thank Mr. W. B. Harris and Mr. F. G. Aflalo for suggesting several emendations in this chapter.

[1] Bul. Geog. Madrid, 1873, vol. 2, p. 21. (B. Mus., Ac. 6018).

[2] Bibl., Arts. 1320, 1365, 1366, 1319, 1399, 1503, 1548, 1670, 1907 and 1908.

Mr. Payton has contributed to the *Field*[1] important notes on the wild-fowl of Southern Morocco.* On the fish in Moorish waters he is also the authority, having collected valuable matter for an illustrated work for the subject, besides having written numerous articles in the *Field* and elsewhere, which one could wish condensed into a volume.[2] Albert Günther (1874) is the only other writer who has taken up the subject, noting some new species.

Conchology, Malacology etc.

The conchology of Morocco was furthered by Lowe on his brief visit to Mogador in 1859, and Paladilhe has described a collection by Dr. Bleicher (1874). Dr. Kobelt also made important conchological notes at Tetuan and Tangier in 1881. Mr. Payton has compiled a list of shells—sea, fresh water and land—comprising 181 species. In the region of malacology, Bourguignat's work and plates of Algerian molluscs (1865) include many Morocco species. Professors Rein and Fritsch had collected fifty-four species in 1872, catalogued with plates by Professor Mousson, and those collected by Dr. Kobelt were reviewed by M. Pechaud. Moorish reptiles and batrachians have been catalogued with plates by Mr. Boulenger of the British Museum, from twenty-three varieties collected by Mr. Vaucher in 1889, and others by Mr. Lataste, forty-four species of the seventy-four discovered in the whole of Barbary. A few Moorish species were also included in the list published by Gervais in 1836.

* Among other birds rare in these parts he shot two brent, and saw one bernicle goose near Mogador.

[1] Bibl, Arts. 1456, 1458, 2002, 2055 and 2056.

[2] Bibl., Arts. 1364, 1549, 1671, 1751, 1752, 1822, 1824 2001, general; 1502, 1673, 1820 1823, azlimzah; 1505, 1820, 1951, bass; 1547, 1750, grey mullet; 1753, 1821, 1950, 1952, 1954, 1957, casergelt; 1818, trout; 1906, barbels; 1946, sardines.

The following note, with much interesting matter elsewhere incorporated, has been kindly furnished to me by Mr. W. H. C. Andrews, of Saffi.

"The plains of Abda, in Central Morocco, afford very excellent coursing ground. Greyhounds and horses are procurable; hares are plentiful. In the hilly districts the jackal and fox are easily found, and the never-failing partridge abounds. On the flat ground, during hot weather, the lesser bustard visits the cooler districts near the sea, and, although a very wary bird of powerful flight, can usually be shot from donkey or mule-back, as he allows the mounted sportsman to approach within reasonable distance, an almost unaccomplishable feat on foot, unless at midday during extreme heat.

Sport in Central Morocco.

"In the farther interior one finds with the partridge the desert partridge and golden grouse, or 'koodri,' also several varieties of plover, and the two larger varieties of bustard, called here 'khabas Sulṭán,' or the ruffed bustard, and 'khabas el kabeer,' or great bustard, a plain-plumed grandee, with a very hoarse, grunting kind of note. Towards the end of the autumn they may be seen in the early morning, feeding under cover of the bushes, usually four or five together. The Arabs catch the big bustard alive by trapping him, but one leg, more often both, will be severely injured by the trap, and a lame bustard in captivity is not a pleasant sight. The trap is concealed amongst a large patch of ashes—in which, it seems, the bustard loves to roll—carefully arranged in the woods by his human enemies, who watch his gambols and eventual discomfiture from some place of concealment near at hand.

Trapping Bustards.

"Wild boar are numerous throughout the country bordering the Tansift, and near Marrákesh the wild-fowl shooting on the river is magnificent, while snipe simply abound in the creeks. The gazelle is usually to be found in the most deserted spots of the Ḥáḥá and Raḥámna plains.

"From Waladîya for some twenty-five miles, parallel with the sea, runs a river or lagoon of salt water, separated from the sea by a narrow tongue of grass land, occupied by few inhabitants, but wherein a number of mares belonging to the Government are placed to graze and breed at leisure. The creeks of the lagoon form a perfect playground for innumerable snipe, wild-fowl, flamingoes, *et hoc genus omne* dear to the sportsman, not to be found in more accessible spots. The lagoon, too, teems with mullet, bass, and various other kinds of fish."

Mr. Andrews has also furnished me with the following measurements of skins which he has inspected in Morocco. *Panther* at Saffi from the Zemmûr district, from nose to extremity of tail, 7 ft. 8 in.: *leopard* (quite different colour and marking, common in Sûs) without head or tail, shoulder to rump, 3 ft. 4 in.: *áûdad*, shoulder to tail, 4 ft. 3 in., breadth 2 ft. 9 in.: *gazelle*, from south of Atlas, between horns to extremity of tail, 3 ft. 8 in., breadth of hind quarters, 1 ft. 9 in., length of horns 9½ in., circumference at base, 3¾ in; skins from north of Atlas, about 2 ft. 7 in. long: *antelope*, female, 4 ft. 2 in. long without head or tail; hind quarters 2 ft. 4 in.; male

Moroccan Skins.

approximately 4 ft. 7 in. long, hind quarters 2 ft. 10 in.: *ichneumon*, nose to end of tail, 3 ft. 3 in. He mentions the skin of a lioness (l'bà) seen some years ago at Casablanca, and attributes the monarch to the sterile plateaus of Tádla, Aït Shokhmán, Beni M'gîld, Aït Attár, etc. The skin of the hyena inspires terror in domestic animals, and in famine years it has been known to attack human beings.

In Northern Morocco, by agreement between the native authorities and the foreign representatives, a close season for game has been ordered, from Feb. 1 to Aug. 15. Anyone shooting hares or partridges between those dates, or selling partridge eggs at any time, is liable to be fined.

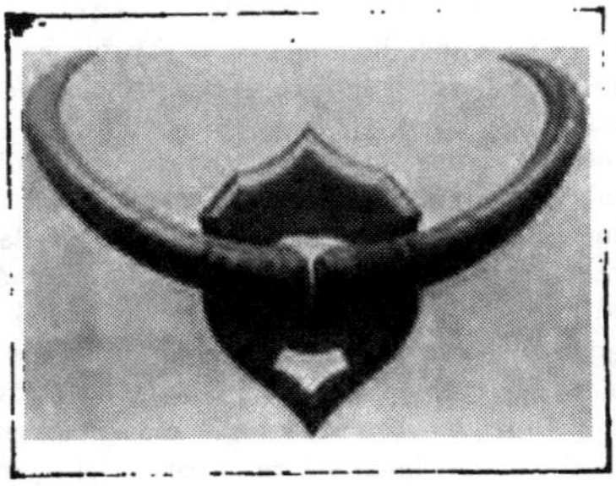

Fez Road. Continental Hotel. Marshán.

TANGIER FROM THE RUINS OF THE ENGLISH MOLE.

(Before erection of Pier.)

Irish Tower. Tannery Gate. Armstrong Battery. Chief Mosque. Customs House. Armstrong Battery. Kasbah or Citadel. Site of York Castle. Armstrong Battery.

Cavilla, Photo., Tangier.

CHAPTER THE FIFTH

OPEN PORTS—I

TANJAH * (TANGIER)

"A castle in the Streights' mouth."—GENERAL MONK.

FOREMOST among the Ports of Morocco, as nearest to Europe, comes Tangier, "Beloved of the Lord" according to one school, but "Devoted to Dogs"—*i.e.* Nazarenes—by another, and that the most numerous. Its situation, as noted by Monk, has throughout its history secured for it a prominent position in the annals of Morocco, and although its origin is shrouded in obscurity and myth, there can be little doubt that all the races which in turn have ruled this portion of North Africa have made of Tangier an important station. It has still not only the largest trade, the largest foreign colony, the best of everything that is not Moorish in Morocco, but it is the diplomatic capital, the residence of all the gentlemen accredited by foreign Powers to the Moorish Court. It is here, too, that the large majority of new arrivals first set foot in Africa, and it is here that almost all of them take leave of the Moorish Empire. Here the sudden

Importance.

Foreign Colony.

* Known to the Moors as "Thighrah Tanjah", *i.e.* "Frontier Tangier." The French and Germans spell it Tanger, the Spaniards Tánger, the Portuguese Tangere, the Italians Tangeri, and uninformed English writers sometimes add that final "s" so frequently indulged in by the uneducated, the accent being at the same time shifted from the first to the second syllable, which should be avoided. In Chesapeake Bay, Virginia, U. S. A. is a small group of "Tangier Islands."

change from West to East first thrills the traveller with the inexplicable magic of the Orient, and here, albeit that in contrast with the inland towns Tangier seems foreign and uninteresting, the departing guest looks back with feelings of regret at what he leaves behind, and having tasted of the lotus, will, if possible, return.

Position: Access.

Only about thirty miles from Gibraltar, the houses of which are distinctly visible against the huge dark Rock, the diagonal passage across the Straits—a four hours' run upon an average *—is seldom smooth, and in winter is often out of the question. From Cadiz the six hours' crossing is somewhat better, but from Tarifa, the nearest of the ports of Spain, there is only an irregular service of *faluchos*. By way of Algeciras Tangier used to be reached from London in sixty hours † by the Sud-Express, or by ordinary trains in four days, while by sea the journey from London or Liverpool may be accomplished in from five to seven days.

View from the Bay.

As the spacious Tangier Bay is entered, although the surrounding hill-sides are bare, the situation and appearance of the city, nestling between two hills on the right, and beyond it the background of Spartel Hill, with summer residences scattered amid gardens, lend it picturesque charms. But the frequency with which the detail of the scene has been recorded by most writers on the country will relieve me from entering minutely into the enchanting panorama.

Prominent Features.

Suffice it to point out the prominent features; on the right the citadel or ḳaṣbah, with the towers of the mosque and palace, and below

* Two and a quarter according to the steamship companies; but on one occasion, when we had started at noon, on our arrival in Gibraltar Bay at 4.15 p. m. the captain shouted to the pratique officer "Two and three-quarters from Tangier!"

† The time taken at present is about eighty hours. By sea Gibraltar may be reached in about four days and a half.

it the remains of the English mole and York Castle: to the left the district where most of the Europeans reside, as indicated by the numerous flagstaffs, though of late years many have gone to live outside: in the central valley lies the commercial quarter, bounded by the Great Mosque on the left, the New Mosque on the right, and below them the pier and the Custom House. The beach below the sand-hills to the left is a favourite promenade, and an excellent bathing-place; along it runs the track to Tetuan.

The Ridge Beyond.

Behind the ḳaṣbah, stretching westward, lies a breezy plateau of common land, the Marshán, where golf and cricket hold sway.[1] Beyond this, in the bottom of a rugged valley flows the Jews' River,* near to which Earl Teviot was cut off with 200 English soldiers when we held the town in 1664. Up the hill beyond runs the zig-zag road to Spartel Light-house on Rás Ashakkar, the north-western point of the dark continent.

Landing Scenes.

On landing, all is confusion and hubbub, but at last the yelling crowd has divided the spoil, and the grave turbaned seigneurs in flowing robes who act as assessors having done their duty, an irregular procession, mounted and on foot, borne on in a vociferating stream of laden porters, donkeys, mules and beggars, makes slow progress up the steep incline through what was once Port Sandwich, to the main street of the town. Steep, narrow, and cobbled, it looks far more

* The Americans once wished to purchase a settlement at the mouth of the Jews' River—so-called from the number of Jewish exiles from Spain who where forced to land there [2]—to serve as an emporium for the Mediterranean, but the offer was refused.[3]

[1] For historical events connected with the Marshán, see *The Moorish Empire*, pp. 109, 153 and 330, and for illustration, p. 138.

[2] MENEZES, p. 5. [3] URQUHART.

picturesque than inviting, but at every step presents some fresh study.

The Interior.

Passing one road on the right, to the Continental Hotel and the ķaşbah, and another on the left, to the beach, the chief mosque lies on the left, with the "college" attached to it on the right; into these none but Muslims can enter. Then begin the notaries' cells, and beyond the British and the Spanish post-offices the street is widened into the Sôķ es-Sagheer, or Small Market,—once much larger, but now sadly encroached upon—seventy-five feet above the sea.*

Straight ahead continues the steep main street, here known by the name of the Seeágheen or "Silversmiths'," though they have long deserted it.[1] Half-way up on the left is "Synagogue Lane," into which no less than six Jewish temples are crowded, sufficient proof that this was once the Jewish quarter, though in Tangier there is no residential restriction. Meanwhile the cupboard-like shops which have not yet given place to European buildings, with their motley assortment of goods for sale, their squatted owners and excited groups of buyers, have attracted our attention, and will demand repeated visits later on. If it be Thursday or Sunday, when markets or şôķs are held on the disused graveyard outside the gate at the top,—Báb-eş-Şôķ, known to the English as Port Catherine, 130 feet above sea-level,—our path must be threaded through densely packed

Markets.

* A minute account of all the streets of Tangier, with their names, was published by the writer in 1888 in *The Times of Morocco*, Nos. 169, 170 and 171. Tangier is by no means so difficult for a stranger to get about in alone as it appears at first sight, and of course it is perfectly safe, though there are streets in which Europeans are rarely seen. It occupies so small a space that it is impossible to get lost in it, as all streets lead eventually to the ķaşbah, the inner market, or one of the gates.

[1] For illustrations see *The Moorish Empire*, pp. 175 and 181.

THE SÔK ES-SAGHEER OR SMALL MARKET, TANGIER.

(As the Author first knew it in 1884, now deformed by foreign shops and "flats.")

Molinari, Photo., Tangier.

crowds of country people, surging and shouting, an experience never forgotten.[1]

Having then picked our way to the ridge beyond the market with all its attractions, crossing roads to the beach and to Fez on the left, we take up our position close beside the tasteful little English Church, mauresque in style, with the great looming Villa de France Hotel behind us, overlooking the town. A background of sea, and a foreground of aloes and cactus in the ill-kept Moorish grave-yards below us, throw up a beautiful picture.[2]

A Vantage Point.

Tangier is seen to be walled, much of the work remaining still from the time of the Portuguese, but even if sufficient to resist marauding tribes, the walls would never stand cannon, for they are in ruinous condition.* To the right or south side of the gate by which we emerged, which in 1897 replaced a much more picturesque predecessor, lie the meat and vegetable markets. Beyond this stretches the most substantial part of the wall – here crowded with houses, †—to the south-west angle, once known as the Irish Tower. Thence a narrow path in the fosse, with the Jewish cemetery on the right, runs past a bricked-up gateway to the beach road, close by a small lighthouse. ‡ The beach road emerges from the Báb Dár Debbágh or Tannery Gate, so-called from the tan-pits beside it, and extends between the Great Mosque and the Oil Mart to the Báb el Marṣà—"the Port Gate"—by which we

Walls and Gates.

* A century ago "'Alî Bey" found these the home until September of great numbers of storks,[3] but now, though plentiful in the interior and in the villages round, these birds have entirely deserted Tangier in favour of Europeans.

† One of them the finest synagogue.

‡ The exact position of the little lighthouse is given as 35° 47′ 12″ N. by 5° 48′ 2″ W.

[1] For illustrations see *The Moorish Empire*, p. 383. [2] Ditto, p. 149. [3] p. 38.

entered. There are no more gates on this side, though the English had a postern by York Castle—35 ft. above the sea—from the quarter now called Dár el Bárood, *i.e.* the "Powder House," 65 ft.

The Citadel (Kasbah.)

There are indeed no other gates to the city proper, or madînah, excepting two which lead into the citadel, Báb Ḥáḥá—named after a province—above Dár el Bárood, and on the top of a steep and ill-paved hill, Báb el 'Aṣá, "Gate of the Stick," where the bastinado used to be given—200 ft. above sea-level,—almost in the centre of the high blank wall which separates the ḳaṣbah from the town, and renders it on this side practically impregnable. No better view is to be obtained than from this point,* especially when, with a full moon shining over one's shoulder, the white town below lies bathed in a soft fairy light, a sight to be secured by all who can possibly do so.

Age of Chief Buildings.

One other gate there is to the ḳaṣbah, Báb Marshán, —260 ft.—once the Peterborough Gate, which, as its present name implies, leads to the plateau outside the town. It was among the gardens which then, as now, extended on this end of the Marshán, that the besieging Portuguese in 1437 were themselves penned in by the Moors beyond, and driven to capitulate; and it was to this gate that the English garrison of Fort Charles had to fight their way across deep trenches on the Marshán when the Moors succeeded in reducing it.† When the English left the town in 1684 all their expensive forts were destroyed, so that these gate-ways date only from that period, as do also the older mosques, the college and the palace,‡ while

* A glimpse of which is afforded on the cover of this volume.

† Just inside it is the pound for strayed cattle, and a supply of public biers is kept here as well as in the mortuary behind the Great Mosque.

‡ Ez-Zaïáni.

from the method of construction employed, it is doubtful whether any of the other buildings have existed so long.*

There is little indeed to be said architecturally for the existing Tangier, as, though many native dwellings are within artistically decorated in glazed tiles and plaster work,—the horse-shoe arch adorning even the plainest,—they are always destitute of plan, and lack design.† The material used in construction, rough stone and mortar work in which there is far too much of the latter, and that of an inferior quality, renders all the local buildings short-lived, so that great things are seldom attempted. Even the *débris* of a fallen house is for the most part useless, so that it is generally employed to fill up the foundations and to elevate them to the level of the street outside, which has been raised by the offal of years far above the inside pavement. From this custom the ages of buildings may often be guessed, new ones requiring two or three steps upward, and old ones as many downward.

Construction.

Formerly the houses were all built round court-yards, and had no windows in the plain outside walls, but the advent of several thousand Spaniards has introduced a less suitable style, although with some pretence at outside decoration, paltry both in style and quality. An exception must, however, be made in the case of the solid, though not beautiful,

Foreign Influence.

* Buffa,[1] writing of Tangier in 1805, tells of a subterraneous passage from the ḳaṣbah to several miles without the gates, "containing many curious remnants of antiquity," having ruinous apartments on either side, "which we may readily suppose to have been designed as places for the concealment of treasures, or receptacles for the dead," adding "from the fragments of some urns I have collected, upon which are to be traced parts of inscriptions in the Punic character, I imagine this subterraneous place to have been built by the Carthaginians, for one or both of these purposes." Where is this to be found? Or does he refer to the conduits?

† Moorish Architecture is fully described in *The Moors*, ch. xi.

[1] p. 24.

erections of the British Government for their Legation and Consulate,* as well as a few private residences of Europeans.

Mosques.

Three of the mosques—already mentioned—have tessellated towers, beyond which and gabled roofs of glazed green tiles, they possess no special exterior feature, while screens have been placed at their doors to prevent even the glimpses which formerly could be obtained of their cool tiled aisles and courts.† The so-called college has sunk till it hardly deserves the name, though a few students still gather there. A fourth mosque, much smaller, that of Sidi Aḥmad bin Náṣr, lies near the centre of the town. Adjoining the chief mosque‡ are the Court of the Ḳáḍî and the morsṭán or sick-house. The latter was recently re-built in a vastly improved, but still unsatisfactory style; here the friendless sick are left to die in filth.

The Palace.

The Palace in the Citadel alone attracts the tourist as a specimen of Moorish architecture, but it is poor and very mixed. The pillared court-yard is fine, nevertheless, the columns dating probably from Roman times, though perhaps imported when the place was re-built.§ The interior decoration was restored in a vulgar fashion when foreign tiles were introduced, in 1889.[1] An inscription in mnemonics on the tile-work in the Ḳoobbah Sidi Bokhári (a chamber off the passage to

* It is a noteworthy fact that the present Legation, erected in 1890, stands on a spot which in the time of the English was known as Whitehall.

† Said to have been built on the site of the English Cathedral.—*Hay's Life.*

‡ Of this "Alî Bey" gives a plan, telling us that in the room over the entrance were two big clocks and a small rude dial. As a memento of his visit he erected and endowed a drinking jar beside the main entrance.[3]

§ For illustration see *The Moorish Empire*, p. 190.

[1] p. 27.

left of the inner door of the court-yard) gives its date as 1064 A.H., = 1684 A.C.*

Courts.

The Lieutenant-Governor's Court is at the end of the Citadel Square, and the Governor dispenses justice at the gate of the palace. Hard by is the treasury, the roof of which, like that of the Khalîfah's Court, is supported by marble pillars, thickly encrusted with white-wash.

Prisons.

Two prisons adjoin the treasury, both opening on to the great square, one reserved chiefly for petty local offenders, the other for country-folk and dangerous criminals, many of whom are kept chained. As the government provides insufficient food for the prisoners, those who have no friends to bring it to them make a livelihood by plaiting baskets or begging. There is a smaller prison for women, Dár el 'Areefah, close inside the Báb el 'Aṣà, to the right.

Saint Houses.

Several saints' shrines stand within the walls; the most important being those of Mulaï Táyib, containing the remains of Sidi Háj 'Abd es-Salám el Wazzáni, built by his English widow in the Haûmat Beni Idder; that of Sidi Mohammed bir-Raîsool, below the Báb el 'Aṣà of the ḳaṣbah; that of Sidi 'Alî bin Dáood in the Dár el Barood—the local head-quarters of the Darḳaweeyah brotherhood;—that of Sidi 'Alî bel Hamedoosh in the street below the French Legation; that of Sidi Aḥmad Bûkoojah in the ḳaṣbah, and that of Sidi 'Alî 'Aleelish in the corner by the Irish Tower. There are also two important Zawîyahs, or brotherhood head-quarters, which are not shrines; that of the 'Aïsáwà,

* The inscription reads يحلّ بيتنا السعد بالاجمالى "Our happy home opens on my total," *i.e.*, on the sum of the numerical value of the letters of which the sentence is composed—*viz.*, 10+8+30+30+2+10+400+50+1÷1+30+300+70+4+2+1+30+1+3+40+1+30+10 = 1064.

close to the new mosque, distinguished by its palm tree, and that of Mûlâï 'Abd el Ķáder, at the foot of the hill to the ķaşbah. The patron saint of Tangier is Sidi Mohammed bel Ḥáj, familiarly known as Bû 'Araķeeyah —"Father of the Perspiration Cap"—whose picturesque white-washed dome stands out amid the foliage on the hill behind the town, surrounded by grave-yards. Another much used grave-yard occupies the far end of the Marshán; and away in the valley below, to the left, are a series of shrines known as the Mujáhhadîn, *i.e.* those who fell in a religious war, tradition says with the English.

Quarters.

Tangier is nominally divided into districts the names of which are known to all native residents, but to few Europeans;* they are derived from the tribes among whom it was divided when abandoned by the English. It has a governor—báshá,—a lieutenant-governor—khalîfa,—the usual irregular police—makháznîs—who have to be paid by the job, and a ķáḍî or judge. These, with the Customs Administrators—Oománà,—the Captain of the Port—Raïs el Marsà,—the Clerk of the Markets—Muthassab,—and the overseer of the mosque-property—Ná-

Local Authorities.

* It may therefore be useful to mention the most important. The Beni Idder Quarter (Haûma) is the largest, between Synagogue Street and Irish Tower, and the lower corner on this side is called the Hofrat ben Sherki, the Quarter of the Tamsamáneeïn. The district round the open space below the French Legation is called the Şakáïah Jadeedah (New Conduit), the Quarter of the Beni Tooft, between which and the ķaşbah lies the Jinán Kabtán (Captain's Garden), a purely native quarter. The next open space, Wád Ahardán, is named after the leading local family, between which and the ķaşbah hill, lie the Haûmat Zawîyah and the Haumat Bookooya. The Dár el Barood has already been mentioned: between this and the Bab Ḥáḥá lie the quarters of the Beni Toozeen and Agmer, who could not accustom themselves to town life, so moved out to a village on the Marshán. Similarly the Temsamáneeïn have moved into the village beyond the M'şallah or field of prayer, beside the *Villa de France.* There is no reliable map of Tangier published; the writer once commenced one, but never found time to complete it. Some dozen years ago he put up name-plates in some of the streets by public subscription.

dhir—are the only important local officials, but Tangier is also the residence of the Sultan's Commissioner for Foreign Affairs.

Defences.

Tangier is presumably protected by a series of antiquated batteries, of which only two, overlooking the landing-place, are kept in repair for saluting purposes; but between these two there is a modern battery with a pair of twenty-ton Armstrongs; a second pair is placed in Dár el Barood, and a third pair on the north side of the ḳaṣbah. It is a question, however, whether these could be used effectively in case of need, as the so-called artillerymen are hopelessly inefficient, and have never seen them fired.* Further round the bay, near Old Tangier, is the useless battery of El Ghanḍoor,† and on the opposite slopes of Rás el Manár, ("Tower Head,") known to Europeans as Cape Malabat, are the two small Ashbar batteries. Another, of more importance, lies on the north side of the Marshán, rather low down, completing the list of local fortifications. Tangier has practically no regular garrison, and in the eyes of the Moors it has no aristocracy, two or three families only taking front rank in native society. It is therefore considered no honour to belong to Tangier, whose traditions are so modern from the point of view of Moorish interests.

Population.

Foreign Residents.

Indeed, the foreign element predominates in influence, if not in numbers, and it is supported by the educated Jews. In a total of perhaps thirty thousand, some six thousand are from Europe, and five thousand of these from Spain, chiefly labouring emigrants, introduced some years ago when the

* When the late sultan inspected the first-named pair of Armstrongs, he commanded that one should be discharged, and it was amusing to stand by, as I did, and listen to the reasons and excuses offered to the autocrat for disobeying his order.

† Guns marked "V. B.," 1718 and 1797.

place was "boomed." Till then the little European colony could hardly secure house-room, and land was to be purchased for next to nothing. But with the rush in the later eighties speculation began; the neighbour-

THE MAIN STREET OF TANGIER IN PROCESS OF TRANSFORMATION.
(Seeágheen or Silversmiths' Street.)
Cavilla, Photo., Tangier.

ing gardens changed hands at fancy prices, and on every side there sprang up "jerry-built" houses, many of which, unoccupied, have been doomed to decay. The Spanish authorities and the Franciscans set to work to erect a whole suburb between the British Legation and

Sidi Mohammed bel Ḥáj, to which they have given the name of Barrio San Francisco, where, in 1887, they erected a handsome hospital.

This influx of needy Spaniards has ousted the Moors from most of their little box-shops, and in spite of the prohibition against the importation of liquor and narcotics except for personal consumption, the majority deal in drink and tobacco. Within a century it could be remarked by a traveller that Tangier was noticeable among towns of its size in not possessing one wine-shop, but to-day they abound and lead to much crime, not only among foreigners, but also, and with steady growth, among natives. Gambling also has been greatly on the increase during these years, and one or two attempts have been made to establish casinos intended to rival Monte Carlo.

Expansion.

Attendant Evils.

On the other hand, the advent of Europeans has brought the Press, and the establishment of Spanish, French and English newspapers in Tangier has worked wonders in arousing it from its former apathy.* Apart from the Health Committee of the Diplomatic Body, entrusted by the Sultan with the supervision of incoming vessels,[1] there has now for some years been a public Sanitary Association to which are due the cleaning and partial lighting of the streets, as well as their re-paving and the making of several new roads outside the town. After many years of jealous rivalry between the Powers, the concession to construct a pier was leased to an Austrian, and for a few years a concrete structure on the back of the town drain,—once the Wád Dukár—inadequately served as landing-jetty, but with a fresh agreement in

Benefits from Europeans.

Pier.

* For an account of journalism in Morocco see *The Moorish Empire*, part iii.

[1] See *The Moorish Empire*, p. 391.

1897 a new wooden pier was erected by an English company, much to public satisfaction. The remains of the English mole, and the reef beyond, still serve as a protection from the north-west, but are otherwise a greater danger than advantage.

Drainage.

Tangier is drained by a primitive system of rough stone channels, which were formerly open here and there, no drains being trapped, but lately they have been entirely closed in, and have become more dangerous. The water-supply, though good, is meagre in quantity, and agitation has for many years been rife to obtain European water-works; but success has here again been frustrated by international jealousy, each power being anxious to secure the contract for a subject of its own. At present the water is brought in by two ancient conduits from wells on the Marshán and beside the Fez road.* When the English were here the water-supply was always a problem. The Portuguese left a special book with details as to all springs, wells and conduit heads,[1] but Peterborough having lost it, they were hard pressed at times,[2] and had to rely chiefly on supplies from Fountain Fort, which stood among the sand-hills on the beach. The Jews' River Valley was once crossed by an aqueduct of which some arches yet remain on the hill-side; but its origin is unknown, although it was mentioned by El Bekri cir. 1050 A.C.

Water.

Healthy Climate.

The health of Tangier is good, in spite of its insanitary state, for it enjoys a delightful climate, if enervating when long experienced without a change. In summer the shade thermometer seldom rises

* The visitor "G. P," who described "The present State of Tangier" in 1676, knew so little of Moroccan geography that he thought the water came by hidden passages from Mount Atlas (p. 18). The Moors used to cut these conduits when besieging the town, but several ancient wells of great depth still exist within the walls.

[1] MENEZES. [2] DAVIS.

above 80° F., while in winter it seldom falls below 40°, ice and snow being in consequence the rarest of visitors. In the hottest weather, during July and August, although the reading in the sun may be thirty degrees higher than in the shade, there is almost always some fresh breeze from the sea, and very seldom any hot wind, nothing like that of Algeria being known, and hardly anything approaching that of Central and Southern Morocco. The most bracing wind to some, and the most trying to others, is the sharḳi or east wind from the Mediterranean, which sometimes sets in for several days in succession, growing very wearisome, and rendering the anchorage unsafe. On such occasions all vessels cross to the opposite shore of the bay, or stand out to sea.

Sea-Bathing.

In the summer sea-bathing is much in vogue among the Europeans and Jews, both sexes together; the majority begin in July, although the water is warm enough all the year round. Some years ago I tested this weekly throughout the winter, taking a thermometer with me, and ascertained that the water never fell below 56° F., even when the air was ten degrees lower. The rainy season commences towards the close of September with night showers, and lasts till April, yet although there may be a few storms lasting several days, with intermissions of glorious sun-shine, it is very seldom that some part of the day is not bright and enjoyable. Rain storms occur rarely during summer, but when they do they are extremely violent, and sadly upset the calculations of those whose sky-lights are removed, and whose stack-pipes are choked, as they usually are in summer. It is the south-west wind only which brings rain, clouds from the east seldom crossing the ridge between Tangier and Tetuan.*

* The steam baths of the Moors are not open to Europeans or Jews, but they have one of their own opposite the Eastern Telegraph Station.

The mildness of the atmosphere has given Tangier an excellent name for such victims of chest-complaints as are not absolute invalids, and many have been the marvellous prolongations of life among those who have come here in time. The mistake most people make is to return for the summer to the chills and damps of the north, instead of staying on to be healed, returning only after their second winter. Artists are attracted in considerable numbers by the oriental picturesqueness of the place and people.

A Health Resort.

For the ever increasing stream of tourists abundant and excellent hotels have arisen, and conveniences of all sorts steadily multiply. For some years past electric light has been provided by private enterprise, and actually two or three wheeled vehicles have put in an appearance. Otherwise the means of locomotion, if not on foot, are horses, mules and donkeys, the last-named being hailed like cabs at the street corners, and employed by ladies when they do not wish to wear habits. The telephone has been established by private enterprise for several years.

Hotels.

Locomotion.

As for European society, the presence of the members of the various consular and diplomatic services provides a polyglot and factious nucleus, for there are Ministers Plenipotentiary and Envoys Extraordinary* of Great Britain, France, Spain, Germany, Austria, Belgium, Portugal and Italy; a Minister Resident of Russia; Consuls-General of Austria, the U. S. of America and Brazil, besides Consuls or Vice-Consuls of most of these nations, with their usual complement of Secretaries, Students, Interpreters and Attachés. There is also a goodly mercantile community, including several Jewish families who mingle with the Europeans,

European Society.

* Who are also Consuls-General.

THE KASBAH AND INTERVENING ROOFS OF TANGIER.

(Viewed from near the Irish Tower. Haûmat Beni Idder.)

Chief mosque and flag-staffs of various consulates and embassies in foreground.

Cavilla, Photo., Tangier.

while increasing numbers of private residents are attracted by the climate and surroundings.

Modern Conveniences.

Several medical men of different tongues reside here, and good foreign shops have been opened, some of them English. Mails for the coast and abroad are made up by every steamer at the British, Spanish and French post-offices, which also maintain couriers to several points inland and along the coast, the Moors only vaguely entering into competition. But what accounts for most of the local services is the facility with which the stamps can be sold to collectors, far more being used for that purpose than for the franking of letters, as the issues are changed whenever the demand falls off. Since 1887 the Eastern Telegraph Co. has had a cable from Gibraltar landed at Old Tangier and conveyed to a fine office outside the town; the Spanish Government had one from Tarifa laid by an Italian Company in 1891, and a French cable from Oran is projected.

Christian Missions, etc.

The Franciscans have had a mission in Tangier since 1750, and maintain schools for boys and girls, a hospital, a church in the main street, and another on Spartel Hill, familiarly known as "The Mountain."* Protestant effort has been represented since 1883 by the Bible Society agent, and since 1884 by the North Africa Mission, whose head-quarters for Morocco are at Hope House, on the Marshân. Here a hospital has been erected, bearing the name of the first of the members who laid down her life in this country, Miss Tulloch.† This Society has charge also of

* Formerly the only Christian church in Tangier was the chapel which still exists between the Spanish and Portuguese Legations. At the time this was built it was stipulated that its exterior should be indistinguishable from a private house, and that it should possess no bell.

† For illustration see *The Moorish Empire*, p. 331.

a woman's hospital in the town,* and of a work among the Spaniards, as well as among the Moors.

English Services.

The building formerly used for the Anglican service now belongs to this Mission, which maintains an undenominational service there all year round. In 1896 this temporary structure was removed from the site of the new church of St. Andrew, previously mentioned, in which services are held in winter under the auspices of the Society for the Propagation of the Gospel. Anglican Churches in Morocco pertain to the diocese of Gibraltar.

Export Trade.

The trade of Tangier is considerable for Morocco, but as few important exports are produced in its vicinity, business is chiefly confined to imports. The leading exports are oxen, meat, fowls and eggs for Gibraltar, and sometimes for Spain, with occasional shipments of slippers and blankets to Egypt. Native curiosities and carpets are shipped, it is true, in growing quantities, especially brass trays, pottery and arms, but still their value remains insignificant, and Tangier itself is almost destitute of manufactures.

Imports.

The imports include almost everything brought to any port of Morocco, for Tangier is on the way to Fez and Mequinez, although as Laraiche is nearer, that route is growing in favour. It is therefore unnecessary to enumerate the various articles which may be seen rudely handled and more rudely taxed at the port, their only peculiarity being the larger proportion of objects for European consumption.

The gardens to the south produce fine oranges, a small and fragrant variety of which, akin to the Mandarin, hence derives its name of Tangerine, but they are not exported, and the bulk even of the Tangier supply

* Formerly the home of the writer, in which most of the work for these volumes was done.

comes from Tetuan. Melons find their way from Laraiche and Rabat, pomegranates from Wazzán, grapes etc.—notably muscatels—from Spain, while abundant fruits of mediocre quality are locally grown. These are, in order of season, figs, early and late, apricots, peaches, damsons, plums, melons—plain and sweet—pomegranates, grapes, prickly pears, blackberries, arbutus, Cape-gooseberries, quinces, lemons, limes and oranges; cherries, pears and apples are also grown, but are poor. Experiments in the production of bananas and Japanese medlars have been successful. Most of the ordinary English vegetables are grown, and potatoes have been introduced with good results, but to such a list must be added abundant egg-plants and tomatoes. The only local mineral product is salt, collected in pans near Old Tangier.

Fruits and Vegetables.

Bullion takes a high place in the import list, as Spanish coinage circulates beside that of corresponding values struck for the Moorish Government in France (1299 A.H. = 1882 A.C.) and Germany (1309 A.H. = 1892 A.C.). Copper pieces, which do not pass elsewhere in Morocco, were only introduced in 1888 by the determined action of the foreign colony. The only native-minted coins at present in circulation are the filthy floos (sing. fils) of infinitesimal value.

Coinage.

Most of the trade of Tangier, both wholesale and retail, is in the hands of the Jews, who here enjoy a liberty and privileges utterly unknown inland; they also control the local banking. Their number can hardly be less than ten or twelve thousand, or a third of the whole population,* and among the natives they are certainly the most progressive and enlightened. At their head is a Grand Rabbi, who is

The Jews of Tangier.

* The estimate of the Grand Rabbi is 12,000 to 15,000, and he gives the average number of deaths per annum of "over 100".

entrusted with judicial functions in disputes among his people. Their eleven synagogues are well attended, and the schools of the *Alliance Israélite* for boys and girls are crowded. These are potent factors in their social rise and growing welfare. Many Jews are employed by foreign governments in official capacities, but their places are being gradually filled by Europeans, and the attention of the Jews is turning to manufactures as well as trade. The poorer classes among them furnish most of the local craftsmen and female domestics; very few of the men do menial work, except as porters or scavengers.

Sport.

The country round Tangier provides facilities for constant sport, the chief attraction being "pig-sticking" in the neighbouring plains and marshes, whence boars are gradually disappearing, in spite of the protection of the Diplomatic Body, which has permission from the Sultan to establish a close season and otherwise regulate local sport.*

Natural Beauties.

To the lover of flowers Tangier offers no slight attractions, for in May the plains are carpeted with bloom, and in the hollows of the hills there are abundant ferns. Of course a great drawback in one sense is the absence of roads, so that during much of the wet season the country is all but impassable, while in summer the sand-hills on two sides make it irksome to get out on foot. But this belt once passed with my machine on a donkey, I have enjoyed excellent bicycle rides in dry weather along the narrow camel- and sheep-tracks beyond.

Among many favourite excursions the chief is to Rás Ashakkar, the ancient Ampelusium or Cottes,† now called

* See note at end of Ch. iv.

† Both names mean "abounding with vines" in the Punic tongue, and it is worthy of note that in sinking the foundations of the lighthouse, where no vines grow now, enormous vine stocks were uprooted.[1]

[1] Tissot, p. 51.

Cape Spartel, to which runs one of the only roads in the Empire,—the work of the Lighthouse Committee,—some eight miles long,* chiefly on the top of the hill—which rises to a little over 1000 feet,—and commands delightful views. This Committee represents the eleven Powers † who by a Convention

Cape Spartel.

THE SPARTEL LIGHTHOUSE.

Cavilla, Photo., Tangier.

Lighthouse.

with the Sultan in 1865, agreed that he should at his own cost erect, repair, and when neces-

* Two and a half hours, travelling pace.

† The signatories were Austria, Belgium, France, Germany, Great Britain, Holland, Italy, Portugal, Spain, Sweden and the United States of America. See *The Moorish Empire*, p. 392.

sary re-construct, a lighthouse on this point, his flag alone to fly there, on condition that the other signatory Powers should share the cost of its maintenance in peace or war "which God forbid"—unless withdrawing on six months' notice—under any circumstances all respecting its neutrality. The lighthouse, which is 312 feet above the sea, is of French construction, excellently kept, with a fixed intermittent white light, visible some thirty-six miles.* Close by is a semaphore controlled by Lloyd's Committee, erected on similar terms in 1892.

Caves of Hercules.

An hour and a half's ride beyond the Cape, at Mediána, are extensive caves opening on to the shore, which have been quarried immemorially for querns or mill-stones, and which are popularly held to be those of Hercules, described by Pomponius Mela.[1] Some have attributed the slight remains of ruins above and near them to Phœnician[2] or to Roman[3] builders, and James declares that urns and statues with Punic inscriptions had been found there, but all this is now very doubtful. What is certain is that they make a delightful, cool place for lunch or a pic-nic, and that they are worth a visit, after which one may return to Tangier by a nearly level road, past the beautifully situated grave-yard of Ziätseen, "The Olives," on a hill-top shaded by a grove of those trees, and past the tombs of the Mujahhadîn.

The Port.

The harbour formed by the bay of Tangier is an extensive one, good in all weathers except during a strong east wind, but vessels of any size have to anchor a mile or so out, as the shore towards the west is shallow and sandy, but on the east side

* Menezes says that in his time, 1660, there existed near the Cape the ruins of a castle built to protect the tunny fishery.[4]

[1] An opinion endorsed by Sir John D. Hay, p. 43.

[2] Urquhart, p. 276.

[3] James, vol i., p. 182.

[4] p. 5.

rocky and shingly. The small river Wád el Ḥalḳ, which meanders in and out, sometimes by one channel, sometimes by another, was once of sufficient depth to admit sailing vessels for repair, if not Roman galleys also, as the pan-tile walls of what appears to have been a dockyard seem to indicate, notwithstanding that they have been long deserted by the river.

The date of the Roman remains has been given as the beginning of the Christian era,[1] but this cannot be certainly proved. Behind them to the east lie the scattered ruins called by the natives Ṭanjah Báliah or "Old Tangier" - the truth of which description may be doubted,—and among them a ruined Portuguese watch-tower stands conspicuous, while another, in better condition, gives Cape Malabat its native name, Rás el Manár—"Tower Head."

Old Tangier.

The history of Tangier has been a very chequered one.* The present city, as will have been gathered from the account of the method of building in vogue, is raised upon a mass of ancient *débris* which would doubtless afford much interest to excavators. When the Danish Consulate—now used as the German Legation—was built, Roman tombs were found

The Present City.

* *The Moorish Empire* contains the following historical references to Tangier: taken by Sicilian corsairs, 11; conquered by the Vandals, 17; 'Okba's arrival, 23; subdued by Mûsà, 23; taken by Merwán, 24; seized by Berber rebels, 28; in possession of El Ḥasan II., 42; captured by the Maghráwà, 44; by Yûsef I., 54; by 'Abd el Mûmin, 71; supremacy of Tunis acknowledged, 92; captured by the Beni Marin, 94-5; captured by El Azfi, 95; made tributary to Ya'ḳûb II., 95; death of 'Amir here, 101; taken by Ibráhîm II., 105; Ahmad II. a prisoner here, 106; attacked by Prince Henry the Navigator, 109; abandoned to the Portuguese, 110; Dom Sebastian lands here, 123; Mohammed XI. in refuge here, 123; the English period, 152, 339, 401-2; abandoned by the English, 153-4; bombarded by the French, 196; printing introduced, 185-7; El Ḥasan III.'s reception, 189; missionaries, 326, 327, 329, 330, 332; Spanish hospital, 328; nominal purchase by Spain, 340, 341, 364-6; Europeans in, 402—5, 413, 419, 420, 429.

[1] *Hay's Life*, p. 193.

only twelve feet down; and, eight feet lower, round black jars with fragments of burnt bones which were sent to Copenhagen.* "G. P." spoke in 1676 of "great store of medals found, of Corinthian brass, copper and silver."[1] The step-like appearance which is still presented by the wall behind the Customs House he regarded as evidence that it had once served as an amphitheatre, a purpose to which it has been informally put on many a modern occasion.†

Roman Remains.

Dom Fernando de Menezes also, the last of the Portuguese governors, tells in his *Historia de Tangere*[2] of the finding of tomb-stones, cinerary urns etc., and of an inscription of twelve lines in Latin to be seen in the ḳaṣbah, recording awards to the soldiers of Nerva, Trajan and subsequent emperors. But a still more interesting monument which he describes,[3] was a stone which formerly existed in the cloister adjoining a mosque, the inscription on which ascribed the foundation of Tangier to Hercules, and its name to Tanjerah ‡ his wife. §

* A description of this find, which included some 200 vases and urns not presenting any special interest in themselves, was given by Prof. Ussing in the *Videnskabemes-Selskap Tidskrift* of 1854. On the death of Christian VIII. the collection was presented to the Ethnographic Museum of Copenhagen.

† Compare the contemporary drawing reproduced on p. 141 of *The Moorish Empire*.

‡ Cf. the neighbouring district of Anjerah, which only lacks the Berber prefix "t."

§ It also recorded its final conquest by a Ya'ḳûb el Manṣûr "Lord of the East and the West, converter to the law of Mohammed, conqueror of empires, and wearer of crowns above all crowns" . . . who "never was Jew nor Christian, but a pious Muslim, who had this inscription written in Arabic, translated from another stone in the Chaldæan language, which was in the castle of this town." It bore a date equivalent to 1015, at which time, however, the Maghráwà Berbers were establishing their dynasty, Ya'ḳûb I. (el Manṣûr) not reigning till 1184, so that the date must have been that of an earlier Ya'ḳûb.

[1] *The Present State of Tangier*, p. 32. See *The Moorish Empire*, p. 535.
[2] pp. 11, 12. [3] p. 6.

The legend referred to is well-known, and finds a place with most historians of Tangier, as far back as the time of Christ, when Pomponius Mela[1] tells of the founding of Tingé—the Tingis of Dion Cassius—by Sophax, son of Hercules by Tingé, widow of the giant Anteus, whom the strong man had slain. As Arab and other ancient authors connect the Berbers and Philistines, while some see in Hercules and Samson a common figure, here is fine ground for speculation.* Menezes, who quotes the story of Anteus,[2] adds that the giant's bones were found by Sertorius,† and that their length was seventy cubits. Be that as it may, the fame of this same 'Antár, as the Arabs call him, still survives in East and West, but the most interesting link is the existence even to our own days of a clan a few miles out from Tangier, on the way to Azîla, still known as the Aôlád (or children of) 'Antár, ordinary mortals though they be.

Origin of Tangier.

Descending even to more certain times, though none will venture after what has been said to dispute the venerable antiquity of this city, once reputed to have had walls of brass and roofs of gold and silver,[3]—the information to be obtained is both scanty and uninteresting. Strabo mixes up Tangier and Laraiche,[4] and tells us that the Romans, who had succeeded the Phœnicians in these parts, transported the people of Tingis and Zilis (Azîla) to Belo, near Tarifa, where Mela says that Julia Transducta was built.[5] Some have held the ruins known as Old Tangier to

The Roman Period.

* "The modern word *Zanata*, applied to the people of Berber origin who occupy the region between the desert and the High Plateaux, is merely the Arabic form of the radical from which *Canaanite* is derived." —Sir Lambert Playfair, *Hand-book for Algeria and Tunis*, p. 21.

† See *The Moorish Empire*, p. 11.

[1] I., 5. [2] p. 5. [3] GIBBON, *Decline and Fall*, vol. vi., p. 347, ed. 1855.
[4] III., 205. [5] IV., 6.

PROSPECT OF TANGIER FROM THE WEST, AS THE PORTUGUESE LEFT IT.

Road to Marshán. 4. Landing Place. 3. Christian Church. 1. Fort Catherine. 2. Irish Tower.

From a drawing by Holler, now in Windsor Castle.

represent Valonis Ostia, but Tissot thinks that this could not have been the site of the original Roman settlement, and that at most it dates from Byzantine times.[1]

The Goths.

Whatever happened in those days, at length, with the rest of Mauretania Tingitana, which had borrowed its name, the city passed out of the hands of the Romans into those of the Goths, on whose rule almost the only light thrown is a passage by an Arab author. Ibn el Kûtîyah * says of Julian, the traitor who invited the Moors to Spain, "The city of Tanjah was his residence, and he ruled it as master: the inhabitants professed the Christian religion."[2] And it appears to have been yielded willingly by Julian to the Muslim general.

Early Muslim Period.

The coming of the Arabs, and the crossings of the Straits which their invasion of Spain involved, made Tangier a centre of struggle and warfare for many a year, and when Mulai Idrees passed this way in coming from Tlemçen to Fez in 788, it was the capital of the Maghrib, "the oldest and most beautiful" of all her cities. Thenceforward, till the Portuguese arrived, it shared the fortunes of the country under changing dynasties, but still existed—notwithstanding all the sieges it had undergone—as a stronghold, against which in 1437 the Portuguese strove in vain with disastrous effect.

Portuguese Period.

The story of that expedition, led by the famous Henry of Portugal, surnamed "the Navigator," and by his brothers Pedro and Fernando, sons of João I.—the Great—and Philippa of Lancaster, daughter of John of Gaunt, is ably told by

* Whose name signifies "Son of the Gothess."

[1] p. 45. [2] See *Journal Asiatique*, série 5, t. 8, p. 435.

Azurára[1] and by Menezes.*[2] Ceuta had been taken by the first two brothers during their father's life-time, in 1415, and under their brother Duarte they made preparations to attack Tangier, landing at Ceuta in September 1437, with 2000 horse and 4000 foot, out of 14,000 who had been levied for the undertaking. Their attempt to cross direct by the Anjerah ridge was frustrated at El Ḳaṣar eṣ-Ṣag͟hîr, so they turned back and came by the Tetuan route, which the Moors had failed to protect, and along which the country-people furnished provisions.[3]

Fight on the Marshán.

Forming an entrenched camp on the Marshán, and erecting towers against the city walls, with big artillery and a co-operating fleet, they besieged it for twenty-five days in vain, although its garrison was only 7000 strong. But by this time 70,000 Moors had collected, and besieging the besieged for twelve days more, they forced them to capitulate, agreeing to retire and to restore Ceuta, Dom Fernando and the son of the governor Salaḥ bin Salaḥ being exchanged as hostages. But as the restoration of Ceuta was refused in Lisbon, and the Pope absolved them from their promise, Dom Fernando was allowed to languish with other noble hostages in Fez, where, after having spent the life of a slave, he was released by death in 1443.†

* The latter writer had inherited its governorship from the first to hold that post in Ceuta, Tangier and Azîla, to whose line also belonged the 7th, 8th, 10th, 11th, 12th, 13th, 16th, 17th, 19th, 21st, 22nd, 27th and 30th Portuguese rulers in Tangier.

† His body was salted to be sold to Portugal, but his fellow-prisoners saved his bowels and hid them as relics, the body of the "martyr" being credited with miraculous powers.[4] See *The Moorish Empire*, p. 323.

[1] *Chronicle* written in 1471 and published 1792 and 1841, translation by Beazley, vol. i., issued by Hakluyt Society, 1896. See p. 16, etc. [2] p. 17, etc.

[3] See also Beazley, *Prince Henry the Navigator*, 1895, p. 181.

[4] An account of his captivity is given in the Bollandist collection, and by Geronimo Ramos in his *Crónica do Infante Fernando*, Lisbon, 1577. See also Camoens (*Lusiadas* iv., 52).

On being defeated at Tangier the Portuguese agreed to make no further war in Barbary for 400 years, but this promise was soon to be broken, and El Kaṣar eṣ-Ṣagheer having yielded to them in 1458,[1] five years later a renewed attack was made on Tangier. This again was unsuccessful,[2] so next year they descended on Anáfa, now Casablanca. Encouraged there by the flight of the inhabitants on their approach,[3] in 1471 they returned to the charge, this time securing Azîla as base; but fighting was needed no longer, for the ámeer had just been assassinated, and the governor of Azîla, Sa'ïd el Waṭṭás, was assuming the reins of authority.* Morocco was in a state of chaos, so the people of Tangier imitated those of Anáfa, and fled.

The Taking of Tangier.

The chief mosque was immediately dedicated to the Holy Spirit; the college which Yûsef bin Táshfîn had built was given to the Franciscans, from whom it passed to Trinitarian Redemptionists, and ultimately to Dominicans.[4] Menezes was installed as governor on 68,568 reis per annum, with bread, meat and wine supplied, nearly the whole of which sum was raised by a tax on the bread, meat and wine of others. Thus the Portuguese were established, and at once set about extending their rule. El Kaṣar was seized,[5] but later dismantled,[6] and an attack was made on Targa, ten leagues to the east, the port nearest to Fez, now long forgotten, but this attack failed on account of divided command.[7] The northern strip of Morocco was almost entirely under Portuguese sway, and they could be ousted from none of their strongholds. A century later, in 1564, the kaṣbah of Tangier was strengthened,

Portuguese Occupation.

* See *The Moorish Empire*, p. 109.

[1] Menezes, p. 25. [2] Ib. p. 30. [3] Leo, Ed. Ram., p. 89.
[4] Menezes, p. 34. [5] Ib. p. 52. [6] Ib. p. 70. [7] Ib. p. 59.

and bastions were added,[1] the magnificent masonry of which still remains. Soon after, however, its maintenance costing more than it was worth, the order went forth to destroy the whole of that part of the city south of the main street, which was only stayed by a petition to the King.[2]

Interval of Spanish Rule.

After the death of Dom Sebastian, the ill-starred invader, at El Ḳaṣar, Tangier passed in 1580 under the rule of Spain, which, when the Portuguese threw off her yoke in 1640, retained it as she also retained Ceuta. Three years later, nevertheless, after some disturbance, it reverted to its former masters, under whom the writer of its history became its governor in 1656. Other foes had in the meantime come against it, for in 1647 Don Juan of Austria had made an attack in vain, and when in 1651 it was still harder pressed by famine, corn was offered from Ceuta if it would return to the Spaniards, but the offer was indignantly rejected, and the vessels bearing it were chased.[3]

A "Little Hinge."

The feelings thus expressed secured a welcome in 1656 for Montague and Blake, servants of "the new republic of Chromuel," who put in here for water, when cruising off Cadiz in search of Spaniards. Yet some of the English sailors, having ventured too far ashore, were killed, and three more were made captive, but on explanation were returned without ransom.[4] The result of this little incident was that the Protector's attention was called to the place by Monk, with a recommendation to secure it.*

* He wrote in September 1657, "I understand the Portugal ambassador is come to London; and I make no question but he will be desiring some favour from my lord Protector. There is a castle in the Streights' mouth, which the Portugals have called Tangar, on Barbary side, and which, if they would part with it withal, it would be very useful to us;

[1] MENEZES, p. 77. [2] Ib. p. 125. [3] Ib. p. 189. [4] Ib. p. 207.

When, however, in arranging a marriage between Charles II. of England and Catherine of Braganza, it was stipulated that Tangier and Bombay should form part of the dowry,* although the harassed Portuguese were doubtless glad enough to be freed from the responsibility without loss of honour, the patriotic governor refused to hand it over to the English, even with the offer of a marquisate, considering that to do so would be to disgrace the family which had been "first its conquerors, and then so long its defenders."[1] He therefore chose as an alternative to give way to a governor of weaker scruples, spurning even the generous offer of the Spanish governor of Ceuta to accept it on behalf of the Pope, and so prevent the heretic English from obtaining a foothold upon that coast.[2]

The Coming of the English.

It was a mournful day when, in 1662, the Portuguese withdrew, and the English entered, according to the ex-governor, robbing and sacking,[3] breaking images and sacred vessels in the hermitages and the convent;[4] nevertheless, by a strange irony, the place was soon to be regarded as a "nest of papacy,[5] where Irish troops and Romish bastards could disport

Changing Hands.

and they make very little use of it, unless it be for getting of Blackamoors; for which his highness may give him leave to trade. An hundred men will keep the castle, and half a dozen frigates there would stop the whole trade in the Streights to such as sha'l be enemies to us."[6]

* According to the Moorish historian Ez-Zaiánî the English *took* Tangier from the enfeebled Portuguese[7]

[1] MENEZES, p. 272.

[2] Ib. p. 275, Canovas del Castillo, "Apuntes para la Historia de Marueccos," *Rev. Cientifica*, Barcelona.

[3] Ib. p. 277. [4] Mss. report of Fitzgerald in Record Office.

[5] See PEPYS' *Diary*, and the address from the Commons, Nov. 29th, 1680.

[6] THURLOE'S 6th vol. State Papers, p. 505. [7] p. 14.

themselves unchecked."* On the other hand, we learn from the records of the in-coming tenants that their disgusted predecessors had carried off with them everything of value on which they could lay their hands, even

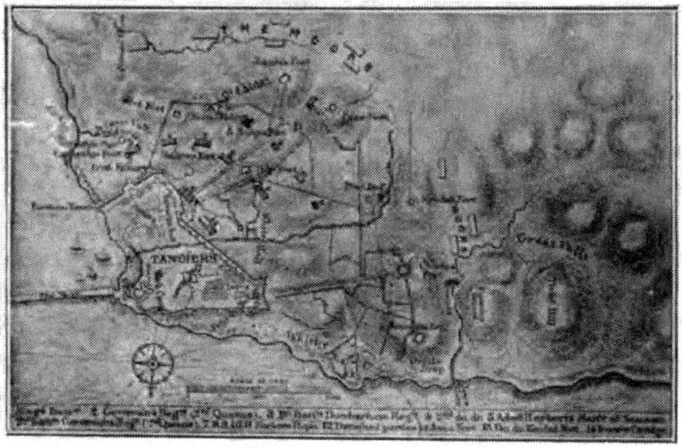

DEFENCES OF TANGIER UNDER THE ENGLISH IN 1680.
From a contemporary official Survey.

to the doors and windows of their houses.[1] The Jews, though not then numerous, received permission to remain, as far too useful to be dispensed with, and became interpreters and go-betweens† as well as traders. They already congregated in "Jewe's Lane," round one syna-

* The ḳaṣbah of Tangier was used for the confinement of Fleetwood, Garland, Mildmay and Wallop, who were among those concerned in the death of King Charles. On their transportion hither from the Tower of London in 1664, Fleetwood's wife petitioned the King "to command her husband to any prison in this Kingdom rather than to Tangier, where food is so dear that she will be unable to relieve him; thanking His Majesty for his unparalleled mercy in sparing his wretched life, forfeited by his heinous sin."[2]

† Chief among them Solomon Pariente.

[1] Davis, p. 31. [2] Calendar of State Papers, Domestic Series, 1663-4, p. 1664.

gogue. During their rule the Portuguese had built seventeen churches and chapels, of which one, with a convent, was maintained by the English for the benefit of those few Portuguese who elected to stay, while the principal church of St. Jago was re-dedicated to "Charles the Martyr."[1] From drawings extant this appears to have occupied the site of the present Great Mosque.

Tangier under the English.

It was with the most exaggerated anticipations, and with the most lamentable ignorance, that the English entered Tangier, mistaking the Moors for Turks, and 'Abd Allah Ghaïlán,—a local chieftain,—for "the emperor or prince of West Barbary." This "Guyland," as they misnamed him,—with whom they were content to make treaties,[2] and from whom they even purchased peace for fifty barrels of powder,—was the leader of the surrounding tribes, eighteen of them Berber, and four Arab, whom Dr. Addison, the Chaplain of the Forces—father of the famous essayist,—reckoned as mustering 21,000 foot and 9000 horse.[3] As a supporter of one of the struggling claimants for the thrones of Fez and Marrákesh, Ghaïlán was besieged by the other, Múláï er-Rasheed,—known to the English as "Tafiletta"—in Azîla, whence he was eventually fain to escape by the aid of the English. But while able to hold his own he was the real foe with whom the foreigners had to contend.

Local Relations.

When the Earl of Peterborough entered on the command, he distributed £400 to the kaïd and sheïkhs of the vicinity "according to the custom of first entrance."[4] By such means peace was purchased for six months, but the Moors were only tempted by these payments to further onsets. Their presents to the

[1] "G. P." pp. 34-5. [2] F. O. Docs., vol. i., contains copies. See Col. Corresp. vol. iv. etc.

[3] *The Moors Baffled, ... being a discourse concerning Tangier*, 1681.

[3] Tho. [4] Davis, p. 25.

garrison consisted chiefly of cattle and victuals, but included at least two lions. When they sent an embassy to treat with Colonel Kirke the secret service money was drawn on for 1000 guineas for the envoy, 100 each for his companion, secretary and interpreter, and 50 for each of his twenty servants, with a coat apiece thrown in, while for conveying a letter to the Emperor £10 was paid. But when it was deemed expedient to offer six brass guns to "Tafiletta,"* it was thought sufficient to substitute on them the name of Charles II. for that of good Queen Bess.[1]

Great Expectations.

Charles stated in Parliament that "the new acquisition of Tangier etc. ought to be looked upon as jewels of an immense magnitude in the royal diadem,"[3] while Pepys expressed the popular faith that Tangier was "likely to become the most considerable place the King of England hath in the world:"[4] and though Earl Teviot, the first to go out as its governor, found life there so dull that when he received a parcel of "news-bookes" from the consul at Cadiz, he regarded it "an act of charity soe to doe with us, who see nothing but Moores and the four Ellements, and are deprived of all civil and state conversation," he did not hesitate to write: "One thing I shall foretell you, that who liveth to be heere two years (without the Place be given away or sold, or civil discords amongst ourselves arise) will find it a very comfortable Place, yea, and very pleasant, too."[5] To most who came, the place itself afforded great attraction: "a most odoriferous smell entertained us, which I conceive to be a mixture of

* In 1668 Col. Norwood, then lieut.-governor, wrote "Revolution in Barbary from North to South soe violent, and all in favour of King Tafiletta."[2]

[1] Davis, p. 201. [2] Col. Corresp. vol. iv.

[3] Clarendon, *Autobiography*, vol iii., p. 313.

[4] *Diary*, Sept. 28th, 1663. All the passages in this diary bearing on Tangier are collected in *The Times of Morocco*, Nos. 155-7. [5] Letters of 25/15 Ap., 1664.

pleasant scents arising from the variety of sweet trees and herbs growing there wild."[1] But a truer note was struck by a poetaster who left on record:

"August the Tenth we sailed away,
And anchored at Tangier next day:
A Place the English now possess
On the Barbarian Shoar it is:
'Tis fortified very strong
Or else we should not keep it long." [2]

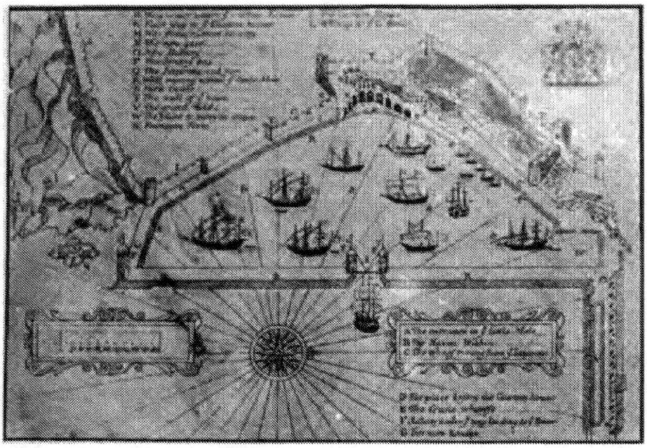

MOLE AND HARBOUR OF TANGIER IN 1675.
Constructed and destroyed by the English.
From a contemporary official Plan.

Fortifications and Mole.

Teviot, at least, was not to outlive his two years, for it was only a few months after the letters quoted were written that he was cut off, and war was renewed. The Portuguese fortifications were insufficient for the new state of things, and not only were the town walls put in repair and towers added,

[1] "G. P.," p. 3. [2] BALTHORPE, *The Streights' Voyage*, 1671.

but a line of forts was erected outside—from the Jews' river across to Old Tangier—which at last numbered fifteen. Between 1665 and 1668 £31,000 were so spent, £3000 going for the repair of the Marshán Gate, or Peterborough Tower. In addition to this the mole was commenced, on which 1000 men worked daily, and Tangier was made a free port.[1] But the Spaniards objected as much as the Moors, and actually hanged one man in "Giblator" for having loaded "lyme for Tanger."[2] The Moors with Spanish assistance built a rival town four miles out, the turrets and bastions of which could be seen from Tangier;[3] but I am aware of no traces of this undertaking, unless this is the true history of "Old Tangier."

The English Garrison.

Nothing, however, daunted the English, and of the "Tangier regiment",—now the Queen's Royal West Surrey, which was raised for service here*—it has well been said by its historian, Lt.-Col. John Davis, "There is really no part of the history of the regiment which shows up more strongly the indomitable pluck and endurance of English soldiers than the defence of the garrison of Tangier, constantly harassed by a fierce, fanatical and relentless foe, and having to fight under every disadvantage that they could labour under."†[4] Even as regards their pay, they were kept in arrears—26 months in 1676—and when three years had passed only fifteen months' pay had been sent, until their condition became such that the mayor had to issue a proclamation forbidding the purchase of their uniforms.

* For costume of Tangier Officers see *The Moorish Empire*, p. 467.

† The Duke of Marlborough's first active service was in Tangier, as a volunteer sixteen years of age.[5]

[1] The warrant is in vol. ii. of the Colonial Office Papers.

[2] Consul Wescombe's letter of May 4, 1664.

[3] Letter of Fitzgerald, July 15, 1664.

[4] p. 131.

[5] *Memoirs* by Cox, 1820, vol. i., pp. 4 and 5.

But while threatened mutiny and misrule within would have proved fatal in time of peace,* the common foe kept them fairly together, and in 1680 Mûláï Isma'îl blotted out their grievances by his great siege. Two years previously two of the advanced forts had been taken by the kaïd of El Ḳaṣar, and now Fort Charles, on the Marsḥán, the strongest of the out-posts, was to fall. On account of the renegades and interpreters in the Moorish army, communication was maintained with the town in Irish, through trumpets, and at last the little garrison of 176 men under Capt. Trelawney, had to withdraw, since they would not yield. To intercept their retreat the Moors had cut three trenches, eight yards wide by four and a half in depth, and in crossing the last, 124 of their number were cut to pieces before they could be succoured by a sortie from the citadel.

Moorish Attacks.

The abandoned fort had been undermined, and was blown up never to be rebuilt: the Moorish mines were constructed by Turks from Candia, and to convince the English of the hopelessness of their position, the Moors invited their officers to inspect them, which they did. Throughout the struggle there was a succession of lulls wherein civilities were interchanged in all good faith; most of the correspondence is still in existence.[1] No little chivalry was often shown, the English being especially careful in their treatment of the bodies of dead Moors, which no doubt went a long way towards securing respect.

Chivalrous Amenities.

Some of the English methods of warfare, strange to us, appear from the evidence of native as well as foreign historians, to have been peculiarly effective.[2] One of

* "No money, no guard" was the watchword of the discontented soldiery.

[1] In the Public Record Office *Colonial Correspondence, Tangier*, in 48 vols.

[2] El Ufrání, p. 444.

these was to strew the ground before their forts with "cultraps," four-spiked instruments of which one point was always upwards ready for the foot of man or beast; of these 36,000 were supplied at one time. In return the Moors prepared "stink-pots," which they cast into the town and forts. The English used St. Malo dogs to give them notice of approaching foes.[1]

Peculiar Warfare.

After the fall of Fort Charles the attack was centred on Pole Fort, on the Fez road, and Norwood Fort, to the South of the present "Villa de France," which commanded the main approach to the town; but Cambridge Fort, on the road to the beach, and Fountain Fort, at the well close by, were held till the last, together with the Bridges Fort out on the sand-hills. Fort Ann, a little further out on the Fez road, seems to have fallen early.

The Outer Forts.

The garrison of Tangier had varied in number, averaging about 1500, with a civil population in 1676 of 700, including 51 Jews, 5 Moors and 130 foreigners, the number of families being estimated at 200.* On account of the abuses committed on entering the town, a commission was appointed to lease and register the available dwellings.[2]

Population.

This little colony had its mayor and corporation[3]—six aldermen, twelve common councilmen, who,—the mayor and aldermen in scarlet, and the councilmen in purple,—went on Sundays with the

How they lived.

* Some twenty families of English labourers were settled in a hamlet known as Whitby, in the cove below the Marshán, where stone was quarried, being brought in carts by a road round the cliff to York Castle.[4]

[1] Addison, *The Moors Baffled.*

[2] Their transactions are in the Record Office, "*Tangier*," vol. xxv.

[3] The Patent for the constitution is in vol. xlviii. of the Col. Office Papers, "*Tangier.*"

[4] "G. P.," p. 35.

governor to church.[1]* They had also a "Court Merchant," of which the annals are still extant.[2] "For maintaining and breeding the orphans, children of soldiers and townsmen," there was an exhibition of £200 a year, and most of our typical English institutions were in full swing. The treaties, however, permitted only a dozen at a time to hunt or divert themselves on the beach, in return for which trading Moors were allowed as far as the Fountain Fort. But the spot known as Whitehall was a place of pleasure in quiet times, with a pretty "bowling base," and on the occasion of Lord Howard's embassy great sports were held on the beach, which included bull-baiting. That the English employed slaves there, possibly Moorish prisoners, is evident from an entry among the State papers referring to "79 slaves belonging to His Majesty's bagnia at Tangier."

On the other hand, the regulations were severe. Theft and robbery of more than the value of twelve pence was punished by death, and the challenger to a duel by "death without mercy." Blasphemy, or attacks on "the known articles of the Christian faith," were punished by boring the tongue with a red-hot iron; drunkenness or frequent swearing by the loss of half a day's pay, besides which drunkards were placed in the stocks.

Mismanagement.

In spite of all this the conduct of affairs in Tangier was disgraceful, as was but to be expected from the class of men sent there by the slovenly Tangier Board in London. They included such notorious characters as Colonel Kirke, the Earls of Inchiquin and Peterborough, and a host of ne'er-do-well adventurers; for, in the language of the Secretary of the Board, the observant Pepys, "this place was to the King, as my Lord Carnarvon says of wood, that it is an

* The first mayor, Bland, absconded.

[1] "G. P.," p. 40. [2] Public Record Office; Col. Office Papers, vol. xxxiv.

excrescence of the Earth, provided by God for the payment of debts."[1] Pepys had already noted that "Unless the King hath the wealth of the Mogul, he would be a beggar to have his businesses disordered in the manner they now are, that his garrisons should be made places of convenience only to particular persons.[2]

Exposure.

Public opinion at last grew too strong for this to continue, and in reply to a royal recommendation to consider what should be done with Tangier[3]—intended to secure a vote of funds,—the Commons impeached the management, refusing to waste more money here. They complained "that the supplies sent thither have been in great part made up of popish officers and soldiers, and that the Irish papists among the soldiers of the garrison were the persons most countenanced and encouraged," thereon hanging a regular anti-popery protest. The Portuguese, seeing the pass to which things had come, asked for the return of Tangier on repayment of the English expenses, the English to be for ever free of the port.[4] The King was willing, but the Duke of York (afterwards James II.) objected, and it was eventually decided to abandon the place to the Moors instead, Lord Dartmouth being sent in 1683 with secret instructions to this effect.

Withdrawal of the English.

Thus was lost at one stroke all that had been gained by Portuguese efforts, and all that had been purchased by the lives of many hundred Englishmen, and over £1,600,000 spent, "more than all the garrisons of England."[5] The first task was to destroy the magnificent mole on which Sir Hugh Cholmondeley had expended so much ingenuity, the remains of which are still to be seen. As early as 1676 it was described as "a very pleasant thing to look on,

[1] *Diary*, May 5th, 1667. [2] Ib. Ap. 16th, 1667. [3] Nov. 29th, 1680.
[4] Menezes. [5] Dartmouth Mss.

near 470 yards long, and 30 broad, with several pretty houses upon it, and many families. Vast numbers of guns are continually kept warm during fair weather, in giving and paying salutes." Manned by 100 gunners,[1] as many as 1000 guns were fired from the mole, the forts, and the ships in the bay when an English frigate arrived.[2] The principal feature of the mole was the then novel method of its construction by sinking "chests" of 2000, 1000 and 600 tons of stone, and the formation of concrete blocks. At low tide the hollows where the mines were laid are still to be distinguished.

The work of Destruction.

Much anxiety was felt lest the Moors should take advantage of the reduced fortifications, but when they observed what was going on they abstained from molestation, and even sent in supplies. The dissatisfaction locally felt * was assuaged by the appointment of a commission to settle all claims for compensation, those of the Portuguese and other foreigners first. At length, the civilians having been embarked, with their horses and moveable property, on February 6th, 1684, "my Lord Dartmouth quitted Tanger, having first levelled it with the ground. There are none of the walls standing, except some of the bottom of Peterborough Tower, which did not blow up, there being 50 or 60 barrills of powder under it which did not take fire."[3] Lord Dartmouth's own despatches tell of the destruction of the houses also, but there is sufficient Portuguese masonry still to be seen in the city walls to show that the destruction was not quite so complete as it was represented to be. The Moors were

* An address of the mayor, aldermen, etc. of Tangier to Charles II., protesting against the abandonment, is to be found among the Dartmouth Mss. (p. 96), and has been reproduced by Dr. Samuel Kinns in his *Six Hundred Years*, 1898, p. 329.

1 "G. P." p. 32. 2 Ib. p. 4.

3 Letter from Frowde, Feb. 10th, 1684. Col. Corresp., vol. xlviii.

warned that one of the batteries had been delayed in exploding, but they were in such a hurry to enter that eight of their number perished when it did blow up.

To Sir Cloudesley Shovel Mulai Ismâïl wrote: "God be praised that you have quitted Tangier and left it to us to whom it did belong: from henceforth we shall manure it, for it is the best part of our dominions."[1] The result of its cultivation, which did indeed commence in earnest by the restoration of defences and public buildings, and the introduction of a new population,[2] was that Tangier was reduced to a second-rate Moorish port, which only the advent of Europeans has raised to its present position. The Moors will never believe that they did not drive out the English, whose departure they attribute to fear. "Tangier," writes El Ufrâni, "was besieged so closely that the Christians had to flee on their vessels and escape by sea, leaving the place ruined from bottom to top."[3]

Tangier under the Moors.

Since then its history has nothing worth recording, even as a pirate harbour; the only events of importance being the removal to it of the foreign consuls in 1770, and its bombardment in 1844 by the French, then at war with Morocco.* At 8 a.m. on August 6th of that year the "Suffren," the "Jemmapes" and the "Argus" opened fire, supported later by the "Triton" and "Belle Poule," the "Rubis" firing the camp outside, while English and Spanish vessels looked on, having first removed the foreign colony. For half an hour the Moors replied well, directed by renegades, but the battery at Old Tangier, which annoyed the "Triton," was soon destroyed, and in three hours all

The French Bombardment.

* See *The Moorish Empire*, p. 196.

[1] Ockley, p. 144. [2] Ez-Zaiáni. [3] *Nozhat Hádi* p. 506.

was over. The losses of the French were insignificant, but the Moors had 220 killed and 400 wounded, and the town was badly knocked about, though the mosque towers stood, according to the Moors because miraculously protected. The year of this disaster is still remembered also as "the year of the snow," which fell then, but not again till 1886, when it lasted only an hour or so.

TANGIER TO TETUAN

THE forty miles of devious track which separate Tangier from Tetuan may be covered easily in one day on good animals, but those unaccustomed to the saddle and dependent on hired mounts, would be wiser to sleep at or near the fandák or caravan-sarai about half way. This involves either "roughing it" as one does in a Persian *chapar khaneh*, rolled in a rug on some straw in a sort of stable, or transporting a tent with its paraphernalia. Either plan has its advantages and disadvantages, which must be individually weighed. Hire of mounts by the journey varies slightly, averaging four or five pesetas—*2s. 6d.* to *3s.*—for ordinary pack beasts, the owners accompanying them on foot. A courier will run to Tetuan and back within twenty-four hours for a dollar. The first half of the way, which strikes inland from the beach between the orange groves, partakes of the nature of the environs of Tangier, shadeless plains and rounded hills with a good deal of cultivation; but the fandák lies in the approach—past an excellent spring—to a more rugged district, similar to Spartel Hill, which extends to near Tetuan. Thus far the east wind, as well as the south-west, sometimes brings rain, which very seldom reaches Tangier from this direction. On this, the more beautiful side, all is changed,—views, soil and vegetation. From Tetuan—which is not served by any regular vessels—Ceuta may be reached by an eight hours' uninteresting ride, (see chapter xix.) and the return to Tangier effected in one or two days by the hills and valleys of the beautiful Anjerah country.

TETUAN FROM THE HILL BEHIND THE TOWN.

Looking South.

(The white spots in the valley are Summer residences.)

Cavilla, Photo., Tangier.

CHAPTER THE SIXTH

OPEN PORTS—2

TETTÁWAN (TETUAN)*

BEAUTIFUL in situation, picturesque in its surroundings, Tetuan lies on the northern slope of a fertile valley down which flows the Wád Martîl † to the western end of the Mediterranean. Behind it tower rugged masses of rock, the southern wall of the Anjera country, peopled, as all mountain regions in this Empire are, by an indomitable race who practically keep it closed to Europeans. Across the valley rises yet another barrier of hills, the northern limits of the still less domitable Rîf. Yonder transverse valley leads to the forbidden Shesháwan and parts unknown, while to the west of it lie routes to the much venerated shrine

Situation.

* The derivation of the word Teṭṭáwan is supposed, with some show of reason, to be from the Rîfian thîṭáwîn,—"eyes" or "springs." A Spanish author[1] quotes a Moorish tradition that "Tet tagüen"[2] was the cry of warning shouted while the walls were being built, and that it meant "Open your eyes!"—*i.e.*, to see the enemy approach—the watchword developing into the name. Leo Africanus[3] says that the city was called Teṭṭáwan, "an eye," because under the Goths it was once governed by a woman with but one organ of vision, but this tale seems rather too far-fetched for credence. Others think that the name implies the eyes, or best part of the land, or perhaps it simply refers to the springs on account of which the site was doubtless chosen, which add such a grateful coolness to the better class of houses. Hence the name may well be rendered "City of Fountains." On a coin of 1793 in the French National collection it appears as Teṭwán, a pronunciation which, though not unknown to-day, is incorrect.

The Name.

† Or Marteen.

[1] CASTELLANOS, p. 43. [2] Pronounced "Tet táwen." [3] Ed. RAM, p. 91.

of Mulai 'Abd es-Slám son of Masheesh,* the goal of thousands of pilgrims each year.

The Valley.

The Tetuan valley itself tells of peace. Orange-gardens, apricot-orchards, vine-yards, corn-fields, grazing wastes, are interspersed and animated by white-dotted villages and garden houses. Especially is this the case at Kîtán, yonder, where the wealth of aristocratic Tetáwan spends the hot season, pic-nicing or camping out, or installed in cool tiled dwellings, with an ever present shade and perfume and water-splash; served at ease by black hand-maids and white to whom the outing is as great a treat as to their masters or their mistresses. The very beasts of burden enjoy it—but for the flies—and set up high jinks whenever the lad in charge of them dozes. Here all the *abandon* of the East finds play, and days pass sleepily, while nights are wakeful with the mirth of music and the voices of the men. Even the gloomy residential lanes in the city itself resound in the small hours with festive life, and ever and anon a creaking portal opens to admit or let pass out some slippered and shrouded form, but otherwise the streets within are silent and deserted—save for the prowling cur—as that vast grave-yard beyond the walls.

Walls and Gates.

From a distance, like all these towns, glistering white, on a nearer approach the walls of Tetuan show themselves crumbling, while the houses they enclose are often lichen-covered, and the narrow streets between them are receptacles for rubbish. Six gates afford access. Báb Nûádhir ("Gate of Sheaves") at the west end, leads to a deserted quarter whence, with tunnel-like turnings up the steep hill to the left, runs a long, straight street to the Ṣôḳ el Fôḳi, the chief business quarter. Through this gate one enters from Tangier by way of the potters' caves, wherein the tessellated pave-

* For genealogy see *The Moorish Empire*, table facing p. 116, col. iii.

ments are prepared, and where the road-side streams are full of maiden-hair. The ordinary entrance from Tangier, Báb Tût ("Mulberry Gate"), lies to the south on the same side, and by a high-walled lane, past slaughter yard, grain market, caravan-sarais, gives on the Feddán or Market Field.* Further round comes Báb er-Ramûz, which leads to another deserted quarter, and then Báb el 'Oḳla—whence issues the road to Martîl—opening on the chief residential quarter, externally dismal, but containing the best houses and their pleasure gardens. Báb Sa'ïda ("Gate Fortune") which comes next, is now disused. Then comes Báb el Mukábar (the "Gate of Tombs") on the north-east, by which one leaves for Ceuta, with tan-pits inside and grave-yard outside; and the last is Báb el Jeef ("Corpse Gate") through which pass all Jewish funerals.

Cemeteries.

On account of the unusual class of built tombs with which it is crowded,—the older ones probably those of refugees from Spain,—the great Muslim cemetery is well worth a visit, and across the terraces of breccicated tufa behind the town, a path winds to the hill above the north-west corner. There, in a high-walled enclosure, repose beneath the wild luxuriance of what were once ornamental plants, the remains of the Spanish army which in 1860 invaded Morocco and took Tetuan. From this coign of vantage, or from the neighbouring high-perched ḳaṣbah or citadel fort, may be studied the whole labyrinth which forms the town, and there are few streets in Morocco constituting a more intricate maze than those which here form the mart of the slipper-workers. In Summer the business streets are rendered pleasant by the grateful shade of vines.

Tetuan is famous for its thick-soled yellow shoes, ex-

* A view of this is given in *The Moorish Empire*, p. 162.

ported to the east, and for its gilt-embroidered velvet slippers, chiefly the work of Jews, but it has also a local name for its footahs—the artistic "towels" which are cape and skirt for the country girls—in repute among Europeans as anti-macassars on account of their fast dyes and strong substance.* Tetuan produces also much esteemed flint-locks, and as the division of labour is well carried out, a high degree of skill and taste is acquired by the workers, to each group of whom a separate street is allotted. One branch of their manufacture, the inlaying, chiefly with silver wire, is also applied to other articles, such as snuff-nuts.

Manufactures.

In almost every instance some peculiarity of workmanship or design enables the native products of this or any other Moorish town to be at once distinguished, and the Tetuan jelláb or hooded woollen sacque is known by its narrow black and white stripes. The small glazed tiles of Tetuan differ from those of Fez, not only in being coarser, but also in being moulded to the shapes required, instead of being baked in squares and then cut to shape one by one, an operation which ensures much closer fitting and a much more level surface. The whole process of manufacture is of the most primitive imaginable. Close to the town wall on the lower side are many corn-mills, turned by the escaping sewers, amid an unhealthy stench, the water rushing from a small spot on to a horizontal wheel directly beneath the stone, beside which hangs a bag to catch the flour.

Distinctive Products.

With the exception of the sale of its manufactures and the local demand for imports, trade is not brisk in Tetuan. Markets are held on Sundays, Wednesdays and Fridays, in the large space near the south side, called the Feddán, or "Enclo-

Business Quarters.

* A reputation being undermined, however, by aniline substitutes.

sure," but they are seldom largely attended, as provisions can always be obtained at the Ṣôḳ el Fôḳi, or "Upper Market," which is little more than a wide street. Near this is a fandáḳ, called El Ûsa', which serves as a sort of club where the better-class Moors meet of an afternoon for coffee and gossip. The palace, usually occupied by the báshá, occupies the north-east corner of the Feddán, which is used for "powder-play" or for imperial receptions as well as for a market; the Customs office adjoins the palace.

A STREET IN THE TETUAN MELLAH.

The Melláḥ or Jewry of Tetuan is remarkable for its regular, parallel streets, frequently crossed by flying arches. The houses in it belong to the Government, and were originally let at very low rentals, but the actual occupiers, being third or fourth tenants, pay accordingly. It is not a century since it was built, its inhabitants being driven from near the chief mosque. The Jews here have very good schools for boys and girls, supported by the *Alliance Israëlite* of Paris.

The Melláh.

The best Moorish houses, belonging chiefly to descendants of the Andalucian families, are congregated near the great mosque, the only one worth noting, situated in the older part of the town. These houses have fine courts, surrounded with arcades, some of which have marble fountains in the centre, with orange and other trees. All have large tanks supplied by ever-running water, which has first filled a marble trough in the wall higher up, serving as a reservoir for the fountains. It is enough if the water rise a couple of inches or so in these, the perpetual, fitful sound of the bubbling water being preferred to the grace of the European jet, since the Moor desires to gratify his ear rather than his eye. The best of them have gardens adjoining, the tiled pathways bounded and covered with trellis supporting vines and other creepers. Nor do the gardens realize the European ideal, though filled with a luxuriance of foliage and flower, heartily appreciable in the warmer climate. Often there is an apartment on one side, beautifully set with tiles and elegantly equipped, which serves as a summer-house, or withdrawing-room for the reception of male visitors.

Moorish Architecture.

Gardens.

Within the house the floors, pillars, stairs and dados are faced with the local glazed tiles in geometrical patterns, and the wooden ceilings are often exquisitely carved and painted in Mauresque designs, such as one finds in the Alhambra. Indeed, in Tetuan

Decoration.

may be seen some of the best relics of the taste which ruled in the construction of those noble halls. This town shares with Fez, Rabat and Salli the distinction of being considered one of the most aristocratic in Morocco, and of all the coast towns it is perhaps the most interesting.

There are few European residents in Tetuan, and the majority of these are Spaniards of a poor class. There is a Spanish consul with a vice-consul, and there are three other vice-consuls and five consular agents, all but the Spanish and British appointments being allotted to Moors and Jews. Attached to the Spanish consulate, on a piece of ground adjoining the Feddán, are a monastery and a church of the Franciscans, whose labours here date from 1672, though abandoned between 1790 and 1860. Several European doctors reside here, and some small hotels have of late years been opened. Many of the Europeans find accommodation in the Moorish quarter, Tetuan being one of the privileged towns in this respect, but it is very difficult to find a house.

Condition.

In point of cleanliness, Tetuan compares favourably with every other town in Morocco save Mogador and Mazagan, though during the last few years Tangier has made strides in this direction. The streets are many of them wide, and more or less straight, but often dark and dismal where they pass under rows of houses. This city occupies a larger area than Tangier within the walls, but its population, of which few live outside, is not so large.

Port.

Although situated about seven miles from the sea, and therefore not strictly speaking a port, since its river is not navigable, Tetuan is reckoned one, its trade being carried on through the port of Martîl at the mouth of the river of that name, little more than a landing-place. Between the port and the town runs the best road in Morocco, made by the Spaniards when occupying the district. The roadstead, sheltered to the west, north-west and south, is exposed to the Levanters which blow so constantly, making it unsafe while they last. Here it was that Nelson took in supplies of water and vegetables before the battle of Abûkîr Bay. The precise position of Martîl is 35° 37′ N., and 5° 18′ W., and it is about thirty-three miles from Tangier, as the crow flies, or forty by road. Ceuta lies to the north a day's journey, and Sheshâwan is a long day inland.

History.[2]

The earliest authentic mention we find of Tetuan only dates back to 1310 A.C.,* when its re-building[1] was ordered by Abû Thâbet 'Amr, ameer of Fez, who was at the time besieging the Moors of Granáda in Ceuta. Ninety years later Tetuan had gained a notoriety through its pirates, and in the year 1400 Enrique III. of Castille destroyed the town and its ships, carrying off many slaves.[3] The present town was not built until the Andalucian Moors settled here in 1492, first setting up the walls, and then filling in the enclosure with houses. Many of them brought the keys of their Spanish homes, and treasured them up in expectation of the day when they should once more be the proud masters of Spain and have use for them, but careful enquiries have not enabled me to hear of any such relics as still existing. The family of El Khaṭîb,

* It had, however, existed for ages prior to this date, and is said to have been the Yagath of the Romans,[4] but it is also spoken of as Tetuanum.[5] Tissot has identified its river as the Tamuda of Pliny, and the Phalouda of Ptolemy.[6]

[1] In RAÔḌ EL ḲARṬÂS this is spoken of as its foundation,—p. 513.

[2] *The Moorish Empire* contains the following historical allusion to Tetuan: taken by Arabs, 24; Abu 'Aînân proclaimed, 103; attacked by Enrique III. of Spain, 108; foreign merchants there, 159, expelled, 393; El Yazeed flees to it, 169; attacked by Spain, 176-7; pledged to Spain, 177, 340; El Ḥasan III.'s reception, 189; missionaries there, 326, 327, 330, 340.

[3] GODARD, p. 394. [4] RICHARDSON, p. 111. [5] JAMES, vol. ii., p. 11. [6] p. 20.

however, preserved not only the key and deeds of their house in Granáda, but also the sword of Bû 'Abd Allah, ("Boabdil"), until they were taken by the Spaniards in the war of 1860.

ENTRANCE TO JEWISH QUARTER, TETUAN.

In 1564 piracy was again flourishing here, for in that year Felipe II. of Spain sent an expedition which destroyed all local vessels.[1] For some time previous to 1772 Tetuan was the residence of the foreign representatives, but in that year they were ordered to Tangier, as considerable ill-feeling towards the Christians had arisen in consequence of the accidental shooting of a Moorish woman by an Englishman, when hunting in the neighbourhood.[2] In 1727 there were living there, in addition to slaves, eight Europeans, four

Piracy.

[1] CASTELLANOS, p. 44. [2] *Annual Register*, vol. xv., pp. 122 and 124.

of them English merchants, one a Greek merchant, and another the French consul.[1] In that year, on the death of Mulai Isma'íl, the palace was ruined, but was subsequently rebuilt, and the fortifications date chiefly from 1757. The Melláḥ, the great mosque and other works were constructed by Malai Sulaïmán in 1808.[2]

Bombardments.

On November 26, 1859, the port and the fort which existed at Point Negro on the way to Ceuta—where it seems there was formerly a small harbour,—were bombarded by the French for having fired at the *St. Louis*, a vessel flying French colours.[3] During the war of 1859—60 between Spain and Morocco, the port of Martîl was bombarded by the enemy, who forthwith marched on the town. On February 6, 1860, it was entered by Marshal O'Donnell, the leader of the Spaniards, no serious opposition being offered by the Moors.*

Whilst in possession of Tetuan, which they evacuated on May 2, 1862, the Spaniards almost transformed it into

Capture by Spain.

* When the Moors saw that a siege was inevitable, knowing that the town was not prepared to resist an attack, notice was given, and in one night nearly the whole population fled to the hills around. As one of their leaders pictured it to me: "We saw the Spaniards coming up from Martîl, and knew that next day they would be upon us. That night we abandoned all our worldly possessions: we took our women and our slaves, and any cash we could lay hands on, but all else we left to the invader. When all were outside, the gates were locked and we fled. We had not whither to go, so we wandered on the hills. Alas, our Teṭṭáwan! Next day the enemy came on the town, and scaling the walls with ladders, they got the gates open and the place was theirs. Everything they found in our houses they destroyed. They broke our fountains and smashed our tile-work. Our mosques and sanctuaries, which we had left locked, they broke into and desecrated.[4] When word of this was brought to us, I and others were sent to General Prim to request that our sacred spots might be respected, and he had the doors closed again in accordance with our desire."

[1] Braithwaite. [2] Castellanos, p. 44. [3] Godard, p. 394.

[4] The chief mosque was dedicated to "Nuestra Señora de la Victoria" and used as a Romish Church, but the others were spared.

a European city. The streets were repaired, lighted and named, and various other improvements were carried out, but so hateful were the traces of the invader to the Moors, that when they returned they destroyed every vestige of the alterations, and reduced it to its former state.* As the foreigners had no friendly communication with the natives, the latter brought them no charcoal, so two whole quarters of the town were pulled down and robbed of their timber for fuel. They still stand in ruins, silent witnesses of the curse of war. Everywhere the visitor goes he is forcibly reminded of this, and the Moor has often cause to remark with bitterness: "Once this—or that—was beautiful, but since the war—."

Spanish Occupation.

* Almost precisely what happened during and after the concurrent occupation of Canton by the British and French.

VIEW OF LARAICHE FROM THE BAR.

Molinari, Photo., Tangier.

CHAPTER THE SEVENTH

OPEN PORTS—3

EL 'ARÁÏSH (LARAICHE) *

FROM the sea Laraiche presents a hardly less imposing appearance than Tangier, for its situation on the cliff which forms the left bank of the estuary of the Wád Lekkûs gives its buildings prominence, and makes the most of its mosque-towers and flag-staffs. *Situation.* The serpentine river debouching below, with its dangerous bar, is supposed by some to have given rise to the picturesque fable of the Hesperides,[1] the gardens of which are said to have existed here. Of these the modern name is held to be a reminiscence, as corrupted from the Arabic for "pleasure-gardens," 'Arási. Such still abound, and in them grow in great profusion the "golden apples" known to us as the familiar oranges.†

* By the Spaniards the name is still further corrupted to Larache, and by them pronounced Laratchi. Among the early atlases showing Laraiche the Catalan map gives Larax (x being pronounced as sh); Battista Agnesi Laraxa, and others have Laraxi.

† "For the orange, now so familiar and cheap that thoughtless people overlook its beauty and delicacy, was once a hidden marvel of the earth, darkly talked of by travellers in far regions, and not so much as tasted by emperors and queens. Note how, in Keats' 'Endymion,' the first thing the hero does in Elysium, on arriving there, is that 'he asketh where the golden apples grow.' *Legend of the Hesperides.* Nobody, surely, knew in the early classical days. The legends ran that somewhere on the Mauretanian or Gaetulian coasts there were groves of dark, glossy, fragrant trees, the fruitage of which had rinds of solid shining gold, and pulp of nectar such as the immortal gods might

[1] PLINY the elder, bk. v., c. 1.

Once, according to the legend, they were guarded by the foaming-mouthed dragon which, perhaps, was no more than the Wád Lekkûs! *

Harbour.

The bar washed up by the Atlantic swell at the river-mouth presents a serious difficulty. Only steamers of specially shallow draught,—about 11 feet—or small sailing vessels, can now enter the port, though it used to accommodate disabled Salli rovers, when they put in here for repairs. The river being fairly deep inside, this was then a favourite port in which to winter. But the large quantity of alluvial soil brought down each winter is slowly decreasing the width of the channel.

There is plenty of room, about three-quarters of a mile by a quarter—with a mean depth of twenty-four feet. The bar has only five or six feet of water at low tide, and vessels of over 100 or 150 tons, unless specially constructed, are unable to cross. Sometimes a storm nearly obliterates the channel, the river escaping by two or more outlets impassable for vessels, and serious fears are raised that the port will be altogether closed. A

desire to eat. They were tended by the delicate hands of the Hesperidean maidens, dusky-skinned, ebony-tressed daughters of Atlas and of the South-West Wind. Their sacred precincts were guarded night and day by enormous dragons or pythons, which coiled their mottled lengths of glowing bronze and purple round each precious stem, making it certain death to approach."

* One ingenious individual points out a lake in the vicinity as the site of an island referred to by ancient writers.[1] This seems to require a good stretch of imagination, but our author reasons with great plausibility that what would cause an island to sink to the level of the surrounding land might cause it to sink still lower, till no trace was left. Tissot[2] considered that the Shammîsh peninsula might once have been an island, or else part of the left bank, the stream passing right before Lixus, where there is now a neck 600 metres broad. Perhaps, too, the lower peninsula was also an island, and the tongue called Rakádah appears recent. See map of 1700 by Pointis, which Tissot reproduces.

[1] ALDRETE, *Varias Antiquidades*, 1774. [2] p. 82.

good dam across the river, with a flood-gate on one side, to clear a channel by a sudden escapement of water, would entirely obviate the difficulty. The number of sailing vessels which are often to be seen at one time inside the bar is remarkable: sometimes thirty or more of half a dozen nationalities will congregate in search of grain or beans or oranges. The lack of sufficient loading accommodation, and the delays in getting out, account for their accumulation, but severely handicap trade. *

Defences.

Laraiche is well situated for defence, its walls are in fair condition, and it has in addition ten forts, all supplied with old-fashioned guns, among them some brass pieces left by the Spaniards. Four gates afford access to it; that of the Ṣòḳ, or market, being one of the finest of its class on the coast, occupying a large space within the walls at the top of the hill. The others are Báb er-Rûá, Báb Baḥar and Báb el Marsà. But the most remarkable feature of Laraiche is its fine, large market-place inside the town, surrounded by a low colonnade in front of diminutive shops. Other-

Buildings.

wise Laraiche is deficient in architectural features, and possesses no palace. The chief mosque, Moorish in design, and of native workmanship, nevertheless includes the remains of a Romish church dedicated to San Antonio.

Saints.

The other mosques of importance are those of the Ḳaṣbah, and of the Záwîahs of Mulai 'Abd el Ḳáḍer, Aûlád Miṣbaḥ, 'Ali bin Ḥamdûsh, and the 'Aïsáwà. The patron saint is Lállah Mannánah el Miṣbaḥ Sîyah, a maiden who is supposed to have saved the

* Riley tells us that the pirate vessels used to get across the bar when lightened and buoyed up, listing to one side and steadied by cables till the ebb tide carried them over. [1]

[1] p. 574.

town from Christian bombs in the good old days of yore. In the large open space of the Kaşbah are two prisons, and before the Customs Gate a fair landing stage was erected a few years ago. Near the mouth of the river is a castle said to have been built by Mulai El Yazeed.[1] The narrow streets, which are frequently steep, are generally paved, so that Laraiche is not as badly off as some towns in this country.

Outside the walls are three Moorish grave-yards, and one each for Jews and Christians. The surrounding country is hilly, and the timber of which the pirate vessels were built was formerly obtainable in the vicinity, from the forest of M'amôra. As late as 1789 it seems that vessels could be fitted and stored here, and fine holm oaks are still to be seen.[2] At present the extensive cork-wood forest is only cut for charcoal, or for the construction of lighters and gun-carriages.

The Country Outside.

Not far from the town are the remains of what is believed to have been a Phœnician city, Shammîsh.* The ruins now to be seen there are insignificant, having shared the fate of so many other ruins in being used as a quarry, the marble being burned for lime! The name Shammîsh, which is also that given to several places in Egypt, is said to be from the Arabic *m'shammish*, sun-burnt, and it has been suggested that it was founded by sun-worshippers from that country, which must have been long before the time of the Arabs.† Yet the equivalent in Hebrew and Phœnician would probably be but slightly different. It is suggested that Shammîsh was founded by one of the four Berber tribes, Zanátà, Ketámà, Sanhajà and Hawárà, who came to Mauretania long before the Arab invasions.[3]

Phœnician Remains.

* Mentioned by Idreesî, who makes no allusion to Laraiche.

† cf. Jer. xliii., 13. Beth-Shemesh = House-of-the-Sun = Heliopolis.

[1] Ali Bey. [2] Lemprière. [3] Ibn Khaldûn, etc.

MARKET PLACE OF LARAICHE.

Molinari, Photo., Tangier.

In a thorough description of the Báshálik of Laraiche, published in the Bulletin of the Madrid Geographical Society in 1883—4, which is the most complete and reliable account yet published of any part of Morocco, Sr. de Cuevas, formerly Spanish Vice-Consul at Laraiche, gives some very interesting information about this place. He points out that the name is neither pure Arabic nor Berber. Syria, he reminds us, is called Shám after Shem, its people's ancestor, worshipped as Jupiter Ammon, and suggests that as Kush was the son of Shem, to this may be due the names of both Shammîsh and the river Lekkûs. It is believed by some that Shammîsh was one of the Carthaginian cities founded by Hanno in his celebrated voyage, about 500 B.C.[1]

A Thorough Description.

Pliny records the founding by Claudius Cæsar in 50 A.C., of Lixion, 32,000 paces from Zilia (Azîla),[2] which is just the distance to Laraiche. The Vandals must have possessed it between 438 and 533 A.C., and they are chargeable with the destruction of its buildings, although Lixus does not appear to have been abandoned until the eighth century. The remains of Shammîsh are chiefly Carthaginian walls with huge hewn stones, truncated columns, bases and capitals of the three orders of a later date, all in confusion, with Berber walls six or seven feet high. Roman inscriptions, coins of Domitian (81 A.C.), Nerva (96 A.C.), Trajan (98 A.C.) and Alexander Severus (222 A.C.) and a Greek tomb-stone have been found there.[3]

Lixus.

Modern Laraiche, if it has not existed since the time of Shammîsh, seems at all events to date from the eighth century, but the actual town was probably not

[1] *Periplus*: see Appendix. [2] Ch. v., Cap. 1.

[3] CUEVAS: HAY, p. 124 and MARTINIÈRE, *Bull. Arch. du Com. des Trav. Hist. et Sc.*, t. viii., pp. 148 and 451, the most complete account of the ruins, with plates.

built till the middle of the thirteenth. A governor of Laraiche is mentioned as having been appointed in 913 A.C. by the third Idreesi ameer.[1] It appears in the Catalan map of 1300, as does also Shammîsh, but it was not mentioned in Idreesi's geography of 1154.

Modern Laraiche.

In the "Raôḍ el Ḳarṭás" it is stated that in 1270 Christians seized Laraiche, slaughtering its inhabitants and carrying off its riches.[2] Who were these Christians? The recorded history of no other country seems to throw light on the story, though Castellanos says that in 1504 it was captured by surprise by the Portuguese, who ten years after lost it,[3] but this statement seems to be a mistake. During the greater part of the fifteenth century it was famous for its pirates, but their activities were checked by the capture of Azîla by the Portuguese in 1471, from which time the rovers found Salli a safer home. In the same year the Portuguese undertook a fruitless expedition up the river to capture the island or peninsula below the ruins of Shammîsh—which they called Graciosa, or "Beautiful."

*History.**

The present walls of the ḳaṣbah were built in 1491 by Mulai en-Náṣir, a brother of the then sultan of Fez, and in 1578, after the battle of El Ḳaṣar, Mulai Ahmad V. (Hamed ed-Dháhebi) added two large castles of tabia—mud concrete,[4] that near the mouth of the river being known as El Kashlah or "the Barracks," and that to the south-east of the ḳaṣbah as El Heri or "the Store." The walls of the town were the work of the Spaniards.

Erection.

* *The Moorish Empire* contains references to Laraiche at pp. 128, 130, 134, 152, 155, 167, 170, 190, 301, 322, 323, 325, 327 (n.), 330, 340, 403 and 413.

[1] Raôḍ el Ḳarṭás. [2] p. 566.
[3] p. 73. [4] El Ufráni.

In 1579 an unsuccessful attempt was made by Felipe II. of Spain to obtain the cession of Laraiche in return for assistance against the Algerian Turks,[1] but in 1610 Mohammed es-Sheikh sold the town to Felipe III. for 100,000 crowns[2] and assistance in his fight for the throne against his brothers.[3] The Spaniards added greatly to the fortifications,* finishing them in 1618, which date is recorded on a stone over the water-port.[4] In 1664 the republic of Salli attacked it, but without success.[5] At length, in 1689, Mulai Ismá'īl, aided by frigates and forces from Louis XIV. of France, besieged it most determinedly, and in November of that year it capitulated, a Franciscan friar being intermediary in the negotiations.† Instead of abiding by his agreement, and letting the garrison return to their country, the sultan only liberated a hundred of the chief among them, carrying off sixteen hundred as slaves to Fez and Mequinez.

Spanish Occupation.

A Moorish historian states that the siege lasted three and a half months, the garrison only surrendering after 1200 had perished, the remaining 2000 being taken prisoners. A breach had been made by the explosion of a powder-magazine in the wall west of the triangular tower called El Heri. The

A Moorish Account.

* Tissot gives their names for the towers as those of St. James, St. Stephen (the latter to the S.W.) and the Jews (this being the oldest), while the castle was dedicated to "our Lady of Europe."

† The first act of the Spaniards had been the erection of a Franciscan convent. During their occupation the chief trade of Laraiche was in charcoal.[6]

[1] An unpublished account is in the Govt. Library at Algiers, C. VI., No. 4.

[2] Menezes, p. 124.

[3] See Rojas, *Relacion de Algunos Sucesos*, Lisbon, 1613, and Guadalajara, *Relacion y Destierro de los Moriscos de Castilla*, Pamplona, 1614, wherein Laraiche is said to have been "taken."

[4] Castellanos, p. 77.

[5] El Ufráni, p. 442. See Alfano, *Vera Relazione*, Rome, 1666. Mouëtte (p. 145) says that on this occasion 12,000 Moors were cut to pieces.

[6] D'Avity.

booty included 180 cannons, of which twenty-two were bronze, the dimensions of one—called El Kissáb—being given as thirty-five feet in length, needing four men to stretch round the breach, and firing a ball of thirty-five rotals (of 850 grammes).[1] By the Convention of Madrid of 1691, published in the *Gaceta* of March 20th of that year, 100 Spaniards were exchanged for 1000 Moors.

Since that time Laraiche has been in the hands of the Moors, who re-peopled it with Rîfîs, but in 1758 it contained only 200 inhabitants.[2] In 1765 the French under Du Chaffault suffered great loss in an attempt to destroy the pirate vessels in the river,* and in 1829 the Austrians met with the same fate, the small force which had been landed being enticed too far up and cut off.[3] In February 1860 Laraiche was bombarded by Spain, then at war with Morocco, but on account of the heavy sea running the damage inflicted was slight.

Bombardments.

In 1780 all the Europeans in Laraiche were expelled by Mohammed XVII.[4] and it seems that as late as 1836 none were resident there, although in 1786 the monopoly of its trade had been for a time granted to Holland, including even the export of wheat.[5] In 1789 the Moors were still building pirate vessels here.[6] Several foreign merchants now reside at this port, their interests being looked after by one consul, six vice consuls, and five consular agents. The Spanish Franciscans have had a mission here for some years past,

European Residents.

* Three chaloups which went up the river to burn the corsairs were stranded and cut off with a loss of 450 men, of whom but 84 survived in slavery. This is hardly the light in which the affair was officially reported, at the time when *l'honneur de la France* required that it should appear otherwise, but in a little book published soon after in Holland by one of the victims the truth appears unvarnished.[7]

[1] EL UFRÁNI, p. 507.
[2] EZ ZAIÁNI, p. 141.
[3] EN-NÁSIRI, vol. iv., p. 183.
[4] JACKSON, p. 65; CHENIER, vol. i., p. 24.
[5] London Encyclopedia, ed. 1836.
[6] GODARD, p. 562.
[7] By BIDÉ DE MAURVILLE: GODARD, p. 551.

although they abandoned their former station in 1822. During the last few years it has also been occupied by various Protestant missionaries, two societies being represented there just now. The population is not, perhaps, more than six or seven thousand, of whom 1000 may be Jews,* and 2/300 "Christians,"†[1] though other estimates run as high as ten thousand.‡[2]

Laraiche is the poorest in every respect of the open ports of Morocco, and contains but few well-to-do Moors. It has no manufactures, and even the greater part of the native clothing is brought from El Ḳaṣar and the interior, but Europeans have established two steam flour mills and a saw mill. There are some 140 shops and six fandáḳs, two of which are devoted to Jews. One European only, and he a Vice-consul, has ventured to build outside the Walls.

* Buffa says that at one time some 200 Jews were expelled for selling spirits to the sailors who then composed the population.[3]

† Half of them Spaniards.

‡ The population of Laraiche has—in my opinion—been considerably under-estimated by De Cuevas at 4000 (reckoning only five to each of 750 to 800 houses) including 500 Jews and 70 Christians.

Population.

But with his usual minuteness that writer gives the occupations of Laraiche as follow: 102 oilmen, 22 grocers, 8 greengrocers, 5 bakers. 1 miller, 15 to 25 breadsellers, 19 café-keepers, 5 salt collectors, 4 Jewish and 4 Moorish butchers, (often weeks or months between killing oxen, but 20 to 25 sheep a week,) 18 drapers, 32 grain-dealers, 18 smiths and farriers, 10 shoe-makers, 9 cobblers, 1 European shoe-maker, 7 tanners, 12 masons, 70 lime-burners owning kilns, 6 weavers, 7 woodcutters, 3 charcoal-dealers, 2 Jewish and 5 Moorish carpenters, 6 sawyers, 4 mat-makers, 1 sword-smith without assistant or apprentice, 12 water-sellers, 1 copper-smith, 1 turner, 6 barbers, 1 Jewish and 2 public Moorish baths, 2 silver-smiths, 1 tin-smith, 4 Jewish and 2 Moorish auctioneers, 18 grain measurers, 4 "horse doctors," 2 Jewish tailors, 4 coopers, 2 tambourine players, 2 oboe blowers, 20 government calkers to repair 5 lighters, 7 notaries, 1 rabbi, 1 military-captain, 2 customs-officers, 1 administrator of taxes. Revenue from Báshálik of Laraiche, 330,198 ducats or Metkals; inhabitants, 143,000.

[1] LEMPRIÈRE, p. 25. [2] Estimate by Mr. FORDE. [3] p. 447.

Pliny mentions this neighbourhood as abounding with olives, and tells us there was an altar to Hercules there. Strabo says that the plain produced 250-fold per annum.[1] There was a time when a good deal of cotton was grown round about. The large quantities of oranges produced in gardens near the town find a ready market in Seville. Its other chief exports are beans, maize, millet, fenugreek and canary seed, chick peas, lentils, linseed, goat-hair and skins, ox-hides, sheep-skins, wool, and fullers' earth—g͟hásool. The wool nearly all goes to Marseilles. There are plenty of shabel (shad), (clupea alosa), mis-named "Barbary salmon," and a fishery of bonitos (*scomber pelamis*) and horse mackerel (*scomber hippos*) is carried on just off this port, mainly by Portuguese. The imports are much the same as at other ports; much of what enters here finding its way to Fez.

Exports.

Were it not for the difficulty of loading, the commerce of Laraiche would be undoubtedly far more important, and would absorb much of that of Tangier, being so much nearer the northern capitals of Fez and Mequinez. From Fez it is about four days, travelling with loaded animals, and from El Ḳaṣar a short day's journey over sand and gravel, which means fair travelling even in winter. It is about twenty-two miles, or a short day's journey, over the sand from Azîla, which is one good day from Tangier, and it is about eighty miles, or two and a half days from Rabat. It is situated in the province of El K͟hlôt, and is the chief town of a Báshálik. The exact position of Laraiche is latitude 35° 13′ N., and longitude 6° 7′ 30″ W. By sea it is 43 miles from Tangier, 77 from Rabat, and 73 from Gibraltar.

Position.

[1] iii., 205.

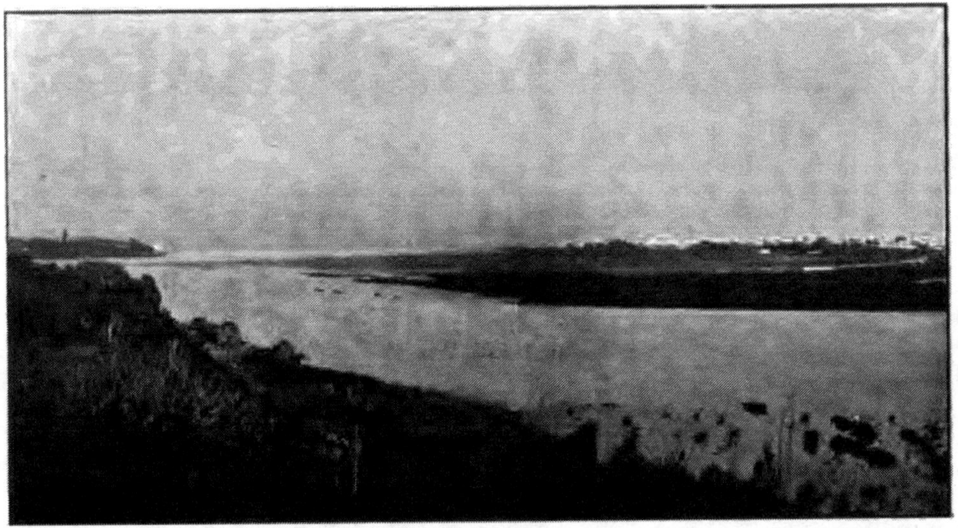

Portion of Rabat.

SALLI, SEEN ACROSS THE BÛ RAGRAG.
(Looking out to sea.)

Cavilla, Photo., Tangier.

CHAPTER THE EIGHTH

OPEN PORTS—4

SALLI-RABAT

I—SLÁ (SALLI)

PIRACY, rather than commerce—unless it be the trade in white slaves which resulted,—has given this ancient town its fame. There is nothing attractive about it, low-lying on the north side of the Bû Ragrág, with the more prominent walls of Rabat on the opposite bank of the river-mouth. Though its white walls gleam, and a few minarets relieve its uninteresting outline, but for its historical associations, Salli would hardly repay a visit, and foreign visitors are not made welcome. Even now, when such appear occasionally in the streets of Salli, they are sometimes received with stones, or at least with curses, but it is usually only the children who indulge in this sport. Europeans are not allowed to reside in the town, though English, Irish, French and other merchants lived there during the piracy days, and consuls were appointed to Salli up to the beginning of the eighteenth century. It is only within the last few months that an otherwise superfluous post-office has been established here by way of re-introducing a foreign element.

Situation.

Fanaticism.

Viewed from Rabat, the rover city seems to be divided into two portions by a central group of gardens, to the left of which rises a low hill, surmounted by the tower of the chief mosque. To the right

Appearance.

lies a still lower hill—if worthy of the name—beyond which stretch other gardens with summer-houses. The melláḥ also, filthy as any, but boasting no less than eight synagogues, is to be found on this, the south, side.

Streets.

The thoroughfares of Salli are neglected and dirty, comparing most unfavourably with those of Rabat: in fact it is a poor place, and in bad condition even for Morocco. Of the few streets in the centre of the town that have been paved, tortuous and narrow as they are, most have foot-room at the sides, with a foul gutter, generally full of garbage, in the centre. There are many gardens, cattle-yards, ruins and open spaces within the walls, outside of which is no security for life or property.

Walls and Gates.

The city wall is said to average thirty-five feet in height, and it is fortified at intervals by good square towers. It is pierced by six gates, Báb M'alḳá, opposite Rabat, Báb El Jeed * or Sidi Bûḥá-jah, Báb el Khabbáz, Báb Fás, Báb Sebta and Báb Seba' Binát (of the "Seven Maids"). † The old ḳaṣbah moat, its great cistern and the subterranean passage from the old ḳaṣbah to the fort intended to command the bar, were cut in the rock when Salli was a republic early in the seventeenth century: the new ḳaṣbah and the fort to the south-west were erected by Mulai Rasheed, and the walls were repaired by Mulai Ismá'ïl.[1]

Defences.

Some of the batteries date from 1744, and there are bomb-proof magazines of more recent construction. To the north are ruins of a suburb built by Ismá'ïl for his black troops. The cemetery set apart

* Meaning "the hanging," a name attributed to some early execution there.

† Said to owe its name to the plucky defence made by seven maidens washing wool, who had been set upon by evilly disposed men.

[1] MOUËTTE, pp. 17—18.

for the foreign slaves was just outside the northern gate,[1] and while they lived they were confined in a subterranean dungeon.

The chief mosque—to which is attached a flourishing college—is a large one, capable, it is said, of holding some thousands of people, and there are several of smaller size, the most important being the modern building of Sidi Ahmad Ḥajji. The chief saint-house is that of Sidi Bin 'Aáshir* in the graveyard towards the sea, which tens of thousands visit every year, and where large numbers are supported by the charitable. The shrine of Sidi 'Abd Allah Ḥasûn, close by the principal mosque, is of sufficient sanctity to close the street to infidels, and no Jew is allowed to pass that of Sidi Bû Ḥájah, near the Báb el Khabbáz or "Baker's Gate," so they always have to make a detour there.

Mosques and Saints.

A short distance from the Sebta gate, on the way to Laraiche, the track is crossed at a great height by a fine stone aqueduct which runs to the north end of the town, having brought the water from Ismîr, about ten miles distant. When it enters the town it is used for washing clothes, the stream running in an open groove in the masonry, about one foot wide and two deep. The building of this aqueduct has been ascribed by many to the Romans, but, judging from a careful inspection, I am of opinion that if they had any hand in it originally, it has been at least rebuilt by the Moors.† Close by the great archway under which the road runs over the bare face of the rock, are extensive quarries.

Aqueduct.

* The origin of the veneration was the part played by S. bin 'Aáshir in resisting the Spaniards in 1260.

† In the *Raôḍ el Ḳarṭás* is recorded the bringing in of the 'Ain Ghabûlah in A.C. 1150 by 'Abd el Mûmin.[2] Keatinge says the main aqueduct was the work of an English renegade,[3] who probably repaired it.

[1] Dan, p. 435. [2] p. 379. [3] Vol. ii., p. 36.

LANDING PLACE, RABAT.

Photograph by John Frost, Esq.

The old water-port of Salli is now high and dry, separated from the present bed of the river by a wide stretch of sand: it was restored by Mulai Ismá'il. Docks also formerly existed here, and vessels were built for the rovers with wood from a forest which then stretched between this town and Laraiche. Chenier believed that the sea was once twenty to twenty-five feet higher than at present, and spoke of the ruins of an older town on an island There is too high a bar at the mouth of the river to allow vessels of more than about two hundred tons to enter, but there is good anchorage on the Rabat side, when once across. *

The Port.

Steamers lie outside, a good distance from the shore, and communication with the port is maintained by means of lighters, great heavy boats of genuine native build, manned by sixteen to twenty descendants of the rovers, who are still called "sailors," by courtesy, that being an hereditary title in Morocco. All goods from abroad for Salli have now to be landed at Rabat, where is the Custom House. Communication between the two towns is brisk, and a number of ferry-boats constantly ply to and fro, the Sultan maintaining for his own use a couple of very respectable barges.

Anchorage.

In spite of the bad name among seamen earned by the bar Bu Ragrág, it would seem from a careful register of its behaviour for several years, compiled by Mr. Frost of Rabat, that the average proportion of good to bad is as three to two, and that including the days when lighters can cross with care, the bar may be reckoned passable four days in six, though that would not be saying much for it were the port doing great trade. A west or north wind almost always renders it impassable, but with an east wind it is in the best of

The Bar.

* See *The Moorish Empire*, p. 662, for the dimensions of the rover vessels.

humour. A little judicious dredging would probably set it right in all weathers.

Position.

The exact position of Salli is latitude 34° 2′ 7″ N. and longitude 6° 46′ W., and it is situated in the province of Beni Ḥasan. From Mequinez it is distant about 45 or 50 miles, by the closed route, but it is about 90 miles by road, or three days' travelling; from Fez 123 miles, or four days; and from Laraiche two and a half days. In the time of the Romans, as Salaconia, it was a town of some importance, marking the limit along the coast of their Mauretanian province,[1] and when the pioneers of Islám came, it soon fell into their hands, and helped to form the nucleus of empire. As early as 1161 it entertained business relations with Genoa, whence it received an envoy who obtained a treaty fixing at 10 % the duty payable there, as also at Azîla, Laraiche and Fedála.[2]

*History.**

Its earliest place in modern history, however, is when, about the year 1260, it was captured by Alfonso X. of Castille, who was soon to be dispossessed by the ameer of Fez.[3] According to Marmol the foreigners only held it ten days, but a Mohammedan historian gives the length of the occupation as fourteen days.[4] Its arsenal and forts towards the sea were then erected, Ya'ḳûb II. (bin 'Abd el Ḥaḳḳ) himself assisting the work, but after this event it is said never to have recovered its magnificence.

* *The Moorish Empire* contains the following historical references to Salli: taken by Idrees I., p. 36; Christians transported to, 61; taken by 'Abd el Mû'min, 62, 71: death of Ya'ḳûb I. there, 81; taken by the Beni Marîn, 93; supports El Ḥádi, 88; Yûsef IV. buried there, 100; 'Amr Abû Thábit buried there, 101; 'Ali V.'s tomb, 103 (n.); ruled by El 'Ayáshi, 134; foreign merchants, 159; conquered by Mohammed XVII., 167; attacked by the French, 167, 175; independence (seventeenth century), 268, 347; trade, 349, 355, 402, 403; French consulate, 404.

[1] See Mela, Pliny, Polybius, etc.

[2] Caffaro.

[3] Ibn Khaldûn, vol. iv., p. 47.

[4] In Raôḍ el Ḳarṭás.

The inhabitants of Slá—called Sláwîs—were always proud and independent, and are still considered aristocratic.* Especially has this been the case since the settlement among them of a number of exiles from Spain in 1610, from which time the sultans experienced no small difficulty in controlling them. Ere long they had established an almost independent republic,†[1] and an ambassador was sent to Charles I. by Zîdán, in 1625, to request assistance for their subjugation. This was at first refused, but was granted in 1636, when the fortifications of Salli were demolished, and in return the King of England received a present of horses and 300 Christian slaves.‡

Independence.

In 1624 and 1629 the town had been bombarded by the French because their subjects had been imprisoned in consequence of the capture of Mulai Zîdán's books.§ Salli was once more reduced in 1666 by Mulai Rasheed—"The Great Tafilatta"—

French Bombardments.

* At one time during the Moorish occupation of Lisbon so many of them settled in the neighbourhood of that city that their descendants and articles produced by them are still known locally as Saloios (*m.*) or Saloias (*f.*).

† Received at first as welcome guests, they soon ousted the natives, while the ameer besieged them in vain. They were protected by El 'Ayáshi, known as a saint, and boasted an independent dîwán or council, which governed them as a republic. When the English were in Tangier, the "Salleteens" sent as envoys to the governor a Moor and a French renegade, with two fine horses, forty selected oxen and eighty sheep, asking for assistance against Ghaïlán: "a great ship to lye at the port between us and the enemy ... and any of your ships that shall come to this port shall drive away whatsoever merchant ships they find there and seize their goods."[2] As late as 1782 the elders still had absolute power over all but state questions, the dîwán being composed of past governors, two of whom were elected each year, one for the town and one for the citadel. In 1784 the kaïd of the kasbah was invited to go to Tunis as Bey.[3]

The Salli Republic.

‡ A translation of the sultan's letter is to be found in the Harleian Library, Cat. vol. ix., p. 490, Cod. 2104, Art. 2.

§ See *The Moorish Empire*, p. 130.

[1] Dan, p. 204; Mouette, p. 14. [2] Addison, *The Moors Baffled.* [3] Thomassy, pp. 312-3.

and recovered from Ghaïlán, who was carving out for himself a kingdom in the north. Then in 1680 the French came again, blockading it without success under the Chevalier de Chateau Renaud, and again in 1718 under Du Chaffault, when their consulate there was suppressed.[1] Thus it remained till Chenier removed there from Saffi half a century later "the better to watch the English at Gibraltar."[2] In those days it was recorded by a French writer that "The French at Salli and Saffi are only known for their bad faith and untrustworthiness," many being simple runaways. In 1690 the Kaïd had been a French renegade named Pillet, but eventually the twin towns were closed to Europeans.

A Curious Fiasco.

In 1851 Salli was once more bombarded by the French, for having plundered a stranded vessel. They demanded £8000 damages, and the punishment of the robbers. Rabat, which always had its quarrels with its sister-city, was bound over not to fire if not fired upon, and the foreigners pounded away for a couple of hours. At the end of that time night fell, and as provisions on board had run short, the admiral took his departure. But before morning the Moors had determined to capitulate, and it is said that an official was sent off at daybreak with the keys of the town and presents, but when he got out of the mist that overhung the river, he found no one to whom to deliver them! So ended the incident.*

The feelings that exist between the two towns may be inferred from the popular saying: Ba'd má tirja' er-riml zabeeb wa el m'gáz ḥaleeb, 'omr er-Sláwi wa er-

* But though only two men then lost their lives, it is said that fifty have done so since by the explosion of the bombs then thrown, which have claimed their victims every few years. The most recent within my knowledge occurred in the governor's house on Oct. 18, 1891. Four were killed and several wounded on the previous occasion.[3]

[1] THOMASSY, p. 211. [2] Ibid., p. 256. [3] cf. KERR, p. 224.

Ribáti ma yakoon ḥabeeb—*i.e.*, "Till the sand becomes raisins, and the river milk, the Ribáte and Sláwi will never be friends."

2—RIBÁṬ EL FÁTIḤ (RABAT)

Facing Salli, looking down upon it from low cliffs below which the river sweeps grandly, lies its modern rival and supplanter, Rabat, in Arabic "The Camp of Victory." † Ya'ḳûb el Manṣûr was its builder, at the close of the twelfth century, employing many thousands of Christian slaves on its works, principally captives from the battle of El Arcos in 1195, whom he eventually formed into the Sha'báni tribe, now lost sight of. El Manṣûr's ḳaṣbah was demolished by Mohammed XVII. in the eighteenth century (1774), when he employed an English renegade to build the three forts facing the sea, and mounted them with guns obtained from England.‡ Then in 1888 a German engineer was engaged to erect more modern fortifications for two 36-ton Krupp guns, intended to carry ten miles. The citadel is principally occupied by the Údäïä, a hereditary mulatto legion.

History. *

Fortifications.

Rabat has two walls, in the inner of which are seven gates, Bab el Marsà, Báb el Baḥar, Báb Shellá, Báb el Jadeed, Báb el Aa'lû, Báb el Ḥád and Báb 'Abîbá, and in the outer wall, some two miles

Gates.

* *The Moorish Empire* contains the following historical references to Rabat: founded, 81; taken by the Beni Marîn, 93; a pirate stronghold, 268; brought into subjection by Mohammed XVII., 167; El Ḥasan III.'s expedition, 187; his entry, 192; missionaries, 317, 330-2; Europeans, 413.

† Its name is said to have been due to a prophecy by Ibn Tûmart, the Mahdi, that after his followers the Muwáḥḥadîs had built a city they would always be victorious.[1] Its plan is said to have been modelled on that of Alexandria, and certainly it is far too regular for Moorish notions.

‡ The embrasures are too close together to be of much service.

[1] 'Abd el Wáḥḥid, p. 262.

RABAT, SEEN ACROSS THE BÛ RAGRAG.

Landing Place. Citadel Bar.

Cavilla, Photo., Tangier.

in circumference, are three, Báb el Jadeed, Báb Támsná and Báb Ḳabîbah. Between these walls are two imperial palaces, one large, one small, the former of which, while of a plain exterior, is decorated inside with considerable taste, especially as regards the tile-work. It contains the tombs of Sidi Mohammed XVII. (bin 'Abd Allah) and of Mulai Ḥasan III. The other is a much humbler dwelling on the sea-shore, seldom used by royalty.

Palaces.

In the ḳaṣbah is a very large mosque, built by Mulai 'Abd Allah V., in addition to which, and to the chief mosque (in the "Slipper Market"), those of Mulai Sulaïmán (in the Ṣûáḳah) and the Sinna (on the Shella road, by the gate of the palace) are worthy of mention. The patron saint, Sidi Lîábûri, is supposed to guard the river, and to him petitions are made when the bar is troublesome. A lady of the same name, Lallah 'Ayeshah Lîábûrîah, buried on the hill above, is also in great repute, and so is Sidi Mukhalûf, to whose shrine the ladies repair in throngs, as they do likewise to that of Sidi Yáḥyà at Shellah. At the shrine of Sidi er-Rázî the insane are confined, and there is a Dár Damána, or sanctuary, held in very great reverence.

Mosques.

Saints.

Both within and without the walls are many beautiful orchards, orange gardens, vine-yards and olive-groves, so that fruit is abundant in season. The surroundings of Rabat and Salli are most picturesque, the sloping hill-sides on the north, and the Zemmûr mountains beyond, contributing charming views. Game, large and small, abounds within easy distance, and the opportunities for fishing are excellent. The air is rich in spring with perfume from innumerable wild flowers, and the flaming red of the pomegranate blossom gleams amid its dark green foliage.

Surroundings.

The winter climate is nowhere surpassed on this coast,

and sufferers from chest complaints would probably here enjoy a more congenial atmosphere than anywhere within so short a distance of London or Paris. From a record of the temperature between October 1874 and June 1877, kindly placed at my disposal by Mr. Frost, it appears that the shade register is never unbearably hot, the highest from July to September being 70° and 80° F., and the average highest for those months, 78°. The lowest registered was only 48° in December and January, and on the coldest days of those months it averaged 50½°. Dr. Kerr informs me that while in some years they have had ice as thick as a sixpence, he has never known the thermometer to register over 82° in the shade on ordinary occasions, although during the continuance of an occasional hot wind lasting sometimes three or four days, he has known it rise to 96° with windows and doors closed. July and October are the most trying months, the latter on account of the effects of rain on the accumulated rubbish of the summer.

Climate.

The markets of Rabat are more than usually interesting for a coast town, because of the local manufactures, among which the most important is carpets. Although when new of very bright colours, these productions have the name of being prepared entirely with vegetable dyes, which, when they fade, leave most harmonious shades. This industry is capable of great extension and improvement, but as the work is all done by women in private houses, it is difficult to control. Excellent Morocco leather is likewise produced here, and there is a large and increasing trade in yellow and red Moorish slippers, many of which find their way to the East Rabat is also famed for its pottery, and the usual handicrafts are pursued.

Manufactures.

When there is a railway here, with a bridge over the Bû Ragrág, it promises to be of some commercial im-

A STREET IN RABAT.
(Báb Sûïḳah.)

Cavilla, Photo., Tangier.

European Residents.

portance. There are at present two European consuls, two vice-consuls, and three consular agents, all engaged in trade, besides whom there are several other foreign merchants. In 1886 Rabat became a station of an English Presbyterian mission, which has developed into the Independent "Central Morocco Mission." The Franciscans have also a mission and school. The town was opened to Europeans by Mohammed XVII. or Abd er-Rahmán II., but the present custom house was only erected in 1848. There are many Jewish traders also, who possess a good sized melláḥ, rebuilt about 1811,[1] which contains sixteen synagogues.

The people of Salli sometimes taunt the Rabátîs with being descended from Jews who have embraced the faith of Mohammed, and whatever foundation there may be for this assertion,* it is certain that the Moors of Rabat are not considered of blue blood, and aristocratic families seldom intermarry with them. An Arab writer who was here in the fourteenth century, on the other hand, declares that Rabat was then almost entirely inhabited by families from Granáda.[2]

The populations of Salli and Rabat have been thus estimated:

	Salli	*Rabat*
Washington	9,000	21,000
Arlett	14,000	24,000
Jackson	18,000	25,000
Gråberg	23,000	27,000
Castellanos		30,000
Kerr	22,000 †	40,000
The writer	20,000	30,000

* The only proof to be offered is the existence in Rabat of a district called the Ḥaumah Baḥaïrah (formerly Derb bilá Soma',—*i.e.*, Mosque-less street) in which may be found many families with such un-Mohammedan names as Toledano, El 'Aôfîr, Bû Yûsef, Bel Mesa'ôd, El Haloo, Ben 'Brahîm, Dadûn, El Azraḳ, etc.

[1] Riley, p. 546.

[2] Ibn el Khateeb, quoted by Gayangos in El Makkari, bk. viii., ch. i., note 40.

† Arrived at by the computation of a well-known Moor, of 10 dwellers in each of 2000 houses, with 1500 Jews. When no oil or barley comes into Salli the Government orders a third of the supply for Rabat to be sent there.

RUINS OF ḤASAN MOSQUE, RABAT.

Cavilla, Photo., Tangier.

Not far from the walls stands the prominent unfinished Hassan tower, sister to the Giralda at Seville and to the Kûtûbîya at Marrákesh, all of them monuments raised about the year 1200 by Ya'ḳûb el Manṣûr.* Its fretted sides are of a beautiful design in weather-worn stone, the huge blocks of which it is built defying time. The ascent by an inclined plain is so gradual that a man could ride up on horse-back, had not the door been built up. Access can now be obtained only by a window some 20 ft. from the ground, to which I once climbed bare-foot, as the Arab boys do, with my toes in the holes they had scooped, but was well rewarded, after dislodging hundreds of pigeons, by the view from the top. †

The Hassan Tower.

The height I ascertained by measurement with a string to be 145 ft.; the thickness of the exterior walls being 8 ft. 6 in., and of the interior walls 5 ft. 6 in., with a 6 ft. 6 in. passage between. In the centre there are five storeys of single rooms, besides the ground floor, and had it been completed there would probably have been seven or eight, with a smaller tower above, and a promenade for the muédhdhin all round. It is said that at one time a determined attempt was made to destroy it, but that its solidity was such that the idea had to be abandoned. At present it forms the land-mark by which vessels steer when approaching Rabat. Its position is 34° 3' 30" N., 6° 48' 50" W.

Dimensions of Tower.

At its base are many massive rough marble columns,

* Illustrations of all these are given in *The Moorish Empire*, Ch. 5, "The Muwáḥḥadi period."

† But not being a sailor, the descent was another matter, not so much so the perpendicular portion, as the initial horizontal journey along the face of the wall, gripping by fingers and toes in holes scooped between the great stones, from the window-sill to the wall by which the ascent had been made, an interesting but unpleasant experience.

MOSQUE TOWER AT SHELLA.
(Surmounted by Stork's Nest.)

Photograph by John Frost, Esq.

erect or in scattered sections, which are said to have once numbered 360, partly surrounding a large quadrangle formed by the ruined walls of what was designed to be a gigantic mosque. Underneath are extensive vaults or cisterns, and in the vicinity are traces of aqueducts and other buildings.

The Hassan Mosque.

A little further out from the town are the ruins of Shella, the first town to proclaim Mulai Idrees, probably the Roman colony which seems to have given its name to Salli; perhaps a Carthaginian settlement. Jackson had heard that the tombs of two Roman Generals were here, revered as those of saints,[1] but this was most likely a confused idea of the Beni Marîn tombs which lend special interest to the spot, though Roman and other ancient coins have been found here. Among the few remains of antiquity are some stone vaults, an arched canal, perhaps Roman, and a piece of old wall.

Shella.

Otherwise, although picturesquely ruinous, and overgrown with vegetation surmounted with storks' nests, the beautiful gate-ways and mosque-tower which still stand are all comparatively modern.* In the time of Idreesi (1154) the ancient Shella had already been abandoned in favour of Salli,[2] so that this magnificence points to another period, when, in the fourteenth and fifteenth centuries, the Beni Marîn revived its glories and employed it as a royal burying place. In a desolate ruin two of the tomb-stones, finely inscribed,† have lain for six hundred years, those of Ali V.—the "Black Sultan,"—and of his wife Shems eṣ-Ṣbáḥi—"Morning Sun,"—who were laid to rest here on May 24th,

The Existing Ruins.

* For illustrations see *The Moorish Empire*, pp. 107 and 114.

† The inscriptions are translated in a note to p. 103 of *The Moorish Empire*, where an illustration of one will be found.

[1] p. 301. [2] p. 83.

1351, and Sept. 18th, 1349, respectively.* On account of the sanctity of such a spot, until quite recently Shella was closed against Christians and Jews, but now its ruins provide a most pleasant spot for picnics.†

From Rabat to Casablanca is 46 miles by sea, and about 50 by land.

* In the *Raôḍ el Ḳarṭás* [1] are given the names of several ameers who were buried here, as Ya'ḳûb II., who died in his new palace at Algeciras in 1286; his son Yûsef IV., assassinated at Tlemçen in 1307, and 'Amr (Abu Thábit) who died at Tangier in 1308, and that of one woman, Umm el 'Az—"The Beloved Mother"—in 1284. Those whose graves remain were of later date than the work in question.

† See the *Athenæum* of Sept. 18 and Oct. 30, 1875, for an account by T. Blackmore.

[1] p. 683.

Gate of Town.

REPAIRING THE LANDING PLACE, DAR EL BAÏḌA, 1897.

Photograph by Dr. Rudduck.

CHAPTER THE NINTH

OPEN PORTS—5

DÁR EL BAÏḌA (CASABLANCA)

NEITHER in point of history nor situation, nor even for what it is in itself, does Dár el Baïḍa offer the slightest attraction. It has never been, and probably never will be, more than a trading port for the provinces of Tádla and Shawîa, in the latter of which it is situated on the south side of an open bay, at 33° 36′ 20″ N. and 70° 33′ 30″ W. It is about 130 m. or five days' journey almost due north of Marrákesh. By sea it is distant from Tangier 160 miles.

Position.

Dár el Baïḍa has passed the stage in which Ali Bey found it, that of "a small village with a great wall round it",[1] but it has not yet assumed the dignity to be imparted only by the march of history. Once, it is true, there existed here a town called Anfa,[2] but all vestiges of that have so long disappeared, that even in imagination one can hardly connect the two. After its capture by the ameer Ya'ḳûb II. in 1260 A.C. (658 A.H.),[3] Anfa seems to have risen steadily in importance as a sort of trading republic, till Leo Africanus was able to describe it as one of the finest and best conditioned cities of Africa.[4] The wonderful fertility of some eighty miles width of tilled land stretching down to the coast, and the mildness of a climate which ripened melons and cucumbers in April—and which, he declares,

History.

[1] p. 132. [2] IDREESÍ, etc. [3] *Raôḍ el Ḳarṭás*, p. 430. [4] Ed. RAMUSIO, p. 58.

enabled them to furnish Fez therewith,—were sources of revenue sufficient to make its people noted for their dress and luxury, and to enable them to trade with Portugal and England. Their buildings were accordingly palatial, and their mosques and shops of the best. But as they were also pirates, and therefore a serious plague on the Portuguese coasts, Alfonso V. of that kingdom came against them in 1468 with an overwhelming armada,—for those days—some fifty ships and much artillery. The effeminate inhabitants, instead of showing fight, fled to Rabat and Salli, leaving Anfà defenceless. When the Portuguese discovered this, they sacked and destroyed the place, leaving it in such a state of desolation that Leo, who visited it shortly afterwards, tells us that he could not keep from tears.

Fate of Anfà.

As the Moors seemed disinclined to rebuild the town, the Portuguese in 1575 undertook the task, since when it has been known as Dár el Baïḍa—"White-house," in Spanish "Casa-blanca." The foreigners held it for some time, but ultimately abandoned it on account of constant trouble with the natives, and the damage done by an earthquake. But the Moors appear to have taken as little interest after this as before, till in 1789 a Madrid corporation, *Los Cinco Gremios Mayores*, obtained the monopoly for this port and Fedála of the commerce in grains, cattle, peas, salt, planks, hemp etc.[1] Next year the surrounding tribes, whom this arrangement probably failed to suit, came down and besieged it, but were repulsed with the aid of the Spanish residents, who received from Mohammed XVII. an autograph letter of thanks, a couple of lions, and compensation for damage received.[2] The present Custom House and adjoining buildings mark the site of the *Cinco Gremios* stores.

Modern Period.

[1] THOMASSY, p. 326; GODARD, p. 562. See *The Moorish Empire*, p. 403.

[2] CASTELLANOS.

Like many another Morocco venture, this one came to nought in face of the treachery of the Moorish Government, who nullified the value of the monopoly by offering facilities attracting the trade to Mazagan and Laraiche. Thenceforward the local history offers little of interest till in 1894, the now important European colony had the satisfaction of seeing the British, Spanish and French vice-consuls, supported by the presence in the bay of war-ships of their several nationalities, the successful arbitrators between rival tribes which had for some time been at war in the vicinity.

NORTH GATE OF DAR EL BAÏḌA.
Photograph by Dr. Rudduck.

At present Dár el Baïḍa holds a prominent place as a rising commercial town, third on the Moorish coast,— and a rival to Mogador for the second place.* Since

* The best account of Casablanca yet published was contributed by Dr. Weisgerber to the *Bulletin de la Société de Géographie* of Paris, 8th series, 1900, pp. 437—448, and is accompanied by excellent maps of the town and the province of Shawîa.

1893 the British consulate has been transferred here from Mogador, and there are three other consuls, while eight more nations are represented by vice-consuls and consular agents, and there are several doctors. The Franciscans have been established here since 1868, and it has been the southernmost station of the North Africa Mission,—which maintains here a hospital—since 1890. The population may be about 20,000, of whom some 4500 are Jews, and 500 Europeans, the majority of the latter being Spaniards of a poor class.

Present Condition.

Unharassed by bar or serious rocks, it is seldom that the Dár el Baïḍa lighters are prevented from working, notwithstanding the absence of port works and all it requires to make a satisfactory landing. The prettiest view of the town is to be obtained from the slight hills behind, as the broken white line of houses and towers stands out clear against the deep blue of the sea. The land on which it stands is perfectly flat; the surroundings are bare, and therefore uninteresting; the gardens are few. Only one or two Europeans venture to live outside.

The Port.

To the east lies a vast Muslim graveyard, and to the west that of the Jews, Romanists and Protestants having their respective resting-places near together on the south. An extension of the walls to the west, without communication with the present town, is still uninhabited, as indeed is a considerable space within the walls at this point, which is otherwise occupied by a vast medley of huts, that half of the town—the Tinakar—being without gates, and therefore forming an undesirable *cul de sac*. The eastern half is of built houses, and in this almost all the Europeans reside. The local wells being brackish, rain-water is collected in cisterns beneath the houses, or brought in from springs

Tinakar.

outside. The drainage is extremely primitive and faulty, but the public health is fair.

The Town.

The gates are four in number, that of the sea, that of the ṣôḳ or market (held on Mondays); the New Gate, and that of Marrákesh, which leads to a lane of huts, disgustingly filthy inside and out. The walls are in fair condition, but of no great strength, and little can be said in favour of their two or three batteries. Some of the streets are comparatively wide, and those most patronized by Europeans are exceptionally well paved. There is a melláḥ in which are many Jews. The great mosque has been outshone by the new mosque of Mulai el Hasan III., built of stone, but very plainly finished, and the patron saint is Sidi Belyout. The water supply is poor, most of the local wells and streams being brackish. The distance by sea to Mazagan is about 52 miles, or by road fourteen hours, say 60 miles.*

* To Aolád Jerár, 3 hours; Dár oold el Ḥáj Ḳásem, 4 hours; to Azammûr 4 hours; crossing river ½ hour; to Mazagan 2½ hours.

Landing Place.

MAZAGAN FROM THE NORTH.

Cavilla, Photo., Tangier,

CHAPTER THE TENTH

OPEN PORTS—6

EL JADÎDA (MAZAGAN)

MAZAGAN affords, perhaps, the only instance in Morocco in which the European name preserves the original appellation, while the native name is no more than half a description, which might suit many another place better, being simply "The New," *i.e.*, "The New Little Fort,"—El Bôrîjah el Jadîdah—the name by which the fortress built by the Portuguese in 1506 became known to the Moors.[1] The older word, Mazagan,* is itself in all probability only a part of the original name of the spot, near to which were in those days heaps of stones which marked a ruined town, for it is evidently a corruption of the word Imazîghán, by which the Morocco Berbers describe themselves. † In the New World, too, it has found a place as the name of the colony established on the shores of Pará, in Brazil, by the Portuguese who in 1769 abandoned this Mazagan—officially known as Castilho Real ‡—to the Moors then besieging it with 100,000 men.

Name.

* The "Marsà Marzîghan" of Idreesi.—Dozy's Edition, p. 73.

† Some Portuguese writers derive the name from "Má-a-cochon" ("still or quiet water"):[2] others from Má' zaghà, a common local term for water in cisterns.[3]

‡ See *Memorias para a historia da praça de Mazagão*, by Da Cunha, Lisbon, 1864.

[1] Cf. Ez-Zaïáni, p. 144.
[2] *Vestigios da lingua arabica em Portugal*, 2nd ed., p. 147.
[3] Antonio Caetano Peirara, Professor of Arabic.

Position. The exact position of Mazagan is 35° 15′ N. by 8° 29′ W, about 110 miles or three to four days' journey from Marrákesh, which lies almost due south, and it is about 220 miles west by south from Fez. Its surroundings are for the most part flat and devoid of interest, gardens even being few in number on account of the meagre water supply. From the sea it presents a very un-Moorish appearance, but its massive Portuguese walls of hewn stone look as strong as ever, though to-day of little use. It marks perhaps the Portus Rutubis of Polybius, the Rousibis of Ptolemy.

Situation. Its situation on the south-west shore of a broad bay on the north-east side of which lies Azammûr, some ten miles distant, is a favourable one for shipping, but large sailing vessels have to anchor some way out to sea, that in the event of a south-westerly gale springing up, they may be able to weather Azammûr Point. Reefs protect the anchorage on either side, and at comparatively slight expense could be utilized for the construction of moles alongside which all vessels could come. Instead of this, however, in the manner of things Moorish, ballast is discharged in spite of regulations, in the very place where depth is needed.

*History.** In 1502 a Portuguese squadron despatched to take possession of Targha, a town which the Goths built beyond Tetuan, was driven by a storm down the west coast instead, and one of the vessels at least was wrecked near where Mazagan now stands. Here the survivors entrenched themselves for fear of the Moors, and held out as they could till 1506, when engineers were sent to erect "The New Little Fort." This refers to the massive construction in the centre of the

* *The Moorish Empire* contains the following references to the history of Mazagan: Portuguese occupation, 111, 152; attacked by El Ayáshi, 112, 134; besieged, 121; recovered by Portuguese, 167.

town, which has been so much quarried and built upon as to be hardly recognizable. Underneath the houses there extends a vast tank which once formed the ground floor of the fort, its roof supported by 70 pillars, of which a number remain * But in course of time neglect and abuse have permitted this most valuable work to become little more than a cesspool of which all orifices have had to be closed. Its masonry is worthy of inspection. In 1513—when Azammûr was captured—a surrounding wall was erected, and in 1541 the present outer wall was finished. The original Borîjah still stands to the south-west of the town.

Portuguese Period.

Under the Portuguese the population was given as 4000 souls, who inhabited 75 streets, but some of the latter must have been small to have been contained in the available space. There were then eight religious houses and four churches.[1] In 1562 the place was unsuccessfully besieged by 200,000 Moors,†[2] but it was finally abandoned when they besieged it in 1769, as not worth the money and the bloodshed required to retain it.‡ In 1825 it was opened to European trade,[3] of which it obtained a good share, as the port of the rich province of Dukalla, and the most convenient landing-place from Europe for Marrâkesh. Chenier, writing but a few years after its evacuation by the Por-

* Chenier counted only twenty-four in 1781, when he described it as well lighted, and reached by stairs.

† In 1591 Ahmad V. offered to exchange Laraiche for Mazagan, but the offer was refused.

‡ The church fittings were thrown into the sea, the houses and property fired, the guns spiked, the horses houghed, other animals killed, and the towers blown up by the retreating Portuguese. The reason was said to be that Pombal, the minister, wanted money, and the products of Papal bulls annually spent at Mazagan. A blacksmith left in the town fired the mines, which killed several thousand Moors.

[1] DA CUNHA. [2] DE SOUSA.

[3] F. O. DOCS. (Morocco), Vol. 34, No. 105.

tuguese, remarked: "The Moors of the province of Dukalla, who carried on a clandestine trade with the Portuguese, greatly regret that it has changed its master. The town of Mazagan is at present entirely ruined and almost uninhabited. The Moors have taken away the timber of the houses and left the walls standing."

Present Condition.

At present there is a considerable European colony, chiefly mercantile, which includes a consul, eight vice-consuls and four consular agents. The Jews seem to flourish here, and to be on the whole better off than in most of the other ports, as a large proportion have foreign protection, and they are confined to no particular quarter. In 1869 the Franciscan Friars were established here, but did not open their church building till nineteen years later, and in 1891 Mazagan became a station of the Southern Morocco Mission. The streets are wide and regular for this part of the world, being also lighted at night, and from a local point of view the place is clean and prosperous. As might be expected, there is nothing to attract in the way of Moorish architecture, even the governor's house and the chief mosque, which adjoin the one entrance in use, being devoid of interest, for Mazagan is not a place in which to study the Moors. The chief local saints are Sidi Mûsà and S. Bû-Nafa'.

Trade.

Outside the gate is the market field, for which the full days are Sunday and Thursday, and beyond it has arisen an extensive settlement of bee-hive huts or nûállahs, which accommodate the greater part of the native population. Several Europeans have also ventured of late years to reside outside. Between the landing-place and market is the Customs yard, and to the left of this, stretching round to the shore, are grouped the stores and business places of the European merchants. The exports purchased here are beans, maize, chick-peas, wool, hides, goat-skins, almonds, wax, canary-seed, fowls and eggs. There is an abundance of fish, and also of lobsters, but the local speciality is ducks—a relic, it is said, of the Portuguese,—rare or of recent introduction elsewhere in Morocco. The climate is equable, suited to complaints of the chest and throat. Whenever Morocco is opened up Mazagan cannot fail to assume importance.

To Saffi.

The distance by land to Saffi is about 85 miles, and there is a choice of three routes: viâ Walîdîya (12 hours distant), beyond which the shore is followed; viâ Dár Ibráhîm Sha'afari and Dár Bû Mehedi; and viâ Saïs. The distance by sea is 84 miles.

CHAPTER THE ELEVENTH

OPEN PORTS—7

ASFI (SAFFI)*

SAFFI is one of the most picturesque and interesting sea-port towns of Morocco, a reputed relic of the Carthaginian times. It has been surmised that its original name was Sophia,†[1] and Tissot had no doubt that it was the Mysocaras of Ptolemy.[2] It is the only town in the province of 'Abda, about 96 miles or three days distant from Marrákesh, which lies to the E.S.E.: its exact position is 32° 18' N. and 9° 12' W. The town is built on the side of a hill, at the mouth of a fertile valley which descends to the sea. It is surrounded by a lofty and substantial wall with three gates, outside which there are a number of strongly built "whited sepulchres," the walls of which, resplendent with fresh lime-wash, gleam amid the green. Antecedent to its seizure and possession by the Portuguese, the town was of great extent, covering a space considerably larger than it now occupies, ‡ but the foreigners, exposed to the continual assaults of the Moors, were unable to defend

Situation.

* In the preparation of this description of Saffi I am much indebted for the kind assistance of Mr. W. H. C. Andrews, long a resident here.

† Others have derived the name from the Berber word Asîf, a river,[3] but this is improbable.

‡ De Sousa, in his *Africa Portuguesa*, 1681, says that Saffi once contained 3500 houses.

[1] Cf. IDREESI, p. 86.
[2] p. 115.
[3] BERBRUGGER, *Expl. Scientifique de l'Algérie*, vol ix., p. 172.

so extensive a front, and razed the ancient structure, which then included the suburbs. They also erected a fort upon the cliffs overlooking the water-port, which was connected by a strong wall with a castle (transformed into a palace, cir. 1760, by Mohammed XVII.), thus restricting the town to its present dimensions.

Portuguese Period. *

According to a Spanish writer,[1] in 1507, Saffi—at that time a species of republic[2]—was in a state of rebellion, which afforded an opportunity for the escape of thirteen Christian slaves, who made their way to the Portuguese castle of Mogador, built the year before. The news they brought of the state of the city reached Lisbon, whence an expedition was sent to try and take advantage of the disorders there. On arrival before the town, the Portuguese endeavoured to induce one of the factions to let them in as supporters, but though promises were made to them, they were not kept, so they were forced to land by night, and attempted to take the place by surprise. An influential Moor undertook to govern the city in their name if they supported him, which they promised to do, but, as might be expected, difficulties soon arose, and next year the foreigners obtained full possession. In 1510 a determined attack was made by the Moors, and the place was besieged for seventeen days, but they were ultimately repulsed. In 1541,† however, when harassed by the Fîlâli Shareefs, the Portuguese abandoned the place, after having burned it, and the Moors, on regaining possession, re-fortified it.

* The following historical references to Saffi will be found in *The Moorish Empire*: taken by Portuguese, p. 111; a republic, 116; evacuated by Portuguese, 118; visit of Sir Anthony Sherley, 131; of Capt. John Smith, 243; attacked by Mulai Zidán, 243; trade, 349, 401, 403, 404.

† Mogador and Mazagan being then respectively non-existent and in process of erection.

[1] Castellanos. [2] Godard, p. 410.

Under the Portuguese régime, Saffi was an important emporium of commerce,* and retained this position till the seventeenth century to such an extent that in 1639 an English Order in Council directed all ships trading with Morocco to go first to Saffi. French factories were also established here at one time, but in 1718 the French Consulate was suppressed,[1] and Saffi was closed to foreigners by the Moors until Mohammed XVII. (bin 'Abd Allah) became its governor,[2] when in 1753, a Danish company secured the exclusive right to trade here.

Trade.

Between 1748 and 1756 the number of vessels which loaded in Saffi roads was 176,[3] and in the latter year an English consul was appointed. It was again closed to trade, and the merchants ordered to Mogador, on the completion of that town in 1760, but was re-opened about 1817, when an influential Jew, named Skrîḳi, having purchased a quantity of wool in the neighbourhood, obtained the sultan's permission to export it, and finding his affair prosper, arranged his abode in Saffi, becoming a successful merchant. At that period the dollar was worth only 12½ okîat, and the peseta passed for 2½. In those "good old days" the Arabs bringing grain to the *raḥbah* or grain market were compelled to give security at the town gates for its removal if unsold, so cheap and plentiful were wheat and barley in that part of Barbary.

Modern Opening.

The houses of Saffi are mostly old, and, as is usual in Eastern cities, present a blank white-washed exterior to the street, only a few modern buildings having windows. The largest shops are naturally to be found in the main street, which also contains the chief mosque, the water-port and the oil, cotton

Buildings.

* Misprinted by Chenier, 1641, and by Thomassy, 1661!

[1] THOMASSY, p. 551. [2] EZ-ZAÏÁNI, p. 124. [3] THOMASSY, p. 229.

cloths, fruit, charcoal and bread markets. The provision markets are fairly well supplied, all varieties of fish and game being abundant, as are also fruits, but vegetables are not plentiful. The northern extremity is occupied chiefly by Jewish shop-keepers and Moorish vendors of Saffi pottery, manufactured close at hand, near the north-west gate, Báb es-Sha'ba. The other gates are those of the landing-place—Marsà,—and the Rabat. A smaller gate, Báb er-Rabaḥ, affords admission to the palace from the Marrákesh road, and in the Rabat are the remains of Báb el Ḥamar—well preserved—and of Báb Kodîat La'fu.

Saffi is by no means a salubrious city, being the least cared for on the Morocco coast. There are the usual number of public baths, washing and watering places common to all Mohammedan towns, but water is scarce, and the system of drainage defective. The people rely almost solely on the rains for their drink and household allowance, collecting the precious liquid in subterranean tanks, one or two being attached to every dwelling. The most pleasant and wholesome spring is at "Sidi Bû Zeed," the Saint House on the cliffs to the north of the town. Its waters are used at table by Europeans and wealthy Moors in preference to the lifeless fluid of the tanks, too often tainted by sewage and other impurities. Besides the Sidi Bû Zeed supply, the garden sánîahs (wells with Persian-wheel-pumps) beyond the Sha'ba gate, contain considerable quantities of brackish water, used perforce in bad seasons. With this exception drinking water can only be procured at the orange groves of Imzoghan, situated a mile and a half from the walls. Some time ago an attempt was made to fertilise the level ground on the cliffs to the south of the town by storing rain water there in cisterns, but this was not a success.

Water Supply.

In point of climate Saffi compares unfavourably with

the other coast towns, but the resident merchants seem to enjoy good health. In winter the floods from the neighbouring plains accumulate in the valleys, inundating the principal thoroughfares to the depth of several feet, occasionally despoiling the low-lying shops of their contents, and making the town inconveniently damp. In summer the hills prevent the north-easterly breeze from extending its cooling influence to

Climate.

COURTYARD OF SAFFI PALACE.
Photograph by Joseph Thomson, Esq.

the town, which then becomes very hot and disagreeable.

Within a stone's throw of the main gate of Saffi is a straggling suburb of about two thousand souls, the Rabat quarter, in which are the merchants' stores. Like the town of the same name on the Wád Bû Ragrág, this suburb probably owes its name to its having been originally a camp—which the word Rîbáṭ signifies,—gradually built up into a town in the Spanish style by Moors expelled from Spain.[1] It

The Rabat.

[1] CHARANT.

contains a celebrated sanctuary much frequented by rebels and bad characters. In 1874 all the prisoners escaped from the town and took refuge there, and during the disturbance attendant on the death of El Hasan III. in 1894, a most stubborn stand was made in the Rabat by rebels, who were only driven out by serious fighting after five months' siege.

Patron Saint.

The Rabat sanctuary consists of a mosque and záwîah dedicated to the patron saint of Saffi, Sidi Bû Mohammed Sálaḥ—known in the East as Mûl 'Amûd es-Swári," "Master of the Yard arm." * Jews and foreigners are not allowed to enter the part of the Rabat which contains the holy place, and during the processions of the 'Aïsáwà and Ḥamádshà, as well as on the occasion of certain holidays and fairs, both Europeans and Jews deem it prudent not to make themselves too prominent. † There was a time when no Jew or Chris-

A Curious Legend.

* It seems that this worthy, travelling to Mekka—how long since none seems to know—found himself one evening near an Arab dûár on the outskirts of Alexandria. He entreated a night's lodging, but was brusquely informed that strangers were unwelcome there, and that he could either rest on the top of a lofty and slender pole that was pointed out, or proceed. To the amazement of the Arabs he ascended the staff and composed himself as comfortably as possible in the air. Alarmed at the accomplishment of an apparently supernatural feat, the Arabs gravely decided to make friends with this extraordinary being, who, they surmised, could demolish themselves and their dwellings by raising his little finger. They therefore hastened to procure a bull, which was sacrificed at the foot of the pole, and their mysterious guest was invited to descend. After threatening them with all sorts of divine plagues, His Saintship consented, but on one condition. Taking off a shoe and casting it into the air, he cried: "Whereso-ever this falls, you must erect and dedicate to my memory a fandaķ for the reception of weary travellers and pilgrims on the road to Mekka, who, like myself, tired, hungry and overtaken by night in a strange land, can find there refreshment and rest." This demand the Arabs promised most devoutly to fulfil, and Bû Mohammed Sálaḥ descended to pursue his journey, and become, on account of his learning and virtues, a saint most highly venerated by Mohammedans from East to West.

† But this fanaticism is dying out, and Europeans now run small risk of being molested.

tian was allowed to ride through this holy quarter, but in 1767, when the French consulate for Morocco was removed from Mogador to Saffi, M. Chenier, the consul, broke through the custom by boldly riding in and daring the people.[1] The same thing was done in 1796 at Agadîr by Jackson.[2]

Fanaticism.

The Rabat also contains the ruins of a mansion once occupied by 'Abd er-Raḥmán ben Náṣir, a son of Mulai el Yazeed, who was born in the palace at Saffi. 'Abd er-Raḥmàn ben Náṣir became a celebrated personage during the days of Mulai Sulaïmán, being known as es-Sultan es-Sagheer, or "Little Sultan." He exercised his authority over the tribes from Rabat to Massa in Sûs, and conducted business with the Spaniards, who assisted him with cannon and gunpowder. 'Abd er-Raḥmán purchased a great deal of property, built mosques and shops, and generally improved the town of Saffi. His house in the Rabat, on account of its isolated position and the approach of the sea undermining the cliff upon which it was erected, was abandoned upon his death, and has fallen to pieces. Some of the rooms preserve traces of the wealth and taste of their celebrated owner, remnants of handsomely painted ceilings, frescoes, richly carved doorframes and marble columns, still fairly bright, clean and distinct.

Interesting Ruins.

Many of the saint houses in the neighbourhood of the town are of quaint design, and possess interesting traditions. Those most worthy of notice commemorate Sidi Bû Zikri, (son of Bû Mohammed) and Sidi Bû Zeed, of Shlûḥ origin, once attendant to Mulài El Waleed, the munificent prince who built Walîdîya, twenty-five miles to the north. The view of the white tombs at the village of Sidi Wáṣil, nestling among the

Saint Houses.

[1] CHENIER, vol. i., p. 42. [2] JACKSON, p. 233.

hills to the south, is much admired, having cultivated land in the foreground.

Saffi Palace. The bold outline of the old palace built by Mohammed XVII. (bin 'Abd Allah) is a prominent object above the town. It contains many large rooms, dweriahs * and beautifully decorated courts in

IN THE SAFFI PALACE.
Photograph by Herbert White, Esq.

tolerable repair. With all its defects, Mauresque architecture presents great attractions to travellers, and in Saffi are many interesting buildings and ruins deserving the attention of both archæologists and artists.

* Small suites for guests.

Some writers mention remains of the chapel of a Gothic church, having Portuguese arms etc. on the centre and side, with its vaults intact, but with the walls buried up to the cornice in rubbish. Dr. Leared speaks of Portuguese stone-work with heraldic devices as being still visible over the principal entrance to the Sultan's palace. There are other relics of Portuguese days, as the bath in the passage beside the chief mosque, and part of the nave and aisle of a church in the street called Derb Sidi 'Abd el Kareem. The madarsah or college is said to have been once a monastery, and in a passage to one of the baths is a reputed hermit's cell. Christian tombs were found on the site of the present Customs warehouse in 1886, the contents of which were removed to the cemetery outside the Sha'ba gate. Underneath the beach, well inside the Portuguese wall, is a second wall with a gateway and a large number of marble columns, all of which have been laid bare occasionally by exceptional storms.

Historic Remains.

The local authorities of Saffi comprise the governor and vice-governor, with the ûmána and their staff in charge of the customs house; the ámîn enkás —who collects market dues and government rents—the ḳáḍi, and two captains of the water-port, who are in charge of lighter-men and boats.

Local Authorities.

The European Powers are represented by eleven vice-consulates or consular agencies,* the holders of which, seven in number, constitute the Sanitary Board, whose duties chiefly consist in imposing quarantine.

The original Muslimîn inhabitants of Saffi, expelled by the Portuguese in 1508, migrated to a fertile district one day's journey to the south-east of Marrákesh, which they named Mesfîwah, and have become a large and pros-

* Neither France nor the United States are represented here.

perous ķabîlah or tribe.* The present Moorish community, in spite of the sanctity of the neighbourhood, is not very fanatical, and requires a vigorous summons to a jeḥád N'ṣárà—anti-Nazarene campaign,—or oppression of the most rigorous description, to stimulate them to action of any kind.

Garrison.

The garrison consists of two käids and one hundred 'askars or regular troops. As these men frequently desert, seventy-five is considered a good muster in attendance upon the governor at the mosque on Fridays. There are also the mûállîn mîzán—"masters of scales"—employed by the merchants as porters and carriers, who form a sort of police or militia, and the tûbjiah or artillerymen in charge of the town batteries, all being townsmen and residents. These corps constitute the defenders and upholders of the peace of the district. They administer "stick," contribute the night-guards and watch,—mûállîn dôr,—and the guards at the gates of the city on feast days, when large numbers of strangers arrive, and sometimes create disturbance. Moorish soldiers, like the Irish dragoons, have not much "janius" for work, but they are sober, patient, and of frugal habit; all good qualities.

The Roadstead.

Saffi Bay, bounded on the north by high cliffs rising four hundred feet, and projecting some two and a half miles to sea, is of considerable depth, and during the summer months affords smoother water than any other harbour on the Moorish coast. There is good anchorage, and vessels of the largest tonnage can lie about three-quarters of a mile from the beach. It is, however, entirely exposed to southern and westerly winds; consequently in winter masters must weigh anchor and proceed to sea at the first appearance of bad weather, or, trusting to the strength of their

* The Arabic word for a man of Saffi is Mesfîwi.

cables, remain and risk being driven ashore. A great many ship-wrecks have occurred here at different periods,

SAFFI BEACH.

Photograph by E. Lee, Esq.

but happily without great loss of life, and there is much speculation in flotsam and jetsam. There are men in Saffi whose grandfathers walked by the sea-side from the water-port to the Tansîft river, distant eighteen miles to the south, but for many years this has become impracticable, owing to the gradual encroachment of the sea.

Landing at Saffi.

The surf here is so strong with certain winds that it is extremely difficult to get ashore. The difficulty consists in rounding a high rock which stands right opposite the landing-place, and when this is attempted in bad weather a man is posted on the rock to give notice of each coming breaker to the occupants of the boat, that they may take advantage of it instead of being swamped. The boats at this port remind one of huge Red Indian canoes, being high and rounded at the ends, and grotesquely ornamented round the edges in black designs on the bare wood. Their oars are the poorest on the coast, and are little more than small spars. The boatmen, however, are so accustomed to take advantage of the waves for each pull, that they seem all but helpless in smooth water, and have no idea of rowing to time. Probably in allusion to the breakers, the boatmen sing in chorus "Here he is, here he is, here!" beginning slowly, but reaching the final "here" with a jerk, as they give a pull together.

Trade.

In busy times twenty or twenty-five sailing vessels may be seen at anchor abreast of the town, awaiting grain cargoes, and of the merchandise imported a considerable quantity is sent to Marrákesh on camels. The chief articles exported are beans, maize, washed wool, olive oil, almonds, bees' wax, cummin seed and gums. The trade of Saffi is principally in the hands of two English firms of long standing, but there are representatives of several other nations in business there, also several younger English firms. Since 1892 it has become a station of the Southern Morocco Mission, and there is a resident English doctor. The Franciscan Friars also have had a work here since 1889.

To Mogador.

The distance by land to Mogador is about 60 miles, or sixteen hours' ride, with a choice of routes, by the shore or inland. If the start by the shore route is timed to meet a falling tide at Sûeïra Ḳadîma, the journey may be performed in about fourteen hours on good animals, or in twelve if a re-mount be arranged at Sidi Is-ḥaḳ, the saint house half way. The reverse journey should be commenced with the fall of tide. By sea the distance is about 56 miles.

A STREET OF MOGADOR.
Photograph by the late Dr. Robert Brown.

CHAPTER THE TWELFTH

OPEN PORTS—8

ES-SÛEÏRA (MOGADOR)

WITH a history dating only from 1760, when it was built by Sidi Mohammed XVII. (bin 'Abd Allah) the town of Mogador lacks the charm of that antiquity possessed by most of the Moorish ports. Low-lying,—on a spit of rock and sand jutting out from the province of Ḥáḥá, which with the island opposite enclose a fairly safe port,—it is hardly even picturesque, and although presenting a welcome glint of white walls from the Ocean, there is little attractive about it. On the land side stretch miles of wearisome sand-dunes, studded with broom—rising here and there to over 400 ft.—beyond which are the argán forests, one of the features of Southern Morocco. Approached from this direction, the city bursts upon one's view like a mirage between sky and sea, for amid the drifting sand the flat white roofs and scattered mosque towers rise against deep blue beyond.* It is this view, if any, which entitles Mogador to be called "the Picture."

Appearance.

Mogador possesses few pleasure gardens, but beside the aqueduct which brings the drinking water several miles into town, an enterprising European has developed

* This port, rather than Mazagan, is described by the lines,

> "Strange town, all glittering, treeless, white,
> Begirt with sand and seething spray!" [1]

[1] MACKENZIE BELL, in *Sunday Morning off Mazagan.*

a moist patch, and there is a large extent of market gardens on the southern side of the town. Gardens belonging to the Kaid and others, are to be found in the Moorish quarter, where the most has been made of some spare courtyard.

But Mogador has more to recommend it than most Moorish ports. It is the best planned and the cleanest town in the Empire, and in consequence of this, as well as on account of its climate, it stands high as a health resort.* "A north-east wind, a cloudless sky, and a glowing sun, are the normal atmospherical conditions of this part of the coast," writes Mr. Payton, for many years British Consul here,[1] "and very delightful is our climate in consequence, the heat of the sun being tempered by the bracing breeze; so that, in Mogador at any rate, it is almost always pleasantly warm, without being relaxing—never cold, yet never nearly so hot as some summer days in London. Our general temperature seems to be 70° to 75° in the shade, though in winter, when it rains, the glass will often go down to 60°, sometimes even a few degrees lower, when we Mogadorians go about shivering and grumbling at the bitter cold.[2] A charming climate this for pulmonary or bronchial complaints, for the north-easter which we have so often is not a keen cutting blast like his namesake in England, but a bracing, invigorating,

Climate.

* Dr. Seux, Chief Hospital Physician of Marseilles, after passing in review the various health resorts of Egypt, Algiers, the Gulf of Lyons and the Biscay Rivieras, Italy, Spain and Madeira, declares the climate of Mogador to surpass them all.[3]

[1] *Moss from a Rolling Stone*, p. 268.

[2] For meteorological observations see BEAUMIER, Bull. Soc. Géog. Paris, 1872, 6 sér., t. iv., pp. 150 and 308: also *Zeitsch. der Oesterrs. Gesell. für Meteorologie*, 1873, t. viii., p. 7: and OLIVIÉ as below.

[3] See also DR. THÉVENIN, *Du climat de Mogador sous le rapport des affections pulmonaires.* Bull. Soc. Géog., Paris, 1868, 5 sér., t. xxii., p. 335; and DR. OLIVIÉ, *Climat de Mogador et son influence sur le phthisie*, l.c. 1876, 6 sér., t. x., p. 365.

health-giving breeze, laden with ozone and iodine, and healthy particles of saline moisture." At the same time this saline moisture produces a relaxing dampness which some find very trying in time, especially the nervous. On the other hand, a desert wind sometimes reaches even to Mogador, but this is a rare visitant, an excess of the north-easter being a more common annoyance.

Position.

This well-favoured spot lies some 358 miles from Tangier by sea, and the same exactly from Las Palmas in the Canaries, with both of which it is in regular communication by steamer.* From the former port vessels usually take three or four nights, the days being spent in Casablanca, Mazagan and Saffi, or longer if other ports are touched at. It is about 80 miles further to Agadir. The inland journey to Marrákesh, about 110 miles E. by N., occupies about three days and a half, or by skirting the Atlas another day or two can be very well spent. Its exact position is 31° 30′ 5″ N. by 9° 46′ 2″ W. Mogador harbour is well sheltered from all winds except the south-west, but is sometimes difficult to escape from when that wind blows, as the channel between the town and the island is shallow and somewhat hazardous. Vessels not drawing over 19 ft. can enter between a small island and the north end of the large one, and anchor some distance from the shore.†

The Landing.

The water-port of Mogador is the best in Morocco. It has a passage cut in the rocks to allow boats to approach the gate except at low water, with a path cut and levelled to the end of the

* The "Mersey Line" (Messrs. Forwood Bros., Crosby Square, London), have of late years done much to encourage the visits of tourists to this coast, and especially to Mogador. They have now a frequent service of fine steamers which make the round from London, returning by way of the Canaries in about a month at moderate fares. French and Spanish steamers also run between the Canaries and Mogador.

† The Admiralty plan is No. 1594.

rocks for use when a nearer approach is impossible. A small dock inside the fortifications, under which the boats pass through arches, is provided for the landing of merchandise, while close by is the customs weighing-house. The customs administrators used to have their office in the main square of the old ḳaṣbah or citadel, but this having been transformed into a State prison, they have been established in a new building at the water-port. In 1863 an English engineer, named Craig, commenced the construction of a jetty, but this was never finished, on account of the obstruction of the authorities. Under the battery of the water-port is a spacious cistern, but the water-supply of the town is carried by an overground closed conduit from a spring near Dîabât, the quality of which is excellent. The water is collected in a large stone tank beneath the sand-hills.

Fortifications.

The fortifications look in good repair, but an English officer[1] who inspected them reported: "As far as parapets, ramparts, embrasures, cavaliers, batteries and casemates constitute a fortress, this town is one; but the walls are flimsy, the cavaliers do not command, the batteries do not flash, and the casemates are not bomb-proof. The embrasures are so close that not one in three upon the ramparts could be worked, if they were mounted, which they are not."

In the circular battery to the south is a gun taken by General Lord Heathfield during the siege of Gibraltar, and given to the Sultan for a ship-load of corn, duty-free. Its carriage is like an eagle, and on opening it reveals the gun inside. The Dutch Government presented the Sultan with the brass eighteen pounders in these forts, which are still in fair condition. The Skalla battery was built by a Genoese, and though graceful in construction, is not strong.

[1] Col. Keatinge.

The town of Mogador is well laid out from the plans of a French engineer named Cornuc, who, after all his labours, which extended over ten years, complained that he left the country poorer than when he arrived.* The work was chiefly done by renegades and other European masons, for Morocco boasts few of this handicraft, since the majority of its buildings are of tabîa or mud concrete. It is said that so great was the desire of Sidi Mohammed to see the work completed, that on some occasions he laboured with his own hands at the walls to encourage the people. When he had finished it, he invited all the foreign merchants to come and settle here, giving them ground, and even permitting them to trade free of duty until he had got them firmly settled. By doing so he cleverly cheated the Royal Danish Company, to whom he had previously sold the monopoly of the trade of Saffi and Salli, which were ruined by this step. To the French merchants, whom he favoured, he gave "a vast and fine garden." Another local concession of peculiar importance was the authority to institute a Tribunal of Commerce at the request of the Genoese in 1770. Its sentences were enforced by the Government, so that the European merchants practically ruled the town. Yet in 1815 Riley reported but six foreign merchants and consular agents, of whom the only account vouchsafed is that one was "formerly respectable."[1] A mint was once established here, but has long since been closed.†

Its Buildings.

Oriental Duplicity.

The madînah or Moorish "quarter,"—more correctly close upon two-thirds,—is divided into the Beni 'Antar,

* Bidé de Maurville says that he was sent to the Emperor by the English, but was dismissed as incapable.[2]

† There is in the French National Collection a coin struck here in 1775.

[1] p. 440. [2] p. 244.

Agadîr and Shabánat districts. The Jewish quarter includes the old melláḥ in the east end of the Beni 'Antar district, and the new melláḥ, which is much smaller, in the east end of the Shabánat district. The entrances are opposite each other, close to the Saffi Gate. As in most other towns, the melláḥs are filthy in the extreme, literally reeking with indescribable nastiness. It is a striking fact that though Jews swarm in almost every part of Morocco, it is stated that there are none in the province of Ḥáḥá except within the walls of Mogador.

Divisions.

The Governor and other Moorish authorities, almost all the foreigners, and a large number of Jews, live in the ḳaṣbahs. That part called "the old," which is considerably the larger, dates from the building of the town, but "the new" was built in 1869, when the accumulated demands for houses for foreigners—which the sultan engages by treaty to supply, since he will not allow them to build for themselves—compelled him to build this little additional wing, containing some of the finest buildings. As the rent to be paid is fixed by treaty at 6 per cent on the cost, in the old ḳaṣbah these are ridiculously low, being only six to ten dollars a month, while in the new ḳaṣbah they are double that amount, owing to the increased cost of building at the later date.* In consequence of disputes about the cost of the work, however, the rents were reduced to 4 per cent. Many houses, especially consulates, are free, but the British consulate here, like all others on this coast, has been taken over by the British Government to avoid continual applications for repair. Thus a measure adopted to prevent the foreigners from obtaining a foothold has resulted in securing one to them.

The Kasbahs.

* But even in the old ḳaṣbah the interest at the same rate on subsequent repairs has in many cases greatly increased the rent.

Europeans were until recently forbidden to live in the madînah, and the Moor who admitted them to stay in his house would soon be thrown into prison. It is only with great difficulty that any have succeeded in obtaining quarters there. The Moors say that if once the foreigners were allowed to take up their abode in their quarter the rents would rise until they themselves would have to turn out. At present the ḳaṣbahs are so full that houses are hardly to be had for love or money. Many have been waiting for years in the hope of the Sultan's granting the requests forwarded to him to supply them with decent dwellings. The houses of the Europeans as a rule consist of a large square patio or courtyard, communicating with the street by a big door and surrounded by long narrow stores, the living rooms being over these, and the "front door" on the landing or arcade which runs round the court, approached by stairs in the corner. The door jambs and facings, as well as the arches and pillars, are of stone, presenting a solid and not unattractive appearance till white-washed.

European Dwellings.

Between the two portions of the ḳaṣbah is an open space used for "powder-play" on festivals, called the "Running Ground," at one end of which a gate opens into another large square, devoted on the left to public washing purposes, and on the right to the building of lighters for the port, between which a few privileged animals graze when there is pasture. On the right, parallel with this gate, is the "Green Gate," of the palace, right opposite which is the Customs' Gate. At the other end of the "Running Ground" is the Bâb el Meshwar or "Gate of Audience,"—where the governor or his lieutenant dispenses "justice,"—which leads to the madînah. A striking proof of the regularity with which Mogador is planned is the fact that standing at the

Regular Plan.

Customs' Gate one can see right through to the Saffi Gate at the far end, up the main street, through no less than four more gates and as many arches. The other main thoroughfare runs from the Marrákesh Gate to the Beni 'Antar Gate, while a third stretches from the heart of the old ķaşbah far into the madînah, parallel to that first mentioned.

Business Quarters.

In the centre of the madînah, where the first and second of these cross, is the new market, a small but fine square, shut off at night by gates on all sides, surrounded by a colonnade under which are the shops of the drapers. Behind these again come the grain and other markets, all being well-built and regular. The main street, running through this, is wide, but somewhat obstructed at night by the numbers of cows and dogs that sleep there. Moreover, as the gates across it are shut after dark, it becomes necessary to take an exceedingly round-about course to get from one section to another. The shops are then guarded by sleepy watchmen and wakeful dogs, who during the day-time viciously bark at passers-by from the shop roofs.

Markets.

There is no special day set apart for a market, as in most other towns, but natives bring in produce any day —except Saturday, when Israel vetoes trade. Formerly of an afternoon the section of the main street between the new ķaşbah and the Lions' Gate used to present quite the appearance of an exchange, with all the Jewish and European merchants walking up and down, ascertaining the last quotations for the arriving camel-loads of produce from Sûs or Marrákesh, and making bids; but of late years declining trade has taken away much of the life of the place.

Mogador was at one time famed for elephants' tusks, ostrich feathers and gold dust, but their day is past, as other countries have been able to produce them more cheaply than Morocco, and a safer outlet to the western Saḥara has been secured by way of Timbuctoo and the Senegal. Now the chief exports are gums, almonds, hides, goat-, sheep- and calf-skins and hair, olive oil, beans, walnuts, wool, maize, citrons, wax; with some esparto grass, orchella weed, sesame seed and various minor products. Several other things, such as colocynth, were once shipped from Mogador, but are so no longer. Nevertheless, of the ports of Morocco, its commerce is second only to that of Tangier. Its imports are much the same as elsewhere on this coast, but its importance is derived from its position as the most southerly port open to foreign trade, so that the whole supplies of the province of Sûs must pass through it, except such as find their way by Marrákesh, which they reach from Mazagan or Saffi. Of late years German firms have made great headway here.

Commerce.

The manufactures of Mogador are brass trays, daggers, woollen cloth for jellábs, ḥáiks and other garments, and articles of furniture made from 'ar'ár wood (the *thuja* or *citrus* of the Romans, and probably the "thyine" of the Revelation to John).

Manufactures.

Of foreign officials there are at Mogador two consuls —each assisted by a vice-consul—six vice-consulates and three consular agencies. Nearly all of these officials are merchants, of whom there is a considerable colony here, but the Jews are rapidly monopolizing the local trade. Mogador boasts two small hotels, besides the excellent Palm Tree House Sanitarium a few miles out—a centre for sport—and there are resident European physicians. Four Jewish schools flourish, two for girls, one supported by the Anglo-Jewish Association, the other private; and two for boys, one of which is French (*Alliance Israëlite*) the other English.

Foreigners.

The three chief mosques are: that of El Ḳaṣbah in the centre of the old ḳaṣbah, that of Sidi Hamed oo Mohammed, close to the Sôḳ Waḳḳa, and that of Sidi Ben Yûsef, near to the new ḳaṣbah.

The Roman Catholics possess a chapel attended by a Spanish Franciscan priest and two lay-brothers, their station here dating from the year 1868. English Protestant services are held in a chapel in

Missions.

MOGADOR BEACH FROM THE AQUEDUCT.
Photograph by the Hon. E. W. Loch.

the Mizpah, a large house built for business purposes, but afterwards for some time the head-quarters of the London Mission to the Jews. This Society has carried on mission work here since 1875—it being the oldest established of those in Morocco,—and the Southern Morocco Mission has been at work here since 1887.

Just outside the Saffi Gate is the European cemetery,

a small walled enclosure, one side of which receives Romanists and the other Protestants. Both are well kept by public subscription, under the direction of the consular Corps. Previous to 1862 foreigners were compelled to bury their dead on a sand-hill. The Jewish cemetery is just beyond, unwalled—as the local community is unable to provide this protection,—and the Moors have their own walled place apart. *Cemeteries.*

To the south of the town is a beautiful beach which forms the fashionable afternoon promenade, admirably adapted for bathing, which nevertheless is not much indulged in: to the north is a long stretch of rocks.

The larger island is about three quarters of a mile long and one quarter wide, and is situated about half a mile from the shore,* to which it lies nearly parallel, rising at one point to about 107 ft. M. Beaumier, a former French consul at Mogador, expressed the opinion that it is diminishing in size, but I have it on the authority of one of the oldest and most observant residents here that during the last fifty years there have been no signs of such shrinkage. There is a tradition that at one time cattle were driven across at low water. This island has long been used as a sort of state prison or convict settlement, and occasionally as a quarantine depôt for ḥájes or pilgrims returning from the East when plague or cholera has been abroad, many of them being destined for the northern parts of the Empire, but doomed to bide their time far away down here in the south. To this latter use it is now put. *Mogador Island.*

On this island are two houses and a mosque, besides a fortress-like prison,—originally destined to confine the prisoners taken in securing the succession of the present

* The length, breadth and distance from the shore are given by one writer as 900, 350 and 700 mètres respectively.[1]

[1] CASTELLANOS.

sultan in 1894,—six small batteries and a couple of cisterns. A notable feature about its defences is that four of the batteries are on the land side, as though Moors were more feared than Nazarenes. When the French bombarded the town in 1844, they landed and took the island, after a severe hand-to-hand fight with the garrison, then consisting of several hundred men, and spiked most of the guns, entering and desecrating the little mosque.*

Buildings on the Island.

Mogador Island is divided near the north end into two portions, the detached part being little more than a huge rock, but interesting because pierced from end to end by a natural tunnel with a ventilating shaft to the surface near the centre, through both of which daylight can be seen, the tunnel being passable by boat in favourable states of the tide. These cavities are the home of legions of blue-rock pigeons. Between this island and the Customs House is a smaller one, just a rock, partly covered at high water, but affording a never-failing supply of sea-shells of many varieties.

Natural Peculiarities.

There is good fishing to be obtained on the larger island, where picnics are often enjoyed by the towns-folk, glad to get among the wild-flowers after a stay in a place laid siege to by sea and sand. Another favourite resort is the village of Dîabát, a Berber settlement, about a mile to the south, near a small river, which is the nearest and most accessible spot on shore where vegetation is to be found in any quantity. The scenery in the neighbourhood of the river is a beautiful alternation of wooded hills and luxuriant valleys, and the flora of the whole district is exceedingly varied.

In the Vicinity.

* An old man who was custodian of this place for a quarter of a century is said to have resided here seventeen years at a stretch. He gave as his reason that people ashore were too wicked for him, yet even he could enjoy "Christian spirits" in his island home!

Game abounds near Mogador, and the sea there is rich in fish. On the way to Dîabát are passed an ancient fort on the beach, a disused palace of the sultan, half-filled with sand, and the shrine of Sidi Megdûl, the patron saint of the place, from whom the town derives its European name. *

Names.

The Arabic name of Mogador, Es-Sûeïra, may be translated either as "The Picture" or "The Beautiful," and by the Shilḥa-speaking Berbers of the neighbouring hills it is transformed into Ta Ṣûárt. † The European name has given rise to much discussion and theorizing. "Mongodor" is to be found on the Pizziani map of 1367, and "Mogodor" on the Catalonian map of 1375, but it is doubtful whether only the saint-house, or a fortress also, was then in existence. ‡

* A fanciful derivation suggested for the name of this saint deserves a record. It is that he was originally a Scotch sailor shipwrecked on the coast just here, of the name of McDougall, [1] though others say he was a Danish Captain. A curious instance, however, of the easy way in which ignorant natives are ready to revere an unknown tomb is afforded by the honours paid to the resting-place of the wife of an English merchant buried not far from the gate. [2] Sidi Megdûl, too, has been in his time almost as much revered by the Jews as the Moors.

† Others render it "The Little Walled Place."

‡ See also the Atlas Minor of Hondius (1608). [3] The older Medicalan map is better, and shows "I. Domegador." "Magador" was one of the places where Ahmad Dhahebi cultivated sugar, [4] and "Magadore" was visited by Capt. John Smith in 1604. [5] Mogador Island is referred to as such in a petition of Gilles Pen to the Conde de Leste, dated 1627, [6] and in 1629 Cardinal Richelieu wrote approving of "the Mogador plan," which was for Razelli to seize the island, of the whereabouts of which, however, he seems to have been very uncertain, for it is described as somewhat removed from the shore, and therefore commanding both Saffi and Salli. [7] Yet Razelli must have known better, for next year he sent a vessel to be cleaned at the island of "Mongador," [8] and strange to say, although the existence of a town previous to 1760 is so stedfastly denied, in 1660 there had existed commerce between the island and Dieppe for thirty years—in gold dust, wool, wax, ostrich feathers, etc. [9]

[1] HARRIS, *Land*, p. 246 [2] RICHARDSON, vol. i., p. 104.
[3] p. 567. [4] "Ro. C.," ch. ii.
[5] p. 913. [6] MSS. in Library of San Isidoro, No. 11.
[7] D'ANGERS, p. 141. [8] ARMAND, p. 77. [9] *Relation Curieuse*, p. 12.

Drake, who visited this spot in 1577, gives an excellent description of "The island Mogador."[2] *

Although the actual town is of such recent construction, the Portuguese had a fortress, if not a settlement near. † In the days before the Indies lured their intrepid sailors away from the Barbary coast, their most important colonies were in Morocco, and they were masters of almost every roadstead or strategical point from Ceuta to Agadîr. It was impossible, therefore, that this island and the harbour formed by it should escape their attention, and as early as 1506 we read of a fort being built there. Whether this is represented by the crumbling fortress described, it is impossible to decide, and soon there will be nothing left even of that. § What remains yet of the masonry is of the usual solidity of Portuguese work, but the foundations have been undermined by the encroaching sea. Another fort once stood on the rock of the smaller island, close to the long

History. ‡

* "It is uninhabited, of about a league in circuit, not very high land, all overgrown with a kind of shrub breast high, not much unlike our privet; very full of doves, and therefore much frequented of goshawks and such-like birds of prey, besides divers sorts of sea-fowl very plenty. At the south side of this island are three hollow rocks, under which are great store of very wholesome but very ugly fish to look to."

† Some think Mogador may have been the site of Pliny's Erythræa, others that Mysocorus is to be looked for here, or perhaps the Cerne of "Annone," (Hanno) the "Cyraunis" of others.[1]

‡ *The Moorish Empire* contains the following allusions to Mogador: Portuguese settlement, 111; building, 167; bombarded by the French, 196; trade, 405, 408-9, 410 (and n.).

§ A correspondent well able to judge throws doubt on the reputed origin of this fort, pointing out that much of it is built of tabîa, or concrete such as the Moors use, but the Portuguese seldom. Its position too, seems one more likely to have been selected by the Moors. Drake spoke of "an old fort built sometime by the King of Portugal, but now ruined by the King of Fesse,"[2] which appears to have been situated at some distance, and was possibly Sûeïra el Ḳadîma.

[1] See Gråberg, p. 289. [2] *Drake's and Dampier's Voyages.*

battery, but this has disappeared under similar action. A short distance north of the mouth of the river Tansîft is another Portuguese fort, called Sûeïra el Ḳadîma —Old Sûeïra—which name may be more then a coincidence.* The Moors have a tradition that it was built in one night by the aid of devils. This has been explained by saying that the Portuguese brought everything necessary for its construction from Lisbon, all prepared and cut, so that they were able to put it together in a remarkably short space of time.

French Bombardment.

On August 13th, 1844, during the French war with Morocco, the Prince de Joinville bombarded Mogador with three ships of the line, a frigate, two steamers and some brigs. But the town suffered more from the neighbouring tribes, who came down and sacked it. When peace was signed in September, the messenger who brought the news found no one there to receive it.[1] During Ramadán 1873, on the accession of Mulai el Ḥasan, four kaids of Ḥáḥá and Shiadhma having taken refuge in Mogador, the tribesmen besieged the place closely As they had no cannon they could only cut off the water-supply and destroy the gardens. But as this meant starvation to the besiegers as well as to the besieged, some of their friends in town let them in for a feed at night!

* This is about 48 m. north of the present Mogador; on the south side of the Tansîft stands a ḳaṣbah of Mulai Ismá'il.

[1] GODARD.

MARKET PLACE OF AZAMMÛR.

Photograph by Herbert White, Esq.

CHAPTER THE THIRTEENTH

CLOSED PORTS

I.—AZÎLA or AṢÎLA * (ARZILLA).

SOME 27 miles, or a good day's ride, south-west by south of Tangier, lies the unfortunate port of Azîla, unfortunate because its situation and its rivals promise it a future no brighter than its past, which has been neither noteworthy nor glorious. Yet even Azîla has its place in history, and can look back to Roman times, though in Morocco the sole patent of nobility would seem to be a Carthaginian strain. To the Romans Azîla was known as Zilia, Constantia Zilia, or Julia Traducta, according to the authority preferred, but it was probably little more than a station on the road from Tingis to Volubilis. It could never have been much of a port, notwithstanding its fair roadstead, so it never gained a reputation for piracy. The little river of Azîla which crosses the sands to the north is of no importance, but a reef of rocks, on which there once stood a dyke, affords indifferent shelter for small boats when they are able to pass the channel; Spanish fishing fleets, which lie a short way out to sea, are the only vessels which now frequent this port, and then but for water. When in 1894, on the death of Mulai el Ḥasan III., some of the European Powers sent men-of-war down the coast, the Spanish

Early History.

Roadstead.

* Spelled Aṣîla by Ibn Baṭûṭa. An inhabitant of Azîla is known as an Azîlashi.

commander foolishly dropped anchor before this relic of the past, which, having neither the means of defence nor of returning the salute which was offered, was evacuated in hot haste. As recently as 1860 the Spaniards had thought it worth a bombardment, which it certainly was not.

CITADEL OF AZÎLA.
Photograph by Herbert White, Esq.

*Early Moorish Period.**

In 713 A.C. Azîla, then possessed by the Goths, fell before the Arabs, who found Christians residing here,[1] and it is reported to have prospered under their dominion until we read of a strange occurrence—looked at in the light of English history,—no less than that it was seized and destroyed by our nation in 933 A.C.[2] At that time we should hardly

* The following historical references to Azîla will be found in *The Moorish Empire:* taken by Arabs, 24; by Ummeyîs, 42; by Portuguese, 110; besieged by Mohammed VIII., 111; Dom Sebastian here, 123; evacuated by Portuguese, 126: Christian martyr, 319; Christian mission, 330.

[1] GAYANGOS, vol. i., p. 252.

[2] LEO, (ed. Ram.) p. 89, and EL BEKRI.

have expected to encounter our ancestors so far afield, and if they did get there, this was possibly the first occasion of relations of any description between our island and the Moors. Leo tells us that the idolatrous English were persuaded by the Christianized Goths to undertake this expedition in order to drive the Moors out of Europe, but he probably referred to Norman pirates.*[1] Then followed thirty years of abandonment until the Córdovan K͟halîfa, El Ḥákim, rebuilt the place,[2] but it was soon afterwards depopulated by the plague, and in 1264 the Moorish governor of Ceuta destroyed its walls and forts.[3] When Prince Fernando of Portugal was brought here as a hostage for Ceuta in 1437, mention is made of a Christian church, and it was here that a century later, in 1556, was martyred the Franciscan Aguilon.[4]

Portuguese Period.

In 1471, on St. Bartholomew's Day, Alfonso V. of Portugal,—"The African"—supported by two hundred vessels, large and small,[5]—or three hundred and four according to others, with an army of thirty thousand,[6]—captured Azîla after a ten days' siege, at the moment when the direct line of the Marînîs was overthrown, and Fez was being besieged by Sa'îd el Waṭṭás. According to custom the chief mosque was converted into a church, and dedicated to "Our Lady of the Assumption." Among the five thousand prisoners were the wives and children of "Mulai Sheïk͟h," who, arriving too late to relieve the town, ransomed his wives by the concession of the tribute of the villages round,[7] and the body of Fernando, which now lies at Belem, near Lisbon. All the other prisoners were carried

* A "Mauritaniensis" appears as a follower of the Conqueror in Domesday Book.

[1] See KEATINGE, vol. i., p. 252, and DOZY, *Recherches*, vol. ii., p. 264.

[2] RAÒḌ EL ḲARṬÁS, p. 129.

[3] Ibid, p. 433.

[4] REMON, *Hist. Gen.*, vol. i., p. 444, and GODARD, p. 400.

[5] CASTELLANOS, p. 65.

[6] GODARD, p. 403.

[7] GODARD, p. 403.

off to Portugal, among them Mohammed, the son and successor of Sa'ïd, with his sister, both being children. Seven years later they were redeemed at great price, but not until they had learned so much of the language and customs that the former was afterwards known as "Mohammed the Portuguese."[1]

Determined Attacks.

This so galled him that thirty years after his liberation—in 1508—he made an attack in which the town was taken and the Moorish prisoners liberated, although four hundred of the garrison were still able to hold out in the castle till relieved from Tangier, Ceuta and Jerez.[2] Yet Sa'ïd would not give up, and two years later recommenced the siege, which was raised this time by a squadron returning from India,[3] but not until the place had been burnt. Once more, in 1516, for twelve days Sa'ïd attacked Azîla, which was again relieved by sea,[4] with a loss to the Moors of five hundred men. Sa'ïd then discovered that the Portuguese had restored the fortifications so thoroughly that the Moors came no more until 1526, when they made one more vain attempt.[5]

Christening Extraordinary.

It was during the Portuguese occupation that many of the Jews expelled from Spain by those "Catholic Sovereigns," Fernando and Isabel, were brought here in Spanish ships, and having been attacked by the Moors on their way to join their co-religionists in Fez, were forced to return and purchase shelter by submitting to a sprinkling from the friars' mops at work above the gateway, as with broken hearts they passed in.[6] At last, in 1545, João III. of Portugal, the persecutor of the Jews, decided to evacuate Azîla, and the Moors retained possession of it till it was re-

[1] LEO, l.c., MENEZES, p. 52. [2] GODARD, p. 412. [3] CASTELLANOS, l.c.
[4] LEO, p. 90. [5] MENEZES, p. 53.
[6] PRESCOTT, *Hist. Ferd. and Is.*, vol. ii., p. 127.

occupied by the Portuguese governor of Tangier in 1577, just before Sebastian's expedition, but it was once more abandoned in 1588,[1] by Felipe II. of Spain and Portugal.[2] Thereafter the foreigners left it alone, and it was re-peopled by the Rîfîs who had been employed in the war with Tangier: they erected the existing mosque.[3] Azîla suffered another siege by Mulai Rasheed in 1666, when it was the stronghold of Ghaïlán, the Anjera chieftain allied to the English, with whose assistance he was enabled to fly the country.

Modern Azîla.

To-day all that remains of Azîla is contained within the small, square Portuguese walls, round the top of which one may walk, so excellent is the state of their preservation, but of the castle there are only picturesque ruins, with an unexplored underground passage. There is practically nothing in the way of Moorish architecture, and very little of Moorish life, for things are sleepy there, and although there is a fair proportion of Jews among a rustic population, which may number some two thousand, there are no Europeans. Probably the only foreign residents within the last three centuries were two English missionary ladies during the eighties, who are still remembered with affection by the natives.*

The Town.

Azîla has two gates, that on the land side bearing even now defaced Portuguese arms, and the other leading straight on to the beach Although there is no Jewish quarter, there are two synagogues. No manufactures of note are carried on, but there are a number of weavers and several silversmiths, the latter being Jews. Most of the local trade is done at the Sunday, Monday, Tuesday, and Wednesday markets in the neighbourhood, and at the one held at home on Thursdays.

* Misses Herdman and Caley, both since at rest.

[1] El Ufráni, p. 263. [2] Suares Montanés. [3] Ez-Zaíáni.

The government is sometimes subject to that of Tangier, but generally to that of the province in which Azîla is situated.

The country round is flat, or covered with low hills fairly cultivated, and the only point of interest in the vicinity is the megalithic circle near the village of M'zôra—about eleven miles inland. This is known to the natives as El Utád—"The Peg"—on account of its principal feature, of which the best description is given by Dr. Spence Watson.* To the caves and lighthouse at Spartel is about twenty-two miles, passing the insignificant remains of Tahaddárt at the mouth of the river Kharrib or Hashîf, which, being tidal, is often not to be forded for several hours. "Mons le G." speaks of this as a port still used by vessels of from fifty to eighty tons in 1670, there being twelve to thirteen feet of water on the bar at high tide.[1]† The site of the Roman station of Ad Mercuri is at the Dshár Jadeed, eight kilomètres distant, or thirty-six from Tangier.[2] At Zaïtûn Aolád ben Hallal, three and a half hours distant, and about as far from Shammîsh, are the ruins of another settlement; and at Lallah Jellallîyah, three hours from Azila and three and a quarter from Shammîsh, is all that remains of what was probably the town of Taberna.[3] To the nearest open port, Laraiche, there is a fairly level road of some twenty-five miles, with nothing of interest on the way, but a very pleasant luncheon place is an oleander grove, at two thirds of the distance.

Neighbouring Interests.

The exact position of the town is 35° 28' N. by 6° 2' W.

* *A Visit to Wazan*, ch. vi. See also TISSOT, *Mauritanie Tingitanie*, pp. 178—181; CAPEL BROOKE, *Sketches*, vol. ii., p. 36, and A. FAIRLIE. For illustrations see *The Moorish Empire*, pp. 5 and 9.

† In 1683 Marseilles traders landed here.[4]

[1] *Relation Curieuse*, p. 4. [2] TISSOT, p. 134.

[3] Ib. p. 137. [4] MOUETTE, *Captivity*, p. 306.

2.—MEHEDÎYA, NEW M'AMÔRA or MEHDÙMA.

No little confusion has been caused in works on this country by the application to the port of Mehedîya*—"The Sheltered,"—which lay on the south side of the estuary of the Sebû, of the name M'amôra—"The Replenished"—which belongs to the forest district behind, and to the

GATEWAY AT MEHEDÎYA.
Photograph by Herbert White, Esq.

remains of another town on the Sebû in that district, some way higher up, near Sidi 'Ali bû Jenán, identified by an inscription found on the spot, with the Roman Colonia Aelia Banasa Valentia.† The other name by

* Tissot thinks it may have been named after Ibn Tûmart, the Mahdi, by his disciple 'Abd el Mû'min, first of the Muwáḥḥadîs, to whom its building is ascribed.

† The historical light thrown by the discovery of this inscription is ably discussed b M. Ernest Desjardins in the *Revue Archéologique* (Paris) for 1872, (vol., xxiii., p. 360). He shows its date to be A.C. 177, and to

which Mehedîya has become known is a consequence of its fate, for Mehdûma signifies "The Ruined." It was probably the Thymaterion of Hanno and Scylax,[1] the first Carthaginian Colony. The Spaniards re-named it San Miguel Ultramar.[2]

Portuguese Attempt.

The port is mentioned as Mehedîya in 941,[3] and in 1158 it was recaptured after a brave defence from the Sicilians into whose hands it had fallen in 1140, being rebuilt and fortified about 1200.[4] Its modern history, however, dates from the landing here in 1515 of a Portuguese force for the purpose of building a castle which should serve as a base of operations against Fez, but before they were ready the Moors came down in such numbers that they were overwhelmed, with a loss of ten thousand men: almost all the survivors were made slaves, as many as 100 vessels were lost, and they had the chagrin of seeing the materials which they had brought employed in the fortification of Fez itself.[5] Leo, who tells us that he saw the whole thing, attributes the defeat to an attempt at dual control among the Portuguese, adding that the original M'amôra had already all but disappeared, having been destroyed by Sa'ïd el Waṭṭás. About a hundred years later, at a date concerning which there is much divergence of opinion,* Felipe IV. of Spain sent a fleet and took possession of what then existed. By his successors it was held till retaken by Mulai Isma'ïl in 1681,

have been part of a monument raised in honour of the Emperor Commodus, son of Marcus Aurelius.

* 1604, Chenier; 1614, d'Avity (1640); 1614, Godard, p. 429; 1617, Castellanos, p. 86; 1644, De la Fuente, *Hist. de España*. But the question is settled as 1614 by Orozco, *Disc. hist. de la Presa . . . de Mamora* (Madrid, 1615).

[1] Tissot, p. 91.

[2] D'Avity.

[3] Raôḍ el Ḳarṭás, p. 108.

[4] Ib. pp. 279, 345, 379. See also El Bekri.

[5] Leo, (ed. Ram.), p. 62; Castellanos, p. 83.

an occupation of which the only vestiges remaining are the ruins of quays and stores.[1]

In Leo's time the river it had been intended to guard had already wandered a mile and a half away, and though it was at one time a favourite refuge of the Corsairs,* as its name implies, the bar being preferred to that of the Bû Ragrág, it has never again been rebuilt, and since that date has only served as the home of some of Mulai Ismá'îl's Bokhárî troops and their descendants. Formerly pearls as well as shabel were found in the river mouth, but at present the only article of export for which it is famed is the black sand found on the beach, much used by the Moors to dry their writing with; of this the sultans yearly receive a sack by way of tribute.

Spanish Period.

Along the coast to the north stretch for many miles immense fresh-water lagoons, the result, no doubt, of one of the periodical rises to which the whole coast has been subjected. These, prolific in ducks and eels which the natives spear, also abound to such an extent with gnats and mosquitos as to afford a good reason why M'amôra should be deserted. One of the most curious sights to greet the visitor to those parts is the moving of the native huts by manual transportation to approach or retire from the waters. At the northern extremity of these merját—as they are called—near the shrine of Mulai Bû Selhám,[2] are the scanty remains of another settlement, also known as old M'amôra. The exact position of Mehedîya is 34° 18′ N. by 6° 36′ W., and the distance to Laraiche is about 72, and from Salli 21 miles. It is the nearest port on this coast to the northern capitals, the distance to Mequinez being about 60 miles, and to Fez 103.

Fresh Water Lagoons.

* See *The Moorish Empire*, p. 267.

[1] DE CAMPOU, p. 253. [2] See TISSOT, p. 86.

3.—MANṢÛRÎYA.

Of a place like this one can hardly say more than that it once existed, having been built near the mouth of Wád Seer at the close of the twelfth century by Ya'ḳûb El Manṣûr, after whom it was named. Up to a certain point it no doubt flourished to the extent that most of the Moorish coast towns did in the Middle Ages, when they could find some one on whom to prey, but when in 1468 the Portuguese appeared before Anfà, now Casablanca, and its inhabitants fled to Rabat, they carried with them those of Manṣûrîya,[1] whom they passed half-way, and thus closed its history. From Casablanca the distance is some 26 miles, and from Rabat about 24.

4.—FEDÁLA.

Although the founding of the now vanished town of Fedála has been most commonly attributed to Mohammed XVII., who both opened and closed it to Europeans —between 1760 and 1773,—Pellow records the commencement of its walls by Mulai Ismá'îl, who only finished the mosque and a little palace,[2] and it had long ago been mentioned by Idreesi as a port.*[3] It was Sidi Mohammed, nevertheless, who completed the town, and conceded the trade in grains here and at Casablanca to the *Cinco Gremios* of Madrid. But since the time of its closing it has all but disappeared. What little remains is some 13 miles S. W. of Manṣûrîya and 15 N. W. of Dar el Baïḍa, near a headland, at a point where the roadstead is good, on the right bank of a little river. It is now but a hamlet where travellers sometimes rest for the night, and where Spanish fishing vessels take water.

* Some have thought it was the Dyos of Ptolemy.

[1] Leo (Hak.), p. 398. [2] Orig. ed., p. 67. [3] p. 81.

5.—AZAMMÛR.

Near the mouth of the Um er-Rabî'a or "Mother of Grass" in Dukálla stands Azammûr, one of the most purely native towns on the coast, its exact position being 33° 18′ 46″ N. by 8° 15′ W. *Position.* With a name dating back to pre-Arab times,—for it means in the Berber language a wild olive tree,—Azammûr knew foreign domination only from 1513, when the Portuguese, with the newly founded Mazagan as a base, were successful in an attempt which five years before had been made in vain. *History.* But in 1541 the Portuguese were fiercely attacked by Mohammed IX., yet were not discouraged, for they held it till João III. determined to abandon it in 1545, at the same time as he abandoned Azîla.* Since that time few Europeans have troubled their heads about the place, and none resided there till the Southern Morocco Mission made it a station in 1898. Of the early history of Azammûr nothing is known, but the French National Collection contains a coin struck there in 1374.

It seems strange that its river should not have secured for Azammûr a larger share of attention, in spite of its rival, Mazagan, but even in the history of the Empire it appears to have played no important *Fisheries.* part, except as the frontier town of the kingdom of Fez. Its principal revenue has always been derived from the supply of shabel or shad in the Um er-Rabî'a, which is here some 150 ft. wide, with a deep, strong-flowing current full of red earth from up country; to span this, Mohammed XVIII. in 1863 ordered from England an iron bridge, which, though landed, was never erect-

* Three saints were buried here to attract a new population, but their bodies were carried off to Mazagan by the Portuguese, one among them, Abd Allah Ibn Kessi, being subsequently ransomed at great price.[1]

[1] GODARD, p. 429.

ed.* When the Portuguese made their attempt of 1508 it was in support of a shareef who undertook to hold it as their vassal, paying 10,000 dried fish per annum, and admitting Portuguese imports duty free, but when he got in he ignored his share of the bargain.[1] The tide runs up the river some twenty miles, but the bar at the mouth would hamper trade if the port were thrown open.

Population.

Castellanos estimated the population of Azammûr at 20,000, but it must be very much less, and Jackson said he thought there were more storks than men in the place. The proportion of Jews is considerable, and in the absence of Europeans they have suffered more here than is usual on the coast, but now so many have European protection that they are well enough off. A growing local trade is done in goods imported through Mazagan, and the gardens along the river keep it very much better supplied with fruit than its rival. The chief market takes place on Friday. Several fine native houses repay a visit, and some of the mosques and shrines are picturesque. The chief mosque became in the Portuguese days the "Church of the Holy Spirit." In a suburb is the sanctuary of Mulai Bû Sha'îb, and the other local saints are Sidis Wadûd, Mohammed bin 'Abd Allah, Bin Náṣir and Ḥamed el Jabîlo; there is also a Jewish shrine. The chief mosques are those of the Darḳáwà, El Maḳ'ád, the Madînah and the Ḳaṣbah.

Ruins of Tît.

Some few miles from Azammûr—seven from Mazagan,—are the ruins of Tît, perhaps the Karikon-Teikhos of Carthaginian times, of which but the scantiest traces remain above ground, though in 1513 it was of sufficient importance for the Portuguese to occupy it temporarily. Its only boast to-day is the well-known shrine of Mulai 'Abd Allah.

* It still lies in the Mazagan Customs House.

[1] GODARD, p. 415.

6.—WALÎDÎYA.

Half-way between Mazagan and Saffi* is a natural harbour which will probably supersede them both as a port when Morocco falls into enlightened hands, for an extensive lagoon exists there which could contain a large fleet in safety, and only requires the removal of one or two rocks at the entrance to fit it for use. In the piracy days it was a well-known and favourite refuge,[1] and the Sultan El Waleed, who succeeded in 1631, built a town here called after himself, Walîdîya, which has long ceased to exist. M. Tissot, who has published an important mémoire on the subject,† considers this to be the "very safe" port of El Ghait mentioned by Idreesi, and it is possibly the Diour of Ptolemy.‡ It is probable also that this is the port of "Ayer," the construction of which cir. 1240 is recorded by Puerto, who says that Christians were employed to remove the rock at the entrance.[2]§ Spanish missionaries landed here in his time,[3] cir. 1660.

Natural Harbour.

All that now remains of human habitation is a curious little walled village, but on the narrow strip of grassy soil which separates the lagoon from the ocean the imperial horses are bred, a number of the finest mares in the kingdom being kept there for the purpose. Their great delight is standing buffalo-like up to their necks in the water, a practice to which their guardians attribute their glossy appearance, and of course they are all splendid swimmers. To the northward is the still larger lagoon, eight or ten miles long, called locally Rijlah dîalt Aolád 'Aïsà.

Horse-Breeding.

* Ten hours' ride from Saffi.

† *Note Sur l'ancien port d'el Ghat,* Bull. Soc. Geog., Paris, 1875, t. x., p. 67.

‡ Leo here placed Conte—20 miles from Saffi.

§ A big village with a saint's tomb, half an hour on the road from Walîdîya to Saffi, is still known as Aíyar.

[1] See PELLOW and MOUETTE. [2] p. 365. [3] p. 462.

VIEW OF A PORTION OF FEZ.
(See p. 247.)

Molinari, Photo., Tangier.

CHAPTER THE FOURTEENTH

IMPERIAL CITIES—I

FAS (FEZ

"Nature and Art have played the Wantons, and have brought forth this Citie, the fruit of their dalliance: or elſe they ſeeme corrivals; both, by all kind offices, ſeeking to winne her love: so doth the Earth ſeeme to dance, in little Hillocks and pretie Vallies diverſifying the Soyle; ſo doth the River diſperſe itſelfe into manifold Channels; no ſooner entring the Citie, but it is divided, as it were, into many Fingers, in varietie of Water Courſes, inſinuating itſelfe unto every Street and Member thereof: and not contented thus in Publike to testifie Affection, finds means of secret Intelligence with his Love by Conduit Pipes ... which still enioying, he wooeth, and ever wooing enioyeth." [1]

IN these quaintly graceful words, two centuries ago an English writer conveyed to his northern readers the native idea of Fez, the true metropolis of Morocco. Lacking all that might render it picturesque, hidden from most points of view in the hollow between two flanks where the plain which has extended all the way from Mequinez dips down to a lower level, Fez is rich in the richest of gifts to the Eastern taste, it has an abundant water-supply, for which the site was undoubtedly chosen.

Its Chief Attraction.

Moorish writers on the subject seem never to tire of singing the praises of Fez and its river. Of the latter

[1] PURCHAS, *Pilgrims*, ed. 1617, vol. v., p. 775.

it is stated by one of its admirers that "it cures the diseases of the stone and ill odours: it softens the skin and destroys insects: one can drink a quantity of it fasting, it is so sweet and light, qualities which it acquires in winding through the cypress and other trees." Moorish "physicians" report that "drunk fasting, this water renders the senses sharper. It whitens clothes without needing soap, and of itself imparts a surprising brilliancy and perfume."

Wonderful Water.

Of the city its native historian[1] says:

"O Fez, all the beauties of the Earth are united in thee!
With what blessing, with what good fortune, are not those overwhelmed that inhabit thee!
Is it thy freshness that I breathe, or is it the health of my soul?
Thy waters, are they white honey or silver?"

To quote once more:

"O Fez! may God preserve thy land and thy gardens, and give thee to drink of the water of snows!
O terrestrial Paradise, surpassing the beauties of the most beautiful, of which the very sight is enchanting!
Dwellings on dwellings, on feet below which flows water sweeter than the sweetest liquor:
Meadows like velvet, bordered with a net-work of brooklets as with gold:
Mosque of the Ḳarûeeïn! O noble name!
Whose court is so fresh in the greatest of heats?
Speaking of thee comforts me, and thinking of thee makes me glad."

In 1300 A.C. a Spanish Moor wrote: "Fez unites in itself sweet water, salubrious air, abundant harvests, excellent grains, beautiful fruits, vast ploughings, marvellous fertility, thick woods close at hand, meadows covered with flowers, immense kitchen-gardens, regular markets connected and crossed by straight roads, pure fountains, inexhaustible streams flowing in haste beneath shady trees with branches interlaced, on

An enchanting Picture.

[1] The author of *Raùd el Ḳarṭâs*, p. 37.

their way to water the gardens with which the town is surrounded."

According to *Raôḍ el Karṭás,** the native annals of Fez, its origin was on this wise: Idrees II., having found his quarters near Walîli (Volubilis) at the foot of Zarhôn, too restricted for the growing Court of the infant Empire, and unfavourably situated, himself went in search of a suitable site for an imperial capital. Jebel Wálîkh was his first choice, and a line was traced for the walls at its base, but hardly had the foundations been laid, when in one night a mountain torrent swept away the work, and that spot was abandoned. Another attempt was made upon the summit of the mountain, and the work proceeded merrily, until the winter tempests rendered it an unsafe dwelling-place, and the already rising walls and partly built mosque, founded by the hands of Idrees himself, were of necessity deserted. The year following a plain watered by the Sebû was chosen, and operations were again begun, but stories of the floods of that river caused the shareef to leave the ground soon after he had cleared it.

Choice of Site.

Tired of seeking a site for himself, Idrees now sent his minister with a commission of experts to do so for him, and they selected the present situation of Fez, enchanted by its broad fields and abundant woods, watered by so many grateful streams. One of the chief springs, 'Aïn Ameer, was so named by the wazeer, who purified himself and worshipped on the spot. The number of the springs was said to be about sixty, and the growth of vegetation was described as correspondingly luxuriant. The land belonged to two hostile tribes of the Zanatà who afterwards became the rulers of the Empire, the Zûághah and Beni Tághîsh,

The Final Selection.

* From which most of the historical information prior to 1320 has been derived.

the former professing Islám, and the latter Christianity; the one occupying the side now known as the Andalûs bank of the river, and the other the Ḳarûeeïn. From these the site was purchased for six thousand dirhams.

Foundation.

Idrees laid the foundation stones on the first Thursday of the holy month, Rabî'a el Awal, 192 A.H. (808 A.C.) on the Andalûs bank, commencing the other side a year after, having already built the Sheïkh's Mosque, his own house, the markets, etc.* When the walls were up, each tribe desiring to inhabit the town was allotted a quarter, wherein each individual was granted a plot for himself. Many are the stories told of the fertility of this well-favoured spot: among them that the trees planted this first year bore fruit the next, and that some bore twice a year! The author of *Raôḍ el Ḳarṭás* attests that he saw corn sown on April 15, 1291, and reaped in the end of May, forty-five days later, after an almost incessant east wind, and without rain since April 12.

The Name.

In Arabic Fás means a hoe, and the city is said to have received this name because Idrees turned the first sod with one of those implements, which are the spades of this country, saying, "Here I plant my fás," or words to that effect,[1] Another legend runs that on the spot were ruins which a priest

* But it now seems that an earlier date must be assigned, for M. de Tiesenhausen has published a dirham struck in Fez in the year 185 (801 A.C.), and in the French National Collection there is one dated four years later, which show El Bekri and Ibn Khaldûn also to be incorrect in giving 191 and 193 respectively as the date of its foundation.[2] Leo also is mistaken in the date. Or perhaps after all this is but a fresh proof of the remarkable accuracy of the author of *Raôḍ el Ḳarṭás*, whose account is quoted in the text, for the earlier dates may have been those of the first foundations laid, if the name had already been chosen. But the credit of selecting the site must rest with the faithful Rasheed, for in 808 Idrees was only twelve years of age, and had but recently "assumed the reins" of government.

[1] IBN BAṬÛṬA. [2] *Revue Belge de Numismatique*, vol. xxxi., p. 358.

of the Berbers pointed out to Idrees as those of an ancient town called Sáf. "Then I will change its name to Fás," was the reply. The neighbouring district is by some authors called Fahs es-Saïs, but whether this name was known before or after the foundation of the city is not clear.*

Political Vicissitudes.†

Like Marrákesh, Fez was once the capital only of a kingdom of the same name, and it was when these two kingdoms were merged into one, that the Moorish Empire, as it has been called by Europeans, was formed. The history of Fez has been chequered, as no less than eight times during the first five hundred years of its existence it was besieged successfully;‡ yet once only has it known foreign masters, when, during the struggle between the Beni Marîn and the Sa'adi shareefs, in 1554, the Turks took

* Other conjectural derivations are given by some authors; a Spaniard believes that the Phut and Lubim of the Bible are Fez and Libya. But *à propos* of the latter word, an ingenious derivation has been suggested: in Rîfian Berber "l" becomes "r," and "b" becomes "f"; thus, without the slightest stretch of imagination, Lybian is the equivalent of Rîfian!

† The *Moorish Empire* contains the following historical allusions to Fez: besieged by 'Obeïd ibn 'Abd Allah, p. 41; repulse of Fáṭimîs, 42, 87; taken by Ya'ála, 44; by Yûsef I., 53-4; improvement, 53-4; taken by 'Abd el Mû'min, 71; lost by El Mortaḍà, 86; Mohammed IV. killed there, 90; taken by Abu Bakr and retaken by 'Ali IV., 92; Abu Bakr's death there, 93; New Fez founded, 96; seized by Turks, 119; by Abu 'Aïnán, 103; Mohammed V. flees to it, 104 (n); besieged by Ahmad II., 106; Prince Fernando dies there, 109; taken by El Waṭṭás, 110; Mohammed VIII. established there, 111; conquered by Sa'adîs, 117; taken by Mohammed X., 119; by 'Abd el Málek I., 122; the "bastions" built, 128; Zîdán proclaimed, 130; Mohammed XII. proclaimed, 130; revolts against Zîdán and is sacked, 132; revolts from Mohammed XIII., 135: Fîláli shareefs take it, 135; Mohammed, son of Mulai es-Shareef, its ruler, 137-8; taken by Rasheed II., 138; pillaged by the Udáïá, 163; 'Abd el Málek flees to it, 164; besieged by Ahmad VII., 164; El Mustáḍà enters, 166; garrisoned with blacks, 167; besieged by Udáïa, 173; refuses to acknowledge El Hasan III, 179; in revolt against El Hasan III., 181-2; 'Abd el Azîz IV. installed there, 194; Friars welcomed there, 315, 322; Euan-Smith mission, 345.

‡ Namely in 960, 979, 1048, 1062, 1069, 1145, 1248, and 1250, A.C.

possession of the old city without a siege. The ameer retired first to the new town, and thence to Marrákesh, leaving the Turks free to occupy both towns for a brief period, until they abandoned them to the Beni Marîn ameer of Bádis (Velez), who remained there until the shareefian ameer retook it.[1]

For a long time Old Fez (Fás el Báli) was divided

PART OF THE WALLS OF FEZ.

Molinari, Photo., Tangier.

into two districts called "banks" (*i.e.*, of the river), the Adûat el Andalûs and the Adûat el Ḳarûeeïn, so-called on account of their respective inhabitants being of Spanish or Eastern extraction.[2] Those who gave their name to the Andalûs bank were driven from Spain by one of the early khalifas there in 820 A.C.,[3] but until 935 A.C. this quarter consisted only of a ḳaṣ-

Rival Sections.

[1] TORRES, p. 427 [2] IDREESI, p. 86.

[3] EL BEKRI, *art. Fás*; IBN KHALDÛN, vol. ii., p. 561.

bah, or citadel.[1] They were said to bear the palm for bravery, strength and successful agriculture, and to boast the most beautiful women, while the inhabitants of the Ḳarûeeïn shore were foremost in learning, in culture and in commerce, their men being considered the most fine-looking. Each section had always its own great mosque, market and mint, and at one time—1060—its own ameer.* The wall separating these rival districts was removed in 1070 A.C. by Yûsef bin Táshfîn, builder of Marrákesh, but the animosity between the two classes of settlers vented itself in bloodshed as late as the last century. Nevertheless, to their presence Fez was much indebted for its rapid rise to importance.

Unification.

In 1204 the whole town was walled in,[2] and seventy years later, in 1274, the town of New Fez (Fás Jadeed), sometimes spoken of as "the White Town," since its walls have ever been whiter than those of the Old Town, was built by one of the Beni Marîn ameers, Ya'ḳûb II. (Abû Yûsef). Since then, with the exception of the rearing of gates, mosques, palaces and mansions in its palmy days, Fez has undergone little in the way of improvement.

Building Completed.

When Mulai Idrees the younger founded the city, he built a fine mosque, still standing, by the side of which his remains lie buried. He has become the patron saint of the city, and the sanctuary of his mosque is considered one of the holiest in the country. The veneration in which the záwîahs of Fez are held has brought thither throngs of pilgrims to whom Mekka was inaccessible. In the seventeenth century the number of shrines and mosques was said to be six hundred and fifty, and that of the fandaḳs three hundred, but these

Sanctity.

* The names of two of the city gates, Ajîsa (pron. Gîsa) and El Fatûḥ, recall the names of the rival ameers. See p. 248.

[1] Ibn Khaldûn, vol. ii., p. 145. [2] Raôd el Ḳarṭás, p. 388.

are the figures given by a writer who made the columns of the Ḳarûeeïn fifteen hundred, about treble their present number.[1]

In the early days of Mohammedan rule in this country Fez was a highly favoured city, the seat of learning and the Empire's pride. When Ḳaïrwan and Córdova were lost, it received their learned and devout refugees,* becoming famous as the Baghdád of the West, already the Imperial metropolis, self-satisfying, self-contained, where letters flourished, and where the most elegant of dialects was spoken.[2] Thither came large numbers of students attracted by its educational advantages.† Its libraries were extensive, if its teachings were not deep,‡ and though what was taught there might seem of small account in our days, it was then esteemed wonderful.

Academic Reputation.

In the middle of the sixteenth century even Christian seekers after knowledge were to be found in Fez, and in 1535 Clenardus (Cleynaerts) went there to study, but already its academic glories had passed, the scholars were few, and the libraries

European Students.

* After one of their intestine struggles, eight thousand families of Andalucian Moors took refuge in Fás Jadeed, another party finding their way to Ceuta.[3]

† The extinct Madarsat el A'alám was built in 1320,[4] the school attached to the Andalûs mosque in 1321,[5] that of the Aṭṭarîn in 1323,[6] and that of the Ḳarûeeïn in 1373. Ali V. (the "Black Sultan") built "the school of Abu Yûsef" at the close of his reign 1348;[7] the Sharráṭîn madarsah was erected by Mulai er-Rasheed in 1671, and another by Abd Allah V. cir. 1757,[8] probably the Madarsat el Wád.[9] Some of the former Madarsahs, though retaining the name, are now no more than ordinary mosques.

‡ The best list of the MSS. remaining in Fez, though incomplete, was obtained by M. Ordèga, and contributed by Prof. Basset to the "Bull. Corresp. Afr.," Algiers, November and December, 1882. It gives two hundred and forty names.

[1] PURRTO, p. 612. [2] ABD EL WAḤEED, p. 261. [3] DOZY, vol. ii., p 76.
[4] EN-NÁṢIRI, vol. iv., p. 54. [5] *Raôd el Kartás*, p. 570. [6] EN-NÁṢIRI, vol. ii., p. 54.
[7] EN-NÁṢIRI, vol. ii., p. 86. [8] EN-NÁṢIRI, vol. iv., p. 91. [9] EZ-ZAIÁNI, p. 22.

had all but vanished: * although occasional auctions of books, for the most part religious, still took place at the Ḳarûeeïn, sales were rare, and purchasers indifferent. † When in the beginning of the eighteenth century "'Ali Bey" tried to find out what remained,[1] all he could come across was a room in the Ḳarûeeïn Mosque, wherein a collection of ancient manuscripts was rotting away, and another full of clocks and various instruments, of which no one knew the proper use.[2] Among the latter were European terrestrial and celestial globes, then about a century old. Euclid existed in great folio volumes, unread. Ptolemy's cosmography was the latest studied, and Aristotle's physics. Sufficient astronomy was understood to take the time by the sun with rude astrolabes constructed for each latitude. With mathematics there was but a slight acquaintance, and with geography even less. Chemistry was unknown, but some notions of alchemy existed. Anatomy was banished, and the ideas of medicine extant were the most rudimentary.

Scientific Attainments.

The luxury of prosperity had brought on its attendant vices, which never fail to induce ruin, and to use the language of Chenier, in his work on Morocco, "Fez, the school of sciences and manners, soon became the sink of every vice."[3] Now but a skeleton remains of what was once so flourishing, and save in its commerce and traditions, Fez has little to distinguish it from, or render it more remarkable than, the other capitals. In these points it undoubtedly takes the lead,

The Fall.

* Yet it is recorded on the authority of Erpenius (Van Erpe), that in 1613 there were 32,000 vols. in the Fez Library.[4] Mohammed XVII., however, distributed many among the ḳâḍîs, in 1760.

† A translation of his account from the Latin of 1556 (Louvain) was published in Ghent in 1845 by Prof. Nève.

[1] p. 66. [2] p. 177. See Prof. René Basset's list, Alger, 1883.

[3] Vol. i., p. 73. [4] G. B. Carta in *Man. Univ. Geog.*; Gråberg, p. 177.

being the great mart of the Empire, and though retaining but the shadow of its former greatness, it is still, so to speak, its university town.

Existing Libraries.

The Ḳarûeeïn mosque has still the best library in Fez: here, in 1285, Ya'ḳûb II., the builder of New Fez, deposited thirteen loads of MSS., which he had taken from the King of Seville, Sancho IV.,—"the Great." Rohlfs, writing in 1861,[1] says that five thousand volumes remained there then, but it is impossible to ascertain the exact number: most estimates are much higher. The library is open on Fridays, when any Moor of known respectability may borrow volumes, on the Ḳaḍi's order, and on signing a receipt for them, but to Jews and foreigners they are prohibited. For many years there has been in connection with this mosque a lithographic establishment,* from which a series of works has been issued, chiefly theological or biographical. Other small collections of MSS. are to be found at the mosques of Mulai Idrees and Erṣîf, but more are to be found in the houses of some of the old Andalucian families, who are quite willing to lend them to other Moors.

Colleges.

Of colleges the only remains are seven madarsahs,† containing chambers which accommodate among them perhaps one thousand five hundred students, who "read" at the Ḳarûeeïn. They pay no

* Mulai el Ḥasan took this over to have a work printed, called "Es-Sheïkh Mortaḍà." Two hundred copies were issued, of which fifty were sent to Mekka and as many to Cairo; twenty to Constantinople, seventy being distributed between the three libraries at Fez, and the remainder kept in the sultan's private library. Most of the works issued from this press are to be found at the British Museum, but those which are unique are of little value.

† These are those of the Ṣeffarîn, about 200 students; the Sharrátîn, 225; the Meṣbáḥîyah, 215; the 'Aṭṭárîn, 175; Báb el Gîsa, 115; Abû 'Ainán, 75, and the Saḥrîj (appertaining to the 'Andalûs mosque), 115. The numbers are the estimates of a student of the first named, based on the number of loaves issued daily for their consumption.

[1] P. 1[illegible]

rent, but buy the keys of the rooms from the last occupants, selling them again on leaving.* At the mosque they are taught by 'ulámà or "wise men" who are supported from property of which part has been bequeathed for the special endowment of "chairs," the same expression being used in Morocco as in Europe. In the mornings religion, which embodies law, is studied, and in the afternoons Arabic. Thursdays and Fridays are holidays.†

Fez has a reputation for learning, and undoubtedly the wisest men in the Empire are to be found here, but by reason of their pride and bigotry the best of them deserve the title someone has bestowed upon them of "ignorant learned." Their sultans have ever found the Fásîs difficult to manage, especially on account of the large number of hereditary saints who so easily rouse their fellow-citizens. It is a noteworthy fact that Fez is at once the most religious and the most wicked city of Morocco, according to the Moors' own reckoning, the saints and sinners being for the most part identical.

"Ignorant Learned."

The position of Fez is in latitude 34° 6′ 3″ N. and 5° 1′ 11″ (or 4° 38′ 15″) W. It is said to be two hundred and thirty miles north-east of Marrákesh, but this cannot be reached by a straight road on account of the unsubdued state of the country, which necessitates a roundabout route extending to near Rabat, though direct roads both from Marrákesh to Fez, and from Fez to Rabat were open two centuries ago. From Mequinez Fez is distant about thirty-six miles, or a long day's journey, and from Tangier by road about six days, or one hundred and sixty miles. The nearest open ports

Position.

* From $20 to $100, according to college and room.

† For further information as to the university system, see *The Moors*, ch. xviii.

are Laraiche and Rabat, the journey to either occupying three and a half days, or four days, respectively; but the nearest point on the coast is about seventy-five miles distant, near Peñon de Velez; and Mehedîya, at the mouth of the Sebû, is the nearest point on the Atlantic, about 103 miles.

Original Walls.

The existing walls of Fez were re-built by the Beni Marîn, by whose time the old ones were found far too restricted. Of these, two of the gates still remain, in the Shrábeleeïn and near the Báb Gîsà, but with two exceptions the gates of the founder are forgotten, even in name, the exceptions being Báb el Ḥadeed, commemorated by a successor, and Báb Sils-lah, the site of which retains its name. The others were called Ifrikîya, Sa'dûn, Fars, Fásîl, Farj, Zaïtûn, Shibbûba and Kinisîá.*

Growth and Destruction.

The growing suburbs were enclosed about 1056 to protect them against the invading Murábtîs, but in vain, for just a century later they were almost entirely destroyed by the Muwáḥḥadi successors of the Murábtis. In 1145 'Abd el Mû'min concluded his long siege by erecting a dam across the plain above the city, until he could deluge it by suddenly cutting a channel. Nearly all that remained of the walls after this operation he destroyed, declaring that in future justice and his sword should defend the town. They were not re-built till the reign of his great-grandson Mohammed III. (en-Náṣir) in 1204. The Beni Marîn restorations of 1282 came next, when New Fez was completed by Ya'ḳûb II. Since this time our sources of information are less complete.

Old Fez has now seven gates. The highest on the

* This last name is curious, as indicating the proximity of a place of Christian worship, which the word means: when rebuilt in 1240 this gate was re-named Khaûkhah.

west side, Báb el Maḥurôḳ—one of the most important—was originally called Báb Shari'à, and dates from 1204, but owes its present name—which means "The Burned"—to the fact that on the day of its completion the head of a rebel was stuck on the top, while his body was burned below.[1] On emerging thence to make the circuit of the town, and turning to the left, a cemetery comes in view, and crenellated walls enclosing gardens, beyond which is the upper gate of New Fez, which bears the remarkable name of Ḳubîbat es-S'min, or "Bucket of Butter:" its western exit is known as Báb Sagma. Between the two towns lies the Ḳaṣbah Bûjilûd ("Father of Skins"), the gates on either side of which are called by the same name, as is also the adjacent mosque. Beyond this ḳaṣbah the connecting suburb bears the title of Baïn el Mudûn, or "Between the Towns."

Gates.

Still bearing round to the left, past a quarter full of gardens with pleasure houses, the Báb el Ḥadeed or "Iron Gate" is reached, then Báb el Jadeed or "New Gate" and Báb el Fatûḥ, named after an early ameer. Between this last and that at the south-east corner, named after Sidi Bûjîda, whose grave lies just outside, is a glorious point of view, a hillock once a resting-place for the dead, now a refuse heap for the living. Fez lies stretched out below like a panorama, with a rival point of view beside the Beni Marîn tombs[2] across the valley. There is nothing imposing, but something awe-inspiring, in the sight of that white-roofed conglomeration of habitations, broken only by occasional mosque-towers, or in the outskirts by luxuriant foliage. All the bustle of the city is hidden, and an air of repose reigns instead, yet beneath that placid surface a great metropolis throbs.

Panorama.

[1] *Raôd el Ḳartás*; and El Makkári, p. 367. For illustration, see *The Moorish Empire*, p. 219.
[2] Ditto, l.c. p. 95.

Close inside the neighbouring gate stands the Jama' el Andalûs, mosque of the refugees from Spain, with a prominent portal of beautiful tile-work, visible over the roof-tops. Between this point and Bab Gîsa,—named in 1063 after Fatûḥ's rival brother—* is a long stretch of wall, down one side of the valley and up the other, with the river passing out at the bottom. Between Báb Gîsa and Báb el Maḥurôḳ stretches the wall completing the circuit of Fás el Báli, "The Old."

New Fez.

New Fez—the "White Town"—has but two gates, that of the "Bucket of Butter," already mentioned, and the Báb Sidi Bû Náfa'. To the left of the former, coming out, lies the open space devoted to "powder-play" on Wednesday, Thursday and Friday afternoons, when the Court is in residence, or on any feast-day, and beyond this the river enters the town, after having traversed part of the palace enclosure.

Water-Supply.

From its peculiar situation Fez has a drainage superior to that of most Moorish towns, and by reason of the abundance of water an organized system became necessary from the outset. The chief source of the supply is a spring some eight miles along the plain, protected by a fort apparently of great strength. It is really the exit of a subterranean river from a low hill known as Rás el Má' or "Water-head." Down below is a beautifully clear pool with a gravel and sandy bottom, into which falls what is thenceforward known as the Wád Fas, or Fez River. The whole plain abounds in excellent springs, and De el Puerto speaks of six hundred "fountains" within the Old City in his day.[1]

* El Fatûḥ ruled this side, and 'Ajîsa the other, and each made a gateway near his palace, but the story runs that when El Fatûḥ at last triumphed, he ordered the name of his brother's gate to be decapitated, whence Jîsa, otherwise Gîsa. It was rebuilt for the second time in 1285 by Ya'ḳûb II.

[1] p. 612.

Even in the hills these springs, usually tepid, are to be found, and to the north of the plain are the hot sulphur springs of Mulai Ya'ḳûb, by some considered the *Aquæ Dacicæ* of the Romans,*— which are thronged by sufferers from all parts

Medicinal Springs.

MAIN BED OF THE FEZ RIVER BETWEEN THE WALLS OF THE CITY.

Molinari, Photo., Tangier.

of Morocco. About four miles from the town are the hot springs of K͟haôlîn, at no great distance from which are others named after Sidi Harázam, who died in 1163. The water of some of the springs supplying the town is much warmer than the air in winter, and cooler in summer, although in winter the river grows cold. Consequently I have seen both tepid and cold water from natural sources laid on side by side in the same house.

* Tissot, however, gives the *Aquæ Dacicæ* as between Volubilis and Sala.

When the river enters the town it is led off in numberless channels, at first more or less open, which are used to turn a number of water-mills. Every house is supplied with this running water, which, after having passed through mosques and private dwellings, finds its way through sewers into the lower reaches of the river, as its branches reunite before leaving the town.* Here, in the main bed, among the rocks and boulders, are perched many corn-mills, and as the turbid stream flows by, it is led off by rudely constructed channels, fringed with maiden-hair, to grind the city's wheat. These mills are extremely simple in their plan: a shaft, passing down from the centre of the upper stone, has on its lower end a wooden fan upon which the water pours with considerable force from a wooden spout, causing the fan to revolve. The wheat is washed in a tank supplied from the same source.

Water System.

In almost every street may be heard the sound of running streams, and often the splashing and grinding of mills is added to the varied sounds with which the air is filled. Under the houses and and through them, its volume swelled by the water from springs in the town, and by conduits bringing special supplies for special people, the river rolls along, and though it affords an excellent means of flushing the drains—which on this account are by no means so odoriferous as in the other towns—it creates an unhealthy dampness, as the countenances of the citizens betoken.†

Drainage.

* Stories are told of houses of ill-fame, having *oubliettes* overhanging the river, into which the bodies drop, and when they float ashore on anyone's property they are promptly pushed off again into the stream to prevent complications.[1]

† It has been asserted that the supply and drainage system are one, which, being an absurdity, is a palpable libel. The drainage system lies below the level of the fresh river water, and was organized by a French renegade rather more than a century ago, under Mohammed XVII.

[1] Erckmann, p. 138.

When the town becomes very dirty and muddy the water is allowed to run down the streets by opening lids for the purpose in the conduits, and stopping the ordinary exits of the water, so that it overflows and cleanses the paving, to the inconvenience of shod, and the delight of unshod, passers-by. Generally the inhabitants of Fez prefer the muddy river water to that of the pure springs which abound in certain quarters of the city, since these latter are mineral, and are called "heavy," while the river water is considered "light." Europeans drink from the springs.

Street-Cleaning.

On account of its peculiar situation in a hollow, Old Fez is protected from the most violent storms, so that when it rains the down-pour is fairly direct, the atmospheric disturbance to which it is due being much higher up, and but slightly affecting the lower strata of air. Thus it is remarkable how slightly the barometer falls for rain, and while for the same reason it becomes hot and close in summer, slight frosts are not unknown in winter. This season is attended by one great inconvenience, that, owing to the absence of roads, communication with the outside world is almost entirely suspended for days together, at all events during the lîáli rains—from December 23 to February 1.

Climate.

The temperature varies in the shade from 30° F. during a few nights in winter, to an occasional 115° in summer, when the heat is dry, depending on the wind; rising rapidly during south and south-east winds to 90° at night and 100° to 110° during the day. After eight or ten days of such heat, clouds gather and irregular squalls are followed by thunder and lightning, but seldom by rain. Then the west or north-west wind sets in, and the glass falls to from 90° to 76°, day and night. In summer there is usually a fresh evening breeze. Some danger to health arises from chills due to the

Temperature.

variation of temperature in the dwelling-houses, which by shade and running water are kept on the ground-floor at about 73° or less, while in the shade on the roof 110° may be registered, 100° on the top floor and 86° to 90° on the second. The height of the melláḥ above the sea-level is given by De Foucauld as 400 métres (1312 ft.), and that of the gardens outside the town by Duveyrier as 352 m., by Desportes as 342 m., and by De la Martinière as 335 m. The upper or New Town may therefore be reckoned as about 1000 ft. above the Atlantic.

Population.

It is impossible to do more than guess at the population of Fez. Among the estimates of writers on this country are twenty, thirty, forty, fifty, eighty-eight, ninety to one hundred, and three hundred and eighty thousand; evidences of the value of "statistics" in Morocco. The numbers are probably under one hundred thousand, even when the Court is here. All that can be said with certainty is that the two towns are estimated to cover an area of about six square miles, and that while there are many gardens and open spaces within the walls, the greater portion is occupied by closely-packed houses, and that the Old Town is the business centre for hundreds of miles in every direction save the north. Consequently its tortuous streets are crowded daily, and while Mequinez or Marrákesh appears full only when the Sultan is in residence, at other times seeming half deserted, these busy thoroughfares are little affected either by the arrival or departure of the Court.

Inhabitants.

No city in Morocco contains so many rich families, finely housed, as does Fez. It is the boast of its inhabitants that they are the most civilized and polished under the sultan's rule. As regards their colour, or even their type of feature, if a regiment were picked haphazard from the upper classes and dressed as Europeans, the proportion which would be recognizable by sight as Africans would be astonishingly small. Even the women slaves are often much whiter than many country people, having the scantiest traces of negro blood in their veins. This is owing to the preference for white female slaves, which tempts people to sell their children by light-coloured slave-mothers, so that the negro strain is perpetuated on the mother's side only, until it is almost altogether lost sight of.

Fâsi Characteristics.

A lazy set are these pale-faced Africans; they consider it quite a long walk from one end of the town to the other, and beneath their dignity to go afoot if they can possibly borrow a mule, should they not already possess one. Few ride horses, save those connected with the Government on duty bent, except for the "powder-play." The mules ridden by the well-to-do are fine creatures, and there are probably more of them to be seen here than anywhere else in the country, for their ambling pace is far more to the taste of the portly, kesksoo-stuffed gentry, or even of the lean and blasé young men of the middle classes, since few have much energy left after reaching the age of twenty.

Fâsî Dress.

The dress of the Fâsî of any position is in summer the k'sá, a fine, semi-transparent, woollen and silk toga, about six yards by one and a quarter, worn in graceful folds over the usual garments of the country, supplemented, in cold weather by a dark blue selhám, of foreign felt cloth, uniform in hue and cut. The women usually fold their thick ḥaïks rather differently from those on the coast. In muddy weather many of the men wear clogs, ḳabâḳab, of the shape of wooden skates, with a broad iron tread under the heel, and another under the ball of the foot. These are worn on the bare soles, being kept in place by simple leather straps across the toes, so that some skill is required to retain them. A prolongation of about six inches in front has a nail underneath at the tip, to prevent the wearer from slipping down hill.

Comparison with the East.

In many ways Fez may be favourably compared with even such famous centres as Shiráz or Baghdád, and with the exception of their colleges, with Samarkand or Bokhára. Constantinople and Cairo are beyond comparison richer and more beautiful; Damascus has better houses, and Jerusalem is more substantially built; no public works in Morocco vie with the architectural glories of Hindustán, and the Moorish counterparts of the "Alhambra" and "Alcassar" of Seville being occupied by royalty, are therefore hidden from public view. But among the cities of Barbary, Tunis alone rivals Fez, and in the picturesqueness of its bazaars surpasses it by reason of its multi-coloured costumes; yet in all the cities mentioned, and in many more, I have seen nothing between Morocco and Central Asia to excel Fez either in interest or in artistic effect.

Streets.

Most of the streets of Fez are exceedingly narrow, and as the houses are higher than is usual in this country, besides being often built over the thoroughfares, these are gloomy and dark, an effect which is heightened in summer by training vines or stretching awnings across the busier avenues—some of which, indeed, are permanently roofed with wood. From this in part results the pallor for which their inhabitants are noted, considered a mark of distinction, and therefore jealously guarded. Many of the houses have to be supported by props and stays across the streets, but there is less of that ruined, half-decayed appearance, so typical of eastern towns. One cause of this difference lies in the fact that the materials employed in building are wooden beams, rough stones, tiles and mortar, in lieu of the tabîah, or mud concrete, which is attended by much outward crumbling.

Style of Houses.

The better-class houses of Fez are invariably built upon the principle of a central court-yard, with pillars and tile-work and bubbling water, cool in summer but dark in winter; with long, narrow, windowless chambers, lit and ventilated by huge, horse-shoe doorways and by perforated plaster-work. Flat roofs they all have, which are reserved for the women, but sometimes usurped by the storks. A six or eight-roomed house in a good position may be rented for from £10 to £12 a year, less than a fourth or fifth of what would be demanded in Tangier. Except in wet weather, or when the army is here, provisions are cheap, but fuel is always dear in comparison, since it must be brought two days' journey Rice is grown in small quantities not far from the town, as are also Indian hemp and tobacco, notwithstanding prohibition, but there are no peculiar local products. Excellent salt is supplied from a hill at Tîssa in Haïaïna.

Sport.

There is but little sport round Fez. On the Wád Fás, west of the city, a few wild ducks, widgeon, wild geese and water-hens may sometimes be found, as also snipe and occasionally sand-grouse. Partridges are more common, and one need go only three or four miles out of town to find them. The wild boar is said to be very numerous in the hills around Sifrû, and at Zarhôn, but the former region is as yet unsafe for Europeans, who have hitherto been neither numerous nor enthusiastic enough to interfere with the Zarhôn boars. Hares and rabbits are scarce. Hyænas have been seen frequently near Sifrû, and occasionally the skins of leopards, and even—though more rarely—those of lions, are on sale in the Fez market. They are said to be found in the districts of the Beni M'gîld, Beni

M'tîr and the country lying between Mequinez and Marrákesh, but these are districts closed to foreigners.

Manufactures.

There was a time when Fez was famous for its manufactures, but although it yet retains a reputation in this country for one or two articles, and the cap which is almost a symbol of Mohammedanism still bears its name, the goods it now produces are in the main paltry and rude. It is said that Cordovan refugees introduced the art of dyeing and preparing the famous Cordovan—now known as Morocco—leather, from the name of which is derived our word cordwainer, as also the French *cordonnier*, an evidence of the early popularity of this article. The author of *Raôḍ el Ḳarṭás* states that previous to about 1242 A.C. (when they were all destroyed by the ameer of that date) there were four hundred paper factories in Fez.

The manufactures still carried on are those of yellow slippers of the famous leather, fine white woollen and silk ḥaïks of which it is justly proud, women's embroidered sashes, various coarse woollen cloths and blankets, cotton and silk handkerchiefs, silk cords and braids, swords and guns, saddlery, Fez caps, felt saddle-cloths, brass trays, Moorish musical instruments, rude painted pottery and coloured tiles. The gold- and silver-smiths also turn out some passable work, and much silk embroidery is produced in private houses.

Markets.

As in the other capitals, each trade has a district or street devoted mainly to its activities, and there is a ḳaïsarîyah, or covered market for the sale of textiles; this, however, bears no comparison with that of Marrákesh, as the passages are narrow and the shops are small: business, nevertheless, is brisker, which is the main point. The entrances are crossed by bars to prevent the ingress of horses, mules and like intruders. By the side of this is the 'Attárîn, or Spice

Bazaar, the most important street for shops, and one of those which is covered in.

Old Fez is decidedly the business section of the town, while New Fez is occupied principally by the Government quarters and the melláḥ. In Old Fez are some very good caravan-sarais or yards surrounded by two or three storeys of mer- *Business Quarters.*

A FANDAK OR PUBLIC PLACE OF BUSINESS.
Photograph by R. J. Moss, Esq.

chants' offices and sample rooms. The most important are those of the Najjárín (Carpenters), the Koṭṭánîn (Cotton-spinners), the Shrabbeleeîn (Slipper-makers), the Sharráṭîn (Rope-makers), the 'Aṭṭárïn (Spicers), and the Ṣárà (or "Shady"), the names being those of the streets in which they are situated, all save one so called from the trades plied therein. Jackson estimated the number of fandáḳs of three storeys a century ago as two hundred, with fifty to one hundred rooms apiece. The Najjárîn, in which several of the leading Jews have their offices, was sacked by the populace in 1747, when three thousand ḳafṭáns* stored there by Mulai 'Abd Allah were taken.[1]

Foreigners.

Till within the last few years there were no Europeans established in business in Fez, but it was frequently visited by travellers† in search of orders, who have, however, grown fewer of late years. In accordance with a long-existing treaty-right, a British vice-consulate was established in 1892, a French one in 1894, soon to be followed by those of other nations, France and Spain alone having hitherto had unofficial agents. The authorities of Fez do not by any means extend a welcome to foreigners, whom they are always sorry to see. Even with letters from the commissioner of foreign affairs at Tangier, it is difficult to get accommodation. During the eighteenth century a special order was required to enable Europeans to enter Fez,[2] and the first free European ladies known to have visited it were the members of Sir John Hay's family who accompanied the embassy of 1868. In 1887 Fez became a station of the North Africa Mission, medical work being courageously opened up by the late Miss Herdman and two other ladies, at a time when they were the only resident Europeans, and everything was to be feared from the fanaticism and ignorance of the Mohammedans. But their labour of love soon made them universally respected, and in 1896 the Gospel Union of America opened a station here also. Centuries ago the Franciscan Friars

* Tunics. † Mostly Germans.

[1] Ez-Zaïáni, p. 113. [2] Chenier, vol. i., p. 78.

had a house here, when they watched over and cared for the foreign slaves until 1790.

Since 1892, the British and French postal systems have been extended to Fez, the couriers making the journey on foot from Tangier in three days, but as yet no regular means of communication exists with other parts of the Empire. The Moors have also an inefficient service, but in all important matters use the European posts, the establishment of which has introduced Arabic newspapers, chiefly from Egypt.

Postal Service.

The police system of Fez, as of the other large towns, is very simple.* During the day there is no patrol, as in European cities, and to the credit of the people be it said, there is not the same need for such a system, since they are generally peaceable and law-abiding. Each house-holder or shop-keeper is held responsible for what occurs before his premises, which makes it both his interest and his duty to suppress all evil-doing, and accounts for the usual quiet. Drunkenness is very rare, although contact with Europeans is slowly but surely adding this to the vices of the Moors. Those who do drink forbidden liquors do so in their houses on the sly, obtaining them chiefly from the Jews, who are permitted to distil for themselves. From the division of the city by doors across the streets into an immense number of little sections, the only way to get about after evening prayers is from roof to roof, so that a crime or outrage committed in any district is easily detected, and the escape of the criminal rendered difficult. The city is divided into eighteen wards, each of which is under the charge of a muḳaddam.

Police.

Fez is provided with several prisons: the chief among them are the Zibbálat en-Naṣárà ("Dunghill of the Nazar-

* See *The Moorish Empire*, p. 224.

enes"), in the Old Town,—said to be so called because it was originally a filthy dungeon in which white slaves were confined,—and the Dakákan, at the entrance to the Dár Makhzen, or Government House, in the New Town. In the Dakákan many of the prisoners live in ordinary Arab tents in the yard, while some have apartments to themselves. Behind these are dark and pestilential underground dungeons in which murderers are kept, often until released by death.

Prisons.

The slave-market is held every afternoon at ten minutes before sunset, in an enclosure used in the early morning for the sale of wool, and afterwards for that of grain. When caravans from the Sahara come in, slaves are plentiful, but, like most other articles of commerce, they become scarce and dear in the wet season, when sales are effected privately through the auctioneers.

Slave-market.

Adjoining the 'Aṭṭarîn is the morstan, or hospital and mad-house of Sidi Farj. This is undoubtedly that referred to by early writers as connected with the mosque of Mulai Idrees, from which it is separated only by a stone's throw. At first it was richly endowed, and some attempts were made to doctor and relieve the suffering, but although the revenues are still large for Morocco, the sick receive slight attention.* Nowadays, instead of all that is not stolen being appropriated to the use for which it was bequeathed, a large proportion is permitted to accumulate, until it is taken over by the Government and is invested in more

Hospital.

* As a specimen of the uses to which these endowments were put may be mentioned the statement of Vincent le Blanc, who says that 'Abd el Málek I. (1576-8), wishing to borrow the golden balls of the Kûtûbîya for his wars, was told by the people that his grandfather had "sold the foundation rents of the Hospitall of Fez, and dyed before he could recover them, so as 'twas lost to the poor." [1]

[1] *The World Surveyed*, trans. T. B. Gent, 1660, p. 256.

mosque property. "'Ali Bey," wrote in 1806 that this money was originally bequeathed for the benefit of sick cranes and storks,[1] the truth being probably as has been recounted elsewhere.[2] The morstán is now divided into three parts, a ground floor in which madmen are chained, a first floor, which serves as a women's prison, and a yard in which a few miserable wretches drag out their weary life, the sole vestiges of a hospital.

Leper Quarter.

There is no regular lepers' quarter in Fez, where this disease is now unknown,* but there was one once on the lower side of the town, so placed that wind and water might reach Fez first. This was on the Tlimṣán road, near the Báb Khaûkhah, but in 1239, after a fearful famine, the lepers were allotted the caves outside the Báb Maḥurôḳ. Some twenty years later, owing to complaints that they polluted the river by washing and bathing in it, they were removed to the caves of the Kaôkáb battery, near the Báb Gîsà.

The Jewish Quarter.

The melláḥ, or Jewish quarter, forms one of the noticeable features of New Fez. Hardly had Fez been founded when a number of Jews took refuge there, being allotted a quarter by Mulai Idrees on the payment of thirty thousand dînárs a year. This tax is still paid, but the sum has changed, and is taken in lieu of military service. In 1276 the mob rose against them, and had killed fourteen when the ameer Ya'kûb II. (Abu Yûsef), riding to the spot, forbade any Moor to approach the Jews' Quarter. Next morning he laid the foundation of New Fez, in which he accorded the Jews their present melláḥ, which contains the largest Jewish colony in the Empire. Yet its synagogues are poor and often dirty, and it can boast

* The Moors say that this complaint practically became extinct after the introduction of lemons from Spain in the eleventh century.[3]

[1] p. 74. [2] See ch. iv., p. 70. [3] See *The Moors*, ch. xii.

nothing of interest save the excellent school of the *Alliance Israëlite*, which has worked wonders already. As yet no effort has been made to educate the girls, and nothing was done for the boys until a few years ago. The disastrous system of child-marriages is here seen at its worst, although as some sort of compensation it is said that there is no worse corruption of the people's morals.

The Jewish Colony.

The Jews go about with white-spotted blue handkerchiefs over their heads, and the Jewesses affect big red ones with white patterns, four of which, woven in one piece, are worn over the head and folded in front, much as the Moorish women wear their ḥaïks. Their indoor dress requires a chapter to itself, but its most noteworthy local features are a high peaked head-dress or silken kerchief, starched cone-shape, and an unusually low and scanty bodice. As in the other inland towns, with a few exceptions the Jews are not allowed to go shod or to ride outside their quarter, and they may not ride horses at all. Except in the business centre and in the portions immediately adjacent to the melláḥ, the number of Jews to be encountered is very small,—especially in bad weather—which is not surprising in view of the restrictions and indignities imposed upon them. The Nazarene Fandaḳ, or Foreigners' Hostel, formerly stood near the melláḥ, just beyond the "Gate of the Lion" (Báb es-Seba'a) * beside which the governor of New Fez sits to do justice.

Admission to the palace—built in 1750[1]— and to the Government offices, is obtained by the Báb Kubîbat es-

* This gate was so named, according to Moorish tradition, because a lion which had been delivered from a serpent by one Alonzo Perez de Guzman, in the reign of Ferdinand the Holy, followed his benefactor to this gate. This De Guzman was the ancestor of the dukes of Medina Sidonia.[2]

[1] Godard, p. 48. [2] Torres, pp. 240—242.

S'min, but the palace enclosure, which occupies a considerable portion of the new town, has its own gates opening outside as well as into the city. Between the "Lion's Gate" and the Báb Kubîbat es-S'min is the large quadrangle in which foreign envoys are received in public audience, and where the country governors present their tribute at the great feasts. The glaringly modern gate-way on the west side, dated 1308 (1891), is the main entrance to the new arms factory, built and managed by the Italian Military Mission, and intended also for use as a mint. Some undershot iron water-wheels in the gardens hard by are also the work of Europeans. The new ḳaṣbah was erected by Mulai er-Rasheed in 1671.[1] *The Palace.*

Outside the walls of Fez are three forts in good repair, still called by the European name "bastions," as they were built by renegades and Christian slaves, about the year 1590.[2] It is said that they were erected on behalf of the towns-people, and opposite the well of 'Aïn 'Alû in the main street is shown the door of a passage understood to communicate with the fort between Gîsa and Maḥurôḳ gates. Near this fort are the great tombs or ḳubbát of the Beni Marîn,* and between it and the town are natural caves enlarged by the extraction of building material, now made use of in winter to stable camels, but, as mentioned earlier, once allotted to the lepers for a residence. *Forts.*

Of the veneration with which Fez has been always regarded something has been said already. It contains more mosques than any other city in Morocco, and their number is reckoned at two hundred *Mosques.*

* For illustration see *The Moorish Empire*, p. 95.

[1] Ez-Zaïáni, p. 22.

[2] El Ufráni, p. 260. Braithwaite (p. 206) says that one of them was the work of an Englishman in 1690.

and six. Ordinary saint-houses are not unusually abundant inside the walls, but these are numerous outside.* The chief mosques of Fez are in the old town, where two prominences noticeable on the general slope of the ground have been utilized for the erection of the most famous temples of Morocco, those of Mulai Idrees and the Ḳarûeeïn.

Mosque of Mulai Idrees.

The former was built by Mulai Idrees the younger, founder of Fez, about the year 810: it was restored on on the same lines in 1308,[1] and rebuilt by Mulai Isma'îl in 1720.[2] The streets which approach its entrance are sacred, and are an inviolable sanctuary, being considered in this respect equal to a mosque, so that Jews, Christians or four-footed beasts are not allowed within, though it is not necessary to remove one's slippers. The ends of these streets have chains or bars across to mark them, and they are very well paved with red bricks. The principal one, which runs up to the Tûmîat door of the saint's tomb, has a pretty arched gate.† In this one the shops are of a better class, and sell special articles. Among them are native bees' wax candles to burn round the tomb, for those of foreign manufacture would not be holy enough.

Numerous refugees are usually to be seen squatting

* In 1190, in the reign of Ya'ḳûb el Manṣûr, there were counted 725 mosques or saint-houses, 42 public lavatories, 80 drinking-spouts and troughs, 22 washing places, 93 public baths, and 472 flour-mills inside the walls as well as many more outside. In the reign of Ya'ḳûb's son were counted 89,236 houses, 1941 lodgings for single men, 467 fandaḳs for merchants and visitors, 9082 shops, 2 bazaars (ḳaïṣariyát), 3064 manufactories, 117 public lavatories, 86 tanneries, 116 dye-works, 12 copper-works, 136 public bread-ovens and 1170 other ovens.[3]

† I was very near trouble in this street one day, when my eye-glasses having aroused suspicion, I was hailed by a shop-keeper with a summons to testify to Mohammed, but removing them. I affected not to hear, and before the lethargic zealot could leave his shop, I was well round the corner, lost in the crowd, as I was clad like a native.

[1] *Raôḍ el Ḳarṭás.* [2] Ez-Zaiáni, p. 22. [3] *Raôḍ el Ḳarṭás.*

about, and the custom prevails for pious Muslims to speak to these poor people, and when they confess, to endeavour to make peace between them and their pursuers, often taking them out of sanctuary under their own protection, when it would be an outrage to arrest the protégé, who is usually provided with an inscribed board or some other patent of protection.

The Sanctuary.

Opposite the Tûmîat door the late sultan rebuilt a refuge for friendless shareefas, where they were fed and lodged under the care of other shareefas—female descendants of Mohammed—and the superintendence of the muḳaddam or "ancient" of the saint's tomb. To the left of this entrance to the shrine, in a side street, is a plain door leading direct into the adjoining mosque, entering which at the evening prayer-hour, I was able to examine the interior.

An Asylum.

Following the sacred street round to the right, there is a fountain, and further on a door which is seldom opened, but which has a hole into which the faithful cast their offerings. Near the Báb Sidi Bûjîda, in the Keddán, is the N'zálah (resting-place) of Mulai Idrees, a tiled seat protected by a bar of wood, with an alms-box in the middle, to mark a spot on which that worthy used to sit. This also is a sanctuary, and alms deposited in the box go to the mosque.

Alms-boxes.

The Tûmîat door was once very beautiful, but it is now much faded. It is of wood, divided into several low arches of equal size, carved and painted in pink and gold, with the creed of Islám worked into a rectangular pattern over the centre. Through these doors is seen a carpeted chamber with mattresses round the walls like an ordinary native reception-room. Beyond this is another antechamber, and then the tomb in the ḳûbbah beyond; but the direct way is barred by a grating. Passing round to the left, the

The Shrine.

visitor enters the body of the mosque—rich in tile-work, the large court in particular,—and an exit is obtained by the M'jedleeïn door, leading into the 'Aṭṭârîn.

The Tomb.

The actual tomb and its surroundings are the finest in Morocco.* Here lie Mulai Idrees II. and his brother Mohammed I. The sarcophagus itself resembles a large casket-shaped chest about seven feet by three, and three feet high to the edge, with a raised lid, flat on the top, about eighteen inches higher, to which the sides slope from the edge. It is covered with rich, gold-embroidered cloth, and both surrounded and surmounted by gilt censers, with a taller one in the centre. These, and most of the gilt ornaments are reputed to be gold, but this it is impossible to ascertain during an ordinary visit.†

Decoration.

Gold-braided hangings adorn the walls, and carpets—both native and European—the floors. Exquisitely carved and painted arabesques give warmth to the ceiling,‡ from which are suspended lanterns and chandeliers in profusion, one of the former being of great size—eight feet high, it is said. These are interspersed with numerous oil-lamps—tumblers with floating wicks,—while several handsome candle-sticks stand on the floor, so that there is no lack of glare, and the heat when the

* For many of these minor details I have relied on the description of my native servant, whom I sent in to make a closer examination than was possible for me.

† Rohlfs speaks of this display as contrary to the teachings of the Ḳor'án, and mentions a massive silver plate under glass, with an inscription in gold letters, which I did not see. [1]

‡ "I have been told that the ceiling of the Mosque of Mulai Idrees is the repository for State documents of high importance, such as, for instance, the papers of allegiance of Fez to successive Sultans, and the like. I remember hearing, when Mulai 'Abd el Aziz succeeded in 1894, that a formal copy of the document attesting the allegiance of Fez to the new sultan had been deposited there."—J. MacIver MacLeod.

place is crowded, must be intense, especially when it is remembered how many of the worshippers bring candles. Among other conspicuous ornaments, after the native fashion, are two large "grand-father" clocks, and three round gilt time-pieces. To the left of the sarcophagus, regarded from the mosque, stands the alms-chest, richly ornamented; and before the tomb is the monbar or pulpit, from the foot of which the motions of the worshippers are led by the imám, so that, while facing the east, they also face the shrine.

Reputed Sanctity.

The reputed sanctity of this spot is so great that although it might mean death or acceptance of Islám for an "infidel" to be found in any mosque in Morocco, this one is by far the most dangerous to visit, and only two or three Europeans have ever entered it.* The natives believe that the angel Gabriel periodically visits the shrine, and that if any worshipper has the good luck to touch the hem of his garment, his admission to Paradise is secured. The chance of such a fortunate event is enough in itself to attract these conscience-stricken sinners, and doubtless accounts in some measure for the crowds who daily pay their respects there.

The Karûeeïn

Separated from the Mosque of Mulai Idrees by the ḳaïṣarîyah, a little further down the hill to the south, is the famous mosque of the Ḳarûeeïn. Its foundations were laid on the first day of Rámaḍan, A.C. 859, by a widow who had bought the ground and supplied the building expenses from a large inherited fortune.† All materials were found upon the spot, the well from which the water was drawn still existing in the courtyard. Since 918 A.C. the Friday

* Caillé did so in 1825.

† Some authors state that a sister of this widow supplied the fund for the building of the Andalûs Mosque.

sermon (khoṭbah) has been heard by the Court or its representative in the Ḳarûeeïn instead of in the Shorfa or Mulai Idrees mosque.

Its History.

According to an inscription over the west door, the present tower was built with a fifth of the booty taken from foreigners. On the top was placed a ball covered with gold and encrusted with precious stones, surmounted by the sword of Idrees II., whose descendants quarrelled with the builders, and in vain endeavoured to recover it. This tower having become the abode of storks and pigeons, it was repaired in 1289 from tribute paid by foreigners. On a dome built where the original tower had stood, were placed talismans on iron spikes, to shield the place from evil,* such as a figure of a bird holding a scorpion in its beak, to prevent the entrance of those insects; a ball to frighten serpents away; and one to keep mice out. Most remarkable stories are told to prove the efficacy of these not very Mohammedan devices. The lavatory was rebuilt in 1120, a special conduit being made to supply the water.

Enlargements.

The next enlargements were made in 1133, when the property of certain Jews which was needed for the building, was seized and paid for at a valuation, as the owners would not sell. The mihrab was at this time richly adorned with gold and colours, and when 'Abd el Mûmin took the city in 1145, the scribes had it papered and whitewashed inside the night before the new ameer was to attend the service, in order to avoid his reproaches for this display.† A large addition, and the door approached by stairs, were made in 1208. The great chair was then added prob-

* Could this, by any chance, have been to protect it from lightning?

† 'Abd el Mû'min changed all the officials on the ground that they could not speak Berber, and were therefore useless, which shows how important a part that language must have then played.

ably the one still in use. In 1898 the Karûeeïn was re-painted and re-plastered by the present sultan, and when the old plaster was scraped off the mihrab the original gilding and painting was revealed after seven centuries and a half, thus confirming the record quoted in the *Raôḍ el Ḳarṭás*, which tells the story.

The most ample details of every improvement made in this mosque are preserved by the Moors, including the number of bricks and tiles used in the work: everything had to be pure and sanctified, and even the money could only be derived from certain sources. The chief court was paved in A.C. 1131 with fifty-two thousand bricks, above which was a layer of tiles, and it was formerly shaded by a movable awning. In the centre is a marble fountain constructed in 1222, supplied by a leaden pipe from the reservoir. In 1325, when the number of columns was two hundred and seventy, the number of worshippers who could be accommodated was calculated at twenty-two thousand, and it is said that it has been frequently filled to overflowing, which must have caused a dense crowd in the narrow streets approaching it. Even now the Friday prayers are a sight worth seeing, and a sound worth hearing, so great is the concourse.

Details Preserved.

The large lamp is stated to weigh 1763 lbs., and to have 509 lights. It is very seldom lit, but at one time this was done each night of Ramaḍán. Now only long rows of lights are lit down the centre of the aisles except on the eve of the 27th of Ramadán, when the mosque is illuminated to the greatest possible extent The total number of lights is given as seventeen hundred, and these are said to require three and a half cwt. of oil for one filling.

Illumination.

During the repairs of 1898 three large brass chandeliers taken down to be cleaned were found to be really old

European bells. The largest is about four feet in height, and twelve feet in circumference at the rim. In bas-relief, about 3 in. deep, forming a sort of band about 15 in. from the rim of this bell, is an inscription in Roman letters, the best available transcription of which is as follows:—

"MEHTSEMSANTA SPONTANANE VOROE. MOECET. PATRE LIBERACIONEMENT 1219."

Between the final T and the initial M there is an ornament resembling a star, knot, or garter. Between the inscription and the rim there are, in bas-relief and at equal distances, four devices, namely an eagle, a lion, a bull, and another which could not be identified.* This bell has lamps fixed to the rim only, so that the inscription and devices are easily seen, but so many lamps have been attached to the outsides of the other bells, that any inscriptions there may have been on them are hidden.†

Description.

The Ḳarûeeïn is celebrated as the largest mosque in Africa, but it is by no means the most magnificent. Its merits have been greatly over-rated by many writers, whose descriptions have been compiled from hearsay, and not from a personal inspection, as has been my privilege. It bears no small resemblance to a vast store, with a roof which, on account of the area covered, appears very low, and is supported by three hundred and sixty-six square pillars of stone, not marble, as is frequently asserted. The side chapel for

* These would be the emblems of the four evangelists, so the last would be a man, and may have been purposely obliterated.

† For this most interesting piece of information the public is indebted to Mr. MacIver MacLeod, British Vice-Consul in Fez, who obtained it by sending in a Moor able to read European characters to report, and who has also very kindly revised this and other chapters both in Mss. and proof.

A PEEP INTO THE ḲARÛEEÏN.
(Moors washing feet before prayers.)
Photograph by R. J. Moss, Esq.

services for the dead contains twenty-four more. All these columns support horse-shoe arches, on which the roof is built, long vistas of which are to be seen from each of its eighteen doors.

Decoration.

The pillars in the main building are covered nearly to the spring of the arches—about six feet—with yellow rush matting, which is also spread over the floor, except in the two courts open to the sky, which are inlaid with coloured tiles. Here are the only marble columns in the mosque: one court containing sixteen, divided between two handsome porticoes at each end, with fountains underneath; the other containing twelve, which bring up the total number of pillars to four hundred and eighteen. One of the marble fountains—that at the foot of the tower—was erected in 1588, being bought for its weight in sugar,[1] while the cupola over the second fountain—the western—was erected in 1620[2]

Nocturnal Chanting.

From the tower of Ḳarûeeïn ten muédhdhins summon the faithful to prayer, and what otherwise might be the silent watches of the night are enlivened for the five hours preceding the dawn by each one mounting the minaret in turn and chanting the praises of the Almighty for half an hour without ceasing, at times with rich voice and in weirdly beautiful cadence. At the Mulai Idrees and Ersîf mosques there are but three muédhdhins, so the chanting only begins an hour and a half before sunrise, when a veritable concert is produced. The necessary funds are provided by a special endowment.

Other Notable Mosques.

The other notable mosques of the old town are as follows. The Andalûs already mentioned, remained as it was built until 1204, when it was repaired, the large north door being then built, and a conduit made from near Báb el Ḥadeed to

[1] El Ufráni, p. 261, where its inscription is given in full. [2] Ib. 397

supply the fountain. In 1297 it was again repaired, and the conduit, broken during a famine, was restored. Its beautiful doorway is a conspicuous object above the surrounding roofs. Close by is the the Jama' Noor, in which are shown some ancient remains, consisting of a piece of very old wall and a bricked-up door, said to have existed long before Fez did, the building of which the Moors ascribe to Nimrod!

The Ersîf, finished by Mulai Sulaïmán II. in the last century, has a fine tiled tower in a good state of preservation, two marble fountains and a large marble laver. These fountains and lavers are in every case of European workmanship, and white in colour.

The Madarsat Abû 'Ainán, with a large round white marble fountain, black, white and red marble pavement, and painting in gold and colours, was formerly the centre from which five hundred pupils received daily allowances, but this fund, called the manîa, is now administered by the Ḳarûeeîn.

Minor Mosques.

The mosque of Sidi Ahmad es-Sháwî, with the handsome tomb of that saint, can be well seen only by turning past the tomb to the left in a street prohibited to Christians. It was built by Mohammed XVIII. El Hasan III., his son, added the handsome shrine and tower of Sidi Hamed ben Yahyà near the Báb el Gîsa, and the present sultan has caused the erection of a new shrine for Sidi Bûjîda, outside the gate named after that saint.

The remaining mosques of the old town are: the Báb el Gîsa mosque, with orange trees and fountain in the court; the Dîwán, with a marble laver; the Shrábeleeïn with two trees and a fountain; the Bûjilûd in the ḳaṣbah of that name; the Madarsat el Wád (so called because the river flows through it), planted with four trees; and that of the Ḳaṣbat en-Nûár,

Mosques of New Fez.

In New Fez the chief mosques are: El Kabeer or the Great, with its fountains and stream, a handsomely decorated building in which the sultan prays in a portion screened off from the public gaze, entering by a door from the palace: that of Mulai 'Abd Allah: and El Ḥamrá or "the Red"—with a prettily tiled roof,—which stands not far from a small old one, called El Baïḍa or "the White," with its minaret all askew, like a miniature tower of Pisa.

Interest.

So much for the Fez of to-day, by far the most interesting town in Morocco, both as to its history and its contents, well worth a visit from the intelligent explorer able to appreciate and study things Moorish. What it may become in a generation it would be bootless to guess. There is just a possibility that it may still be the rambling city it now is, but the chances are all in favour of its seeing many alterations ere that, in its inhabitants, if not in its stones. It is by no means improbable that by that time the proud Fásîs may have to own a different master from the easy-going shareefs of the present dynasty. Who can say?

PANORAMA OF MEQUINEZ.

Molinari, Photo., Tangier.

CHAPTER THE FIFTEENTH

IMPERIAL CITIES—2

MIKNÁS (MEQUINEZ)

LEAST imposing of the three imperial cities, hardly metropolitan in character, Mequinez has none the less its special interests, and an important place in modern Moorish history.* Here Ismá'īl the blood-thirsty held his Court, and here, in days when Moorish pirates swept the seas, the European captives fared their worst. From very early times some settlement appears to have existed on this spot, which is referred to under its present name in the tenth century,[1] but Idreesi, writing about 1100, describes the place, which he calls Takarárt,[2] as still an ordinary agadîr or citadel, surrounded by villages which afterwards coalesced to form the city. Consequently its foundation was marked by no flourish of trumpets, as it gradually rose out of a Berber settlement.

Interest.

Origin.

Away to the south-east, between Fez and Oojda, lies the home of what remains of the Miknása tribe, whose members played so important a part in building up the Empire, and became the masters

History. †

* M. Houdas has translated a historical description of this city dating from 1533, entitled *Er-Raôḍ el Hátûn fi Akhbár Miknásat ez-Zaïtûn*, by one of its ḳáḍîs, but it is only the usual unsatisfactory discursive mélange and record of trivialities, containing practically nothing of present importance.

† *The Moorish Empire* contains the following historical references to Mequinez: Christians transported there, p. 61; taken by Abd el Mû'min,

[1] *Raôḍ el Kartás*, p. 61 (ann. 941). [2] p. 88.

of a kingdom in it during the tenth and eleventh centuries. To them Miknás owes its present name, for they supplied the original settlers. These were supplemented in 1126 by tributary Christians exiled from Granáda by Ali III. The existing city dates only from 1150, when its predecessor was destroyed at the close of a seven years' siege, and the new city built by 'Abd el Mû'min the Muwáḥḥadi, who had massacred its men and pillaged its ḥareems.[1] Under the Beni Marîn a citadel and mosque were built in 1276 by Ya'ḳûb II. (bin 'Abd el Ḥaḳḳ) at the same time as New Fez, but this mosque was destroyed by lightning, and has long since been rebuilt.[2] Towards the close of the eighteenth century Sulaïmán II. was besieged in Mequinez by 15,000 Berber supporters of one of his rival brothers, and surrounded as it is by semi-independent tribes, the city has always been subject to their raids.

Position.

Mequinez is situated at the western end of the plain which has Fez at the other extremity—about 36 m. distant,—and the nearest town is the forbidden Mulai Idrees Zarhôn, among the hills, a short day's journey to the north. The nearest port is Rabat, which, however, cannot be reached direct, but by way of Mehedîya, a journey of three or three and a half days. Its position is 33° 56′ N. and 5° 50′ W., and its height above the sea-level is about sixteen hundred feet.

Situation.

Viewed from the hills of Zarhôn, Mequinez presents a more striking appearance than any town of Morocco excepting Marrákesh. Lying almost on a level, with a series of little valleys between it and

62, 71; rebuilt, 73; lost by 'Ali IV., 86; supremacy of Tunis acknowledged, 92; taken by Abu Bakr, and retaken by 'Ali IV., 92; buildings by Ya'ḳûb II., 96; taken by Mohammed X., 118-9: Mulai Ismá'îl's building mania, 159-60; 'Abd Allah V. recalled, 165; dîwán of black troops removed here, 166; El Ḥasan III.'s expedition, 187-9; 'Abd el Azîz IV. passes through, 194; effects of Lisbon earthquake, 263 (n.).

[1] *Raúd el Kartás*, p. 379.

[2] *Raúd el Hátûn.*

the base of the hills, and a background of mountains wherein dwell the Beni M'gîld and other fierce tribes, it is seen to advantage, appearing a city of palaces, with its many mosque towers and the extensive buildings of Mulai Ismá'îl away to the left. On approaching from this quarter, it is ever and anon concealed from view by undulating ground, only to appear again in diminishing splendour, till the dingy-looking walls, relieved by the fine tile-work on the Báb Barda'în, are reached. On the Fez side, after passing out through the Báb Bû 'Amáïr, the city is speedily hidden from sight, as the road descends through the vast grove of olives with which the town is encircled, and which lend it the distinctive epithet of Miknásat ez-Zaïtûnah—"Mequinez the Olivet." "Beware," writes a native author, "of denying the beauty of Mequinez, which has never failed to be appreciated. If the hand of time were to efface all land-marks of the town, its beauty would assuredly have left some traces."[1] But for Europeans these picturesque groves derive a melancholy interest from the remembrance that they were planted by Christian slaves.[2]

Walls and Gates.

The walls are of the usual mud-concrete type, grim but crumbling, fairly high, defended by quadrangular towers, and pierced by nine gates. These are: Es-Shîba, Bardáïn, El Melláḥ, Zeen el 'Abdîn, Bû 'Amáïr,* Bilķári, El Ķaṣdîr, Tîrîmi and Ṣôķ el 'Azád. Of these the Báb Barda'în, already mentioned, is the most imposing, but the Báb Manṣûr el 'Alj ("the Renegade"), which leads to the palace, is by far the finest specimen of that class of architecture in Mequinez, and probably in Morocco. It was finished in 1732, at the same time as the ramparts of the ķáṣbah.†[3] On

* So called from a former name of the river.

† For illustrations, see *The Moorish Empire*, p. 165.

[1] Jábir el Ghassári, quoted in *Er-Raôḍ el Hátûn*.

[2] Puerto, bk. xi, ch. xv.

[3] Ez-Zaïáni, p. 71.

the right, close to the Báb Zeen el 'Abdîn,—a mere hole in the low wall,—are the ruins of a large mosque known as the Jama' Rûá, or "Stable Mosque," from having adjoined Ismá'íl's vast stable accommodation.

Ancient Remains.

Passing through the Gate of the Renegade, the governor's seat of justice is reached. Its style of architecture is curious, to say the least of it, with its ancient pillars, which are reputed to have been brought with others from old Roman works at Salli. Perchance they, as well as many more of the huge pillars and blocks of stone to be seen along this road and elsewhere, came from the ruins called Ḳaṣar Faráôn or Volubilis, in the plain below Mulai Idrees Zarhôn. Part of the road between these ruins and Mequinez is strewn with huge blocks, just as they were left by the hundreds of slaves who were transporting them when word was passed along that their tyrant Ismá'íl was dead. There they let them drop, and there they lie yet, a century and a half later.

The Palace.

The Palace, which is still used as an occasional place of residence by the sultans, was the work of Mulai Ismá'íl in the latter part of the seventeenth century. It is a big, rambling place, with massive tabìa (mud-concrete) walls, some of them stated to be twenty-five feet thick.* A good description of it is given in the account by Windus of Commodore Stewart's Embassy in 1721, when it was in its glory. The writer says it was nearly square, and about four miles in circumference, the outside walls extending for a mile.[1] The interior is composed of oblong courtyards, many of them of greater area than Lincoln's Inn Fields, surrounded by buildings and arcades, the ver-

* As a memorial of their labour spent upon them the Christian slaves affixed to them three fleurs de lys, and the date, 1677.[2]

[1] p. 112. [2] MOUETTE, p. 147.

andahs under which are decorated with chequered tiles. Several of these squares contained gardens, in some

COURT OF HOUSE IN MEQUINEZ.
(In which a Belgian Embassy was lodged.)
Photograph by H. E. the Baron Whettnall.

instances, says Windus, sunk sixty or seventy feet, which must be somewhat exaggerated, *Gardens.*

although he attempts to strengthen his assertion by adding that they were planted with cypresses of which only the tops were to be seen; but then all cypresses are not twenty yards high. One of these gardens was spanned by a bridge, five yards wide. They were shaded by vines trained over trellises, and carpeted with clover. A different taste this from that of a better known tyrant, who indulged in "hanging gardens!" This wretch was wont to take the air, not as Cowper describes the London citizens of his day, "close-packed and smiling in a chaise and pair," but alone in a peculiar vehicle on springs, drawn by his women and eunuchs, whom alone he suffered to approach him.[1]

Decoration of Palace.

The palace contains many buildings, called ḳûbbahs—of which our word "alcove" is a corruption through the Spanish. These are more or less square, with a large doorway on one side, and pyramidal roofs ornamented outside with green glazed tiles, and inside with richly carved and painted wood-work in Mauresque style. The walls are tiled to a height of four or five feet in the geometrical mosaics of cut glazed tiles for which Fez is famous: above this height they are finished in plaster, plainly white-washed or carved into exquisite filigree work. Tiles are frequently employed throughout all the apartments; walks, stores, passages and arches being thus adorned. One of the passages is described as thirty feet wide and a quarter of a mile long: this served as a portion of Mulai Ismá'íl's armoury, for it was bordered from end to end by three rows of rails with saddles, and above were cases of arms.[2]

Marble Pillars.

Many pillars of marble and other stones, with finely-worked plaster arches are to be seen, but now all are more or less coated and disfigured with white-wash, often over an eighth of an inch thick,

[1] WINDUS, p. 129. [2] Ib., p. 108.

even on the beautiful tile-work. Some of the pillars were brought from Salli, others are Italian, forty having been brought from Genoa at one time, early in the eighteenth century, by the renegade Pillet, for $16,000, chiefly paid in Christian slaves.[1] The gates of Laraiche, taken from the Spaniards, also figured here, much of the iron-work and many of the swords being of similar origin. The amount of manual labour expended in the completion of this palace was, of course, enormous. It has been computed that no fewer than thirty thousand men, including a large number of Christian slaves, and ten thousand animals, were employed upon it at one time. In the park which surrounds the palace—called Agudál, like that in Marrákesh—wild beasts were formerly kept, and more recently ostriches.[2]

European Slaves.

Until Ismá'íl had them destroyed in 1693, and replaced them by some of its numerous buildings, immense underground dwellings in the old Tannery Quarter were allotted to the Christian captives. This great "bagnio" is stated to have been 155 varas long by 7 or 8 wide, having twenty-four arches, and a bridge across, with water running down the middle and across an open court. In it there was a church, and when the palace was destroyed the friars bought the ruins and built a hospital with eighty beds upon the site.* This was destroyed in 1790,[3] but portions of the subterranean dungeons continue to exist beside their builder's tomb, and are occasionally used for "barracks."[4] The remains of the ḳaṣbahs of Dár Dabîbah, near Fez, and Bû Fakrán, near Mequinez, are monuments of the piracy

* The friars also treated the natives medically, until they found their prescriptions abused, and had recourse to a decoction of herbs and honey which was given to all applicants as "dûá-shareef" or "noble physic."[5]

[1] De la Mercy, p. 275. [2] Erckmann, p. 29.
[3] See *The Moorish Empire*, p. 201.
[4] Harris, *Land*, p. 81. For illustration, see Montbart. [5] Jackson, p. 121.

period, for they were rebuilt in 1746—50 by the crews of the English privateer *Inspector*.*[1]

Most of the existing buildings of Mequinez owe their origin to Mulai Ismá'il's mania for public works—although his brother Rasheed had built the palace of En-Náṣir in the ḳaṣbah—but the suburb of Er-Rîáḍ, which Ismá'il built for his Court, was destroyed by his son 'Abd Allah V. in 1733,[2] and the city suffered seriously from the earthquake of 1755.[3] The melláḥ dates from the same reign, the Christian slaves having completed it in 1682 after three years of labour, which the Jews escaped by the payment of a ransom.[4]

Buildings.

Mequinez has earned the worst possible reputation for morals, rivalling Sodom and Gomorrah in the tale of its wickedness. Nevertheless it has the orthodox plenitude of mosques, five of which may be mentioned as worthy of note. These are: the Kabeer or "Great," the Najjárîn or "Carpenters," that of the Báb Barda'ín, the Tût, and that of Lallah (or Lady) 'Odah. Under the Beni Marîn the number of mosques is said to have reached four hundred,[5] and in the seventeenth century one hundred and fifty mosques and shrines were reported by Puerto, in thirty of which the khoṭbah was recited on Fridays.[6]

Mosques.

The patron saint of the city is Sidi Mohammed bin 'Aïsà, the founder of the 'Aïsàwi brotherhood, whose orgies at the feast of Mohammed's birth-day are degrading and revolting in their bestiality.[7] Mequinez is consequently its head-quarters, which fact adds not a little to the city's reputation for bigotry and

Saints.

* A day's ride distant is the ḳaṣbah of Agûrai, still peopled by the descendants of the European slaves established there two hundred years ago.

[1] TROUGHTON'S *Narrative*.
[2] EZ-ZAIANI, p. 72. EN-NÁSIRI, vol. iv., p. 63.
[3] Ib. p. 121.
[4] PHELPS, p. 13.
[5] *Raód el Ḳártás*.
[6] p. 642
[7] Described in *The Moors*, ch. xiv.

fanaticism. The other rijál el blád or "men of the place" —that is, its saints,—are Ḳaddûr el 'Alámi, Aḥmad bin Khádîr, 'Asa'ïd Busáṭmán and Mulai 'Abd Allah bin Aḥmad. To the shrines of each of these is ascribed great sanctity, and they attract large numbers of pilgrims to Mequinez as a centre, while others flock directly to the tombs of Mulai Ismá'il and his countless sons. Up in the hills of Zarhôn, on the right of the road to Mulai Idrees, is a large village containing the shrine of Sidi 'Ali ben Ḥamdûsh, the founder of the Ḥamádshà brotherhood, whose rites are in some respects akin to those of the 'Aïsáwà.

Present Condition.

The streets of Mequinez are typical thoroughfares for Morocco, but, being more or less on a level, are absolutely impassable in winter, except by wading up to the ankles in mud, which entails the use of the pattens called "ḳabáḳab."* The Jewish quarter is as usual the worst in this respect, for which it alone is remarkable, although the best streets of the madinah bear a strong resemblance to an English farm-yard. A line of straw, house-rubbish and filth of every description borders each side of the way, which when fairly trodden down, forms a rude pavement, as distinguished from the gutter of liquid mire and slush in the centre.

Business Quarters.

The markets will not compare with those of Fez and Marrákesh, nor do many of the shops have the same appearance of prosperity, although in the best streets they do not suffer by comparison. In spite of numerous fandaḳs, the amount of business accomplished is small in proportion to that of Fez, and the paucity of the means of communication with

* Pory has well made Leo say in his translation, "This towne is so durtie in the spring-time, that it would irke a man to walke the streets."[1]

[1] Hak. ed., p 414.

other cities suffices to show how small is the commerce of Mequinez. No regular couriers ran to any other town, till the Moors started one to Fez a few years ago, and a second was established by private venture. No foreign Governments are represented here, nor were there any resident Europeans till the American Gospel Union made it a mission station in 1895. There is one prison, which the Government succeeds in keeping well-occupied, using it both for criminals and State victims.

Inhabitants.

The population has been varyingly estimated at twenty, forty and fifty thousand, the truth probably lying between thirty and forty, but there is no possibility of verifying these figures. A goodly proportion of mulattos represent the Bokhárà, Ûdáïà and other troops imported from Timbuctoo by Mulai Ismá'īl, and the many white slaves brought in at the same time cannot fail to have left a considerable trace among the inhabitants of the town. The men have a good name for bravery, and the women are famed throughout Morocco for their beauty, which is not, however, of a type to captivate Europeans.

Manufactures.

The occasional presence of the Court alone rescues Mequinez for a time from its "dead-alive" condition. Its manufactures are by no means important, yet they include gun-locks, ploughs, swords, knives, pack-saddles, pattens and turned-wood articles, such as rosaries. In the sixteenth century this town was famous for its selhâms, and much silk was cultivated in the neighbourhood,[1] but these are things of the past, although the Miknásîs are no whit behind the Fásîs and Marrákshîs in dyeing and weaving. The little stream outside the gate which waters the gardens and turns the corn-mills is called Bû-Fakrán—"Father of Tortoises"—

[1] TORRES, p. 204.

a name as applicable to the town, by reason of the character of its inhabitants. The streets have by no means a busy look, and though of the regulation width —or rather narrowness—they are seldom crowded like those of Fez, or even of Marrákesh or the ports. In short, its glories, such as they were, have departed, and nothing remains save decay and ruin.

Kûtûbîya Tower.

PANORAMA OF MARRÁKESH.

Photograph by Herbert White, Esq.

CHAPTER THE SIXTEENTH

IMPERIAL CITIES — 3

MARRÁKESH (MOROCCO CITY)

"MARRÁKESH* the Red!" What a picture the name conjures up! Near the edge of the great red plain—Bláḍ el Ḥamrá—of Central Morocco, north of the principal Great Atlas group, Yûsef bin Táshfîn built him a city nine hundred years ago.† Historians talk of Bocanum Hemerum, a Roman station, as having existed near here,[1] perhaps on the spot, but who knows? Traces there certainly are not, and the native story runs that in 1062 Yûsef purchased the virgin soil for his camp, erecting thereon a town which 'Ali III., his son, enclosed with a wall in 1132. Probably little remains of those walls, for many have been the sieges through which the Red City has passed, and its circumvallation has never been more substantial than hard-rammed mud concrete, dug close by.‡ *Origin.*

* There is no record as to the origin of this word, but the ingenious Louis Rinn derives it from *ar* or *ur* = sons, and the name Kush, with an M prefixed.[2]

† Its immediate predecessor as the capital of the kingdom was Aghmáṭ, some hours' ride to the south on the slopes of the Atlas, which has since been abandoned, and is now little more than a name, though still a place of pilgrimage in 1765.[3] It is commonly pronounced by the Moors Ghomáṭ. See *The Moorish Empire*, pp. 47, 58 and 71.

‡ *The Moorish Empire* contains the following historical allusions to Marrákesh: building, p. 53; Ibn Tûmart defeated there, 70; taken by

[1] CHENIER, vol. i., p. 55; GRÅBERG p. 291.
[2] *Origines Berbères*, p. 332
[3] EZ-ZAIÁNI, p. 141.

The Walls.

See them as they crumble on, dinted and riven and undermined, but serving their purpose; twenty or thirty feet high, flanked with frequent square towers; pierced only by seven grim portals—though in Abu'l Fîda's time there were seventeen. The foundations and the gate-ways are, it is true, of stone, but the superstructure is incapable of resisting serious attacks, even without artillery. Including the Agudál parks, the walls are some seven miles round, but the city wall proper measures rather less than half as much. Although rebuilt in 1756,—when also the mosque of El Manṣûr in the ḳaṣbah, and the Barîma mosque were restored[1]—they are in many places sadly out of repair. The gardens through which one approaches under the palm-groves are divided by walls of similar, but much inferior, substance, and impart a misconception as to the durability of these hoary masses of concrete, more impressive at close quarters in that from a distance they appear so mean.

Appearance.

Above them rise innumerable mosque and saint-house towers, here and there one made conspicuous by fretted stone-work, but higher than any the Kûtûbîya, monument of the Muwáḥḥadi Ya'ḳûb el Manṣûr—seven centuries a witness of his might,—the landmark for a day's journey. Ragged storks' nests add a picturesqueness to some of these towers, and to many of the higher roofs, which are as usual flat and whitewashed. The houses themselves are of the same red earth as the walls—but with a greater admixture of brown,

Abd el Mû'min, 71; monuments of Ya'ḳûb I., 81; Christian bishopric founded here, 85, and deserted 109; church rebuilt, 325, 347, 352; taken by Ya'ḳûb II., 86; regained by Ali V., 103; besieged by Ahmad II., 106; taken by Ahmad IV., 117; buildings in 1563, 121; foreign artisans settled here, 126; visited by Capt. John Smith, 243; Dár el Bidee'a built, 128; taken and sacked by Mohammed XII., 130; by Abu Maḥalli, 132; by Abd Allah el Hispáni, 135; by Er-Rasheed II, 135, 138; in revolt, 181.

[1] Ez-Zaiáni.

—and white streaks where the water-courses, lined with gypsum, protect the surface. Here and there the green-tiled gabled roof of mosque or shrine breaks the monotony, and yonder rise the whitened walls and green-hipped roofs of Dár el Ma<u>k</u><u>h</u>zan—"Government House,"—or the Palace.

Round the Walls.

Hard by this is the Báb er-Rubb, one of the most important gates, as it serves in a measure both madînah and ḳaṣbah, and from it issues a principal track to the Atlas, the foot-slopes of which are five hours' ride over the plain. Some distance beyond Báb er-Rubb are two smaller gates, called those of the Ḳ'ṣábi, leading into the citadel, and beyond them runs the straight wall of the Agudál for nearly an hour's ride before the corner is turned by a disused sugar-mill, erected by an Englishman * several decades ago for the sultan of that day. From this point across the plain may be traced—by the line of Government corn-mills which it turns,—the over-ground water-course from Tasultánt, † supplying the park. To the right branches off the track to Amsmiz, past the Ṣahrîj el Baḳár—"Cattle Tank"—a reservoir about 400 yards square.

Báb Dukálla and Leper Town.

Retracing our steps to the Báb er-Rubb, almost hidden from without by a saint-house and mountains of rubbish, and skirting the walls now on our right, the next gate reached ‡ takes its name from the great province towards which it looks, the fertile Dukálla. A special interest attaches itself to this spot, for here sit the out-cast lepers, forbidden admission, who in lugubrious accents beg of the passers-by. Their own peculiar quarters are situated near here, on the Mogador

* Archibald Fairlie.

† *Anglicé,* "The Sultaness."

‡ The one between has been built up.

track, a miserable village or Hárah of tumble-down hovels, the inmates of which may be known afar by their bowl-like wooden hats or wide-awakes of palmetto. At the various feasts they receive a certain allowance in food and clothes from the Government, but this appears only to have induced non-lepers to settle among them, for theirs is not the contagious Eastern leprosy, such as I have met with in Burma, India, Kashmir and Siberia. In the opinion of some it is but an aggravated form of syphilis, the national disease,* and there is certainly an absence of the revolting sights seen elsewhere. The people themselves have no great fear of the complaint, and occasionally marriages take place between the victims and healthy outsiders, the offspring of which are not all lepers, so that instead of spreading, it is fortunately dying out.

View from Jebel Gîlîz.

From the Dukálla Gate it is a pleasant ride or walk among the palms to Jebel Gîlîz, the only eminence in the immediate vicinity, an isolated rock which rises amid palm groves to a height of some 200 ft. from the plain, here about 1650 ft. above sea-level. It is like a miniature Trichinopoly, and the view from its summit takes one back to another Indian scene, much further north: the general effect of the roof-view of the city spread out below is not unlike that of Delhi, though the sky-line lacks the chaste relief of the peculiar architecture of Hindustán. In many respects, too, the mud-built walls and bazaars recall those of Central Asia, of Bokhára in particular, while parts resemble Baghdád or even tumble-down Bushire.

Palm Groves and Gardens.

But Marrákesh is surrounded by a girdle of date-palms and gardens which add to its picturesqueness, though in summer looking sadly withered and dry at close quarters, but enlivened by innumerable blue-rollers, bee-eaters, doves, and, beside

* See *The Moors*, ch. xii.

the river, king-fishers. These palms, which have become a great source of wealth, are not altogether indigenous, the finest having been introduced from Tafîlált long

BÁB DUKÁLLA MOSQUE, MARRAKESH.

(See p. 308.) *Photograph by Herbert White, Esq.*

ago.* Beyond this setting of green, away in the distance, rises the hoary Atlas, its crevasses indicated by eternal snows, which light up and make *The Atlas.*

* It is said that when the Fîlális besieged Marrákesh, the stones of the dates which were their staple provision being thrown away, took root. The original Marrákesh dates are known as balûḥ, those of Tafîlált as thamr.

prominent its barren peaks. Almost due south of the city the crowning summit, Tûbkál, looms majestic in clear weather, on the Tizi-n Tag͟harat. From its valleys flow cool breezes and cooler streams, refreshing the sultry plain. Well may Ibn Baṭûṭa break forth into verse [1] as he describes the charms of this view, and what the nearness of such mountains means to the city, but unfortunately their recesses are closed to the plainsmen by the hostile Berbers, and the Marrákshîs only get as far on their picnics as the favourite shrine of Mulai Ibrahîm, two days' ride distant.

Báb el K͟hamees Market.

Descending, it is more interesting to pass through the town than to skirt the long stretch of wall to the northern Báb el K͟hamees, the "Gate of the Thursday Market" held close outside. This market is one of the sights of the place,* where cattle and horses and mules are sold, as well as every conceivable country product, and not a few of the coarser foreign importations. Hard by, on the banks of the Issîl, is a reeking slaughter-ground, such as is always to be found outside these towns, and the landscape is diversified by heaps of rubbish which have raised the ground beside it till the gate-way seems to lead into some cave. The track which issues from it leads across the Tansîft by a low bridge of twenty-seven arches,† and through the Jabîlát ridge to the plains of Raḥámna and Mazagan. In summer, though at first increased by melting snow, the Tansîft runs almost dry here, and its tributary the Issîl altogether so.

Báb ed-Dabbág͟h, the "Tannery Gate", is the next in order, on the track to Sidi Raḥal, Damnát, and the Glawi Pass for Tafilált. The neighbouring tan-pits have

* Described in *The Moors*, ch. i.

† Built originally in 1170 by Spanish architects, according to Idreesi. [2]

[1] p. 229. [2] p. 79.

STREET SCENE IN MARRÁKESH.
(Vegetable Market.)

Photograph by Dr. Rudduck.

made the name of Morocco so famous that they deserve a visit, and the primitive methods from which the most advanced have not widely departed are extremely interesting. Further round still, on the south-east comes Báb 'Aïlán, and then Báb Aghmáṭ, the sole reminder, by its name, of the former metropolis in the Ûrîka valley towards which it looks.

Remaining Gates.

Near this latter is the entrance to the melláḥ,—to which admission is gained by way either of the Rîáḍ Zîtûn el Jadeed or of el Ḳadeem (the Olive Garden, New or Old)—and on the other side of the melláḥ is the Báb Barîma, which gives access to the ḳaṣbah and the palace. Government grain stores line the road, which traverses the negro quarter peopled by the mulatto descendants of Mulai Ismá'îl's black troops. Past the handsome Báb Agudál, on the right. the entrance to the palace, the Báb H'már or "Red Gate" is reached, so called on account of the colour in which it is painted, as it is kept in better repair than the other.*

Re-entering the city by this gate, straight in front lies the first of the palace yards, in which state functions take place. Great arched gates—not quite opposite one another—lead into the second and third courts, walls and gates alike being here kept in fair condition. At the side of the third yard is the favourite ḳûbbah or summer-house of the sultan, and close by stand several brass field-guns which afford sanctuary to people bringing complaints to their ruler.

The Great Court Yard.

Returning to the madînah or town by the Báb Barîma,

* Said to have been brought piece-meal from Spain, together with the brass-covered leaves of the Báb el Khamees Several authors state that the Kûtûbîya possessed these bronze-plaqued doors,[1] but others correct them with the assertion that they have seen them on another old mosque;[2] the truth seems to be that the natives do not know which were so procured.

[1] As Puerto, p. 80. [2] As Keatinge, vol. i., p. 289.

and following the ķaşbah wall to the left, the gate called that of the Ķaşbat en-N'hás, or "the Brazen Citadel" is reached, which, like the next, Báb Dár el Bidee'a—Gate of the Mint—leads also into the ķaşbah.* Just inside the latter stands the State Prison, Ḥabs min Ş'baḥ, on the site of the Bidee'a palace built by Aḥmad V., and destroyed by Ismá'íl.[1] By this gate anyone lodged in the Agudál gardens passes in and out of the town, but the public use of these last two is forbidden. Beyond them comes the Báb er-Rubb, which completes the circuit, and in this quarter, known as the Ķ'şûr, surrounded by gardens and open spaces, rises the tower of the Kûtûbîya.

The Circuit Completed.

Beyond the ķaşbah and the palace lie the imperial parks of Agudál,† extended and embellished by Mulai 'Abd er Raḥmán II. in the second quarter of this century,[2] when he brought the water from Tasultánt. The inner Agudál ‡ is reserved for

The Agudal Parks.

* One ancient stone gate of the ķaşbah which had been long closed, was specially opened by the ameer in 1549, and was apparently of foreign workmanship.[3]

† The name implies twists or mazes, being more correctly pronounced Ajdál.

‡ Of this Pellow wrote: "What I was most delighted with, without the walls of Marrákesh, was a most curious and spacious garden for the King's pleasure, when he came to the city, it being by far the finest of all I had ever seen before, being kept in the most exquisite manner, as to its curious and regular walks and arbours, and laid with large collections of most kinds of fruits and flowers, the fruit-trees being very large, and dressed and pruned in a very elegant manner; so that their wood, and especially that of their orange-trees, was always in a prosperous condition, almost ever green, blooming and bearing fruit."

The fruit is sold on the trees by auction when the Sultan is not there. In this park are several gardens, such as the Mámûnîah, where foreign embassies are quartered, and another where foreign merchants visiting the sultans used to be accommodated. The walls of the outer Agudál are in a ruinous condition. The best recent description is by Harris.[4]

[1] El Ufráni, p. 167. [2] En-Násiri, vol. iv., p. 177.
[3] Torres, p. 217. [4] *Land*, p. 198.

the Sultan's exclusive use, and has in it a large reservoir called Ṣaḥrîj el Haná ("Tank of Health"), on which Mulai el Ḥasan III. used to keep a little steamboat for his own amusement.

A MARRAKESH STREET.
Photograph by Dr. Rudduck.

Water-supply.

At one time the water supply of Marrákesh was very abundant, and it is still ample: it dates from the earliest days,[1] and was extended in 1189 by Ya'ḳûb el Manṣûr.[2] Chenier[3] says that six thousand springs (wells?) watered the plain, but that in 1768 it was with difficulty that twelve hundred could be restored. The water is conveyed from a considerable distance—perhaps twenty miles—from the foot of the mountains by under-ground channels (khoṭárát) which might almost be called burrows. As these are seldom bricked or

[1] Idreesi, p. 78. [2] *Raud el Kartás*, p. 386. [3] Vol. i., p. 55.

propped, in order to keep them clear, open man-holes are provided at intervals, and on the side of the city towards the Atlas the ground is full of lines of these pits, old and new.

Although not confined to Marrákesh, this system is not common elsewhere in Morocco, but it is identical with that which I found in Shîráz and other Persian cities. One drawback to it is its great expense. Puerto quotes a local tradition that 20,000 Christians were employed in digging the conduits,[1] referring probably to the El Arcos captives. The water of the Tansîft is strongly tinged by the red earth which is so conspicuous in this district; so also is the salt produced in the vicinity. The natives, however, do not object to the sediment which settles in their water-pots, but consider both waters wholesome. *Peculiar System.*

The Jewry was once well laid out, with streets at right angles, but it has been disgracefully neglected, and is in as bad a state as any melláḥ which approaches it in size. From its one entrance the main street leads round three corners to a market in the centre, the level of which is raised to an extraordinary height by offal. Twelve to fifteen feet would be a moderate estimate of the depth of this accumulation, from which there are steep descents to the houses and side-streets, in which the average depth of the rubbish may be three or four feet. Occasional drinking-troughs alone preserve the original level, and here all day in pools of reeking black slush there is a struggling crowd: needless to say that even in summer the stenches are awful, almost rivalling those of a Chinese city.* *The Melláḥ.*

* De Mairault records the finding about 1766 of a large subterranean vaulted chamber in the melláḥ, containing a coarse marble sarcophagus filled with dust, which bore "hieroglyphic" inscriptions, and a second marble box containing arms.[2]

[1] p. 81. [2] p. 344.

Throughout this quarter there is hardly one house with a passable exterior, the walls being generally built of tiles, with mud which gets washed out from the face by heavy rains, leaving the tiles protruding. It is only by their height that the better class houses are to be distinguished; some are really large and commodious, or increased accommodation is secured by communication between several of them. The interiors of these Jewish mansions are grand indeed beside the tumble-down neglected courtyards adjoining, but wherever there is an attempt at display it is tawdry; the colours are glaring, and the effect is an extravagant vulgarity, different far from the Moorish houses of similar rank. All that is really fine in any of them is the Mauresque plaster carving on the frieze beneath the ceiling, or round the door, and the painting of the same school on the ceilings. European furniture—beds, tables, chairs and chests of drawers —look strangely out of place where they have been introduced, and they are seldom put to their intended uses.

Style of Dwellings.

Decoration.

The ground-floors—often almost converted into basements by the accumulation outside—are entered by low door-ways giving no promise of what is within, and indeed the court-yards themselves afford no clue to what is to be found up the winding stair in the corner. Stores, counting-house, corn-sheds and stables surround the yard, in which are gathered six days in the week a noisy knot of buyers and sellers, for this is the business part of the house.

Business Premises.

In keeping with their surroundings, the Marrákesh synagogues are mean and dirty, more like school-yards than sanctuaries on week-days, when incompetent Rabbis attempt to instruct the youth of the congregation. So fanatical and prejudiced are they

Synagogues.

and those whom they lead, that the proposal of the *Alliance Israëlite* to open schools here has met with their successful opposition, and every effort to improve their lot has failed. A few wealthy proprietors thrive on this state of things, and even when on the urgent entreaty of the over-crowded poor, the late Sultan proposed to extend the melláḥ by including a portion of the adjoining Jinán el 'A'fîah, they were able to circumvent an improvement which would have lowered their rents.

Dress.

In the streets the distinctive feature of the dress of the Jews here, as throughout Central Morocco, is the blue head-kerchief spotted with white, by no means becoming, as it rather increases the abject, cringing look of the unfortunate wearers. But there is always a sprinkling of a more stalwart class from the Atlas, wearing the black Berber cloaks, and sporting great "sheafs" of hair on their temples, for this is an important centre of trade, and there is also an increasing number from the ports who have adopted European clothes, or an adaptation of them. The Jewesses dress in a style which differs little from that of the coast, save that out-of-doors they to a certain extent imitate their Moorish neighbours by going veiled in a white cotton sheet. The better class paint and blacken their eyebrows till they look hideous, and disport themselves in low-necked dresses which resemble gay handkerchiefs pinned together.

Condition.

No Jews, unless foreign-protected, are allowed to ride or walk shod through the town, and they are subject to all the usual indignities. They live, for the most part, in degrading misery and filth, sleeping on the ground amid an abundance of loathsome creatures, in dread of scorpions and snakes. Surrounded as they are by dirt, it is not surprising that they suffer much more from ophthalmia than their Moorish neighbours, but on the whole their health is probably as good. Very many of them do not leave the mellâḥ from year's end to year's end, as so many Moors come in daily for business, and outside there are few attractions for them: some of their women have never once crossed the threshold, which is closed from sunset to sunrise, as well as all day on Sabbaths, new moons, festivals and fasts. There is, however, an overflow of several Jewish craftsmen, such as tin-smiths, carpenters and cobblers, to the streets immediately outside.

Kaïsarîyah.

In the central part of the madînah or Mohammedan portion—which is therefore the most expensive district—the various trades are grouped together, the best shops for European goods and most native products being in the ḳaïsarîyah, the best in the Empire. This is a large covered market, consisting chiefly of short, straight, parallel streets lined with the regulation little Moorish box-shops, the entrance being crossed by bars to keep out beasts of burden. In the corners of some of these avenues may be seen drinking-jars built into the wall and endowed by charitable persons, such as are also found in many of the streets outside, but like them they are often dirty and neglected.

Auction Sales.

Every day, from the mid-afternoon prayers to sunset, a busy, vociferous throng occupies the bazaar, rival auctioneers parading up and down with their goods on their shoulders, yelling the latest bids, and people calling from shop to shop or haggling over bargains already struck. In one of the corner shops the sûnk or duty on all sales effected, is levied by gorgeous publicans "at the receipt of custom," and in the crowd there is a good-humoured jostling of portly officials or merchants and filthy paupers, men and women and children; black, brown and white, as though this were the recreation of the day, which for many it is.

Second-hand clothing is sold in the same way in the Jûtîyah, a small square market hard by, truly deserving its familiar name of Ṣôḳ el Ḳamil—the mart of the unmentionable creeping thing. Near this again is the dilapidated Ṣôḳ el Ghazil, an open-air

Other Markets.

GATE OF ḲAÏSARÎYAH, MARRÁKESH.

Photograph by Herbert White, Esq.

market, where, just before sunset on Wednesdays, Thursdays and Fridays, the auctions of slaves are held;* at other times used for sales of wool. Close at hand, too, are the Raḥbat el Ḳamḥ or grain market, and the streets

* For illustration see *The Moors*, ch. viii.

devoted to the smiths and copper workers, for this is the business centre.

In addition to the outside Thursday market already mentioned, there is an inside Thursday market in the open space called Jumû'a el Faná, where business is done, too, on Friday, and a considerable trade in country produce is conducted every day. Here is the great centre for jugglers, snake-charmers, acrobats, story-tellers and mountebanks generally; on feast days also for "powder-play," which is likewise indulged in outside the Báb el Khamees and near the shrine of Sidi bel 'Abbás.

Jumû'a el Faná.

To the south-west of the Jumû'a el Faná, in the midst of the gardens which fill most of the space beyond within the walls, towards Báb er-Rubb, stands the most prominent feature in all Marrákesh, the Kûtûbîya tower, sister to the Giralda of Seville and the Borj el Ḥassan of Rabat. The mosque at its base can be but a portion of that erected with it about the year 1200, at the same time as the ḳaṣbah and its mosque.[1] All that the foreigner now sees is some elegant stone-work adorning a sunken exterior wall, of an age and style corresponding to those of the tower, and a glimpse of theinterior. The roof is supported by large square columns, said to be of marble, which is very likely, although they are white-washed. It is said that there is a tank beneath of the size of the mosque, such as once existed underneath its fellow at Rabat.

The Kûtûbîya Mosque.

The tower itself, commanding in simplicity, straight and square, with crenellated parapet, and then a lanthorn tower, rises to the height of about 250 feet.* Its massive walls of hewn stone enclose seven

The Tower.

* Or 270 ft., according to another calculation. Jackson makes it 200 ft., Beaumier 70 mètres, but it has been estimated at 120 mètres. Cape Cantin

[1] *Raôḍ el Ḳarṭâs.*

storeys, each consisting of a single, vaulted chamber, round which an inclined way, solidly arched, conducts to the summit. Those narrow slits, as the windows appear from below, are splayed within, so that there is plenty of light, and it is said that the interior is richly decorated, but from what one knows of kindred buildings this statement is rendered doubtful. At various stages three blind muédhdhins chant the calls to prayer, their salary being provided by the produce of certain olive groves. The name of this mosque is said by Leo Africanus to be derived from the book shops which at one time surrounded it, no less than two hundred in number! The funds with which it was erected were largely the ameer's fifth of the booty taken from Spain, and European workmen, if not architects, were employed in its construction. Close by is the unpretentious grave of the builder of Marrákesh, surrounded only by a ruinous wall, of which tradition says that whenever a shrine has been raised there it has fallen as soon as the tower was finished.

The lanthorn is surmounted, in the quaint words of Pory's Leo, by "a golden halfe moone, vpon a barre of iron, with three spheares of golde vnder it; which golden spheares are so fastened vnto the saide iron barre that the greatest is lowest, and the least highest," which "spheares" have given rise to much discussion and some confusion with a similar set on the ḳaṣbah mosque tower.* Both sets seem to have roused the cupidity of impecunious ameers and others, but still they remain—or their successors do—for when some years ago they had to be restored after

The Golden Globes.

is said by Leo to be visible from its summit. The west face measures 12 m. 30 c. across, or 3 m. 20 c. less than that of Rabat. For illustration see *The Moorish Empire*, p. 77.

* Captain John Smith understood that "these golden Bals of Affrica" were on the Christian church—surely the mistake of some copyist.

20

a gale, they were found to be but copper gilt.* Jackson estimates their weight at 1250 lbs. English, but Pellow, who makes them four in number, puts them down as 1250 lbs., and claims a place among those unsuccessful in attempting to steal them.†

THE KÛTÛBÎYA MOSQUE.

Photograph by the Hon. E. W. Loch.

* Torres, however, (1535) declared these to be silver, and those of the kaṣbah gold.[1]

† "These four globes are, by computation, seven hundred pounds, Barbary weight, each pound consisting of twenty-four ounces, which make in all 1050 pounds English; and frequent attempts had been made to take them away, but without success; for, as the notion ran, any attempting it were soon glad to desist from it, they being affrighted, and especially at their near approach to them, in a very strange and surprising manner, and seized with an extraordinary faintness and trembling, hearing at the same time a great rumbling noise, like as if the whole fabric was tumbling down about their ears; so that, in great confusion, they all returned faster than they advanced.

Pellow's Account.

"This did I often hear, yet had I a very strong itching to try the

He says that they were removed here from the sultan's palace about 1620 as part of the penance of a sultána for having encroached for three hours in the Ramaḍán fast, the remaining penance including the building of bridges on the Wád Um er-Rabî'a, and the Wád el 'Abeed. That some grain of truth is to be found in this story seems probable from the fact that every legend with regard to their origin points to some "Queen of Morocco," whether a wife of Abd el Mû min—said to have had them made for her grandson's mosque out of the jewels she had received from her husband,—or whether the "King's Daughter of Etheopea,"—to whom a prince of Morocco had been betrothed—set them up as his monument, when he died before their marriage.* But Leo tells a kindred story to the second of these—making it the wife of Ya'ḳûb el Manṣûr who gave the balls, not to this tower, but to the ḳaṣbah mosque, "to the ende she might be famous in time to come."

Curious Legends.

truth of it; and to gratify my curiosity, I one night (having before communicated my intentions to two of my men, and persuaded them to go with me, and provided myself with candles, flint, steel and tinder) entered the foot of the tower, lighted my candles, and advanced with my comrades close at my heels, till I had gained at least two-thirds of the height; I still going on, when really, to my seeming, I both felt and heard such a dismal rumbling noise, and shaking of the tower, (my lights, at that very instant going out) as I thought far surpassed that of common fame; yet was I resolved to proceed, and called to my comrades to be of good courage; but having no answer from them, I soon found they had left me in the lurch; upon which, falling into a very great sweat, I went back also, and found them in the bottom in a terrible condition. And so ended my mad project; which was, I think, a very bad one indeed, for had I obtained the globes, in what could it have bettered my deplorable condition? being always obliged to follow the Emperor's pleasure, and with whom it was a most sufficient crime to be rich. So much for my foolish attempt on the golden globes."—Pellow, p. 96, Orig. Ed.

His Attempt on the Globes.

* Captain John Smith and Jean Mocquet, who visited Marrákesh within a year of one another.

When Charant asked why they had not been taken down by victorious soldiers, "They durst not," said one, "for they are sacred,"[1] but it is of the ḳaṣbah globes again, that Leo writes, "the common people thinke it verie dangerous if a man doth but offer to touch the said sphears with his hand." [By the way, how could he do so?] "Some affirme that they are there placed by so forcible an influence of the planets, that they cannot be removed from thence by any cunning or diuice. Some others report that a certain spirite is adiured by Arte-magique to defend those sphears from al assaults and iniuries whatsoeuer."[2] Though these be but legends, they add a certain interest to one's first sight of what seem after all quite ordinary metal globes, but which for centuries have exercised men's minds.

Spiritual Guardianship.

Of the other notable mosques of Marrákesh, the most important is that of Sidi Yûsef (bin Tashfîn) built by 'Abd el Mû'min (1147—1163) on the site of one erected by 'Ali III. (1106—1143), son of the great ameer whose name it perpetuated in spite of its builder's wish that it should henceforth bear his own.[3] The only others worthy of mention are those of El Mûásîn and Sidi 'Abd el 'Aziz, and that of the Báb Dukálla, erected in 1558 by the mother of Ahmad V. (El Manṣûr ed-Dhahebi).[4] The patron saint of the city is Sidi bel 'Abbas of Ceuta—"the Sheïkh who knew God"—and attached to his mosque, built in 1603 by 'Abd el 'Azîz III. (Abu Fáris),[5] is the morsṭán or hospital yard in which Ali Bey[6] says that in his day (1800) no less than 1800 sick of both sexes were maintained.

Other Mosques and Shrines.

Smaller mosques and saint-shrines abound, but the city is supposed to be under the special tutelage of

[1] See Brown's PELLOW, note, p. 341. [2] Hakluyt ed., p. 267.
[3] LEO, Hakluyt ed., p. 263. [4] EL UFRÁNI, p. 140. [5] Ib., p. 309. [6] p. 250.

seven holy men, whence it derives its name of Seb'àtu Rijál—"the [city of] seven men." These are, in addition to Sidi bel 'Abbás, the Mûl' el Ḳ'ṣûr, Sidi Sulaïmán, Sidi 'Abd el 'Azîz, Sidi Ḳáḍi 'Aïyád, Sidi Yûsef ibn 'Ali, and Sidi Imám Swahîli. In consequence of the possession of their graves, Marrákesh tries to rival Fez in sanctity, and whenever an approaching pious Muslim sights it he adds his stone to the already formidable way-side cairn. In 1893, in consequence of the number of Europeans who occasionally passed that way, the streets approaching the záwîah of Sidi 'Abd el 'Azîz were closed to outsiders by hanging a chain across, though for some time afterwards they continued to be used by residents. Christian slaves were formerly admitted even to the Ḳûbbát es-Shorfà, where many of the Sa'adi dynasty lie buried.[1]

Patron Saints.

With the exception of the palace and the mosques mentioned, Marrákesh boasts few architectural features, except the handsome portals of the ḳaïsarîyah and one or two of the many fandaḳs and several well-designed fountains, notably one surmounted by a carved wooden cornice, and called from its beauty Shráb oo Shûf—"Drink and Look." The best houses have to be reached by foul blind alleys strewn with garbage and dead cats, winding in the darkness under rooms which have been thrown across them, designedly treacherous to all who do not know them well.

Architectural Features.

Very little paving is seen, even in the best streets, which are fairly level, and wide for Morocco, terribly dusty in summer and fearful in winter. Many in the busiest quarters are covered over with stakes and matting or vines, and here the concourse is very great during the daytime. The quantity of sweet

Streets.

[1] Charant.

herbs consumed, chiefly in tea, must be enormous, to judge from the vast piles which distribute a most refreshing odour from the middle of some streets. These thoroughfares are crossed at intervals by clumsy gates

PUBLIC WATER-TROUGH
Adjoining a mosque in Marrákesh.
Photograph by Dr. Rudduck.

which are closed at night, thus dividing the city up into wards; one of these gates, Bâb Kûs, is but three feet high, and rather less in width.

The ḳaṣbah and madînah are administered by separate governors and officials, the jurisdiction of the ḳáïd of the town including only the huts and gardens beyond the walls. The prison in the ḳaṣbah, Ḥabs min Ṣ'báḥ, is principally used for those accused of serious crimes or for political prisoners, that in the madînah for civil and minor offenders, who in part support themselves by platting palmetto, a speciality of the place being fans with bits of coloured cloth interwoven. There is also a women's prison, chiefly for bad characters from the street, and at the morsṭán there is a kind of prison for madmen, where those miserable wretches are left in chains. Soldiers are lodged in the citadel, near the palace.

Administration.

Here, as elsewhere, much of the business is done in caravan-sarais or fandaḳs, of which the best is that of Háj el 'Arbi, the resort of merchants from Fez. In the sixteenth century the European colony inhabited a specially erected fandaḳ of forty-six rooms,[1] and as late as 1816 there was quite a little foreign colony,[2] but that has long since disappeared. Earlier still a quarter seems to have been allotted to discontented nobles from Spain in the ameer's service,[3] and subsequently there was maintained for centuries a Spanish friary with special permission to use bells on the church,[4] which right is still enjoyed where churches exist. Here the first missionaries suffered martyrdom in 1220. There is no accommodation for Europeans, and those arriving without letters from the Moorish Commissioner for Foreign Affairs in Tangier, or without friends in the town, must put up where they can in the melláḥ, as in that case no Moor would dare to let them a house or garden. Although there is a growing trade with Europe, and several foreign merchants have of late years resided here, strange to say no European nation is as yet represented

Foreigners.

[1] Torres, p. 8. [2] Keatinge.

[3] Chenier, vol. i., p. 55. See *The Moorish Empire*, p. 242. [4] Ib. p. 325.

in Marrákesh. In 1890, however, the Southern Morocco Mission established a station here, where medical work is carried on, by which the natives learn that some foreigners, at least, seek their welfare.

The population may be some 50 or 60,000; Richardson suggests 40 to 50,000, Erckmann 55,000, and Washington 80 to 100,000, while native authors dream of a time when Marrákesh gave shelter to 700,000!

CHAPTER THE SEVENTEENTH

SACRED TOWNS

I.—MULAI IDREES ZARHÒN

OF all the many saints of Morocco, none has better claim to veneration than "My lord Idrees" the First, whose ashes lend unrivalled sanctity to Zarhôn, one of the mountains north of Mequinez. Nestling on the hill-side in a fertile valley, is a town known only by the name of the saint buried there just eleven hundred years ago, in 791 of our era, when the Danes were in England. There is no doubt as to the spot, which has been ever since revered and visited as the most holy place in Morocco, and to this day no non-Mohammedan, Jew or Christian, is allowed to set foot within the gates of the town. It is probable that any unsuccessful attempt to evade this law by entrance in disguise would meet with serious results.

Position.

Sanctity.

The only European who has claimed to have entered the town is Jackson, but the statement even of so careful a writer that in 1801 he spent a night in the guest-chamber of the sanctuary,* has been called in question. Neither Rohlfs nor Lenz, although in disguise, had the temerity to enter, and I was myself frustrated when making the attempt.† Clad as a

A Futile Attempt.

* *Account of Housa and Timbuctoo*, p. 119.

† Colonel Trotter, in foreign dress, was turned back by an angry crowd three-quarters of a mile from the gate, and more recently Messrs. Elson and Rockafellar, American missionaries, were stoned on attempting to enter.

native, fortified by introductions from natives who knew me only by a native name, I was resting outside the gates while my man went in to spy out the land, and if possible find us a lodging, when he met a friend who recognized him as my servant. The secret was out, and I too had to turn back discomfited.

So, as no European has been able to describe the town and its shrine, I have to rely on the careful account of my man, taken down from his lips and checked by the descriptions of other natives, as I sat beneath the olive-trees in view of the forbidden ground. Beside us ran the pathway to Volubilis—Ḳaṣar Faráôn or "Pharoah's Castle,"—and the world beyond, traversing well-tilled fields and this luxuriant grove. Just before the gate is reached it crosses the stream which supplies the town, beyond which runs a high wall to the left.

General Description.

Of the five gates, that on this, the lower, side is Báb el Ḥajar, and the street which passes through it gives access to a market-place surrounded by a colonnade. On the right—that is the south side—of this market-place lies the famous shrine, wherein reposes the body of the founder of the Moorish Empire. It is hardly to be supposed that the town already existed here, especially as it has not yet acquired a distinctive name, and lies aside from the routes of commerce. The neighbouring Roman city had been the first home of Idrees in Morocco, and might have become the capital, had not his son and successor preferred to build Fez.

Market.

The approach to the tomb was described by my man as being by a plain door and a passage crossed by a bar to prevent the ingress of beasts of burden. Here were posted many beggars, most of whom were also sick folk. Descending some steps at the end of the passage, turning first to the left and then

The Shrine.

to the right,—the principal court-yard is reached. In the centre a white marble fountain scatters delightful coolness, and round the walls runs a marble colonnade said to have been brought from Ḳaṣar Faráôn. White marble interspersed with coloured tiles makes an effective floor, and the ceilings, supported by arches carved and painted, glitter with rich decoration. On the left of this Court is the Treasury door, adorned in the same style, and on the right the portal, raised one step, which admits to the holy of holies.

Guardian.

Beside this sits the guardian shareef on duty, well-dressed, and provided with a staff wherewith to prevent unauthorized persons from gaining admission. Before him, on the right, stands the great alms chest. Ordinary visitors kiss the step and make their offerings here, as the most sacred chamber is closed even to Mohammedans, except when the reigning sultan enters with his wazeers. This he does on certain state occasions, and it is imperative for each successor to the imperial parasol to pay his respects at the tomb of the saint. A tale is told of a pretender who had gained a formidable following, and visited the shrine for this purpose. The guardian was of course in a dilemma, wondering whom it would pay best to serve, but finally he was advised that if this pilgrim was the rightful ameer steel could not kill him. So he tried the effect of plunging into his breast a sword, which proved him to be quite an ordinary mortal.

The Tomb.

In the centre of the small inner shrine, the original ḳûbbah—hung with rich carpets and crowded with chandeliers interspersed with ostrich eggs and silvered glass balls—is the holy tomb, sheathed in gold embroidery. On the ground stand gold and silver candle-sticks, and round the walls is ranged an assortment of clocks, the majority of the "grand-father" type, with visible pendulums all at work, some striking the quarters and chiming, so that there is a continual concert. Gaudy ornaments on native brackets occupy the intermediate spaces, and the whole effect is, even in the daytime, quite beyond comparison in native eyes, while at night the scene baffles description.

Offerings.

The offerings made to this shrine are often of great value, and the late sultan used from time to time to send large sums in cash. Each Friday the receipts are divided by the shareefs in charge – themselves his descendants—among the chief heirs of Idrees. The whole town is considered sanctuary, pays no taxes, and supplies no soldiers. A deputy of the Báshá of Mequinez represents the sultan, but the shareefs are practically masters. In the upper part of the town pious pilgrims visit the hardly less sacred shrine of Rasheed, faithful henchman of Idrees, and guardian of his son. The buildings are reported to have suffered greatly from the earthquake of 1755.[1]

2.—SHEFSHÁWAN

Origin of Sanctity.

Shefsháwan—or as it is vulgarly pronounced Sheshá-wan,* or even Sháwan—owes its sanctity to the neighbouring shrine of Mulai 'Abd es-Slám bin Masheesh, in whose honour the whole district of Akhmás† is held sacred, and to its having been built by shareefs as a base of operations against the Portuguese in Ceuta.[2] This occurred in 1471—the year in which the Portuguese took Tangier—but it was not completed and peopled till 1511. Its builder was the Fokîh

* Spelled by the Portuguese *Nixuao*.

† Anglicé "Fifths," so called because the tribe in question is divided into that number of sections instead of four, as is generally the case.

[1] Ez-Zaiáni, p. 121.

[2] En-Náṣiri, vol. ii., p. 261. See also *Nashar el Mathâni* and *El Maraḥ*.

El Ḥasan (Abu'l Ḥasan) bin Mohammed, a descendant of the famous Mulai 'Abd es-Slám, and through him of Mulai Idrees and Mohammed of Mekka. Yet there is a local tradition that a fortress, the ruins of which form the present prison, occupied this site long before the introduction of Islám, when it was taken by 'Ali bir-Rasheed, conqueror of Tetuan, who built a town here.* *History.*

Shefsháwan lies some sixty miles south of Tetuan, in a beautiful valley between two arms of a mountain of the same name. Like most Moorish towns, it is surrounded by gardens, orchards and vineyards, and so beautiful is the view which greets the traveller, that he instinctively recalls the scenes of the "Arabian Nights." Especially is this the case as the setting sun casts its rays on the spot,—for its aspect is western,—when the squalor and the filth of Moorish civilization are forgotten in the glory of Nature. *Situation.*

The town is about the size of Tangier, and is surrounded by an apology for a wall, pierced by five gates. It has seven mosques, as well as many smaller places of worship, and in order that the true "son of the prophet" may cleanse his body (which seems to be reckoned of more consequence than his soul), there are two large baths provided for him. The houses are of different structure from those of the other towns of Morocco; instead of flat roofs, terraces and blank walls, here we find sloping roofs covered with tiles, and a number of latticed windows, which give the streets a brighter and more attractive appearance. The general aspect is one of cleanliness and good repair. *The Town.*

* For this and most of the facts in the following description I am indebted to Mr. William Summers of the North African Mission, one of the very few Europeans who have ventured within these walls. Others who have done so are Mr. W. B. Harris and M. de la Martinière.

Business is carried on chiefly in five large fandaḳs or caravan sarais, the lower part of the largest of which is monopolised by Jewish pack-saddle makers. Other principal industries are tanning—the majority of the hides coming from Tangier,—weaving, slipper-making, and rope-spinning.

Trade.

One of the sights of Shefsháwan is the Rás el Má' ("Water-head") whence issues an abundant rivulet. It consists of three natural cavities in the side of Jebel Shefsháwan, through which flows a constant stream of clear and most refreshing water. Before being led off to the town and gardens, the stream falls over a low precipice, forming a charming cascade. When Mulai el Ḥasan visited the town in 1889, having remained in it about half an hour, he ascended to the "Rás el Má'," where he dismounted and drank of the crystal stream. Afterwards, to their intense amusement, he made the remark that if the people of Shefsháwan possessed nothing but plenty of stones and water, they *were* good.

Water-supply.

The Mohammedan population consists mainly of shareefs, and nearly everyone "knows his letters." The majority are engaged in that most difficult of occupations, doing nothing: they sit about in groups in the market-place, listening to the latest story-teller, as he retails the corruptions and distortions of his imagination, or they lounge about in the cafés complacently sipping their cups of coffee, just purchased for the large sum of "k͟hams-ooja" each,—nearly a half-penny. As becomes true children of Islám, they wear severely plain garments of natural wool. The principal reason for this simplicity is poverty, for, as most of them are shareefs, they lay claim to contributions from the "faithful," but find, as most religious parasites do, that these contributions have a tendency to grow uncomfortably small.

Population.

Strange to say, in spite of its sanctity, Jews are allowed

to live in Shefsháwan. Their dress and mode of life here are much the same as elsewhere, but they look stronger, and have a more manly appearance. The community numbers about three hundred, and they do their best to live in the thirty houses allotted to them. The name of the quarter is of course, el melláḥ; and when a pious Muslim utters it he begs leave to be excused for polluting the ears of his listener by such a sound. They possess one synagogue with two schools, and all their religious requirements are performed by a much respected Rabbi, who comes all the way from Táza. The Jewish merchants have a fandaḳ of their own in the town, where they sell principally Manchester goods. They are much oppressed and abused, and are so despised that when they pass a mosque or shrine, they are compelled to take off their shoes and even to doff their caps. They are all filled with hope, however, that better days are coming, and hail with delight the increase of European influence in this country, trusting that it will soon extend to Shefsháwan.

Jews.

Before the late sultan's march through this part of the country, the central authority was ignored, and even now the local officials are afraid to assert it. The town is supposed to be governed by a khalîfa of the Báshá of Tetuan, but he is a mere figure-head. If he dispenses justice, the surrounding mountaineers object to it, and should he imprison anyone, they will at once storm the prison and set him free. Many of the Akhmás people owe money to the people of Shefsháwan, and most of the accounts are of long standing, but the governor is afraid to extend a helping hand to recover their property. It is a case of everyone doing what is right in his own eyes. In this district, as throughout the Berber tribes, there exists a native protection system, the more powerful village chiefs of

Administration.

Akhmás taking certain individuals under their care, and defending them from all supposed wrong and injury. This gives them great influence with the towns-people, and in proportion to their influence the authority of the sultan is crippled.

WAZZÁN.
Photograph by Herbert White, Esq.

3.—WAZZÁN

Reason of Sanctity.

Wazzán derives its sanctity from living saints as well as dead, for it is the head-quarters of one of the most widely revered branches of the Idreesi family, honoured throughout the Barbary States. As descendants of the saint of Zarhôn, practically his principal representatives,* the shareefs of Wazzán in some respects claim precedence of even the reigning Fîlálîs, who have so much more recently come to this

* For Genealogical Table, see *The Moorish Empire*, p. 116.

country,* and have only usurped the Empire which the ancestors of the Wazzánîs had founded, but which their family had lost some hundreds of years previously. Thus the influence of the Wazzán house is religious, rather than political, although it is the custom for new sultans to seek its blessing on assuming the umbrella.

It was not, however, till the close of the seventeenth century of our era that this family settled on the spot from which it now derives a name. Its original home, built by its ancestor Mohammed bin Idrees II., had been called by him Baṣra, after the city of that name in Arabia Felix,[1] but in the wars of the Middle Ages it had been destroyed, and there only exist to-day mere traces of what it once was.†

The Wazzán Shorfâ.

---

* See *The Moorish Empire*, p. 135.

† With regard to the ruins of Baṣra, De la Martinière remarks,[2] "The complete destruction of the city, the absence of historical documents relative to the incidents which attended the fall of this unhappy place—a small portion of its walls only having been left standing,—are instances of the rapidity with which some towns of Morocco have disappeared, without leaving a trace in history, for little is known of the origin of the city, and still less of the events which brought about its fall."

Ruins of Baṣra.

Tissot thinks it was once one of the Roman military stations, Tremulæ, which is probable from its commanding the road to Volubilis. All that remains is a wall of about 700 yards from the N.E. angle, and a shapeless heap of stones, half hidden by vegetation. Leo Africanus says that it once included some two thousand households.[3] El Bekrî says it had ten gates and a fine mosque with seven naves and two baths. Idreesi says that in 1100, although in decadence, it was still a town, while an unwalled town existed at Kort, and a ruined town, Maslna, to the south of Baṣra. Abu'l Fîda says that when the Idreesi shareefs lived there it was called Baṣra ed-Dibbán, on account of its numerous dairies, but it seems also to have been styled "the red," as Marrákesh is, from the colour of the earth with which it was built. The neighbouring hill of Kort is conspicuous for many a mile round from its red colour. The ruins are a little less than half-way from El Ḳaṣar to Wazzán, soon after descending Jebel Ṣarṣar, and almost due south of the crest, being therefore to the right of the Wazzán road, on Jebel Sîdî Ámár el Ḥáj, and overlooking the Ḳarîat Ben 'Oda.

[1] Leo, ed. Ram., p. 88.   [2] p. 97.   [3] Hak. ed. p. 503.

Various spots seem to have been favoured before Wazzán was selected, most of them around the conspicuous Jebel Ṣarṣár, which is crossed between this and El Ḳaṣár. In 1727 Mulai 'Abd Allah es-Shareef, to whom the present glory of his house is due, was still residing at a neighbouring spot called Harash, now neglected, where the English envoy Russel visited him.[1] His reputation for sanctity was so great that at Wazzán, where he ultimately settled, his tomb has become a venerated shrine, the nucleus of a town the proudest name of which is Dár D'mánah – House of Safety,—for, like the old-time cities of refuge, it is sanctuary for all who gain its limits, and those perpetrating crimes within its limits may still find sanctuary in one of its numerous mosques or shrines. Not only the greater part of the town, but also much of the country round, belongs to the shareefs, whose retainers farm it, ready at a moment's notice to follow their bidding. All over the country there are isolated farms or 'azáïb, bequeathed to the shareefs by the pious, the tenants of which are under their direct control, and pay no dues to the sultan. The result is that within the territories of Wazzán the shareef is as supreme as a feudal lord, his estate a literal *imperium in imperio.*

A City of Refuge.

By degrees upon that hill-side, high above the valley, across which is a glorious view, there has grown up one of the most picturesque towns of Morocco. Its peculiar feature is the large number of tiled and thatched gables, so unlike the style prevailing in other parts of this country, just what old prints show the roofs of Tangier to have been. Very few flat-roofed or white-washed buildings appear, but domes and mosque-towers lend its outline dignity. Prominent among them is the tower of the chief mosque in the shareefs' quarters,

Situation.

[1] Braithwaite, pp. 129—133.

that of Sidi Háj el 'Arbi, faced with green tiles. The Jama' Kabeer or Great Mosque, the original mosque of Mulai 'Abd Allah es-Shareef, the Jama' Jinán 'Ali—that of "'Alî's Garden;"—and the mosque of the suburb of Kashereeïn are also conspicuous.

The mosque in honour of Mulai 'Abd Allah was built by his son Mohammed, and is the great centre of attraction. Mulai 'Abd Allah is known as the Káteb el 'A'shar, and is the patron saint of the place, but two of his grandsons, Thámi and Ṭáïb, became founders respectively of the great Tuháma and Ṭáïbeen Orders, of which the shareefs are the hereditary heads.*

Religious Orders.

The shrine attached to the mosque of Mulai 'Abd Allah es-Shareef, (*anglicè* "My Lord Slave-of-God, the Noble,") rivals even that of Mulai Idrees II. at Fez. It is built and decorated much in the same style, with walls tiled up to a certain height, then whitewashed, with coloured inscriptions from the Ḳor'án. In form it is a large square room with the tomb of the saint in the middle. The floor is marble, and the roof of arabesques in painted wood inside, and green glazed tiles outside. Among the ornaments are four huge gilt candelabras and a glass chandelier, beside which hang ostrich eggs and glass balls. There is nothing remarkable about the other mosques.

The Shrine.

Situated in the midst of a group of semi-independent hill-tribes, Wazzán has become their mart, which makes it, for Morocco, a place of no little trade, but the only manufacture for which it has a name is that of a coarse white cloth with rough surface, of which the hooded cloaks called jellàb are made. In a detailed account of Wazzán published by the *Sociedad*

Population and Trade.

* The present Shareef is the eighth in descent from 'Abd Allah. For further particulars as to these Orders see *The Moors*, ch. xviii.

Geográfica de Madrid, from the pen of Sr. Dn. Teodoro de Cuevas, then Spanish Vice-Consul at Laraiche—drawn up with his accustomed exactitude and minuteness,—the author calculates the number of dwellings at about 2250, and the total population at over eleven thousand.* Of these a hundred or so are Jews engaged in trade; but there are no Europeans.

Jews.

Even Jews are not made over welcome in Wazzán, however advantageous their presence may prove to be commercially, and the few there are there live chiefly as lodgers in seven fandaḳs, for neither Jews nor Christians are permitted to take up their abode permanently in so holy (?) a spot. Even in death they must rest far away from it, for it is considered the Gate of Heaven, and blessed be the man who dies and is buried there! For this reason the Jewish burial-ground is on an opposite hill, near some ancient ruins. The Muslims find their lest resting-place in six cemeteries which surround the town.

Position.

Wazzán is perched on the north-east slope of a hill called Boo Halál, and its northern and southern boundaries are the suburbs of Kashereeïn and the Báb Fátiḥah. The latter spot, the "Gate of the Opening," (*i.e.* of the first chapter of the Ḳor'án) is in

Occupations.

* Sr. de Cuevas thus enumerates the occupations of the inhabitants: 195 weavers, 140 tanners, 72 grocers, 48 drapers, 44 shoe-makers, 40 bread-women, 39 oilmen, 34 water-carriers, 32 cobblers, 27 café-keepers, 27 auctioneers, 25 blacksmiths, 21 charcoal-burners, 18 embroiderers, 16 knife-grinders, 14 masons, 13 Jewish silversmiths, 12 oil-expressers, 12 tailors, 12 soap-makers, 11 gun-lock-smiths, 10 butchers, 9 farriers, 9 eating-house keepers, 9 woollen sash makers, 8 carpenters, 8 barbers, 8 gun-powder makers, 6 pack-saddle makers, 6 sawyers, 4 makers of skin bottles, 4 potters, 3 gun-barrel makers, 2 brick-makers, 200 public women.

Although this may at first sight seem rather an uninteresting list, if it is looked into it will be found far otherwise, as it gives a very good idea as to what industries are carried on in the town, and the proportion of the people they support.

reality no gate, but the spot at which this chapter is read before the local army goes forth to war at the command of the Shareef. The origin of the name Wazzán is unknown, but Sr. de Cuevas suggests a probable derivation from the words Wád Zaïn or "River of Beauty," which might apply to one of the rivers below.*

As a protection against the hardy mountaineers who now and again attempt a raid on the town, in spite of its sanctity, the various markets have their entrances closed by doors at night, as also do some of the quarters, and the district inhabited by the family of the Shareef. In addition to this, a most elaborate system of night police is in force, so that in one way or another the place is pretty well guarded. Almost every man goes armed, usually with flint-lock and dirk, often with several weapons. The strength of the town is calculated by "gun-locks," *i.e.* so many capable men under arms, about 2250. These share the night duty among them. Scant mercy is shown to strangers found alone after dark. Each night fifty-eight men are told off for the watch, so many for each particular district, each man doing duty in the one in which he resides. Fifty of them are stationary, seated, and the remaining eight patrol the town four at a time, one in each quarter. The Shareef pays those on duty £3 a month, and the available men are employed in turns, a month at a time. There is of course a prison, near the door of which sits the representative of the Government, a khalîfa (lieutenant) of the Governor of Laraiche. There are three public steam baths. The town and suburbs are divided into fourteen wards.

Police Regulations.

The streets of Wazzán are of the usual narrow type, but being all more or less steep, soon run dry after rain, and are rendered passable by being strewn with large

* It is referred to as Wád Zán by De Neveu, *Les Khouan*, p. 43.

stones, though without attempt at regularity or pretence of paving. Below the town is the market-place, well filled on Wednesdays and Thursdays. In the bottom of the valley below is the minzah or summer residence of the Shareef, built in a semi-European style, with green Venetians, standing out from a background of fine trees.

Streets.

To the left is the hamlet of Kashereeïn, and away in the distance little villages are dotted over the landscape. On the other side of a broad, well-watered valley rise the hills of the Beni M'sárà and kindred fierce tribes. The neighbourhood is well stocked with olives and other trees, while a low shrubbery extends for miles in some directions, adding beauty to the scenery. Altogether Wazzán is a delightful spot, and were it easier of access, and opened up to Europeans as a place of residence, it would undoubtedly become a favourite resort.

Surroundings.

The water-supply is good, and fairly abundant, from two springs in the hill above the town, which are led by stone conduits, and unite in a sort of open sewer on the lower side of the hill above the market. Notwithstanding this, the inhabitants are very fond of the intoxicating drinks which they manufacture for themselves. They distil a sort of fiery spirit, chiefly from raisins and figs, by soaking them, and after well mashing them, burying them in an earthen pitcher for some months in a manure heap where there is plenty of heat. "After that," they say, "the liquor distilled has imbibed so much heat that a naked man can sleep warm if he drinks enough." *

Water and Strong Drink.

* Although such practices are strictly forbidden by the Ḳor'an, these precepts are as much disregarded by some Moors as most of the others contained in that volume. Drunkenness is most common in Morocco among the mountaineers, Berbers who had already become addicted to it before the comparatively temperate

Drunkenness.

The morals of the people of Wazzán are in other respects no worse than those of dwellers elsewhere in this country, but if anything are better than those of the inhabitants of the large towns, although, owing to drink, and their independent spirit, quarrels and brawls are frequent.

Morals.

A notable fact in connection with Wazzán—especially considering the position it holds among Mohammedans,—is that it is also famous as the last resting-place of a Hebrew saint, probably the most revered of his class in Morocco. This worthy, when in the flesh, was Rabbi 'Omrán ben Dîwád, and was a celebrated teacher from Jerusalem, who ended his earthly wanderings in the course of one of them about a century ago, at Wazzán. No monument, not even a grave-stone, marks his sepulchre, but there it is, as well known as the shrine of Mulai Idrees himself, a mere spot pointed out to pilgrims on one side of the Jewish cemetery near the ruins of Asján, shaded by a row of pomegranate trees, where the rabbi lies amid saints of less note. His fame is no myth, for each Rosh Hodesh, or New Moon—the political and hygrometric state of the country permitting—sees a gathering of supplicants, offering petitions to the great I AM in a manner directly opposed to the accepted teachings of His law-giver Moses. The 33rd night of the Omer is also a great day for visits to this quasi holy spot, to which flock visitors from Morocco, Gibraltar (!) and Algeria.

A Hebrew Saint.

Wondrous are the miracles ascribed to the agency of

Arabs came and seized their country. Their favourite drink, described above, is called "samit," which Sir John Hay, when he published his little book, thought had some connection with the Scotch word "somet," denoting a sort of intoxicating drink. There are two varieties of samit, the one referred to, and another of sweet syrupy description, with a sickly, burnt-sugar taste.[1]

[1] See *The Moors*, chapter vi.

his defunct holiness, to which the worthy Grand Rabbi of Tangier informs me he is willing to testify, having visited the spot himself in search of health. Among the most common petitions offered through this medium are those of childless women for a Hannah's blessing, and I have been solemnly assured that oftentimes the fair supplicants have afterwards been granted their hearts' desire! When the aspirant for the honours of maternity is unable to visit the spot in person, she sends her girdle by a trusty friend, to lay it on the grave, with candles to burn there while she, at home, makes known her request. Even this system of proxy is reported to have frequently been followed by wonderful results. Trees, old cannon, rocks, and numerous other commonplace objects are likewise believed in Morocco to be imbued with this magic power, and similar efforts are made to get a hearing through their medium, sitting on the revered object usually forming part of the programme.

Superstition.

Strange to say, not only is it among the children of Israel that Rabbi 'Omrán is held in veneration, but also among the Children of Ishmaël in whose alien territory he has found a grave: Moorish women have just as much faith in him as Jewish. Other instances of a similar nature could be given, showing that race hatred in life does not always cross the border-land of "that unknown bourne," when the unreturning traveller has earned a reputation for sanctity here on earth.

Strange Popularity.

Wazzán is no more easy of approach in bad weather than the other towns of Morocco; indeed, owing to its elevated position, it is often extremely difficult to reach, along the slippery hill-sides under the olive-groves. In ordinary weather the distance from El Ḳaṣár is a good day's journey over a mountainous

Approach.

and picturesque track among the vine-yards and cultivated fields of Jebel Ṣarṣár, and over three fords often impassable in winter, the worst one on the Wád Lekkûs,* and the other two on the smaller Wàd M'ḍá. From Wazzán to Fez or Mequinez the distance is about three and a half days, the road to the former lying over Jebel Gibgib, and that to the latter past the ruins of Volubilis. These roads cross the rivers Beit, R'ḍát, Wárghah and

ASJÁN.

Photograph by Herbert White, Esq.

Sebû, so that in the absence of bridges they are impracticable in winter.

Barth and Renou think that Wazzán itself may have been the site of the Roman station of Vopiscianæ, but nothing has been adduced in support of the theory beyond a statement of the late Shareef, quoted by Tissot, that pottery and ancient coins are to be found there, and that a few years ago

Questionable Antiquity.

* See illustration on p. 7.

three rows of tombs placed over one another had been dug out. There was once another town near here, named Asján, of which nought remains but a few ruins, though when Leo wrote,[1] (the translator spelling the name Exaggen – Idreesi calls it Zaddjan) it was of some importance, and was fortified against the Portuguese. The ruins are situated about two hours to the N.E. of Wazzán, and are evidently those of a large place. Part of the wall of immense concrete blocks is still visible, as also are many of the houses, which are nearly perfect, standing twenty to thirty feet high, though the interiors are completely ruined.[2] Idreesi says it was famous for its wine, and that a Tuesday market was held there. The wine business has been monopolised by Wazzán, and the market on that day has been long since abandoned.

Asján.

[1] Cir. 1525. Ed. Ram., p. 88.

[2] See SPENCE WATSON, p. 218.

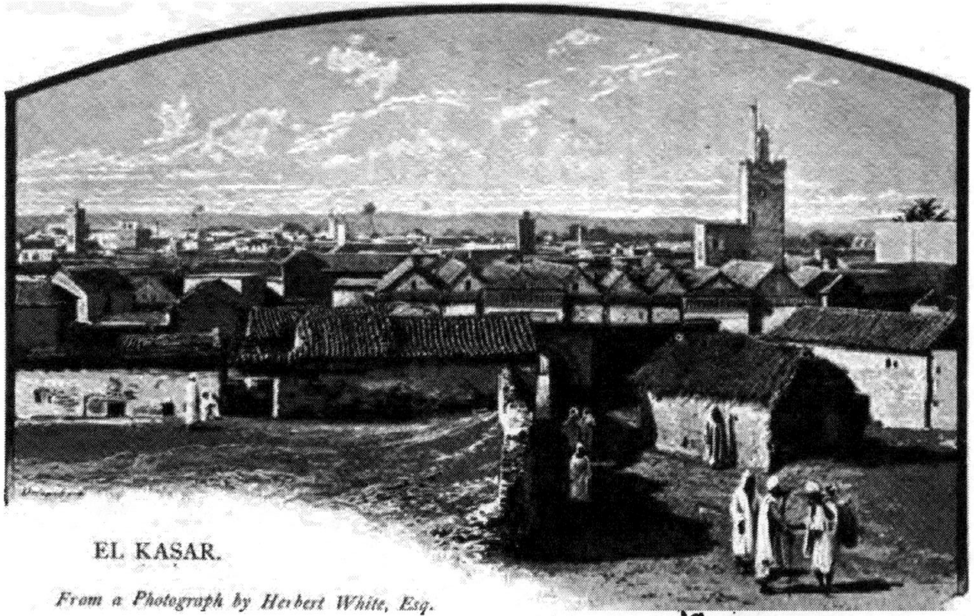

EL KAṢAR.

From a Photograph by Herbert White, Esq.

CHAPTER THE EIGHTEENTH

MINOR TOWNS

1.—EL KAṢAR EL KABEER

BEST known among the minor towns of Morocco, El Kaṣar—although its full name does mean "The Great Castle"—has not much to commend it. Situated near the western edge of the plain of El Gharb, by the meandering river Lekkûs, it commands no prospect, and presents no attractive features. Hardly does it deserve the name of town, as, except by its size and compactness, it is not to be distinguished from an over-grown village.

Situation.

Its mud and pan-tile dwellings, confined by no wall, are only here and there relieved by a mosque-tower or green hipped roof, and are far from inviting; while the figures which people its ill-kept streets exhibit few signs of wealth. There is, indeed, a certain appearance of bustle on market days—Sundays—when the country-folk flock in, and trade is brisk in years of good harvest. The kaïṣarîyah or business quarter is most creditable for the size of the town, as it has to serve a large district. The weekly market, held close by, is crossed by a canal which so comports itself in winter that the only dry place is the bridge, which then becomes thronged with buyers and sellers, who, to cross the market, have to wade shoeless.

Appearance.

About a quarter of an hour to the west of the town, at a place called Es-Sûd, is a cutting from the river, about three yards above the surface at low water. From this a channel runs to the town and out to the river again lower down, through the gardens. This channel is used as a road in dry weather, but when the river rises, the water runs along it and cleanses the town, which is one of the most filthy in Morocco. Houses, mosques and all are flooded. A place so low and damp may well have a name for fever. Windus was informed that it had been cursed by a saint who foretold that it should be burned in summer and drowned in winter, which it very nearly is, but in his day the people were wont to set fire to some one building each summer, as a "scape-house," that other heat might be averted.[1]

Irrigation.

Climate.

Whatever walls El Ḳaṣar once boasted were razed by Mulai Ismá'íl in 1673, since which time it has been altogether unprotected, except by the doors which close the entrance to the ḳaïsarîyah at night. Soon after taking Tangier, the Portuguese had seized it, but had ere long dismantled and abandoned it. At that time it possessed a fine hospital.[2] As recently as 1800 "Ali Bey" considered it larger than Tangier,[3] and Dr. Addison, father of the essayist, who was chaplain at Tangier under the British, states that once the town boasted more than fifteen mosques, whereas at the present time the number is reduced to only two or three of importance. These are "the Great," the Jáma' Sidi el Hazmîri and the Jáma' Sa'ídah.

Decay.

The chief patron saints are Mulai 'Ali bu Ghálib, Sidi Ḳásem ben Z'baïr, and Lalla Fáṭmah el Andalûsîyah (Lady Fáṭmah of Andalucia). The záwîaḥ of Mulai bu Ghálib is a fine one, having a beautiful tiled court-yard open to the sky, with a marble fountain in the centre. Opposite the entrance is a smaller

Patron Saints.

[1] p. 79. [2] MENEZES, pp. 52 and 70. [3] p. 58.

door finely carved and painted in colours, with an inscription over the archway which leads into the ḳûbbah. In the centre of this is the tomb, a large, oblong, wooden structure, covered with scarlet felt cloth with a pattern in green cloth. Above hangs a large candelabra surrounded by numerous oil lamps, and there are of course several clocks. Petroleum and "Nazarene" candles being tabooed as unholy, native bees' wax and olive oil only are used. The ceiling is exquisitely decorated in "Alhambra" style, and round the wall run intricate quotations from the Ḳor'án.

The town is divided into two wards, Es-Shrî'ah and Báb el Wád, divided by the main street. It is reckoned that the one can supply three hundred and fifty armed men, and the other five hundred. The government of the town is unique,—though typical of most of the minor towns of Morocco, - owing to the multitude of jurisdictions, all native. The Báshá of Laraiche appoints a vice-governor for the town, and the sultan another for the country round,—the Khlôt. Similarly there are two ḳáḍîs or judges, and two administrators of mosque property, but only one market clerk.

Administration.

So far all would go well, were it not that those who frequent the place, especially on market days, instead of becoming subject to the jurisdiction of the representatives of Government in the town, remain amenable only to their own respective ḳaïds, who are usually in attendance on these occasions to the number of a dozen or more. Even this delightful state of confusion is increased when one of the parties to a suit claims foreign protection. France and England are represented in El Ḳaṣar by agents, and there is a French Post Office. The only other Europeans are the members of the Gospel Union Mission of America, established here in 1896.

Conflicting Jurisdictions.

The population of El Kaṣar has been set down by various writers at five, eight, nine and fourteen thousand, but as an equally warrantable surmise I would suggest between eight and ten thousand as an approximate figure, a considerable proportion being Jews, who inhabit no particular quarter. A large number of them live in fandaḳs, and most of them trade with Tangier and Laraiche, as the chief business of the place is supplying European manufactures to the townless district beyond.

Population.

With his characteristic minuteness, Sr. de Cuevas has made a list of the trades followed in El Kaṣar in 1882,[1] from which the following data are quoted. Fifteen cows and sixty-five sheep were killed weekly by twenty Moorish butchers, and two cows by four Jewish butchers. Fifteen mills and twenty ovens furnished about three thousand loaves daily, and sixty women sold them in the streets. There were four oil mills, eighty oilmen, ninety-two grocers, twenty Jewish drinking-dens and thirty Moorish cafés and keef shops; twenty-four fandaḳs or inns with some five hundred rooms in all, averaging 1s. 4d. per month; eighty-five shops selling Manchester goods, seven hundred and fifty wool-workers, two hundred and fifty cleaners, six hundred and fifty weavers, one hundred and fifty-five shoe-makers, sixty cobblers, twenty tailors, a silk worker, eighty tanners, thirty pack-saddle makers, twenty masons, thirty carpenters, fourteen blacksmiths, twenty gun-smiths: fifteen brick-kilns employing one hundred and twenty men, twenty-eight pottery-kilns with as many men and twenty-four wheels; six copper-smiths, four tin-smiths, eleven silver-smiths, three gun-barrel-makers, three musical-instrument-makers, four sawyers, one hundred water-men, a quack, and sixteen barbers. There were seventeen Moorish schools,

Occupations.

[1] *Estudio General del Bajalato de Laracke.*

and four Jewish; four public baths, fifteen public and about a thousand private wells: the dead were disposed of in three Moorish cemeteries and one Jewish. There is one prison, in which all the various authorities confine those whom they desire to punish. Close to the town on the south-west side is a spot called El Ḥárah, the site of a lepers' quarter, of which only ruins remain.

Position.

From Tangier El Ḳaṣar is distant about sixty miles in a southerly direction, making two days' journey, although it is *possible* to ride through, unburdened, in a long day. From Laraiche the distance is about twenty miles south-east, a short day's travelling across a plain for the most part sandy, and therefore passable in winter at times when the road to Tangier,—especially the part between that port and the Sunday market of G͟harbîyah—is impracticable.*

View from Jebel Sarsar.

To Wazzán it is a longish day's ride over Jebel Ṣarṣar, but a most enjoyable one when dry under foot. From near the summit a magnificent view of the G͟harb is obtainable, El Ḳaṣar nestling down below in the midst of its gardens on the other side of the Wád Lekkûs, which makes a great bend, passing close by the town, and after meandering across the plain, empties itself into the sea at Laraiche, that little dot of green and white far away at the water's edge. On a clear day another such dot is seen on the right, the still more distant little quondam port of Azîla, while the broad Atlantic is represented by a silver strip along the horizon.

Ancient History.

The early history of El Ḳaṣar, like that of most towns in this country, is shrouded in uncertainty, forming a fruitful subject of discussion among self-confident authors,—one cannot always say au-

* The exact situation of El Ḳaṣar is about 34° 58′ or 35° 1′ 10″ N., (according to different authorities) and 5° 49′ or 5° 55′ W.

thorities. * Notwithstanding the supposition that El Ḳaṣar stands on the site of a Roman station, I have never heard of any discoveries on the spot or in the neighbourhood which would tend to prove that this was the case, except that the tower of the chief mosque—constructed largely of material which has served before,—contains a stone on which are the remains of a Greek epitaph of one Alexander, son of Euripides,[1] but as it is about twenty feet from the ground, it is too high to be read without assistance.

Modern History.

Idreesi mentioned, about 1100 A.C. the existence, presumably here, of El Ḳaṣar Maṣmûda, but Leo Africamus gives 1186 to 1200 as the date of the foundation of El Ḳaṣar el Kabeer by Ya'ḳûb el Manṣûr, and relates a very pretty story to account for his selection of the site.[2] The celebrated monarch is said to have been out hunting, and—after the fashion of monarchs in such tales —getting separated from his suite, to have lighted upon the solitary hut of a fisherman, who ignorant of his rank, treated him so hospitably, that he took a fancy to the spot, and decided to build there a castle. As he built, or re-built, another smaller castle on the straits of Gibraltar, and gave neither

Attempted Identifications.

* While El Ḳaṣar has been variously identified by some with the Kernë of Plato, (capital of Atlanta) and by some with the Roman station of Oppidium Novum, these findings are strongly opposed by others, among whom Sr. de Cuevas of Laraiche, an authority on this part of Morocco, has published a pamphlet to combat both ideas.[3] Don Joaquin Costa has endeavoured to prove its identity with Kernë, and M. Tissot has satisfied himself that it was the Oppidum Novum,[4] in which opinion he is followed by M. de la Martinière.[5] Sr. de Cuevas is satisfied that Kernë was somewhere in Sûs, that the site of Oppidum Novum is unknown, and that the neighbouring Baṣra was of purely African origin, and did not replace the Roman station of Tremulæ, as suggested by the writers referred to.

[1] TISSOT, p. 162. [2] LEO, Ed. Ram., p. 87.

[3] *Informe à la Real Academia de la Historia—El Ksar el Acabir;* Tanger. Imp. J. Lúgaro y Cia., 1887. [4] p. 161. [5] p. 76.

any specific name, this became known as El Ḳaṣar el Kabeer, and the other as El Ḳaṣar es-Sagheer, or the "Little Castle."*

Ruins.

The only ruins worthy of notice at El Ḳaṣar el Kabeer are those of the palace of Ghaïlán, the mountain chief who played such a conspicuous part at the time when the English held Tangier. It was for sheltering him that Mulai Ismá'il destroyed the walls and the palace, which was to some extent re-built between 1840 and 1846 by a Báshá of Laraiche. Half an hour's ride to the east side of the town is a spot called Ed-Dûámar, said to have been the original site chosen for El Ḳaṣar. It is related that when the walls were commenced there each morning the workmen found their tools transported to the spot on which now stands the chief mosque. The only remains at Dûámar are ruins of what were evidently buildings of considerable size, of the regulation mud-concrete with brick angles. Near by are other ruins, apparently those of an ancient bridge.

2.—SIFRÛ

With the exception of El Ḳaṣar, and perhaps of Wazzán, the smaller towns of the interior are little known

El Kasar es-Sagheer.

* El Ḳaṣar es-Sagheer, with which care must be taken not to confound the "Great Castle," has long since been laid in ruins, but in the days of the incursions into Spain, it was important as a place for the embarkation of troops, as the only one on the Anjerah coast, except the bay at Ḳanḳôsh, nearer Tangier. This port was rebuilt in 1192 by Ya'ḳûb el Manṣûr, and in 1458 it was taken by Alfonso the African of Portugal, when its mosque was dedicated to the Immaculate Conception.[1] The Moors besieged it in 1503, when it was relieved, but it was abandoned in 1540. In *Raôḍ el Ḳarṭás* it is variously styled El Ḳaṣar 'Abd el Kareem, El Ḳaṣar Ketámi or El Ḳaṣar el Ġûáz or el Mejáz, the first two epithets referring to one 'Abd el Kareem el Ketámi, credited with having been its builder: the last two mean 'the place of the crossing,' that is, of the Straits. To-day a few scattered ruins on land now owned by Englishmen mark its site, and the Portuguese arms may still be seen on some of its massive gates.

[1] MENEZES, p. 25.

to Europeans, communication with them being difficult, and often dangerous. Among the most accessible, well worthy of a visit, is Sifrû, a charmingly

Situation.

GORGE OF IMINIFIRI, ABOVE DAMNAT.
(See p. 346.) *Photograph by Dr. Rudduck.*

situated walled town nestling in a valley high on an Atlas spur, about twenty miles south of Fez.* †

* For most of this description I am indebted to the late Miss Herdman, of the North African Mission, which has now two ladies stationed there. No other Europeans are known to have resided at Sifrû, and very few have paid even flying visits to this little known spot. Only a few years ago, when I gave an item of news from Sifrû in *The Times of Morocco*, a local contemporary took me to task for inventing new Moorish towns. Yet the editor was a native.

† 7° 4′ 30″ W. (De Foucauld.)

It is the meeting-place for caravans to Fez from east and south-east, from Algeria by Oojdah, and from Tafílált, and it is consequently an important commercial centre, although numbering only about four thousand inhabitants.* About a third of these are Jews occupying a mellàḥ in the heart of the town, and a large fandaḳ just outside the gate.†

Trade.

One quarter of the town is evidently ancient, where there are a few ruined houses, and others partially rebuilt for stables, or wholly for habitation. The present street is on a level with the first floors of former times, and the ground floors are like underground cellars. Most of the houses are of one storey, their courts shaded by vines, but richer folk often add a room or two on the roof. These homes afford shelter alike to human beings, horses, mules, a sheep or two, milch cows and their calves. The bulk of the cattle owned in Sifrû is kept in the Berber villages in the mountains, but all that go out to feed near the town by day are driven home at night.

Description.

Money is scarce, and the Moors of Sifrû live largely on milk food, to the great advantage of the children, who are healthy and well-grown. The Jews, on the contrary, do not use milk, but keep their cattle on the mountains, and have the butter sent to them on market days. For this reason their children are weak and pale, as well as from overcrowding. Although they own lofty dwellings, each room is occupied by a whole family, not even the richest among them having houses to themselves.

Inhabitants.

The gardens around Sifrû are its chief attraction.

* De Foucauld says 3000, with the same large proportion of Jews, who consider Sifrû and Damnát their happiest homes in Morocco.

† Sifrû is referred to in *Raôḍ el Ḳarṭás* as a town in existence in A.H. 455, or A.D. 1063.[1] See *The Moorish Empire*, p. 53.

[1] p. 196.

Even in the height of summer they are dazzlingly green above and below, for they are watered by numerous streams which rush down the mountains on every side, and do not fail in the hottest weather, since they flow from springs. The whole valley and the slopes of the mountains are occupied by these gardens, the irrigation of which reminds one of the great plain below Granada,—the Vega—watered in the same way by the Moors hundreds of years ago, an oasis in the desert of the Spanish mountains. The greater part of the fertile land between Fez and Sifrû is an uncultivated wilderness, presumably from want of water, for but three wells and two small streams are met with in the twenty miles.

Gardens.

The soil is of a deep red, light and rich, extending to a good depth below the surface. Everything that suits the climate thrives to perfection, with hot sun, good soil, and a never-failing water-supply. As Sifrû is twenty-two hundred feet above the sea-level, oranges are cut off by winter frosts, and only a very few orange and lemon trees have survived in sheltered spots. The place is, however, famous for its cherries, which carry better than many fruits, and are sent to great distances. The cherry trees grow to forest height, as indeed do several fruit-bearing species. Each garden has a belt of these, interspersed with ash and other trees on which vines are trained; below them is a thick undergrowth of damson trees. These seem to be planted thus to get shelter from spring frosts, and the fruit ripens well, if late, in the partial shade. The inhabitants exchange damsons for wheat with the country people.

Produce.

The more level gardens, though green, are monotonous, each being a rectangle, with one crop occupying its centre, in summer generally maize, or cucumbers and melons mixed. But the gardens on

Agriculture.

the slopes, with their streams, waterfalls, rocks and caves, are perfect for beauty. Beyond all is an outer belt of very fine olive trees. The prettiest spot close to Sifrû, a slope above the west gate, is occupied by a cemetery, an olive garden and a saint's tomb, all interdicted to Christians and Jews. The peaks of the mountains nearly overhang the town, and can be reached within an hour. Those to the west are remarkably picturesque lime-stone crags, full of caves occupied by serpents and jackals.

Administration.

Sifrû is peopled chiefly by Arabs, with a small sprinkling of Berbers. It is governed by the ḳaïd of the neighbouring Berber tribe, but even the gardens around it are the scene of many robberies and murders, and the whole country is unsafe. The prison is generally full. It is small, and neither better nor worse than those of other parts of Morocco, except in this, that the Berbers when thrown into it suffer much from hunger, as there is no supply of food whatever from the Government, and their friends dare not enter the city walls for fear of being captured, for the inhabitants of Sifrû show the Berbers no mercy, since they suffer so much at their hands. Sifrû has two large mosques with towers, and three smaller ones, besides the shrine of Sidi Ḥasan el Mûsi (cir. 1592—1640), author of "El Muhadarát."[1]

Jewish Colony.

The Jews have five synagogues. The children of both Moors and Jews go early to work in the gardens, and few are educated. The Jews have Hebrew classes in the synagogues for boys only, and not one Jewess can read or write in that or any other language. Yet they would be apt scholars, had they the opportunity of learning. Time hangs heavy on their hands, for they have no garden work and cattle to attend to, like the poorer Moorish women. Since many of the

[1] De Foucauld, p. 38.

Jews have obtained European protection, they are becoming rapidly wealthy by their energy and thrift, and much of the valuable property about Sifrû is passing into their hands. They are very industrious: many employ Moors in their gardens, and buy and sell in the mountains, chiefly for barter. Some are skilled as brass-workers, and send their productions to Fez. The Moors weave a few carpets and their own woollen garments, but are not pushing, being content to live on the produce of their farms and gardens.

Distant only some ten minutes' walk from Sifrû, is another little walled town, Ḳlá, close under the mountains.

Kla and Bahalîl.

There is no market, nor are there shops, for its inhabitants trade in Sifrû. Close to its one gate in the lime-stone rock, are many large caves, one reported to have been inhabited by Christ and His disciples. The road from Sifrû passing the gate lies through an apparently artificial gorge, and leads on to a saint's tomb on the summit of the mountain close by, which perhaps accounts for the cutting. On the way between Fez and Sifrû, perched on the slopes of Jebel Kandar, is the little town of Bahalîl, (*i.e.* "fools"), the inhabitants of which are said to be of Christian origin.[1]

3.—THE TADLA DISTRICT.

Tádla is one of those districts of Central Morocco of which next to nothing is known to the outside world,

Nature.

for being on the borders of a Berber country on the northern slopes of the Atlas, it has been visited by few Europeans.* Sometimes spoken of

* The following historical references of Tádla occur in *The Moorish Empire:* Warfare in the province, 36; conquered by the Lamtûna, 50, 117; projected wall, 159; Ahmad VII. summoned there, 163; subdued, 183 and 185; devastated, 187.

[1] Martinière, p. 398; De Foucauld, p. 37. See *The Moorish Empire*, pp. 36(n) and 311.

as a town, it is really a province dotted with ḳaṣbahs, one of which, on the right bank of the Um er-Rabî'a—here already thirty to forty yards wide—is known by the name of Tádla. But the ḳaṣbahs of Aït Ráḥá and Beni Mellál or Bel Kûsh are the most important,—with perhaps as many as fifteen hundred and one thousand inhabitants respectively.[1] That of Fishtála, three hours from that of Tádla, protects about seven hundred and fifty; both of these were built by Mulai Ismá'íl, who also erected a bridge of ten arches opposite the Ḳaṣbah Tádla, and the existing mosque. A local peculiarity is that the ḳaṣbah proper has but few inhabitants, the majority living in two groups outside the crenellated fortress.[2] The country round is bare, and but scantily cultivated, the only water supply being that of the river, here a trifle salt, from the abundant saline deposits in the vicinity.

Kasbah Tádla.

At the Aït Ráḥá ḳaṣbah the Um er-Rabî'a is crossed by a bridge of one hundred and sixty yards, and here is to be found the palace built by Mulai Ahmad Dhahebi II., while governor during the lifetime of his father, Mulai Ismá'íl, for here at one time he intended to construct his capital. It has, however, no minaret, though the streets and houses are good for this part of the World. It is a four days' journey hence to Marrákesh or Casablanca. Unlike Tádla proper, it is surrounded by excellent gardens, on the produce of which it chiefly subsists.

Aït Ráḥá Kasbah.

The ḳaṣbah of Benî Mellál is situated opposite a defile leading to the pass of the Aït Serî, defended by three small forts. In the time of Leo the town of Táfza, now but a village on the Wád Dernah, a tributary of the Um er-Rabî'a, was the most important settlement in Tádla, practically a republic,

Beni Mellál Kasbah.

[1] Erckmann, p. 64. [2] De Foucauld, pp. 57-8.

prosperous beyond its neighbours, and exporting hooded cloaks to Spain and Italy,

At the present time the most important place in the Tádla district is perhaps Bû Ja'd, somewhat nearer the coast than these kaṣbahs, in the centre of an immense plain, badly watered, and with few gardens. It has no walls, but boasts two large mosques and four mausoleums, for it is the home of one of the great religious families of Morocco. The so-called shareef, Sidi Ben Dáûd, is not, however, a shareef in reality, but a descendant of the Khalîfa 'Omar bin el Khaṭṭáb, whose family came to Morocco three and a half centuries ago,—twelve generations—in the fourth of which they founded Bû Ja'd.[1] Not only is the representative of the Bû Ja'd family in as great repute for the adjustment of quarrels as are the shareefs of Wazzán and Tazirwált in their respective districts, but he does no inconsiderable import trade by way of Casablanca, to say nothing of his vast receipts from tribute. Thursday is the local market day, when most of the men go armed, and carry bayonets on their shoulder-straps.

Bû Ja'd.

4.—DAMNAT.

Few towns in Morocco are so beautifully situated as Damnát, which occupies a lovely valley of the Atlas, two days' north-east of Marrákesh,* with a halt for the night at the small town of Sidi Rahal.† Being abundantly watered from springs which gush from the hill-side beneath a natural arch known as Imin-i-firi,—"the mouth of the river"—a short walk from the gates, the valley is highly cultivated, countless olive-trees forming a prominent feature. For irrigating

Situation.

* 9° 11' 15" W. (De F.)

† 9° 33' 45" W. (De F.); 31° 38' 45" N. (De F.)

[1] De Foucauld, pp. 52-6.

DAMNÁT.

Photograph by the late Joseph Thomson, Esq.

the lower part of the valley there exists a very creditable dam.

The town itself is strongly walled, and has three exterior gates besides those leading into an extensive mellāḥ and the citadel. Within the latter are the governor's palace, the chief mosque and other public buildings of a more solid construction; the ordinary dwellings being almost entirely built of earth-concrete, present a ruinous appearance. A good trade is done with Marrákesh, and until many of them were driven by persecution to the capital, it was the home of a large number of well-to-do Jews, but now the mellāḥ is the scene of poverty and filth alone.

Jewish Centre.

The surrounding Berbers, who on the death of Mulai el Ḥasan descended and sacked the ḳaṣbah, are a source of fear to even the Mohammedan residents. Otherwise Damnát lies too far off the main routes to have played a part of much importance in Moorish history. It may have some three thousand inhabitants, a third of whom are Jews.

5.—TAZA.

Táza, chief town of the province of Haïáïna, south of the Rîf, is another of those less known to Europeans.* Its situation—about two days from Fez, and four from Oojda—is on a high rock described by De Foucauld [1] as eighty-three metres above the river Faḥḥámah, near the point where it falls into the Înáwî, one hundred and thirty metres below the town.† It is

Situation.

* The following historical references to Táza occur in *The Moorish Empire:* Conflict with Fez, 41; taken by Abu Bakr, 92; Mohammed XI. defeated there, 122; taken by Er-Rasheed II., 138; campaigns against it, 270 and 429.

† Its position is given by Ali Bey as 34° 30′ 7″ N. by 6° 0′ 15″ W. (of Paris) [2] and by De Foucauld as 34° 12′ 54″ N.

walled, in some places with a double line, but the walls are old, low and thin, leaving the place an easy prey to the periodical attacks of the Miknása and Ghäïáta Berbers, between whose districts it lies. The full name of the place appears to have been Rabat Táza,[1] although the author of *Raôḍ el Hátûn* calls it Miknásat Táza.

Strategic Importance.

In the days when Tlemçen belonged to Morocco, Táza, being on the high road to Fez, was of some importance, a character which it may be said to have forfeited altogether, except in view of the possibility of a French invasion by this route. Ruins of those days still surround the town, and the once famous mosque survives, in the court of which lies the ameer Abu 'Abd er-Raḥman, who died at New Tlemçen. This mosque was built in 1294, and was said to accommodate ten to twelve thousand persons: its huge lamps of copper, which still exist, gave five hundred and fourteen lights, and cost eight thousand dinars, weighing thirty-two hundredweight.[2]

History.

Táza is mentioned as existing in 828, and it was rebuilt by 'Abd el Mû'min in 1135;[3] in the time of Leo Africanus that writer found it in a most prosperous state, rich and well-peopled, though the Berbers were as much in the habit of cutting off the water-supply by deflecting it as they are now. Its palace had been destroyed by a king of Tlemçen, who besieged it in 1382.[4] The Jews there, Leo tells us, made the finest of wine from the local white grapes, and a good trade in dates and grain was done with Tafîlált.[5] Its gardens have later been famed for nightingales, and its streams for tortoises.*

* A meagre description is given by Scott, p. 24.

[1] cf. 'Abd el Waḥeed, p 260. [2] *Raôḍ el Kartás.* [3] Ib., p. 266.

[4] Mercier, vol. ii. [5] Ed. Ram., p. 52.

6.—DIBDÛ.

Jewish Centre.

It is chiefly as a Jewish centre trading between Melilla —almost due north—and the East Morocco oases, that the small town of Dibdû, is known. It was built in ancient times, however, on a tributary of the Melwîya, and in the sixteenth century was of considerable importance. To-day it has a population of only two to four thousand, of whom De Foucauld, our only modern authority, estimates three-quarters to be Jews.[1] It is unwalled. Situated at the bottom of a green valley abounding in springs, the surroundings could not fail to be beautiful. The distance from Melilla is two and a half days, from Táza two long days, and from Oojda three days.

7.—OOJDA.

Strategic Importance.

From its strategical position on the main route from Algeria to Fez, on the south side of the valley which lies behind the Rîf mountains, the little town of Oojda has ever been the victim of the frontier wars of Morocco, and is likely one day to be either wiped out of existence, or rejuvenated by the inrush of the French.* At present it is otherwise of no importance, though it does a fair amount of local trade, the bulk of which now enters from Algeria. Its population is perhaps only five or six thousand, and its appearance is unpromising, as decayed and ruinous as most inland towns of Morocco. Oojda is situated on

Description.

the lower slopes of a hill-side, and is surrounded by olive groves. Every Thursday a market

* Notices of some of these vicissitudes will be found in *The Moorish Empire:* Oojda destroyed, 96; taken by 'Ali V., 102; recovered by 'Abd er-Raḥmán II., 173; seized by the French, 174; revolt and reduction, 182; Berbers sent here, 302, 429.

[1] p. 248.

is held outside its tottering walls, whereat wool and grains are the staples, and its sheep are famous for both flesh and coats. Though on the borders of the Angad desert, it is copiously watered from a spring, and its gardens furnish abundant fruit. It is, however, famous for no manufactures, and even its local saint, Sidi Yûnas (Jonah) has no wide-spread reputation. Architecturally there is nothing to describe, beyond the citadel and the mosques, the chief of which is in the Sheikian quarter. The other quarters are those of Aôlád el Ḥasan, Aôlád 'Amrán, Ahl Oojda, Aôlád el Ḳáḍi, and the mellàḥ, which is in the centre. Of its four gates the most important are Báb Záwîah, on the Tlemçen road, and Báb Genáïn, on the Táza road.

The exact position of Oojda is given as 34° 40′ 54″ N. by 1° 47′ 30″ W., and its distance from Tlemçen is seventy-five kilomètres, the artificial frontier being at Sidi Záher, fifteen kilomètres distant. *Position.* It is easily reached from Lallah Maghnîah, (Marnia, twenty-six kilomètres) which is connected with Ghazawát (Nemours) and Tlemçen by *diligence*. But the French are apt to look on foreign visitors to so out-of-the-way a spot with suspicion, and when I was there I was officially examined on two occasions. To Fez viâ Táza it is about ten days' journey, which has been reckoned to mean three hundred and twenty kilomètres.[1] De Foucauld gives as the principal stages to Fez, Ḳaṣbat el 'Aïûn, Gersîf, Ḳaṣbat Miknása, Haïáïna and Fez.

The origin of Oojda is attributed to the Zanáta Berbers, whose leader Zîri ibn Athîr built it in 994.[2] Its fortifications were renewed in 1208 by Mohammed III. (En Náṣir), but in 1271 it was destroyed by Ya'ḳûb II. (bin 'Abd el Ḥaḳḳ), and is said to have been re-built in 1297,[3] when the new town of *History.*

[1] De Campou. [2] *Raôd el Kartas*, p. 144. [3] Ib. p. 329.

Tlemçen was founded. Yet little more than a generation had passed, when in 1333 it was destroyed once more by 'Ali V. (Abu'l Ḥasan) on his way to Tlemçen, and in 1336 its walls were razed entirely. Thus whoever was victor it suffered, sometimes being under Tlemçen, sometimes under Fez. On the death of Yazeed, in 1792, the Algerian Turks appropriated it, but abandoned it a few years later on the approach of a Moorish army. Sixteen miles to the north-west are traces of Roman entrenchments, known from a mile-stone to have been the camp of Numerus Severianus.*

* An interesting little brochure recounting a single visit with a few historical details, a plan and views, was published at Oran in 1886 by J. Canal.

THE TOWN OF CEUTA.
(Looking westward from the hill, towards Morocco.)

CHAPTER THE NINETEENTH

SPANISH POSSESSIONS

1.—"SANTA CRUZ DE MAR PEQUEÑA"

OF all the ports which Portugal and Spain at one time possessed on the Moorish coast, only four remain in the hands of Spain, * and all are situated east of the Straits, though Spain indeed claims a somewhat mythical port on the coast of Sûs, known as "Santa Cruz de Mar Pequeña," a claim which she forced the Moors to recognize by treaty † after the war of 1860, although her own authorities have never yet been able to agree as to its whereabouts. It appears to have been established in 1476 somewhere on the extreme frontier of the Morocco of those days, by the Duke of Herrera, ‡ [1] but since to have been lost

"Santa Cruz de Mar Pequeña."

* General descriptions of these "presidios" or penal settlements have been written by Santoja, *España en el Riff*, 2 vols., 1881; and Pezzi, *Los Presidios menores de Africa*, 1 vol., 1893. A more pretentious but less satisfactory account is that of Galindo, Madrid, 1884.

† Treaty of Wád Rás, art. 8. The insertion in the treaty of this stipulation with regard to the vanished possession is attributed by Duro to an offer received while the peace negotiations were proceeding, from the Sheïkh ben Baïrûk of Wád Nûn, to support the Spaniards by rebelling against the Sultan, if the Spaniards would in turn assist him.[2] See *The Moorish Empire*, p. 177.

‡ Herrera was the successor of Jean de Bethencourt, a French nobleman who had entered the service of Enrique III. of Spain about the year 1400, and was sent in charge of an expedition to the Canaries, of which he was made nominal king. "Santa Cruz de Mar Pequeña" was founded at midnight near a place called "Guader"—33 leagues from the Canaries—at the mouth of a river navigable for three leagues. Herrera's exploit was considered of sufficient importance to find mention twice in the inscription on his tomb in the monastery of Buenaventura in the Canaries.[3]

[1] THOMASSY, p. 113. [2] p. 210.

[3] FERNANDEZ DURO, *Bol. Soc. Geog.*, Madrid, 1878, p. 161.

sight of, as it was destroyed by the Moors in 1524. In 1494 a papal bull had been obtained from Alexander IV., confirming Spain in her possession, but her right to stations on the coast being questioned by Portugal, international complications arose.*

A Fruitless Commission.

In 1877 a joint commission of Spaniards and Moors was conveyed down the coast by a Spanish vessel of war, but failed to arrive at any conclusion.† For five months they sat at Mogador, and then they journeyed by land for 110 kilometres south of Agadîr Ighîr, proceeding thence by sea, inspecting all the rivers and landing-places as far as Puerto Cansado and Juby. With them went two Spanish engineers, and two inspectors of public works on behalf of the sultan, to advise as to the best port to throw open to trade. The general opinion seems to have been in favour of Ifni (29° 24′ 10″ N.,‡ 10° 12′ 3″ W.), and a most able report to this effect was published by Captain Fernandez Duro, of the vessel *Blasco de Garay*, which conveyed the expedition. Ruins were there discovered, and documents were signed by the local sheïkhs and the Spanish officials.

Rival Sites.

But the opinion of Captain Galiano in favour of the mouth of the Shibîka, half-way between Capes Nûn and Juby, was upheld by the Spanish Minister of Marine.§ Among the rival sites, Messrs. Coello

* According to an unpublished Mss. in the Library of the Academy of History in Madrid,[1] the Spaniards obtained the adhesion of a number of the neighbouring tribes in the early years of the fifteenth century.[2]

† Among the conflicting reports which have appeared may be mentioned those of Capt. Galiano, Madrid, 1878 (2nd. ed. with maps); an anonymous writer in the *Rev. Gen. de Marina*, Madrid, 1870, vol. iii., pt. 2; Fernandez Duro, *Bol. Soc. Geog.*, Madrid, vol. iv., 1878, p. 64; vol. v., 1879, p. 193, with a good map of the coast, and plan of the bay of Ifni; and Merle, *Rev. de Géog.*, Paris, 1885, p. 169.

‡ Or 29° 26′. § Royal Order of Marine Office, July 19th, 1879.

[1] *Papeles de Salazar*, A. 11: Rey Católico, 1480-1505, fol. 201-206.

[2] See JIMÉNEZ DE LA ESPADA, *Espana en Berberia*, Madrid 1880, and GALINDO, p. 71.

and Ferreiro contended for the mouth of the Nûn, or failing that, of the Dra'a. Gatell,[1] not without some show of reason, claims the identity of a place between Cape Nûn and the Assáka still known as Ṣôķ en-Naṣárà ("Christian Market") or Jorba, two hours inland from which are ruins called Tarûmît, (the "Roman," *i.e.* the Foreign-Place). The probability is that Herrera's castle was, as several early writers averred, erected on the shores of the lagoon known as "Puerto Cansado," doubtless the "little sea" which lent its name to the vanished settlement. Care must be taken not to confuse this place with the Santa Cruz of the Portuguese, Agadîr Ig͟hîr, the position of which was never in doubt.

Abortive Schemes.

Notwithstanding the failure of this commission, great schemes were set on foot by the Spanish Geographical Congress, on the supposition that Ifnî was to be ceded: an Arabic journal was established for gratuitous circulation, and free Arabic classes were announced in the Canaries. On the more practical side, in Nov. 1882 the Spanish Government despatched two companies of marines to Teneriffe, fully officered, with tent accommodation for four hundred, assembly marquees, tent-ovens, provisions, wine, rice, peas, pork, and twenty thousand rations of biscuits, to take possession of the "Fishery," but nothing has yet been done. Were it not for the opposition of France and Great Britain,[2] Spain might possibly at one time have secured in exchange for so unsatisfactory a "possession" another foot-hold on the Straits of Gibraltar.

2.—SIBTA (CEUTA)

Ceuta is by far the most important of the Spanish possessions in Morocco, and can make the proud boast of

[1] *Bull. Soc. Géog.* Paris., 1871, p. 95.

[2] Merle, p. 170.

having been the last North African stronghold to be overwhelmed by the tide of Arab invasion. Although at one time nominally under the authority of the Greek ruler of Constantinople, Ceuta was too remote to obtain assistance, and it was to Spain that its governor turned, to Roderick, Visigoth king of Toledo.* But hereby hangs the tale of the Moorish invasion of Spain, for it was this same governor, Count Julian, who is recorded to have invited his old foes the Moors to cross the Straits under Ṭárik in 710, in revenge for the betrayal of his daughter by his king. And it seems almost just that Spain's last footing in Morocco of any importance should be this same Ceuta, though she did not obtain it by conquest, only by withholding it from Portugal at the close of the period during which the two crowns were united, from 1580 to 1640. In 1688 its retention was secured by the Treaty of Lisbon.[1]

Importance.

After having in all likelihood afforded shelter to a Carthaginian colony, the Bay of Ceuta and the town there nestled passed to Rome, becoming known as Exilissa,[2] later on as Lissa only, or perhaps accompanied by "Civitas," since Leo gives the latter word as the original of *Cibta*,[3] which the Portuguese have rendered *Seupta*, the modern Spaniards pronouncing it "*Thaota*," though spelling it *Ceuta*. This indeed seems a more likely derivation than the rival one from

Early History.

* See *The Moorish Empire*, p. 26. Other historical references to Ceuta contained in that volume are: Attack by the Berber rebels, p. 29; by Yûsef I., 54; its walls razed, 73; supremacy of Tunis acknowledged, 92; tributes paid to the Beni Marîn, 94; taken by Sulaïmân I., 101; by Ibrâhîm II., 105; from Granáda, 107-8; by Enrique III. of Spain, 108; by the Portuguese, 110; by Mohammed X., 119.

[1] See *Recuerdos de Africa: historia de la plaza de Ceuta*, by the Marquez de Prado, with map, Madrid, 1859-60. [2] Ptolemy. [3] Ed. Ramusio, p. 90.

Septem Fratres, or *Arx Septensis*, because of the seven neighbouring hills, though to Byzantium it was known as Septon.* It was also known as Julia Trajecta, in contradistinction to Tarifa on the opposite shore, called Julia Traducta,[1] and it afterwards became the chief town of Hispania Transfretana,[2] a title which it might appropriately use to-day.

Having passed into the hands of the Vandals, on their fall Justinian restored its forts in 534,[3] and in 618 the Goths became its masters. By that time it is probable that the rocky heights of the peninsula to which the Arabs gave the name of Jebel el Mîna—recalled by the name of its westernmost point, Almina, †—had been preferred to the more accessible bay on the mainland, now known as Old Ceuta; or the ruins so-called may be only remains of some besieging camp. Idreesi says that the walled stronghold of which remains still stand on Almina point was built at the time of the invasion by Mohammed ibn Abû Ameer, the town being built on the adjoining hills, the peninsula bearing then the name of Munkoṭgha.[4]

Gothic Period.

The Arabs obtained possession in 711 A.C.,—presumably by Julian's peaceful surrender, since there is no account of its capture[5]—but did not long retain it. In 740 they were forced to garrison it with troops brought specially from Syria, whom the Berbers, under the leadership of Maïṣará,

Arab Period.

* Strabo says that Mons Abyla (Ape's Hill or Jebel Mûsà) contained the tombs of the "seven brothers,"[6] but Marcus, that like so many other popular sites, it had seven peaks.

† On this headland, 476 ft. above the sea-level, now stands a light which is visible for 23 miles. Mt. Actio, the highest point, attains an altitude of 629 ft., and its exact position is given as 35° 53′ 6″ N., and 5° 17′ W.

[1] James, vol i., p. 54. [2] Leo. [3] Mannert, p. 543. [4] p. 199
[5] Gayangos on El Makkari, bk. iv., ch. ii., note 19. [6] Bk. xvii., § vi.

eventually ejected.* The town was then re-built by Majákîs, who re-named it after himself, Majákîsa. For nearly two hundred years his successors maintained their independence, until 'Abd er-Raḥmán I. of Córdova took it in 931, after which it passed into the hands of the Central Morocco Berghwátà till the Murábṭîs took it in 1083, and its separate history ended.† When the Murábṭîs fell it was twice sacked and ruined during the revolution, first by 'Abd el-Mû'min, when establishing the dynasty of the Muwáḥḥadîs in 1148,[1]—though in 1172 he endowed it with an arsenal,[2]—and subsequently by an ameer of Granáda. Ceuta was seldom free from foreign enemies also, for both in 1180 and 1182 the Portuguese admiral Rompinho fought against it, but only succeeded in capturing several vessels.[3]

Forty years later Ceuta became independent, as the capital of the Rîf country. It had by this time obtained renown for articles in brass, which Leo tells us fetched the price of silver in Italian marts, while caravans from the interior brought ivory and gold and slaves.[4]‡ So much of the important trade which these supplies created lay in the hands of the Genoese, that they even kept galleys here to protect the place and her vessels against Spanish pirates. In 1234 they arranged with the governor for the Moors to defray half the cost of an expedition against these foes, for which they sent twenty-eight galleys under Spinola.[5] But as no battle was fought, the Moors objected to pay, and the Genoese getting impatient, broils took place in the street, in which merchandise

Trade.

Relations with the Genoese.

* See *The Moorish Empire*, p. 29. † Ib. p. 45.

‡ Ceuta is said to have been the first place in the West where paper was manufactured. (*Enc. Brit.*)

[1] *Raôd el Kartâs*, p. 272. [2] El Makkari, bk. viii., p. 319. [3] Thomassy, p. 111.

[4] Ib. p. 102. [5] Mas Latrie, *Relations*, p. 102; Godard, p. 344.

belonging to the foreigners was burnt. In revenge the Genoese brought "war machines," and commenced a siege which lasted into the following year, when the Moors were glad enough to settle the matter for 400,000 dînars, [1] the Genoese leaving a few ships as before.

Soon after this, in the Beni Marîn invasion, Ceuta changed hands again, falling into the power of Granáda, and in 1274 a treaty was signed at Barcelona by the ameer Ya'ḳûb II. in person, and Iago I. of Aragon, by which the latter undertook to send ten ships and five hundred knights for the re-conquest of Ceuta; and in 1309 Iago or Jaime II. of Castille made another treaty of similar tenor, * with which assistance Ceuta finally passed to the Beni Marîn.

Subject to Granáda.

Then came the Portuguese again under Joao I., with a fleet of thirty-three galleys, twenty-seven triremes, twenty pinnaces, and transports bearing thirty thousand soldiers on their way to the crusade of 1415. † To them Ceuta yielded on the eve of the Feast of the Assumption. [2] "Prince Henry the Navigator," who was afterwards to do so much to make Africa known, and two of his brothers who had also been distinguished for their bravery, were knighted next day in the mosque, ‡ which had been newly dedicated to the Name of Christ. [3] It was said that from the Moorish palace the Conde de Barcellos—afterwards the Duque de Braganza—carried away to his own home in Barce-

Portuguese Period.

* Mas Latrie gives the treaties in his supplement, pp. 285 and 297. See *The Moorish Empire*, pp. 96 and 241.

† It is recorded that on this occasion they were assisted by the English. [4] *Note:* the date 1414 for this event in the Chronological Chart in *The Moorish Empire* is a printer's error, and should be corrected.

‡ See *Vida do Infante D. Henrique*, Lisbon, 1758, by Laudido Lusitano; and Azurara's *Chronicle*, Hakluyt Ed., p. 17.

[1] *Raôd el Karțâs*, p. 394.
[2] THOMASSY, p. 98.
[3] GODARD, p. 395.
[4] HAKLUYT, vol. ii., pt. ii., p. 1.

lona no less than six hundred marble and alabaster columns, which were in all probability relics of the earlier Roman Period. *

Moorish Sieges.

Three years later the Moors made an unsuccessful attack with one hundred thousand men, supported by troops from Granáda and Tunis,[1] and in 1694 Mulai Ismá'íl commenced a siege which dragged on wearily for six and twenty years, till Felipe V. drove the Báshá of Tetuan out of his trenches, and reduced the investment—which still continued—to a mere formality. The besieging army had averaged twenty-five thousand, including five hundred archers of Fez, who were changed every six months.[2] † It had been the pet scheme of Ismá'íl to regain Ceuta, for which he had striven in vain to obtain the assistance of France. Ruins of his built-up camp may still be seen about two hours' ride along the Tangier track. His son, Abd Allah V., was equally unfortunate in his attempt of 1732.

Strategical Value.

When the Portuguese took it, their chronicler Azurara declared that "Of a surety no one can deny that Ceuta is the very key of all the Mediterranean Sea,"[3] and although, since England has held Gibraltar, so much more has been made of it than of Ceuta that we have learned to think our fortress the key, it is certain that until the introduction of steamships, Ceuta had at least as many natural strategical advantages as "Gib." But it is a question now whether in time of war either would be of much real use, except as a coaling station, of which Spain has no need at that point. After having captured Gibraltar in 1704,

* C. R. Beazley, *Henry the Navigator*, 1895, p. 154.

† It is said that the cause of a sudden retreat by the Moors from a part of the fortifications captured in the first year of the siege, was their fright at the hitherto unheard sound of a booming alarm bell![4]

[1] Beazley, l.c. p. 149.
[2] Ez-Zaiáni.
[3] Hakluyt Edition, vol i., p. 16.
[4] Godard, p. 518.

the English and Hessian fleet called on Ceuta also to capitulate, but being unable to arrange an attack, left it undisturbed. A century afterwards, nevertheless, the English occupied it for a short time, in 1810, under Fraser.*

A Prince's Ransom.

The feeling with regard to Ceuta on the part of Moors and Europeans may be judged from an incident of the times: an unfortunate brother of the king of Portugal who had been taken prisoner at the attack on Tangier in 1437, was set to turn a mill in Fez, where, as no other ransom than Ceuta would be accepted, and that was refused by the Pope as well as by the Portuguese, he was left to die.[1] The olive wand of Pedro de Menezes, whom the Portuguese made their first governor, is handed still to his successors as a symbol of investiture: since 1774 it has been kept in the hand of "Our Lady of Africa," in the cathedral[2] into which the chief mosque was transformed in 1432.[3] A Roman bishopric had been established in 1421,[4] and in 1570 Pius V. united this see with that of Tangier.[5] It was maintained by the sale of indulgences under one of the four papal bulls granted exclusively to Spain in consequence of the African expedition of Cardinal Ximenes, known as the "Milk Bull," permitting the consumption of flesh, butter, cheese and eggs in Lent.[6] The palace and cathedral of Ceuta are among its most important buildings.

Bishopric.

* A proposal has been several times put forward unofficially to exchange Gibraltar for Ceuta, Spain refunding the cost of all public works on "the Rock," but on account of local opposition and British sentiment, the idea has never met with favour. Owing to the manner in which Spain acquired Ceuta no considerations of sentiment weigh with her, and she may at any time dispose of it to a Power whom we should find a troublesome neighbour.

[1] Torres, ch. 104, p. 185. See p. 117; and *The Moorish Empire*, pp. 109 and 123.
[2] Prado, p. 56; Godard, p. 395. [3] Prado.
[4] Prado. [5] Wadding, *Annales Minorum*, Vol. xix p. 76.
[6] Clark, *Spanish Nation*, pt. ii., pp. 45-6.

It would be out of place to dwell here on Ceuta as it exists to-day, since for nearly five hundred years it has been in European hands. The town, the penitentiary, and the fortifications which still require annoying formalities before the stranger can pass through them, are essentially Spanish, and as such have no special interest for students of Morocco. Towards the mainland Ceuta is protected by a citadel upon the narrow neck of the isthmus, threaded by a circuitous thoroughfare, and guarded by moats on either side. I shall never forget the relief with which I re-crossed the brook which forms the Moorish frontier, after having had to dare the bare-footed Spanish sentries, who removed the stoppers from their guns and threatened to shoot us if we would not ride some miles back a second time for a pass which should have been provided at a previous barrier. But a cup of green tea at the Moorish guard-house on the opposite hill made us forget the worries of an excursion into civilization. Hard by is a Moorish Customs House, through which passes merchandize for Anjera and even Tetuan. There are a number of Moors residing in Ceuta, including the few descendants of those transferred from Oran, when that town was abandoned by Spain in 1796.

Modern Ceuta.

The Frontier.

Communication by *faluchos* and steamers is maintained with the neighbouring Spanish ports and Gibraltar, but the most picturesque route is up hill and down dale from Tangier, a long day's journey through beautiful country. The much shorter road from Tetuan is less pleasant unless the slight tide is out, since for nearly eight hours it follows a sandy beach.

Communication.

3.—BÁDIS (PEÑON DE VELEZ DE LA GOMERA)

The next Spanish possession, travelling from Ceuta westward, has also an ancient, if scanty, record. Probably the Belis of the Carthaginians, or perhaps Parietina, it is mentioned later as a Christian bishopric. [1] But it first appears in modern history when we read that, like N'kôr, it was re-built by Mohammed III. (En-Náṣir) in 1207. [2] In the time of Leo,—who says that some authors ascribed its foundation to the Goths, [3]— it was a flourishing place whose inhabitants were half of them fishers, and half of them—owners of a small ship-building-yard—pirates, while among them were many Jews who made excellent wine. Every year or two there came Venetian galleys laden with rich merchandize, and the rulers of Fez held Bádis in high repute as the nearest port to their metropolis. *

History.

In 1508 Don Pedro de Navarro took the rock or "*peñon*" which stands a mile from the site of the ancient city, but only held it until 1522, when the garrison was cut to pieces on its capture by the Turk Sálaḥ Raïs. [4] The town was then re-built, and piracy flourished once more, not only under the Rifîs, but under the Algerians, who had recently taken Fez, [5] and were now also masters of Bádis. In 1525 and 1563 the Spaniards made unsuccessful attempts to recover the "*peñon*," but in 1564 they sent a fleet of no less than one hundred and ten vessels, carrying fifteen thousand men, enlisted in Genoa, Malta and Portugal, as well as in Spain, under the leadership of Garcia de Toledo, who soon obtained possession, and his nation has held it since. ‡

Spanish Period.†

* This was about 1500, yet Ufráni says it was built in 1509! [6]

† See *The Moorish Empire*, pp. 111, 116, 119 and 152.

‡ Lafuente, *Historia de Espana*; Forneron, *Historia de Felipe III.*: see also *Public Record Office*, Colonial State Papers, Foreign Series, vol. for 1564, pp. 194 and 216.

[1] Hooker and Ball.
[2] *Raôd el Kartás*, p. 330
[3] Ed. Ramusio, p. 93
[4] Leo; Torres, p. 433.
[5] El Ufráni, p. 89; Torres, p. 420; Godard, pp. 425 and 470.
[6] p. 69.

During this time the only events in its history worth recording seem to have been misfortunes. It was besieged by the Moors under Ismá'íl in 1680, 1687 and 1702—3: it was visited by the plague in 1743, and by scurvy in 1752 and 1799: between 1791 and 1801 it suffered from four earthquakes, and from yellow fever in 1821.* The lot of those confined to its limits on such occasions can be imagined, for there is no intercourse with the mainland, so that they have frequently been threatened with famine.

Misfortunes.

Ferdinand VII. once offered its return to the Moors in exchange for horses, and in 1872 its abandonment and the destruction of the rock were urged on the Cortes.† Even as a relic it is hardly worth retaining without a slice of the wooded and fertile country of Ghomára beyond, for in dry years the rock is dependent for much of its water on Spain or Morocco. Although no Customs arrangements exist, there is both here and at Alhucemas a small local trade with the well-to-do Bukûya tribe on the mainland. Velez is situated in 35° 12' 45" N.; the height of the rock is two hundred and seventy-three feet.

Proposed Abandonment.

4.—ḤAJRAT N'KÔR (ALHUCEMAS)

The island or "rock" of N'kôr, to which the Spaniards have given the name of Alhucemas, came into their hands somewhat strangely, for it was given over to them by the Moorish ameer when the

History.‡

* The yellow fever was introduced to Europe and America (and subsequently to Morocco) by the West African slave-trade, if, indeed, it did not, as some believe, originate in the inhuman treatment of the "Middle Passage."

† See the *Diario de Sesiones,* No. 13, Apl. 3rd., and Pezzi, p. 39, for the speeches on this occasion.

‡ See *The Moorish Empire,* pp. 45, 111(*n*) and 402.

Algerian Turks were at Bádis, in 1554, in order to keep it out of their hands.[1] Of its earlier history little is known, except that it once boasted its own dynasty, and that it became a refuge of a branch of the Idreesîs.[2] It was re-built by Mohammed III. (En-Náṣir) in 1207,[3] and was probably the "Mazemma"* of Idreesi, Abu'l Fîda and Leo, "a great city set on a little mountain" by the river N'kôr, of which the ruins only remained. It had been twice destroyed, first by the shareef of Kaïrwán for refusing tribute in 930 A.C.,—when the governor's head was sent on a lance to the suzerain city,—and a second time in 1487 A.C. by a Córdovan ameer, who observed with jealousy the rising power of so near a neighbour.[4]

Trade.

In 1665 a futile attempt was made by a French "Compagnie d'Abouzème" to establish a business here, and Roland Fréjus visited Rasheed II. at Táza on its behalf, with letters from Louis XIV.† It was not till 1673 that the Spanish really occupied Alhucemas, under the Prince of Montesacro. In 1771 it was ordered that only such offenders as might develop into honourable citizens and soldiers should be deported to Alhucemas, for it is also a convict station.

Situation.

Alhucemas consists of a little island only forty-eight feet high, about a mile from the shore, in a bay some five miles deep and nine across, from north to south. There are also three small islands near the shore, and three more distant. A fair anchorage exists across the bay, and goods are landed at the

* Possibly this should be read "El Hozma," which would account for the Spanish name, but neither is now known.

† See his *Rel. d'un Voyage*, Paris, 1670, and *The Moorish Empire*, pp. 402 and 473.

[1] Torres, p. 420.

[2] *Raôd el Kartás*, p. 330

[3] *Raôd el Kartás*, p. 61; Ibn Khaldûn, vol. ii, p. 275.

[4] Leo, ed. Ramusio. p. 93.

MELILLA FROM THE EAST.

Drawn by E. F. Skinner.

side of the rock by cranes. Water is as usual scarce, and there being no intercourse with the mainland, life here is not to be envied. From Velez it is twenty-seven miles, from Melilla fifty-three, and from Malaga ninety-three; its precise position is 34° 35′ 15″ N., and 3° 46′ 30″ W.

5.—MELILÎYA (MELILLA)

Situation.

On the east side of the bare forbidding headland of Rás Hûrák, known through the Spaniards as "Cabo Tres Forcas," one hundred and thirty-five miles from Ceuta,* on the coast of Er-Rîf, standing out from hills behind, is the huge rock on which the town and fortress of Melilla have been built.† It is not an inviting spot, and could hardly have been better chosen for the use to which, in common with the other four Spanish "presidios," it has been put,—that of a convict station. Beyond a strip of so-called neutral ground, bounded by a line of small forts, the erection of one of which by the side of a saint-house nearly plunged Morocco and Spain into war in 1893, the Spaniards dare not venture afield, and the draw-bridge is kept shut at night.

Appearance.

From the landing-place a steep ascent leads to the upper town, a little chip of Spain, with its cafés and plazas, its bands and its cigarettes; but the view, which I have seen only in summer, could not then be described as enchanting; simply the rolling, sun-browned hills, rising one behind the other, with hardly a sign of habitation. A good many Rîfîs come with their produce to the market below the town, while in quiet times not a few enter within the walls,

* The distance to Alhucemas is 53 miles, to the Zaffarines 27, and to Malaga 113.

† The dimensions are given as 121 yds. by 95; and its exact position as 35° 27′ N., by 2° 59′ W.

and a growing trade in European manufactures with Dibdû* and the Rîf provides an occupation for a certain number of the inhabitants, but with this exception almost all are military. Close to the gate of the town is the Moorish Customs Office, established by special arrangement in 1866,† through which pass most of the European imports, arms and ammunition excepted, these being landed from sailing vessels along the coast. The mole is cut from the solid rock.

Spanish Period. ‡

It was in 1497 that Melilla fell into the hands of Spain, or rather into those of the Duke of Medina Sidonia,[1] whose general, Juan de Guzman, to punish the pirates, in that year took and rebuilt a fortress which had been erected in 1205 by one Yaïsh, described as a Christian governor under the ameer Mohammed III. (En-Nâṣir).[2] Till the end of the fifteenth century the place remained in the possession of the Duke's descendants, after which it lapsed to the crown in 1506.

Kasása.

Near by was in those days another town trading with Venice, Kasása; this was taken by the Duke at the same time,[3] but has since disappeared. Oysters and pearls were formerly found on this coast in sufficient quantities to make the place worth holding. In 1534 it was lost to the Spaniards through treachery, and ere long it was razed to the ground by the Rîfîs.

Moorish Attacks.

From the outset troubles with the native neighbours of Melilla seem to have continued with slight interruption. In 1563 the Moors made repeated attacks under a saint who professed to be able to cast a spell over the Spaniards, but twice

* Two and a half days' journey almost due south.

† For text, see Pezzi, p. 303, from the *Gaceta Oficial* of March 3rd, 1867.

‡ See *The Moorish Empire*, pp. 110, 167, 177 and 349.

[1] GODARD, p. 405. [2] *Raôḍ el Kartâs*, p. 388. [3] GODARD, p. 405.

the governor let in a portion of the enemy and massacred them.[1] In 1660 an earthquake destroyed the fortifications, and with this exception its history is but a round of famines and sieges, the most important having been those of Mulai Isma'îl in 1694 and 1715—16, after which a blockade was maintained until his death in 1727.

Abandonment Urged.

In 1764 the Spanish Government was urged to abandon all these useless possessions, retaining only Ceuta and O'ran, but the good advice went unheeded, and in 1774 Melilla had to withstand a serious attack at the hands of Mohammed XVII.—while pretending to be at peace with Spain at sea,—an attack in which a thousand Jews are said to have been forced to take part.[2] Again in 1823 abandonment was urged in vain, and in 1829 the prisoners mutinied with the intention of giving it up to the Moors. The Carlists exiled here in 1838 were more successful, for they held the place until in the following year they were promised freedom to return to their leader.

Relations with the Rîf.

An attempt by Spain in 1854 to exercise her treaty rights by chastising the neighbouring Rîfîs without the intervention of the Moorish Government * led indirectly to the war of 1859—60, and again in 1893 to reprisals which necessitated a campaign by the Spaniards to revenge the serious losses received at first. This ended with the payment by El Ḥasan III., just before his death, of an indemnity of twenty million pesetas, (about £666,000).

Attempted Development.

In 1884 a Royal Order had been issued permitting the establishment of an agricultural colony on an adjoining strip of the mainland, the thirty-four colonists to be drawn by preference from a certain place in the province of Malaga, and

* Treaty of 1779.

[1] GODARD, p. 470.

[2] PEZZI, p. 123.

not to include more than one Moor—who should have accepted Spanish rule—among ten foreigners. By treaty no Europeans may enter Morocco from Melilla, and all traffic with the interior must be in native hands.

Name.

The name Meliliya is supposed by some to be connected with the honey (mela) for which, together with wax, the district round has always been famous. Probably there was a Carthaginian settlement here, perhaps the ancient Russadeiron, or Sustiaría Akra. Anchorage in the offing is ample and good, but the constantly strained relations with the mainland have prevented any great development of its resources, although since 1863 Melilla, Ceuta and the Zaffarines have been free ports.

6.—JAZÁÏR ZAFRÁN, or THE ZAFFARINE ISLANDS

(In Spanish, Las Chafarinás)

Acquisition.

One trifling possession alone has been added by Spain to the list since the Middle Ages, that of a little group of three rocky islets, slight in value, near the mouth of the Melwîya and the French frontier. These were secured, not by force of arms, but by forestalling the French in claiming them after the war of 1844, and although this was not done until January 6, 1848, the French general MacMahon, sent on a similar errand, arrived but a few days late.

Description.

The most westerly island is the highest, 441 ft., but the centre one contains the chief establishment, and previous to the Spanish war of 1859 it was well fortified, in addition to having perpendicular cliffs. The easternmost of the three, Isla del Rey, and the westernmost, Isla del Congreso, boast but one house apiece, the convict settlement being on the central island, Isabel Segunda. This is nearly round, and about a kilometre across at the widest part, the greatest height being 136 ft. At the north-west point is a light-house, 226 ft. above the sea.

Value and Formation.

The actual value of the Zaffarines is very slight, and purely strategical, as protecting the best roadstead on this coast. In 1885 the repair of the fortifications was commenced in fear of the Germans, but when the war alarm blew over the works were discontinued. The formation of the islands is granitic, and the water-supply is so poor that this precious liquid has to be brought from Spain, with which there is no regular communication. The distance from Cape Agua is 1235 metres, or nearly a mile, and the precise position of the highest point is in 35° 11′ 7″ N., by 2° 5′ 7″ W.*

* A good plan of the Zaffarines is given in the *Gazette Géographique*, N. Sér, t. xxi., 1886, p. 281. (B. Mus., PP. 3937 c.)

CHAPTER THE TWENTIETH

MOROCCO BEYOND THE ATLAS

SÛS

AS the *terra incognita* nearest to Europe, the so-called "Kingdom of Sûs" has always had an especial attraction for Englishmen, and in view of the fabulous natural riches so freely declared to exist there – an assertion which, from ignorance, few can dispute—it is not strange that for over a century past a succession of venturesome traders and hardy exploiters have essayed to open up relations with its people, but all in vain. The difficulty is, and always has been, that the Berbers of Sûs, who accept the religious supremacy of the Moorish sultans as the descendants and successors of Mohammed, while fretting under such additional authority as has been gained from time to time by force of arms, have never known the power of combination to resist them; in the long run they have always been compelled to yield.

A Tempting Province. *

Between the family of the Hamed û Mûsà Shareefs, whose stronghold is at Ilîgh, and that of the reigning

* The following historical references to Sûs will be found in *The Moorish Empire:* Its Berbers, p. 6; Phœnicians there, 8; Berber rebels, 28; Sulaimán migrates thither, 39; abandoned by the Lamtûna, 50, 65; in revolt, 94; conquered by Ahmad el A'araj, 118; separate administration under 'Ali es-Simlâli, 134-5; Mulai es-Shareef supported, 137; captured by er-Rasheed II., 138; fishing-station on coast granted to Spain, 177; first invasion by El Ḥasan III., 183-4; second, 187-9; third, 191-2; piracy on the coast, 271; sugar exported, 399; adventurers on the coast, 412, 413.

Fîláli Shareefs, there has always been war since the time when, in 1637, the founder of the present dynasty was carried off from Tafîlált to Ilîgh by the "King of Sûs," and with him his women, of whom he was only allowed to retain the ugly negress who became the mother of the tyrant Mulai Ismá'îl. Yet from the time of the latter's brother and predecessor, Mulai er-Rasheed, known to the English of that day as "Tafilatta," Sûs has formed part of an empire whose rulers have held the title of sultan since 1627.

A Family Story.

At various times contenders for the umbrella—one can hardly use the term "pretender" in Morocco, where Succession Acts have not yet come—have seized on this province, and for a time have secured its independence, but it was only in 1810 that any real advantage was gained. In that year independence * was achieved by Sidi Ḥashem of the Hamed û Mûsà, who made his head-quarters at Talent, near to Ilîgh, hard by the shrine of his ancestor, Sidi Ḥamed û Mûsà, † the patron saint of that country, in Tasirwált. But this independence was not to last, and Sûs has never yet obtained the chance which it deserves; it was finally reduced to its present dependent condition by the expeditions of Mulai el Ḥasan III. in 1881 and 1886. It was only in this latter year that Sidi Ḥosaïn, chief of the Aït Bû 'Amrán, who had tried in vain to enter into independent relations with Europe, was subdued, and his death soon after was, as usual, attributed to foul play.

Independence.

Not only has the absolute nature of the sultan's rule

* An independence never recognized, however, by Europe, which has acknowledged Sûs to be part of Morocco at least since the days of Queen Elizabeth, who addressed the ameer as "Xerif of Marocco, Fes and Sus." [1]

† Cousin of Mulai 'Abd es-Slám bin Masheesh: see genealogical table in *The Moorish Empire*, facing p. 116.

[1] Bib. Harl. Cat., vol. i., p. 176, cod. 269, arc. 11.

over Sûs received the recognition of Europe,* but by the purchase of the settlement made by an English company at Cape Juby, far beyond Sûs, the limit of his dominions has been pushed much further south than ever before. And now, in consequence of the last of a series of unsuccessful attempts to establish a trade with the tribes of that coast in 1898, the British Government has given notice that "the coast as far as Cape Bojador, on the 26th parallel of north latitude, has been recognized by Her Britannic Majesty's Government as forming part of the dominions of His Majesty, the Sultan of Morocco." In consequence of this the public is warned, as it has been so often before in vain, that "no trading or other operations can be undertaken in that territory without the consent of the Sultan of Morocco having been previously obtained."†

Imperial Limits.

Independently of this, the province of Sûs is extensive, and in some parts very fertile, but its qualities have been greatly exaggerated. Notwithstanding many specious promises, no new port has been opened since Agadîr Ighîr was closed, although the main caravans from the western Sûdán pass through this province to Mogador. Most nations interested have attempted to evade this policy, either by official or private ventures, making so-called treaties with semi-independent chieftains, who, though not more warmly disposed than the Government towards foreigners as such, would welcome anything that would improve their prospects, and increase their chances in the next revolution.‡ The number of English companies alone

Relations with Europe.

* Spain recognized the Wád Nûn as the southern limit of Morocco by her treaty of 1767 (art. 18), and by her treaty of 1799 (art. 22).

† *Daily Papers*, Aug. 4, 1898.

‡ The family of the Sheïkhs Baïrûk, for instance, have been attempting this for nearly a century past, negotiating with Cochelet in 1819, and with the French again in 1839, when the consul at Mogador was sent

which have been lured to destruction by the vain hope of "doing something" by this means, is not small, but they are generally confined to so restricted a circle of speculators that the noise of their collapse does not reach their successors. *

The Moorish Policy.

It is the determined policy of the Morocco Government to keep Sûs closed, in order to prevent any kind of complications, and until it has put its home quarters in order it cannot be blamed for so doing. With such corrupt machinery, the best of men at the head would find it very difficult to deal with European questions in that distant province, and tantalizing as it may be to financiers, manufacturers and traders, prejudicial even to the pent-up people, one cannot honestly commend the opening up of Sûs until the most pressing administrative reforms have been at least set on foot. †

Agadîr Ighîr *(Santa Cruz).*

The only town in Sûs in which Europeans have been permanently settled is Agadîr Ighîr, and it is the only one of which much is known. ‡ Under the name of "Gartguessem", which is probably only a corruption of some disused local name, this most northerly port of Sûs, afterwards de-

down the coast in a vessel-of-war, *La Malouine*, and on his second visit obtained a treaty which established a nominal protectorate of which nothing came. In 1867 Messrs. Puyano and Butler, who were afterwards enslaved, took Bairûk's son to Lanzarote, and there induced him to sign a treaty with Spain. This man subsequently entered into similar negotiations with English capitalists, and some of the sheikhs came to London.

* For some account of these, see p. 389.

† Among the many projects for the colonization of Sûs, one of the most interesting was put forward in 1698 by the Marquis of Canales, ambassador of Spain in London, recommending that thirteen hundred Huguenot refugees who had arrived in England should be afforded an asylum at Santa Cruz under the Spanish flag, but the Council disapproved of the idea. (Archives of the *Supremo Consejo de Guerra y Marina.*)

‡ For historical references, see *The Moorish Empire*, pp. 111, 117, 183.

scribed as "the gate of the Ṣûdan," calls for very little attention from Leo, as it had not long been taken—in 1536—from the Portuguese, who had built a fort there in 1503, which was re-built in 1540.[1] There is a possibility that the Arambys of Hanno, or the Rusadir of Pliny the Elder may have been in this vicinity, but there is no reason to suppose that the modern town in any way represents the ancient settlements, unless it be its peculiar position.

Name.

The native Berbers call it either Agadîr Ighîr, i.e the "Stronghold of the Cliff"—from its situation at a considerable height above the sea,*—or simply Tigimi (in Arabic, Dár) Rûmî, "The House of the Romans" *i.e.* Foreigners. The portion of its Berber name by which it is now most commonly known to Europeans is of very general application throughout Morocco to any well-protected town or village, pronounced by the Arabs, Agadîr, and by the Berbers, Tagdîrt: it is the same word from which, after various transmutations, the Phœnician settlement of Cadiz has derived its name.[2] †

Fonté.

At the foot of the cliff is a little fort which the Portuguese built to protect the spring, called Fonté, restored by the Moors after the Spanish war of 1859—60. Fonté has always been noted for its fisheries, but its people are warlike, and command the road to Sûs, their village, through which all must pass, having gates at each end which are shut at night. A line of rocks off Fonté was probably that once used for the erection of a mole two hundred yards long.[3]

Agadîr boasts only some three hundred inhabitants,

* About 600 feet.

† Tissot regards Agadîr as the Semitic Gadir.

[1] El Ufrání, p. 76.

[2] Rawlinson, *Phœnicia*, pp. 67, 68 and 290. [3] Gatell.

and Fonté two hundred. The existing battlemented town is described by Payton[1]—who visited it in 1882 on board a steamer loaded with grain for the Government—as "picturesquely perched on the very top of a high brown hill, its slopes adorned with bright green patches of vines and cacti, with the old fort half-way down, the two little brown fishing villages and their protecting white-domed sanctuaries at the base of the hill, the dark crags and rocky coves below them, the far-reaching promontory to the north, which shelters the lovely bay."

Description.

From Mogador to Agadir is a distance by land of about seventy-six miles, two long days' journey. Its exact position is 30° 26' N. by 9° 32' W., some three miles and a half north of the Wád Sûs, up which it is about thirty miles or more,—one day's journey—to Tarudant, while Cape Ghîr lies eighteen miles to the north. * Its roadstead is the best in Morocco, well defended from all winds.

Position.

According to Faria,[2] in 1503 a Portuguese officer erected here a wooden castle, which he called Santa Cruz. This appears to have been done without the knowledge of his government, but as soon as the king heard of it, he purchased the building and surrounded it with a town. After thirty years' occupation, the Moors made such a determined attack with fifty thousand men, that in spite of the foreigners having twice received reinforcements from home, on a breach being made in the wall by the explosion of a powder-magazine, the Moors were able to regain possession, which since that time has been undisputed, although in 1755 the Danish envoy and suite were imprisoned

History.

* The height of this cape, otherwise Rás Aferni, is given as 1200 feet.

[1] *Field*, September 2, 1882. [2] *Africa Portuguesa*, 1681.

because of a Danish attempt to erect a fort here.[1] The Moors used to permit Spanish fishing vessels to land thereat for wood and water on payment of a small tax, and provided them with safe conducts.[2] Since 1773 Agadîr has been closed to European commerce, for Mohammed XVII. besieging it in that year to put down an insurrection, turned all the foreigners out, and destroyed the place, lest the Spaniards should seize it while he was attacking Melilla in 1774. An effort to secure its re-opening is stated to have been made by the Dutch towards the close of the last century, the natives flocking into the works set on foot, but all came to nought. From that time it has but rarely been visited by travellers, as it offers no attractions, and cannot always be safely approached. Yet Great Britain appears to have continued to appoint a vice-consul for Agadîr, at least nominally, until the end of the eighteenth century. English trade with this port dates from the sixteenth century, * and in 1670 the only French house in Morocco was established here.[3]

Port Closed.

The existing remains consist chiefly of the quadrilateral Portuguese citadel, in a good state of preservation, over one of the gates of which, looking towards Mogador, may be deciphered a heart and cross surmounted by the initials "S. C." Rohlfs records a Dutch inscription over the gate, "VREEST GOD. ENDE EERT DEN KONING, 1746,"[4] † a relic of the effort mentioned. ‡ On some of the cannon are

Historic Remains.

* See *Thomas Wyndham's Voyage* in 1552; *Kerr's Voyages*, vol. vii., or Astley's *New General Collection*, 1745, vol. i.; and in Hakluyt, vol. ii., pt. ii.

† "Fear God, and honour the King."

‡ Probably the attempts variously described as Dutch and Danish refer to the same affair.

[1] CHENIER, vol. ii., p. 360. See *The Moorish Empire*, p. 403.

[2] TORRES.

[3] CHARANT, p. 35.

[4] p. 324.

to be seen the Portuguese arms dated 1782,[1] which show them to be of comparatively recent introduction, and on a bronze mortar is an inscription in Arabic, saying that it was cast in London for Sidi Mohammed XVII. (bin 'Abd Allah).[2]

TARUDANT.

Tarudant, the capital of Sûs, lies south of the Atlas spur which runs down to Cape Ghîr.* It has never known a foreign master, and has almost always enjoyed a certain amount of independence, yet it never seems to have grown to be a great city, and whatever importance it once possessed, save as the seat of government, has vanished since the closure of the port of Agadîr Ighîr.† It was already flourishing in the twelfth century on account of the neighbouring mines,[3] and in 1687 it was re-peopled by Rîfians transported from Fez by Mulai Ismá'îl when he drove out his rival brother Haran.[4]

Natural Wealth.

Work in copper produced from mines not far off, at Taurirt Ûwanas, near Izerbi ‡ in the Atlas, always formed a leading industry among the Rudánîs—as its people are called, §—who were also formerly noted for weaving and dyeing, but now have no special reputation for either. Saltpetre, which is prepared in some quantity, remains the sole important product. The rivers Sûs and El Wár supply abundant irrigation for the surrounding gardens, which contain large numbers of date palms. Among these

* The best account of it is by Gatell, *Bul. Soc. Géog.*, Paris, Mars—Avril, 1871, p. 86. See also Lenz, vol. i., p. 302. For historical allusions in *The Moorish Empire*, see pp. 117, 164, 183, 187.

† Jackson surmises from rings then visible along the walls,[5] that the ships of those days could reach Tarudant by means of the river Sûs—to the north of which it is built.

‡ Smelted at Tazalaght.

§ From its Arab name Rudánah; cf. Ez-Zaïánî, l.c.

[1] De Campou, p. 177. [2] Gatell. [3] 'Abd el Wahhíd, p. 263.

[4] Ez-Zaiáni, p. 40. [5] p. 132.

gardens rises the Dár el Baïḍah, or "White House," a palace built by a former sultan, possibly dating in part from the re-building of the town by the Sa'adî shareefs, early in the sixteenth century.

Inside the walls, which have five gates—Ḳaṣbah, (E.) Khamîs (for Marrakesh), Aôlád Ben-Nûna (Mogador), Tergûnt (for Agadîr Ighîr) and Ez-Zorgán (S.), —there is a good deal of waste space, besides gardens and palms. The ḳaṣbah occupies the north-west corner, quite apart from the business centre and the melláḥ, while the market-place is right in the centre, two markets being held weekly, on Sundays and Thursdays. The mosques, which are three in number, are those of the ḳaṣbah, of Sidi û Sidi, and "the Great." There are two prisons, and fifteen or sixteen fandaḳs, one of which, that of Es-Slá, serves as ḳaïṣarîyah.

The Town.

The population was estimated by Gatell in 1861 at eight thousand three hundred, though Rohlfs had put it down as from thirty to forty thousand.* Great hostility exists between the Slûḥ, who inhabit the town, and the soi-disant Hawárá of the vicinity. Tarudant, which is some five hundred and fifty feet above the sea, lies about twenty miles to the south of the Atlas, and Marrákesh—some 110 miles north-west—may be reached by the Bîbáwan Pass in three or four days.

Inhabitants.

With the exception of Tarudant, the most important inland town in the northern half of Sûs is probably Ilîgh (1300 ft.), the residence of the shareefian family referred to, although Gatell described it as consisting of only some two hundred and fifty houses, half of which were occupied by Jews.† An hour distant,

Ilîgh.

* Torres described it in 1550 as being as large as Seville was at that date.[1] It was then famous for its sugar-canes.

† See *The Moorish Empire*, pp. 137, 147(*n*) and 184.

[1] p. 278.

situated 1500 ft. above the sea on a small hill-side plateau,[1] is the zawîah of Sidi Hamed û Mûsà, where the great market called Mogár Imjád is held thrice a year.* The local shareef guarantees protection for both the persons and the goods of patrons of these fairs,[2] and his guards keep order.

Tisnît.

The vicissitudes of life in these regions are such, that what is a village of mud-huts to-day may be a flourishing town with a crowded mart ten years hence, walled and strong—for the time being,—under the protection of some powerful chief, while in another decade only its ruins and a name may remain. Gatell, in 1862, found Tisnît—which lies a day and a half to the northward of Ilîgh, and nearer the coast, one day from Massa,—just another large village with a Thursday market, but as a result of Mulai el Ḥasan's policy, Andrews found it in 1883, though still unwalled, with a population of probably seven thousand,† since which time it has been surrounded by a wall perhaps a mile and a half or two miles in circumference,[3] pierced with six gates.‡ The spread of the central power is always marked by the founding of cities to supersede the informal clusters of

* In August, October and March. The first is the most important, but the second is remarkable for the fights with slings and stones between the Aït 'Ali and Ait Mussi, two divisions of the ḳabîla of Imjád. Jews are not admitted to these markets, but pitch their tents on the outskirts. Even men and women have separate sections on these occasions.

† *Times of Morocco*, No. 22.

‡ Tisnît is built almost entirely of red mud concrete, and is destitute of gardens, though the space enclosed is far from being built over. Grey describes camping ground for 20,000 men inside the gates, whereas he estimates the normal population at but 2000 or 3000; there is another large square before the kaid's house. The ḳaṣbah was not yet completed in 1898. One or two lovely palm-trees raised their tufted heads above the dull monochrome of dirty red, but they only served to accentuate the monotony by contrast.

[1] LENZ, *Rev. Géog.*, Paris, p. 375. See also BENLIEZ, p. 61.

[2] LENZ. vol. i., p. 332.

[3] GREY, p. 250.

KAṢBAH GLÁWI.

(Government Fortress surrounded by Houses, on the Road from Marrákesh to Tafílált—beyond the Atlas.)

Photograph by the Hon. E. W. Loch.

dwellings around the fortresses of chieftains, that in them the people may develop settled habits, and interests which tend to peace, as well as for use as garrison towns.

Further south, not far from the Wád Nûn, is the more important town of Agelmîn, or Glîmîn, the headquarters of the Sheïkh Baïrûk and his tribe, the principal people of the district. * Gatell informs us that it consisted of the ḳaṣbah, the agadîr, and the ḳaṣar el madînah, having five gates in its broken wall, which enclosed a population of some three thousand. Each of the three sections had its mosque, but neither of these had minarets, and there were no shrines. The Jews were packed in one street with gates, in which they had two synagogues, and there was a Sunday market. [1] †

Agelmîn or Glîmîn.

Regarding the rest of the province of Sûs, we must remain content with the most meagre data, especially as to the interior. ‡ The experiences of venturesome traders and ship-wrecked crews have taught us something of its coast strip, which would lead us to imagine no great difference between it and the adjacent portions of Morocco proper.

A Little Known Province.

In several parts of Sûs are traces of foreign settlements, but of their history nothing is known. Davidson heard of the remains of a Christian church and Christian villages near Tazalt, to the east of Tarudant, [2] and other travellers have seen such ruins. Gatell mentions two at Tînkur, near the Ifran district to the south-east of Tazîrwált, and another, with the remains of an aqueduct, half a day

Foreign Remains.

* Lenz described it in vol. i., p. 334. and Panet had already done so in 1850.

† See *Bibliography*, Art. 950.

‡ As far as possible what is here stated has been checked by interrogating natives of the various districts.

[1] Oct. 1869, p. 264. [2] p. 81.

south of Talyûnt, near the junction of the Wád Sîád and the Wád Assáka, called Agwîdîr ("the little Agadîr" or fortress) or Nûna, [1]—whence the name Wád Nûn,—said to have been derived from that of a foreign queen. Lenz speaks of Gada, near Tarudant, with ruined foreign buildings, and a bridge across the Wád Sibûya.[2] Close to Arksîs are the remains of a martello tower of Portuguese origin, still known as Ṣôḳ en-Naṣárà—"the Nazarenes' Market"—probably a relic of some early trading venture.[3]

Possible Ports.

Along the coast are many spots which would serve as road-steads or ports if trading were permitted, the first one of importance being Massa,* (30° 4′ N.) some sixty miles beyond Agadîr Ighîr, at the mouth of the river of the same name, with lovely and fertile surroundings, well irrigated.[4] Two miles distant there is a small town called Aghbalû, half a mile from the sea.[5] The bar seems to have been crossed by the Portuguese, the landing-place being on the south bank, near Sidi Wassaï,[6] but in local annals this spot is famous as the landing-place of Jonah after his piscatorial exploration. A few miles further south, in latitude 29° 50′, is Aglû, formerly a town, now consisting only of perhaps nine hundred houses, with a Monday market. As a port its landing is unsatisfactory and difficult.[7]

Landing Places.

Leaving the plains of Sûs, crossing a spur of the Lower Atlas, and entering the hilly region of Aït Bû 'Amrán, we reach Wád Gharizîm (29° 36′), which possesses a perfect little creek, absolutely protected from north-east winds: Mîrlift, (29° 30′) which is not so good: Sidi Mohammed Ben 'Abd Allah, a little further south, (29° 28′) which is preferable, and finally Ifni—easily

* Or Mastah.

[1] Oct. 1869, p. 267.
[2] Vol. i., p. 322
[3] ANDREWS, *Times of Morocco*, No. 23.
[4] ANDREWS, l.c.
[5] DAVIDSON, p. 175.
[6] ERCKMANN, p. 55.
[7] ANDREWS, *Al-moghreb*, Jan. 22, '98

distinguishable by the saint-house in the centre—in latitude 29° 20'. Here the steamer *Anjou* made a vain attempt to effect a landing for a London and Marseilles company in 1880, after which the governor of St. Louis sent a ship to make investigations.

Physical Formation.

One of the features of this coast as seen from the sea here is a remarkable table-land, varying from two to five miles in width, behind which rises a spur of the Lower Atlas, stretching from a little south of Aglû to Assáka, nearly fifty-two miles. It is cultivated near Rás Gharizîm (C. Agula, 29° 25'), but in the vicinity of Arksîs (29° 10') its rocky nature renders it useless for this purpose, though affording good pasturage. "A long unbroken line of red-brown cliffs, rising perpendicularly from the water, or from a narrow strip of sandy yellow beach, against which the great Atlantic rollers broke in clouds of spray with one unceasing roar; and behind, the rugged outline of the mountain ranges, lifting their lowering peaks to kiss the azure sky:" such is the description of the latest writer on this coast[1] of Arksîs as seen from the sea.

ARKSÎS.

In the event of the Moorish Government's deciding to open a port south of the Sûs river, Arksîs—taking into consideration its favourable landing-places—seems the most suitable spot.* A small town could be built on the high land to the north of the cove, and a Custom House on the upper part of the beach. Situated in the heart of the Aït Bû 'Amrán country, between the Mistîten and Sibûya tribes, and near main tracks, the Bû 'Amrán and Wád Nûn traders would lose no time in making use of it. The precipitous cliffs are broken here by a shelving sandy beach, protected by a reef of rocks to the north. Just

* See *The Moorish Empire*, pp. 187 and 403.

[1] GREY, p. 43.

south of this is the Arksîs cove, a remarkable opening in the cliffs, ending in a small beach. The cove is easy of access in southerly weather, while the beach offers a favourable landing-place in north-east winds, ships finding good anchorage in clay and sand about half a mile from the shore, in eight or nine fathoms of water.[1] *

Arksîs is described on several charts as Port Hillsborough, † having been so named by a Captain Glass, who in 1760 ransomed there some Europeans detained in slavery by the Berbers. Glass attempted to establish a trading station, but at the instance of Spain, in 1764, Lord Hillsborough caused his withdrawal. ‡ From a name of its little river, Gwîder, it has also been called "Isgueder" by Davidson, and is probably the "Yedouecsai" at which in 1859 the French were understood to be erecting a factory,

Unsuccessful Ventures.

* To this description may be added a quotation from Grey.[2] "A mariner sailing casually down the coast of Sûs might pass Arksîs a score of times without discovering that there was a harbour for even as much as a row-boat. This is to be accounted for by the peculiar formation of the coast at this spot. At the southern extremity of a gently sloping beach, from the other end of which a reef of rocks, almost submerged at high-water, runs at right angles with the sea, the land rises, almost perpendicular from the water, to the height of 170 feet. A close scrutiny reveals a break in the cliffs, and through this narrow opening the sea has rushed in . . . and washed out for herself a snug little land-locked cove. A more perfect ideal of the smuggler's cove of romance could not well be imagined, for the bay, as soon as the entrance is gained, trends sharply to the right, and is then almost entirely screened by the friendly cliff."

† After the then Secretary of State.

‡ Glass was arrested while on a visit to the Canaries on a charge of defrauding the Customs, and he and his family were assassinated on their way home by some of the crew, who turned pirates.[3] For his adventures see his *History of the Discovery and Conquest of the Canaries*, London, 1764; as also Barker-Webb and Berthelot; and José Alvarez-Perez in "El Pais del Misterio" in *La Ilustracion Española*, vol. xiv., Ap. 15th, 1878.[4]

[1] ANDREWS, l.c. (here quoted verbatim). See also separate brochure.

[2] p. 57. [3] See the *Gaceta de Madrid*, Jan. 28th, 1766.

[4] GALINDO, p. 315. See also GRIMALDI, Spanish Minister; official letters.

though the idea was abandoned in the face of the sultan's remonstrances.[1] Davidson had previously induced Lord Palmerston to send a British vessel of war to open up negotiations with the local sheïkhs, but the *Scorpion* found it too rough to communicate, and nothing came of the idea.[2]

A Remarkable Scheme.

Perhaps the most remarkable of these schemes was that set on foot by a Captain Sleigh in 1851, intended to develop into a "United Service of Enterprise and Commerce," "for the acquirement of wealth and position in a province within eight days' sail of England," and "for the spread of civilization, anti-slavery and Christianity." Sleigh's remarkable brochure and prospectus* shows that he had in view the establishment of another empire such as that which by similar means had been established in India. It is probable from what he says that he too would have made Arksîs his port, had he succeeded, and it was here that in 1883 the Sûs and North-West African Trading Company's vessel *Garrawalt* attempted in vain, under Messrs. Andrews and Curtis, to establish a trade, an experience which was repeated in 1898 by the Globe Venture Syndicate's vessel *Tourmaline*, under Major Gybbon Spilsbury.† The first two adventurers named were carried on parole direct to Mogador, and there released: five of the second party suffered several months' imprisonment inland, and on being delivered at Tangier, were tried and sentenced to some

The "Tourmaline" Venture.

* *A preliminary Treatise on the Resources of Ancient Mauritania*, etc. See *The Moorish Empire*, p. 510.

† See *The Moorish Empire*, p. 352, note. An account of his experiences by one of the party, Mr. Henry M. Grey, has recently been published under the title of *In Moorish Captivity*. London, 1899. It is an excellent and faithful description, marred only by misconceptions regarding the Sultan and the attitude of the British Government.

[1] RICHARDSON, vol. i., p. 276. [2] Ib. p. 279.

months of imprisonment for smuggling, the director of the expedition also being arrested in England and brought back for trial, but acquitted by a Gibraltar jury.*

Assáka or Wád Nûn.

In May 1882 the late sultan made an expedition to Sûs with an army of twenty-seven thousand men. In consequence of the famine the late Sidi Ḥosaïn bin Ḥishám had threatened to open up direct relations with foreign commerce on his own account, so His Majesty wisely promised the opening of a new port, and fixed upon Assáka (28° 59′ N.) at the mouth of the Wád Nûn, although the inhabitants of Agadîr, Massa, Aglû and Ifni were equally anxious for the opening of their respective ports, each lauding his own. From the fifteenth of September of that year Agadîr and Assáka were opened for six months for the importation of food stuffs, on which the usual duty of ten per cent. *ad valorem* was to be levied, but then they were closed. In 1886 it was announced with confidence in Tangier that the Sultan had promised the German Ambassador then at the Court to re-open Assáka, but from that day to this nothing more has been heard of the project, which had already appeared ripe long ago.

A Buried Project.

Had it not been for the breaking out of a terrible famine and plague toward the close of the last century, many of the foreign merchants established at Mogador would doubtless have carried out their intention of establishing themselves at or near Assáka. Jackson, who wrote in 1809, remarks: "Most probably Buonaparte, if he succeed in the final conquest of Spain, will turn his mind decidedly to an

* A sequel to this was a shareholder's action against the directors for having issued a misleading prospectus, which resulted in the compulsory winding up of the Company, and the repayment of the capital by the Chairman of the Board. The whole speculation was shown to be an imposition on a greedy and gullible public.

extensive factory somewhere here, which (beside many other advantages which existing circumstances prevent me explaining here) would effectually open a direct communication with Timbuctoo and the Ṣûdán, and supply that immense territory with European manufactures at the second hand, which they now receive at the fifth and sixth."

Assáka as a Port.

But Assáka is much inferior to Arksîs as a port, the sea there shallowing and breaking at a distance from the land. Neither is there any secure landing-place for boats save in the finest weather. Its importance lies in its being within reach of the Wád Nûn markets and Glîmîn—the home of the Aôlád D'leem traders and slave dealers, the most venturesome in all Morocco—some thirty miles up the river, which is navigable so far in small boats.

The Sûsîs.

To the north of Wád Nûn, in what may be styled Sûs proper, the customs are not very different from those of the Ḥaûz. The short, sturdy, white-faced Sûsîs,—who are so well known in the marts of the north as able tradesmen, and in eastern Barbary as guards and watchmen,—the clever metal-workers of Morocco, dress chiefly in white woollen shirts with short sleeves, and woollen selháms to match, or in the local khaïdûs, their heads being bare, or bound with a camel-hair cord, their women going veiled.[1] They, too, live a simple and frugal round, prodigal only in powder and human lives. Their language is almost exclusively Shilḥah, acquaintance with Arabic showing some education.

Great Fairs.

Most of the business of Sûs and Wád Nûn is transacted at great fairs lasting eight or fifteen days, during which all roads of approach are guaranteed safe by the tribesmen, that trade may be unhampered. The most important of these are held at

Ilîgh in August and March for a fortnight, at Sidi Bûbker in Aït Bû 'Amrán, at Glîmîn in July for five days, and at Asîrn (Azwáfit) in August for three days, the last two always opening on a Wednesday.[1] Substantial buildings are only erected for fortification, and mosques with minarets exist only at such large centres as Tarudant, Agadîr, Ilîgh and Aglû.

Political Divisions.

The principal divisions of the country south of the river Sûs are Shtûka, Ilálen and Iberkákin, through which the river passes in inverse order, while to the south of Shtûka, occupying the coast to Wád Nûn, lies the Aït Bû 'Amrán, with Tazirwált as a hinterland, beyond the mountains to the east of which lies the great caravan centre of Akka. South-east of Tazirwált is the Aït M'rábiṭ, and south of Aït Bû 'Amrán the Wád Nûn district, beyond which lies Tekna, bounded on the far side by the Dra'a. Then comes that portion of the desert known as El Gádû, in which is the great mart of Tindûf.

BEYOND WÁD NÙN

Natural Features.

From Assáka to Ûïna, beyond the Dra'a, the district adjoining the coast is fairly fertile, but after that it flattens, becoming sandy and barren, for here we are on the edge of the desert. Half a day's journey inland, however, the country is extremely pleasing, and the plains of Wád Nûn offer advantages for the cultivation of cereals as great as those of 'Abda and Dukálla. At various levels árgans, date-palms, olives, almonds, aloes, junipers and cedars flourish, the mountains shielding them from the hot winds, or shoom, of the Saḥara, and the climate is described as delightful.[2] The Tekna district, which lies behind, though

[1] Gatell. [2] Andrews, *Times of Morocco*, No. 20.

the furthest removed, is not the least important division of Sûs.

The Dra'a River.

South of Assáka there are no landing-places deserving the name of ports, and even the mouth of the Dra'a, (28° 43′ N.)—which, though of considerable length, is to a great extent absorbed by the sands of the desert,—does not seem to have attracted adventurers. The next well-known spot is Ûïna (28° 30′), whence the late Mr. James Butler endeavoured to trade in 1866, for which he was detained in slavery for several years, being ransomed at last for $27,000.* The Spaniards also landed there in April 1886. Beyond this comes a much smaller river, the Shibîka, (28° 18′ N., 11° 29′ W.) visited in March 1886 by the German trading steamer *Gottorp.*† About half-way between Ûïna and Shibîka are the foreign ruins referred to, possibly after all the real "Santa Cruz de Mar Pequeña," but not a spot for the Spaniards to covet.

"Puerto Cansado."

There are also several less important landing-places between the rivers, well-known to the fishermen of the Canaries, but otherwise the only possible port until "Cape Juby" is reached is an arm of the sea which enters the land at latitude 28° 2′, called "Argîla," and by the Spaniards "Puerto Cansado." From one to two and a half miles by four miles, in breadth and length respectively, it is nevertheless too shallow to form a natural harbour, though vessels can enter at high tide.[1]

* Documents relating to this attempt were published in Cadiz in 1869. See *Bibliography*, Art. 1046.

† To this expedition we are indebted for the best map of this coast, some of its members having travelled a short way inland, as far as latitude 29°, when they turned off to Glimîn, then bearing north to 30°, and thence through Tisnît to the Wád Sûs, along which they returned to the coast. See the able report by Jannasch, the director; *Die Deutsche Handelsexpedition*, 1886.

[1] GATELL, Oct. 1869, p. 220.

Right opposite to the Canaries—and distant only seventy miles—is Rás Bûibisha, ("Cape Juby", 27° 58′ 41″ N. and 12° 56′ W.) or Tarfaïah,* to the south of which the North-West Africa Trading Company in 1879 established first a hulk, and then a factory, proudly called "Port Victoria," at that time beyond the recognized limits of Moorish rule.† But this was not to be permitted by the sultan, who in 1887, after much negotiation, bought the company out to its great advantage for £50,000.‡ Since then the British Government has recognized the sultan's jurisdiction, as has been stated, as far as Cape Bojador,§ a district about which the Moors know less than we do.||

"Cape Juby."

One of the principal caravan centres of the Moorish Saḥara is Tindûf,¶ also an important slave depôt, rather over four degrees almost due south of Marrákesh, and about 1300 feet above the sea. Lenz speaks of it as dating only from the middle of the century, with well-built houses inhabited by Tajakant Arabs.[1] Douls, who visited it in 1887, describes it as a small town (bourg) situated at the foot of a hill, founded in 1857 by a m'rábiṭ named Bel Hammej, and built of dried mud, with one mosque tower, and the kûbbah of the saint. Here the roads meet from Wád Nûn and Glîmîn, from the district of the Sagîat el Ḥamra—the river which debouches below Tarfaïah—from Tûát, Tafîlált

Tindûf.

* Otherwise "Las Matas de San Bartolomeo."

† In 1881 the Foreign Office gave notice that "the boundary of Morocco as understood by Her Majesty's Government, extends along the coast of the Atlantic as far south as the Wád Dra'a, about a day's journey south of Wád Nûn."—(Letter to the Sûs and N. W. African Trading Co.)

‡ See *The Moorish Empire*, pp. 84 and 412.

§ The agreement, dated March 13th, 1895, is given in Herstlet's *Map of Africa by Treaty*, 1896, vol. iii., p. 1064.

|| The French have published a survey of this coast as far as the Senegal.

¶ Otherwise Tunfoo.

[1] p. 377. [2] p. 23.

and Akka; from Marrákesh and Mogador. The next great centre on the way to Timbuctoo is 'Arawán, a town in the midst of boundless sand-dunes, but with abundant water.[1] Shingît, which marks the Moroccan limits, is to us little more than a name.

The Arabs of the South

With the people of this interesting region we are better acquainted than with their country, since so many ship-wrecked mariners and others have found their way among them, and so many of them venture northward to trade. Except in being much more primitive in their habits—in which they resemble the inhabitants of the south side of the Atlas,—they do not differ greatly from the country folk of Central Morocco. The bulk of the population is Berber, and the prevailing language is therefore Shilḥah, but on the plains, and especially towards the desert, the admixture of Arabs is so great as to supersede the native stock. These desert wanderers who "follow the grass" are quite distinct from those of the north, much more nearly resembling their connections in Arabia itself. Tall, sturdy fellows, they have thick, black, curly hair, which is not shaved off, as by the Moors.

Dress.

Their principal garments are of the blue "selampore" called khunt—a strip of which is also wrapped round the head on a journey,—with a white woollen haddûn or selhám,* or a haïk thrown over the shoulders, while south of the main Atlas sandals are universally worn.[2] Armed with double-barrelled flint-locks purchased from the French in Senegal, they are a venturesome and formidable race, who can maintain their own against all comers.[3] Douls[4] describes the nomads

* The "burnûs" of Algeria. For description of these garments see *The Moors*, ch. iv.

[1] Lenz, p. 378.
[2] Rohlfs, p. 342; cf. Benitez, p. 58.
[3] Andrews.
[4] pp. 30 and 31.

of the Moroccan Saḥara as most fanatical, spending much time in the study of the Ḳor'án, especially among the wandering Fîlálîs, and one wife apiece is the rule.

Independence.

Gatell speaks of them as "the most demoralized and fanatical under Moorish rule," who in the southern parts form for themselves a chaotic republic under the strongest man of the district, every man pleasing himself, and the elders judging. There are among them two great divisions, the Aït Jimmel and the Aït Billah, each including a large group of tribes. Horsemen are not plentiful among them: it is the region of camels. Their food is "stodgy" barley-porridge ('asîdah) and parched flour (zummîtah); such luxuries as tea, coffee, or strong drink, being all but unknown.[1]

The DRA'A Country.

These tribes live beyond the sultan's actual rule, but within what will now probably be called his "sphere of influence." The river Dra'a, or the advancing and retreating desert, may be said to mark the southern limits of Morocco, and to include an important though little known district which goes by its name.* Rohlfs and De Foucauld alone have skirted it; Lenz has crossed it: beyond this our information is entirely from native sources.† Rohlfs tells of its sacred town Tamgrût, from which Jews are excluded, where is the shrine of Sidi Hamed bin Náṣir, and of another, "Adaûfil" inhabited by Arab shareefs.‡ The principal place in this district is, however, Beni S'beeḥ, in the Kitáwà, the largest and most southerly province, with perhaps a hundred ḳ'ṣûr, peopled chiefly by Arabs, the

* A fairly detailed map of the Dra'a country was nevertheless published by Lieut. de Castries at Sebdou (Algeria) in 1879.

† For historical allusions in *The Moorish Empire*, see pp. 24, 71, 93, 116, 118, 137, 301 and 311.

‡ *Adventures*, pp. 346—9.

[1] GATELL.

Berbers holding the country outside. The same writer estimated the population of the Tarnáta province at some two hundred and fifty thousand.

The Dra'a Lake.

The one feature on which all writers are agreed is the Dabiaïah or marsh-lake formed by the Dra'a in winter, and partly cultivated in summer. The soil is in many parts saline, the streams from the Atlas being often of that nature. As a date growing country the Dra'a rivals Tafîlált, and it was from a family of shareefs—descendants of Mohammed—settled here, whose coming was supposed to have increased the date crop, that the Sa'adî Dynasty—the one before the present—1574-1668—arose. The people are a good-natured, thick-lipped, flat-nosed, brown-skinned lot, with a fair admixture of the negro, but never to be confused with him, or to be considered mulattos (haráteen) for they have become a distinct race, however their origins may have intermingled. To call a Dra'wi a hartáni is the height of insult.

The Dra'wîs.

The typical inhabitants of the Dra'a valley (Dra'wîs), are short and thick-set, brown and wiry. Over their scanty and dirty under-garment, usually a ragged shirt, they adopt a square piece of striped woollen material (tibbán), thrown over the shoulders and fastened in place at the neck by two braided buttons, in winter throwing over this a dark brown goat-hair cloak (akhnîf), made rather short, with a startling assegai-shaped design in yellow and black at the back. They are inveterate smokers.[1]

Dress.

De Foucauld[2] describes the people of Aït Yaḥyá, living to the north of the Dra'a, as wearing a brown akhnîf (khaïdûs) with black and white or grey stripes; white or brown haïks, and a small black or white turban, or a cord, if the head be not left bare.

[1] ANDREWS. [2] p. 216.

The richer women dress in khunt, the poorer in white or brown wool. In Dádes, between this and Tafilált, the men appear in black or dark blue selháms, armed with long guns and curved daggers; silk-embroidered leather powder-pouches hanging by their sides. A narrow band of white cotton serves some as head gear, or a twist of camel-hair or silk, and silver rings are worn in the ears.

TAFÎLÁLT

Of all the territory subject to the Moorish sultans south of the Atlas, the district of Tafilált is by far the most important.* Its boundaries would be difficult to define, but its nucleus, the seat of government, is at Rissáni, built by Mulai Ismá'îl, in the district of Wád Ifli,† some ten days by caravan from Fez, and twelve from Marrákesh. Close by, at Abû 'Aám, live most of the wealthy merchants who trade with Fez and the Ṣûdán, the great market being the Arba'á of Mulai 'Alî Shareef, near the tombs of that worthy and his son who founded the existing dynasty.[1] *Situation.*

In Ifli—the central portion—formerly existed the extensive town of Sajilmása, founded by the Miknásà Berbers of the Metgára tribe in 757 A.C.[2]‡ Of this we know but little, for it was destroyed *Sajlimása.*

* The following historical allusions will be found in *The Moorish Empire:* The Romans there, p. 12; Mûsà here, 24, change of name, 33; 'Obeïd ibn 'Abd Allah a prisoner there, 41; subdued by the Lamtûna, 50; supremacy of Tunis acknowledged, 92; conquered by the Beni Marîn, 93, 96; established as independent kingdom, 102; Mohammed, son of Mulai es-Shareef, ruler there, 137; El Ḥasan III.'s expedition, 191.

† Known to the Berbers as "Tarissant" in "Tifalit."

‡ Leo fancifully derives its name from the Latin *Sigillum Massæ*, or the seal set on the victories of a Roman commander in Massa, as this district appears to have then been called.

[1] HARRIS, *Tafilet*, p 274.

[2] IBN KHALDÛN, vol. i., pp. 220 and 262. See also EL BEKRI and EN-NOWEÏRI.

IN TAFÎLALT.

Drawn by Herr Romberg.
From a photograph by Walter B. Harris, Esq.

as far back as the time of Yûsef bin Táshfîn[1] at the end of the eleventh century, but its ruins still extend five miles along the river bank. Since it fell the people have lived entirely in the fortresses called ķ'şûr (pl. of ķ'şar) with which the oasis is dotted, and which form its distinguishing feature. In these the pugnacious Fîlâlîs entrench themselves and live at war, each tribe with its neighbour, some of them being Arabs and some of them Berbers, between whom no love is lost.

The Fîlálî Shareefs.

But the world-wide fame of Tafîlált comes from its exquisite dates, the finest of which that will bear transport find their way to our tables in England. To an improvement of the date crop subsequent to the settlement there of Hîlâli Arabs, the country owes its modern name,* and Morocco its present dynasty, for it was the ascription of the improvement to Mulai 'Ali Shareef † that gave him power, and set his son on the throne of Morocco in 1648. Since that time it has been the custom for Moorish sultans to despatch superfluous sons and daughters to this distant province, in which every other man is therefore more or less a shareef, or descendant of Mohammed on the male side. ‡

Explorers.

This state of things does not induce the Fîlâlîs to extend a welcome to Europeans, and the few who have visited it, except in the sultan's service, namely Caillé, § Rohlfs, || Delbel, ¶ and Harris, **

* First recorded by Marmol in 1573.

† Mouëtte tells now the arrival of a Spanish slave in the disguise of a shareef proved equally beneficial.[2]

‡ The local sanctity is such that Jews have often to go bare-foot, and all may be made to loosen their sandals before a shareef.

§ *Journal d'un Voyage*, etc., French and English editions, 1830.

|| *Reise durch Marokko*, Bremen, 1867; *Sigilmassa und Tafilet*, Norden, 1887. *Adventures in Morocco*, London, 1874, and *Uebersteigung des Atlas*, 2nd ed.; also Petermann's *Mittheilungen*, 1865.

¶ *Journ. Soc. Géog. de Paris.*

** *Tafilet*, London, 1895.

[1] Leo, ed. Ram., p. 133. [2] p. 194.

have done so at the risk of their lives, all of course in the guise of Moors. It is to the last-named that we owe the most recent and complete information about Tafilált and the route from Marrákesh. The Gurlan ḳ'sar of Caillé has since his time sunk into insignificance, but otherwise his description is still applicable.

Caravan Trade.

A considerable source of wealth is the caravan trade with the Ṣûdán and Tûát (seventy days), which here bifurcates to Fez and Marrákesh. Tafîlált was formerly famous for its dromedaries, of whose fleetness marvellous stories are told, the pace being given as eight days' horse-ride in twenty-four hours.[1] Caillé speaks of a fine breed of white sheep, and of the horses as being mostly the property of the Berbers. Harris estimates the irrigated surface, almost entirely devoted to the growth of date-palms, at four hundred square miles, so the total value of the harvest must be very great. The inhabitants—as to a great extent do their animals—subsist chiefly on dates, and in spite of the law of the Ḳor'án, make brandy thereof.

Date Crop.

"To realize the enormous quantity of dates grown at Tafilált," says the writer quoted, "one must see the oasis. The palms, planted so thickly and so closely together as to obstruct one's vision in every direction, form a gigantic forest, to pass through which by the narrow lanes is bewildering . . . The groves of the finest palms are in the direction of Abû 'Aám, nearly all enclosed in high walls. It is these dates, the Bû S'kri and Bû K'fûs, that are most prized, and luscious they are indeed, though they spoil by travelling. The dates were ripe at the time of my visit, in November.[2] The only other articles of importance produced are the famous Fîlalî skins, and ḥaïks made of the fine local

[1] PELLOW, original edition, p. 119; see p. 64. [2] *Tafilet*, p. 292.

SORTING DATES IN TAFÎLÂLT

Drawn by Herr Romberg. *From a photograph by Walter B. Harris, Esq.*

wool. Tafîlâlt is naturally a great slave-depôt, although larger numbers arrive in Morocco by way of Sûs.

Fîlâlî Types and Dress.

From the description of the people given by Harris the following extracts are of special interest. "The Tafîlâlt Arabs consist probably of a mixture of tribes, and have unmistakeable signs of Berber blood. Gentle, of kindly nature, but fierce when roused, they are an excellent people, and have a certain charm of manner which is indescribable, due not a little to their melodious voices and the beautiful Arabic they talk. Their colour is usually dark, and their faces rather expressionless, though lacking the coarseness of those of the other Arab tribes . . .

Dress.

"The costumes worn by the Berbers and Arabs of Tafîlâlt are almost identical: in the former case the long tshamîrah is never belted at the waist, the Berbers, for some reason which I was unable to discover, objecting to this. The jellâb is unknown, the ḥaïk and the ḥaïdûs forming the costume of both peoples. The akhnîf, or black cloak with its strange red mark on the back, is seldom seen, except in cases of Shlûḥ from the mountains . . . The women wear indigo blue dyed cotton or jute, called khunt, or else coarse woollen ḥaïks of native manufacture. Leo Africanus mentions that large quantities of indigo were grown there, but nowadays all the blue khunt is imported from London or Bombay. Amber beads, silver and coral necklaces, silver anklets and bracelets are worn, according to the wealth of the families.

Occupation.

"The women are usually short and coarse in appearance, dirty and loud-voiced . . . They perform all the house-work, mind the cattle, collect firewood and take vegetables, etc. to the market,—in fact every duty except fighting seems to fall to their lot. The men are armed with guns and swords . . . Although the most common weapon is the flint-lock of the country, a quantity of cheap double-barrelled guns, all muzzle-loading, are to be found . . . Little quarter is given: in the case of fighting between Arabs and Berbers all males taken prisoners who are able to carry arms are mercilessly killed, usually stabbed with knives,—powder and shot being too expensive."[1] A curious peculiarity noticed by this writer is that unlike the children of the northern plains, those of this region may be seen modelling from life in clay, while in the architecture and adornment of their ḳ'ṣûr considerable taste is shown.

FÎGÎG and TÛÁT

Beyond Tafîlált, to the north-east, lies the important oasis of Fîgîg, to tap which the French have run a line of railway as far south as 'Aïn Sefra, eighty-eight kilometres distant. It is in the same meridian as Tlemçen, which lies three hundred and eighty kilometres to the north, Fez being five hundred kilometres to the north-west. There are nine ḳ'ṣûr, or fortified villages, counting some fifteen thousand men with three thousand guns, according to Canal. Its importance was much greater when the Mekkah caravan passed that way, and it is capable of considerable development. It has been long dependent on Morocco, but was lost during the wars of succession in the seventeenth century, and only recovered in 1806, when the blacks were reinstated as a garrison in the citadel built by Mulai Ismá'îl.[2] This is the most northerly spot which produces marketable dates.

Situation.

Description.

Still further out in the desert, an indeterminate distance—seventy days from Tafîlált according to Pellow's

[1] *Tafilet*, pp. 287-290.

[2] Ez-Zaïáni, p. 189.

experience, he having made eleven days from Mequinez to Tafîlált,[1]—is the Tûát oasis, of which our knowledge is even less.* In Mulai Ismá'îl's time it had a Moorish garrison, which Pellow was sent to relieve, and the Arabs of the place brought an annual tribute of gold, ivory, indigo, etc., received from the Guinea Coast. Pellow describes them as olive-coloured, with uncut curly hair, wearing shirt and drawers of khunt, and dwelling in tents made of the skins of wild beasts. They had a breed of sheep with long shiny hair instead of wool, which supplied them with mutton, and large herds of cattle fed on a peculiar weed. Rain, which falls very seldom south of the Atlas, is not seen in Tûát, it is said, once in twenty years.

Position.

Inhabitants.

Although the French acknowledged Tûát as a Moorish dependency by their maps after the frontier was settled in 1845,† in 1891 an attempt was made to take possession of it, which was only frustrated by a visit from the late Shareef of Wazzán,‡ but in 1900 a pretext was found for its annexation. A scientific mission had been attacked in that region some

Annexation by France.

* See *The Moorish Empire*, invasion of Tûát, p. 126; French recognition of Moorish suzerainty, 174-5; French attempt, 190.

† Art. iv. of the Franco-Moroccan treaty of 1845 [2] runs:—

"In the Sahara (desert) there is no territorial limit to be established between the two countries, since the land cannot be tilled, and can only be used as pasture ground for the Arabs of the two empires who come and camp to find pasturage, and the water which they may require. The two Sovereigns shall exercise in what manner they please the fulness of their rights over their respective subjects in the Sahara."

The k'şûrs of Fîgîg and Ya'sh are in the next article expressly named as belonging to Morocco.

‡ See Com. V. Desportes, *La Question de Touat*, Algiers, 1891, with map, and *À propos du Trans-Saharien*, Algiers, 1890; and Press of February to May 1900.

[1] p. 120. [2] Hertslet's *Map of Africa by Treaty*.

months before, to punish which a French expedition raided 'Aïn Salaḥ in December 1899. This roused the neighbouring tribes, and fresh French troops were poured in, which defeated the natives in March and April at 'Aïn Ghar and Igli, with cruel slaughter. The railway had meanwhile been pushed on towards Fîgîg, and was sanctioned to Tûát and Tidikelt, a district adjoining, also hitherto part of the Moorish Empire.

Effect on the Government.

France being in a position to make her occupation effective, and communication with the Moorish capital being difficult and tedious, the end of the matter was never in doubt. When the Sultan's Government learned what had occurred—from telegrams viâ Paris to Tangier, and thence by courier,—it of course launched vigorous protests, and appealed for justice to those other Powers to whom it had so often refused that boon. But while such action was rendered necessary to stay threatened risings in Tafîlált and elsewhere, provoked by short-sighted fanatics, saner views were held by those in power, and the Government recognizes the necessity of acquiescence in the inevitable.

What next?

The only question now of interest to us is, what will France take next, and when? France alone is to be feared in the Land of the Moors, which, as things trend to-day, must in time form part of her colony. There is no use disguising this fact, and, as England certainly would not be prepared to go to war with her neighbour to prevent her repeating in Morocco what she has done in Tunis, it were better not to grumble at her action. All England cares about is the mouth of the Mediterranean, and if this were secured to her, or even guaranteed neutral—were that possible,—she could have no cause to object to the French extension. Our Moorish friends will not listen to our advice; they keep their country closed as far as they can, refusing administrative reforms which would prevent excuses for annexation. Why should we trouble them? It were better far to come to an agreement with France, and to acknowledge what will prove itself one day, that France is the normal heir to Morocco whenever the present Empire breaks up.

NOTE.—For such facts concerning "Unknown Morocco" as it has been possible for foreigners to glean from natives, the reader is referred to *Le Maroc Inconnu*, by M. Mulieras. MM. De la Martinière and De la Croix also have compiled four large volumes of *Documents sur le Nord-ouest Afrique*, but as these are French Government property, their circulation is prohibited. The method adopted by these scholars, of piecing together native reports, is most ingenious, and pending exploration, invaluable. From time to time we are presented with fresh maps produced by this system, in which nothing is left in doubt, but the minutest details are filled in with the precision of a trigonometrical survey. The Frenchman as a student is nothing if not sublimely self-confident. Yet a map of North-Morocco published by our own War-Office within a decade shows an arm of the sea running up the hill behind Tangier: but perhaps this information was intended for the French.

"CAMPING OUT" IN MOROCCO.

Photograph by Herbert White, Esq.

CHAPTER THE TWENTY-FIRST

REMINISCENCES OF TRAVEL

THAT first night out in Barbary! How can I forget it? And to how many others has it not led in many a land! Cook had not then invaded Morocco, and travellers made their own arrangements, as residents still do, keeping their outfit in store. Indeed, an important part is played in the fully equipped establishment in Morocco, whether European or Moorish, by the tents and their furniture, requisitioned from time to time for an outing or journey, since he who travels in Morocco must take house and provender with him.

True Independence.

A formidable undertaking, therefore, is the start, with forty things to be remembered, and a constant determination to do without this or that which will be an encumbrance. The trouble is to learn how many of the things in everyday use within walls can in camp be dispensed with, and how many trifling matters of which one would never think at other times are essential to comfort. After all the ordinary articles are packed in boxes and bundles and panniers, there are fire-grates and lanterns, charcoal and barley, tether-pins and chains and ropes, and odds and ends innumerable, to say nothing of trappings and extra pegs.

Camp Outfit.

The very list of them all would alarm the novice, and as something is *always* forgotten, only to be remembered when in camp the first night, he is wise who, like Sydney Smith, makes a "screaming gate" of the first halt, not too far from the base of

A "Screaming Gate."

supplies, so that a messenger can be despatched to obtain what is lacking. So many delays occur in getting started, that the old hand never hopes to get far the first day, and makes early for camp, to start afresh in earnest on the morrow. It is only thus that a proper inspection is practicable, with everything at last in use—a sort of final full-dress rehearsal,—on which much of the future success of the journey depends.

Transport and Service.

Some hire, some buy, mules and horses, or even camels and donkeys, and now comes the re-adjustment of loads and saddles, with the task of apportioning duties among the motley crew of servants. These will have been picked up in all directions, and are seldom to be relied on, for, sad to relate, nothing corrupts their morals like working for Europeans. It therefore happens, not infrequently, that mounts, and even servants, have to be changed at this moment, when some little insight has been obtained into tricks and failings. Nothing seems more hopeless than the confusion presented on such an occasion, unless most practically supervised, but by degrees things "arrange themselves," and the chances are that by the time night falls a marvellous calm will have succeeded, and whatever the real state of affairs, the supper works magic.

A Continuous Picnic.

The luxurious way to travel is to have a separate outfit for lunch, so that while a hasty breakfast is being accomplished amid the bustle of re-packing, the lunch and attendants can ride on ahead to some shady spot, there to prepare the first square meal of the day, with rugs and cushions for the siesta to follow. Starting at sunrise, by nine or ten, just when in summer it begins to grow hot, the best part of the day's work is done, and conscience permits of rest till three or four, when, after afternoon tea, a fresh start is made for the spot at which the camp has been pitched, those responsible for it having halted for a short time only at noon. The long stay made by their employers affords time for reading or sketching or sport, according to taste, and except when spent perforce upon a barren and shadeless plain, is by no means the least pleasant part of what becomes a continuous picnic. In this sort of thing an experienced guide is essential, and the rate of progress must be sacrificed to pleasure. The distance thus travelled will seldom reach five-and-twenty miles a day, whereas the ordinary caravan rate is about thirty or thirty-five.

Deceptive Distances.

Nothing is more deceptive and annoying than the Moorish idea of distance. The Scotch "mile-and-a-bittock" is not to be named beside the Moorish subḥîyah or "morning's ride," and ḳareeb, which in English means "near," in the mouth of a Moor means anything under half a day's ride. Frequently the state of the country requires that a certain point be reached before camping—whether on account of lawlessness or lack of provision,—and the last hours are apt to grow remarkably tedious, although it is surprising what a pace the animals will often make when the sun goes down, and the halting-place is supposed to be near.

Halting Places.

Unless this be at a village or governor's house, all the stores that are carried will come into use, but while the country-folk supply only eggs and chicken, butter and milk, and grain for the steeds, official hospitality furnishes all that the traveller needs, down to firing and candles. Ushered into the bare-walled guest-room, which his servants forthwith proceed to clean out and furnish, the traveller is refreshed by green tea, a pound or so of which is brought in with loaves of sugar and packets of candles, samovar and tray complete. Later in the evening come stews and other dishes for supper, after which, as well as minute bed-fellows will permit him, he sleeps the traveller's sleep.*

The freedom and fresh air of such a life is delightful: with a regular, healthy fatigue, the rule becomes "early to bed and early to rise," and sleep soon grows sound in spite of the barking and shouting and neighing that make things lively, or the wedding in the adjoining village. The inconveniences come in wet weather, or when an unexpected storm brings the tent down about the sleeper's ears. Sometimes the ground is almost too bad to pitch the tent, or the only safe place is a filthy farm-yard-like n'zálah or government camping-ground, but a water-proof sheet sets things right; if the pegs only hold. If the dry ropes are not slackened before rain falls, the sudden shrinkage will be so severe as to up-root the pegs, which accounts for many unexpected mishaps; besides which, a trough is required round the tent as a precaution against floods. In really bad weather a tent with waterproof bottom and sides in one piece is to be recommended.

Winter Travelling.

No one who has not actually proved what travelling in Morocco in winter means can fully appreciate all that it involves. So a few personal experiences of one who has gone through it may in some measure serve to enlighten the fortunate uninitiated. In the first place it must be remembered that this is an absolutely roadless country, and that the traveller rides on and on,—not across a pathless waste, by any means, for the multitudinous and oft-diverging tracks are most perplexing,—but with no other indication of his being on a permanent highway, even between two important towns, than an occasional bridge or ferry-boat across an otherwise impassable river. The approaches to these are often almost impassable, and one frequently

* For an account of Moorish hospitality, see *The Moors*, ch. xvii.

sees a bad ford preferred to a good bridge close by, on account of the quagmires at either end. The bridges are few, and far between, being placed only where absolutely necessary almost all the year round, for if a river is fordable during the greater part of the year, the Moor is content not to pass that way during the remainder, resignedly exclaiming "Má shá Allah!"—"What God wills!"

TRAVELLING COMPANIONS.
Photograph by Dr. Rudduck.

Approaches to Towns.

The same course is adopted with the entrances to towns, and with the specially bad places on the main roads. The more important the town, the more awful its approaches are in wet weather, in consequence of the continual traffic, till the time arrives when they become absolutely impassable, and fresh provisions rise inside to almost famine price. During the rains, Fez itself is often for days almost without fresh meat,—or when none is to be found in the market. The well-to-do are then obliged to go shares in purchasing cows kept in town for their milk, to kill for themselves, and the poor have to go without. The daily visit to the country pasturage of the cattle and animals in the towns works the roads up into a fearful state, and none can come out or in but such as are content to do so barefooted, and that with immense labour. The recital of one experience will suffice.

A Memorable Experience.

Our party consisted of two, a Moor and the writer, dressed alike, and "a jolly lot we were." One fine evening we encamped in excellent spirits a couple of hours outside Mequinez. It was so fine that we thought it needless to surround our tent with a ditch, and after supper, being near our journey's end, went to sleep with our fine clothes set out to make our entry in becoming style on the morrow. But "the best laid schemes o' men and mice gang aft agley," and this is how it happened with us.

Forewarned not Forearmed.

Some time after we had gone to sleep I awoke with a presentiment that it was coming on to rain. Mindful of the un-dug trench, I wakened my man, who, putting his head outside, declared that it was a beautiful night, and the ground dry, so we foolishly turned and slept again.

In the middle of the night I dreamed that I was sleeping in my tent, pitched in a Moorish room, quite dry, while in the adjoining room the rain was pouring in torrents which that famous sportsman "Sarcelle" was vainly attempting to stem, wading about with his trousers rolled up to his knees. As for me, I was floating bravely on the stream on my mattress and waterproof sheet, the edges of which I was holding up. Just then my impromptu punt sprang a leak, and I felt cold water at my back. In a moment I was awake, shouting at my man to tell him that the ground was an inch or two under water, and that our mattresses, spare clothes, and all our belongings, were soaking wet.

A Fine Situation.

Alas for pleasant prospects! We had hardly a dry garment between us, and barely enough food for breakfast, for we had calculated on reaching our destination the previous evening.

Mistaking the dull moon-light through the clouds for the commencement of day-break, we rejoiced that our troubles would soon be over, and dressed in the driest rig we could find, disregarding appearances. Then, after consuming our scanty rations, and swallowing doses of quinine and spirits of camphor to prevent any possible evil effects, we packed up and wakened a native to show us the way to town. But this he refused to do before actual day-break, for the few remaining miles were through the haunts of highwaymen, so we dejectedly sat on our sodden equipment, and dozed for the remaining hours of night, awaking numbed and hungry to the tune of a tropical downpour.

Battling with the Elements.

The first streak of dawn saw us start with encouraging visions of food and shelter, and on we rode merrily through the mud, for although under ordinary circumstances a halt until a change of weather would have been advisable, our plight made that out of the question, with succour so near at hand. Presently a fresh storm burst, which the rising wind drove almost straight in our faces, to the great discomfort of men and beasts. From the moment when the water had awakened us, we had been in constant laughter at each other's jokes, as a precaution against "dumps," and now the only thing to keep our spirits up was to sing, and sing we did right lustily—being some distance apart,—each to his own time and tune, till both were hoarse.

A Weary Trudge.

The road now became so atrocious that the poor beasts had hard work to keep from falling. Our path lay by the side of a stream winding in and out between low rounded hills along the bases of which we rode. The soil was clayey and fearfully slippery, worked up by the cattle into the consistency of damp soft soap, and pathways there were not.

Between each hill we had to descend a steep and treacherous declivity to the dividing brook, and then to mount as bad a place on the other side. Finally the tired beasts began to fall, first one slipping down the side of the hill, then the other sinking in the mire of a gully. Laden with our outfit, they were unable to rise unless we lifted the pack—one on either side,—so we had a fairly bad time of it. Our slippers soon became sodden and full of clay, till they twisted round our feet, and we had to take them off and walk barefoot.

The "Skate-Step."

Even this was no easy matter, for at each step we slipped. At last a couple of country Moors came along, and attentively watching their mode of progress as they overtook and passed us, I noticed that it more resembled skating than walking, so with a yearning thought of the good times others were doubtless enjoying at the moment on some well-remembered ponds, I furbished up my recollections of the use of skates, and soon got far ahead of my poor man, who laboriously floundered along, as though "half seas over."

The "couple of hours to town" was thus rendered nearly six, and when at length we arrived at our longed-for destination, starved, wearied, footsore and soaking wet, it was long before we could get at all passably settled, for Moorish towns by no means excel in convenience or accommodation for travellers.*

Such was the experience of one day, but it has had

* Only once, in all my wanderings, have I had a worse experience, and that was when becalmed for twenty-eight hours in a basket-boat on a flood between the Tigris and Euphrates, within sight of Baghdád: a horse, two donkeys, four boatmen, a married couple, a soldier and myself in a circular ḳoffa—"pitched within and without"—ten feet in diameter; a cold wind driving spray which froze. Further details are better imagined. During the night the boatmen ate my store of biscuits for the month's ride to Damascus.

fellows. Sometimes for many a weary mile the roads lie over rich loamy soil, little the better for several days' sun, cut up for a hundred yards on either side by the feet of cattle. The best-looking paths are sun-dried but on top, and as soon as a luckless rider gets well on, the crust gives way, and his poor beast, after a plunge or two, meekly settles down with *Quagmires.*

A WAYSIDE WELL.
(Province of Raḥámna.)
The Author's servant drawing water.
Photograph by Dr. Rudduck.

his legs buried over the houghs, needing several men to extricate it, one or two at each side, and one at the tail. Treacherous and muddy streams have constantly to be crossed, a bare-legged man going first to sound for a bottom, and the riders following down one steep bank, through a bog, and up another, "liver in mouth."

I have seen eleven out of seventeen loaded beasts sink one after another more quickly than I could count, in a comparatively passable-looking slough of some twenty yards wide on a level plain. When an animal goes in thus, it lies down patiently: if it has a rider he must dismount, although he may go in himself halfway up his calves, and if it is loaded, unless there are men at hand to lend assistance, its load will probably have to be taken off and repacked when on firmer ground.

Sloughs.

When a wide river has to be crossed by a ferry, there is a fearful struggle to get close up to the high-sided boat, and the beasts, having had their fore-legs hoisted in, are cursed and beaten, lugged and pushed, till they drag the remainder of their bodies after them. Getting out is a somewhat similar process. Unless the animal be a specially lively one, it usually endures the whole process, whether of hauling out of a hole or into a boat, with a meekness which is almost affecting, its great round eyes looking piteously at its persecutors, "as a sheep before its shearers."

Crossing Rivers.

At some places the rivers are crossed by treacherous rafts made of bundles of sticks and rubbish, fearful to contemplate—when half-way over,—or supported by inflated skins, which are more satisfactory. Often fording is the only means of crossing, and this, when the current is strong, needs one man at the bridle, and another at the tail of a loaded beast, while even then a fall with a consequent floating off of one's property sometimes occurs.

Primitive Methods.

But it is the poor camels which seem to suffer most. They may be detained for months by some comparatively short piece of bad road. Although they can get along better than other beasts when the mud is half dried—as their big spongy feet press it down instead of sinking in, in which way these animals are the "real and only genuine" road-makers

Effects on Camels.

in Morocco,—yet when the mud is slippery they become unable to proceed at all. If one leg slips, the ponderous, ungainly creature comes down with a crash, and has no power to draw in its limbs when once spread apart, so it is killed there and cut up for food, as many a road-side skeleton testifies.

A State of Siege.

A heavy or continued rain often detains the traveller for days or even weeks in one place, and sometimes he can move neither backwards nor forwards, as was the case some years ago with a British officer caught between a swollen river in front, and the bog into which the plain he had crossed had become converted. Three weeks he stood this siege, till his leave was outstayed, and he barely escaped more serious trouble at home. In such a case the question of provisions becomes formidable, and the traveller is in sorry plight. I say this feelingly, for I write in my tent in Shrárda in the month of January, detained by pouring rain, unable to set foot outside. *

Advice.

All things considered, therefore, the best advice to be given to those who have any idea of travelling inland here in winter is "don't," unless for some special reason apart from pleasure, except in a very dry season, but even then there is a risk of particularly heavy rains to finish up with. The worst period is called "lîalî," and extends from December 11th to January 21st, Old Style,—as the natives reckon,—or from December 23rd to February 1st, according to our calendar. The corresponding hot season in summer, called the "smaïm," equally to be avoided, comprises the forty days from July 11th O.S. to Aug. 21st, corresponding to our July 23rd to Sept. 1st.

* Written in 1889.

THE AUTHOR.
(In Moorish Guise).
Photograph by Elliot & Fry, Baker St., W.

CHAPTER THE TWENTY-SECOND

IN MOORISH GUISE

TO those who have not themselves experienced what the attempt to see an eastern country in native guise entails, a few stray notes of what it has been my lot to encounter in seeking for knowledge in this style, will no doubt be of interest. Such an undertaking, like every other style of adventure, has both its advantages and disadvantages. To the student of the people the former are immense, and if he can put up with whatever comes, he will be well repaid for all the trials by the way. In no other manner can a European mix with any freedom with the natives of this country. When once he has discarded the outward distinguishing features of what they consider a hostile infidelity, and has as far as possible adopted their dress and their mode of life, he has spanned one of the great gulfs which have hitherto yawned between them.

Advantages.

Squatted on the floor, one of a circle round a low table on which is a steaming dish into which each plunges his fist in search of dainty morsels, the once distant Moor thaws to an astonishing extent, becoming really friendly and communicative, in a manner totally impossible towards the starchy European who sits uneasily on a chair, conversing with his host at ease on the floor. And when the third cup of tea syrup comes, and each lolls contentedly on the cushions, there is manifested a brotherly feeling not unnoted in western circles under analagous circumstances,

A Typical Instance.

here fortunately without a suggestion of anything stronger than "gunpowder."

A Dual Existence.

Yes, this style of thing decidedly has its delights—of which the above must not be taken as the most elevating specimen,—and many are the pleasant memories which come before me as I mentally review my life "as a Moor." In doing so I seem to be again transported to another world, to live another life, as was my continual feeling at the time. Everything around me was so different, my very actions and thoughts so complete a change from what they were under civilization, that when the courier brought the periodical budget of letters and papers I felt as one in a dream, even my mother tongue sounding strange after not having heard it so long. I seemed to be living two lives, interchangeable, and yet distinct, and so still seem its memories.

Object.

I like the Moors, with all their faults, and am not ashamed to confess it, and I would enjoy the opportunity of once more mixing with them in the same congenial style. My object on previous occasions was to seize every opportunity of becoming acquainted with things Moorish, especially with the habits and opinions of the people, and the result was in every way satisfactory. But such a task was one of varied, sometimes strange, experience.

Strange Quarters.

Often I have had to "put up" in strange quarters; sometimes without any quarters at all. I have slept in the mansions of Moorish merchants, and rolled up in my cloak in the street. I have occupied the guest chambers of country governors and sheïkhs, and I have passed the night on the wheat in a granary, wondering whether fleas or grains were more numerous. I have been accommodated in the house of a Jewish Rabbi, making a somewhat similar observation with regard to an insect of far worse type with which it swarmed, and I have been the guest of a Jewish Consular Agent of a Foreign Power, where the awful stench from the drains was not exceeded by that of the worst hovel I ever entered. I have even succeeded in wooing Morpheus out on the sea-shore, under the lea of a rock, and I have found the débris by the side of a straw rick an excellent couch till it came on to rain. Yet again, I

"A NIGHT'S LODGING" IN RAḤAMNA.
Photograph by Dr. Rudduck.

have been one of half a dozen on the floor of a windowless and doorless summer-house in the middle of the rainy season. The tent of the wandering Arab has afforded me shelter, along with calves and chickens and legions of fleas, and I have actually passed the night in a village mosque.

Once my lodging was a hut in which a quadruple murder had been committed, empty and even uncleaned for the couple of months which had elapsed since that ghastly event, the blood-stains being still on the walls.

Writing under Difficulties.

On other occasions I had the utmost difficulty to select a spot where I could sit without being under some hole in the roof, through which the rain poured incessantly, and when I lay down I had to be protected by my waterproof. The room, a large garret, the thatched roof of which permitted one to stand up only in the middle third, was packed with field labourers, while in the midst there crackled a fire of thorns, casting a lurid glare on the scene, the only light I had to write by, till it died out and was replaced by a dim and spluttering oil lamp, ever and anon extinguished by a fierce gust through the large holes which served as windows at either end. It was under these befitting circumstances that I wrote the greater portion of these jottings, besides covering a quire or so with general descriptive notes.

Curious Contrasts.

I have one day, behind my mule, in mud and sun, trudged the country barefoot, getting my feet cut and my legs scratched in a manner which prevented their use for weeks, and in the course of the same journey I have ridden bravely amid an escort of a dozen armed men renewed from stage to stage. I have crossed the country as a well-to-do merchant in flowing garments on an ambling mule, and I have gone long distances as a poor countryman, in dirty garments the worse for wear, legs muddy and feet bare, on the top of the load of a stumbling pack-beast. At one time travelling in a style that was a continuous picnic, at another I have been roasted with heat, and parched with thirst; soaked with rain, and pierced with cold, with hardly a dry garment in my possession.

I have had my skin rubbed off by wear and tear, and have been bitten by loathsome insects, but I have hitherto been fortunate in escaping anything venomous, and by most careful precautions as to personal cleanliness and contact with the natives—even to carrying my own tea-glass in my satchel, and never using any other,—and by making free use of carbolic for my hands, I have likewise kept clear of the many contagious diseases from which they so commonly suffer. Among other safeguards of general health, I have placed great reliance in a rigid observance of the rule to boil and filter all my drinking water—except perhaps a sip after a full meal of kesksoo,—and to select rising ground for my camp if possible, by which means I have thus far also been free from the traveller's great enemies, dysentery and fever, or any approach to either.

Personal Experiences.

And here I may say that although I have visited every country of Europe, every kingdom of Asia save Afghanistan and Tibet, all those of North Africa, and nearly all in North America, I have never found it needful to use any form of strong drink. *

A Testimony.

* My principle has been fearlessly to drink the local water after due enquiry and examination, filtering and boiling whenever that precaution appeared necessary, but *filtering first*. Many who make soup by reversing the process complain that "boiled water tastes!" Of course it does, if you cook living creatures in it. But the strict test has been the closely noted effect on the digestive organs, and whenever the water has been doubtful, I have when possible made use of natural mineral waters, or the manufactured article; always at least as pure as the wines I have seen made—and for which I have trodden the grapes myself in Spain.

Precautions with Water.

But a word of warning about filters. All stone or charcoal blocks systems are a delusion, unless an unlimited stock of blocks can be carried, for the moment they are clogged they are worse than useless. Only such filters can be relied on as Maignen's, which can be recharged in a few moments with an absolutely fresh medium. Thus, notwithstanding the somewhat immoderate use of water to which I must confess, I have never had cause to regret it, and I never met a wine-drinker who enjoyed better health. Nor have I yet learned to smoke; there is always time for that. And I may add that few things have more strongly recommended me to my Moorish friends than this abstention from alcohol and narcotics.

When I set out on my travels in Moorish guise, it was with no thought of penetrating spots so venerated by the Moors that all non-Muslims are excluded, but the idea grew upon me as I journeyed, and the Moors themselves were the cause. This is how it came about. Having become acquainted to some extent with the language and customs of the people during a residence of several years among them as a European, when I travelled—with the view of rendering myself less conspicuous, and mixing more easily with the natives,—I adopted their dress and followed their style of life, making, however, no attempt to conceal my nationality. After a while I found that when I went where I was not known, all took me for a Moor till they heard my speech, and recognised the foreign accent and the blunders which no native could make. My Moorish friends would often remark that were it not for this I could enter mosques and saint-houses with impunity.

"Out of Bounds."

For convenience' sake I had instructed the one faithful attendant who accompanied me to call me by a Muslim name resembling my own, and I afterwards added a corruption of my surname which sounded well, and soon began to seem quite natural.* This prevented the attention of the bystanders being arrested when I was addressed by my man, who was careful also always to refer to me as "Seyyïd," Master, a term which is never applied to Europeans or Jews.

'Nom de Guerre."

Having got so far, a plan occurred to me to account for my way of speaking. I had seen a lad from Manchester, born there of an English mother, but the son of a Moor, who knew not a word of Arabic when sent to Morocco by his father. Why could

My "Rôle."

* A similar practice is of necessity followed by foreign residents in China, who never attempt to teach the natives their real names, but adopt Chinese pseudonyms, by which alone they are recognized.

I not pass as such an one, who had not yet perfected himself in the Arabic tongue? Happy thought! Was I not born in Europe, and educated there? Of course I was, and here was the whole affair complete. I remember, too, that on one or two occasions I had had quite a difficulty to persuade natives that I was *not* similarly situated to this lad. On the first occasion I was taken by surprise, as one among a party of English people, the only one dressed in Moorish costume, which I thought under those circumstances would deceive no one. When asked whence I came, I replied "England," and was then asked "Is there a mosque there?" I answered that I was not aware that there was one, but that I knew a project had been set on foot to build one near London.* Other questions followed, as to my family and what my father's occupation was, till I was astonished at the enquiry, "Has your father been to Mekka yet?"

"Why, no," I answered, as it dawned upon me what had been my interrogator's idea—"he's not a Muslim!"

"Don't say that!" said the man.

"But we are not," I reiterated, "we are Christians."

It was as difficult to persuade him that I was not at least a convert to Christianity from Islám, as I should have thought it would have been to persuade him that I was a Muslim. Bearing this in mind, I had no doubt that by simply telling the strict truth about myself, and allowing them to draw their own conclusions, I should generally pass for the son of a Moorish merchant settled in England, and thus it proved. Once, during a day's ride in Moorish dress, I counted the number of people saluted by the way, and was gratified to find that although on a European saddle

Proof of Success.

* Since erected at Woking in Indian style. Quite small, but pleasingly designed. The Liverpool "mosque" has been exposed by the Muslims in England themselves.

and near Tangier, about ninety per cent replied in the formula which showed that they thought me a Moor. A considerable number saluted me first, and among these was an old employé, who was fairly astonished when I made myself known to him.

"MY FAITHFUL MOHAMMED" EN ROUTE.
(Riding a pack-mule with the "batterie de cuisine.")
Photograph by R. J. Moss, Esq.

A Remarkable Instance.

Another striking instance of this occurred in Fez, where, before entering any house, I paid an unintentional visit to the very shrine I wished to see. Outside the gates I had stopped to change my costume, and passing in apart from my faithful Mohammed, after a stroll to about the centre of the city, I asked at a shop the way to a certain house.

The owner called a lad who knew the neighbourhood, to whom I explained what I wanted, and off we started. In a few minutes I paused on the threshold of a finely ornamented building, different from any other I had seen. All unsuspicious, I inquired what it was, and learned that we were in a street as sacred as a mosque, and that my guide was taking me a short cut through the sanctuary of Mulai Idrees!

In the Fes Mosques.

Some days later, lantern and slippers in one hand, and rosary in the other, I entered with the crowd for sunset prayers. Perspiring freely within, but outwardly with the calmest appearance I could muster, I spread my prayer-cloth and went through the motions prescribed by law, making my observations in the pauses, and concluding by a guarded survey of the place. I need hardly say that I breathed with a feeling of relief when I found myself in the pure air again, and felt better after I had had my supper and sat down to commit my notes to paper. In the Ḳarûeeïn I once caught a suspicious stare at my glasses, so, pausing, I returned the stare with a contemptuous indignation that made my critic slink off abashed. There was nothing to do but to "face it out."

"An Arab of the Arabs."

One kaid even complimented me upon being evidently an "Arab of the Arabs"—and therefore no Berber,—and gave me a letter of introduction to the kaid of the first holy place I proposed to visit, for now I made no secret of my intentions. I simply told my man to reply to the inquisitive that his master, the Foḳeeḥ (learned one) Sî Ṭahar bel Mikkî, the son of a merchant from Europe, was completing his education by visiting the chief cities and shrines of Morocco, a secondary object being the study of Arabic, as his knowledge of it was faulty, since he had been brought up abroad. An interview usually suggested to the thoughtful that my mother must have been a European, and I heard one or two ask my man whether she was a legal wife or a slave! In conversation, however, I was proud and grateful to proclaim myself a Christian and an Englishman. My native dress meant after all no more than European dress does on an Oriental in England: it brought me in touch with the Moors, and it enabled me to pass among them unobserved.

My Moorish Education.

Each evening quite an enthusiastic crowd used to gather round my tent door—only kaids and sheïkhs got inside—to sip three friendly cups of green tea syrup in approved native style, and each vied with the other, as occasion offered, to initiate me into the rites of Mohammedanism. As for improving my Arabic, that was by no means forgotten, and many a score of words were thus added to the goodly stock in my ever ready note-book. Oh that I could introduce you who read this into that picturesque circle! What times we had! Inside, the cosy quarters for the night, a bright, warm light, with a group of Moors round the tea-tray; outside, a larger group, warming their hands at the charcoal embers, as they diligently use the bellows to hasten the boiling of our tiny kettle for the sixth or seventh time. The darkness beyond is deepened by the ruddy glow which flickers on their faces. The expression of their swarthy features is intensified as they listen with rapt attention to some thrilling tale, or would-be words of wisdom from the lips of the village sage, or the description of some wonder of "Nazarene Land" which the traveller tells. *That's* the way to pick up Arabic, and how to get acquainted with the Moors!

CHAPTER THE TWENTY-THIRD

TO MARRAKESH ON A BICYCLE

WHETHER cycling without roads is pleasant or not, depends, like so many another question, on the way in which you look at it. For my part, I enjoyed it in Morocco immensely, but the other man—for there were two of us—found it less funny. To begin with, I was a novice at "wheeling," having had but one week's practice, and had not learned what a good road means to the cyclist; whereas my friend had just been cycling through France. Then, too, knowing the country and speaking the language, I derived full benefit from the remarks overheard, which often lost much in translation. But the inexhaustible good-humour and wit of my comrade, Dr. Rudduck, kept us bright, and one realized fully the force of the Moorish proverb: "Choose your companion before your road." The novelty was something, too, both for us and the natives, although when at times we had perforce to walk, it was rather trying to be pitied by passers-by, who wondered why we had not hired mules to transport such awkward "luggage" as our machines.

Cycling without Roads.

Not only has Morocco no roads, it has also no inns or hotels after leaving the coast, and the prospect of unprepared native quarters was not exactly relished, especially as we knew from experience what they were like. So we schemed to carry what we could on our machines, which were rigged up with frames and carriers on which we were

Baggage Arrangements.

able to pack some sixty pounds apiece. Thus, indeed, we started, but soon relinquished our loads to a horseman whom we had engaged for the journey.

Nevertheless, from time to time I had occasion to reload my machine—a "Rover," which, with carriers, etc., weighed 40 lbs.—till it and I and the baggage together scaled 300 lbs., in which condition I rode it easily over pavements and stony roads, or up slight hills. On my return, in crossing Paris like this, the greatest interest was aroused, and I was more than once asked if I were not moving house! A well-filled 18in. "Gladstone" on the frame behind; a good-sized hold-all above the handles; a luncheon basket below, containing spirit-lamp, kettle, and tea things; a packed valise inside the frame, with a sun umbrella strapped alongside; a water-can between the cranks, and a tin of oil below the seat, formed the full equipment: I found it enough.

Apologies for Roads.

Such tracks as there are in Morocco are those formed by beasts of burden, eight or nine inches wide, frequently worn so deep that our pedals struck on one bank or the other in descending, sometimes with such sudden force that the machine was lifted off the ground. Often so many stones or so much sand filled the track that we had to run outside on the grass or ploughed land, over which I soon got accustomed to bowl with ease, if not pleasure. Such careful guiding too, was required on account of these stones, that I expected to be duly qualified for tight-rope riding upon my return. Often the tracks led down into gullies, into which one would wildly plunge—since they were almost always dry—rising up the other side with a bound that was most delicious.

Other variations in a ride which might have grown monotonous were constantly afforded by the wonder and astonishment of all whom we encountered. The time was that of harvest—in May—and right and left the reapers started up with shouts to one another and raced after us. Some, no doubt, thought we were "flying devils," but they could not make out our machines.

A GOOD PIECE OF ROAD IN RAḤAMNA.
(Through a disused grave-yard.)
Photograph by Dr. Rudduck.

"But what sort of beast are you riding? We thought it must be a 'drinker of wind,'"—whereby is denoted a certain fleet camel used on the desert, seldom now seen in Morocco. *Effect on the Natives.*

"Why, dear no; it's only a mule, a Nazarene mule, you know,"—for everything outside Morocco is either called Roman or Nazarene.

"You don't mean to say so! How do you breed them?"

"Well, you can see for yourself from its speed that

its mother must have been a gazelle, and from these round parts and iron that its father must have been a reaping-hook."

Bicycle Breeding.

A moment's stare while trying to realize whether this could be the truth or not, and out they burst in a hearty laugh, for the Moors do enjoy a joke, and this was one which specially appealed to them, so to every new-comer it was repeated as fact in most solemn tones. Others, taking up the idea, would ask particulars as to its feed, and whether it kicked, or had any evil habits.

WONDERING ON-LOOKERS.
Photograph by Dr. Rudduck.

"Stand away from his heels there!"

"Hold his head, Mohammed, and see that his girths are tight!"

"Whew, what a stirrup! Why, they're not the same length! Pull them tight? Now then, the Nazarene's mounting—clear away!"

Then all would set off to race us, girding up their loins and promising great things.

"Wait a bit, though! It's not a fair start!"

But we were clear of a crowd to which we had no desire to return, and, as far as the ground would allow, forged ahead. Sometimes we offered fabulous prizes to any who might outstrip us, riding sedately alongside of some old farmer, whom we tempted to spur on his mare till both panted, while we coolly spurted ahead with "good morning!"

A safe Challenge.

Whenever we overtook such riders, we had to yell our warnings, for our bells were not understood, and on several occasions, in spite of precautions, caused such alarm to fellow-travellers that they and their mounts parted company, one dashing over the plain, the other picking himself up to see what had happened.

Once I met an old man whose donkey so suddenly shied at the apparition that in a moment he found himself seated where there was no fear of falling. I really felt sorry, but was hesitating whether I should stop to be abused or not, when, looking backward, my machine ran into a tuft of grass and seated me likewise, to the unbounded delight of a party of natives, while the old man and I looked at each other solemnly.

Amusing Spills.

Another time, while riding across the market at Tangier, a Moor who tried to get out of my way, as women do even in England, by running right across my track, tripped over his cloak at the critical moment, whereupon I landed head foremost into the soft heap he provided, but before he could collect his brains or his limbs I was mounted, and the crowd enjoyed his discomfiture richly, for neither of us was damaged.

On no occasion did we suffer rudeness or interference at the hands of the Moors, notwithstanding the prognostications of our friends, though their inquisitiveness often proved amusing. Sometimes, if they could get near, they would turn the nut of the tyre valve, or threaten to try our "Dunlops" with their daggers, assured that if not pork

Behaviour of Natives.

sausage, they must be made of pig-skin, since they were the work of pig-eating unbelievers. But they liked the idea of air for fodder, especially as a famine was threatened, and they were urgent in their requests for a ride, which no assurance of danger could stay.

"Let me try, Consul; there's not a horse in the province that I can't ride; I'll break her in."

At one halting-place our only way out of the difficulty was to declare that none should on any account be permitted to try but the sedate and portly governor whose guests we were, who would sooner have stood on his head. Our only real trouble was when we had to wheel our machines—which occurred so often that my companion thought we ought to call it a walking tour with bicycle variations,—when the crowd was apt to grow unpleasantly large and close. While standing we could keep their curious fingers at bay, but walking we could not.

Beneath Contempt.

One day, at lunch beneath a hedge of cactus, all the wonder and amazement of the circle around us was dispelled by a travelled Moor, who exclaimed scornfully: "Bah! *These* are nothing: what do you look at *them* for? Why, these things have only *two* wheels, and in Algeria I have seen things with *four!*"

Their wonder is to be explained, since in Morocco there are practically no wheeled vehicles; of one thing, however, all had heard, that the "Romans" have a wonderful contrivance by which they get about with incredible speed, known in Morocco as the "land steamer," which they naturally took our innocent "cykes" to be.

"Alas! Alas! Woe is me! The Christians have taken our country at last; why, here's a railway train! Woe to me! Woe to me!"*

Those who felt less desponding, although no less

* See illustration by Dr. Rudduck on p. 396 of *The Moorish Empire.*

certain, yelled at us lustily: "Give them fire! Give them fire!" and from the remarks overheard I found that my red-cloth-covered water-can was usually taken for the furnace. None could conceive how moving the pedals could make them go.

As for accommodation at night, the less said the better. The first night we made for a governor's residence, whither we had been preceded by a mounted messenger from the governor of Mazagan, whence we started, an old friend who had not only given us a dinner, but had come out to see us off. On arrival we were shown into the bare and comfortless guest room. Already a Jewish trader was installed there with his baggage, and after a while came tea and sugar and candles for all. Then, after a visit from the governor, supper, a big dish of stew with abundant bread. After this we lay down and slept, when the fleas would permit us, even the case-hardened Jew complaining next day that they had kept him awake, so it may be guessed how we suffered. Next day the old governor, fat, grey, and nearly blind, wrapped in his blanket and white-hooded cloak, came round to be doctored while we doctored a punctured tyre—our first and last, since the stones on these tracks being worn and unbroken, the tyres do not suffer in this way anything like so much as in England.

Wayside Quarters.

But from the heat and jolting they suffered more than ever tyres were meant to stand. On both our machines the rear tubes gave way at the joints, but when replaced by tropical "Dunlops," caused us no more trouble, although in one case a 30 in. tube had to do for a 28 in. wheel. Towards noon the heat of the ground and the sun was so great that the air in the tubes extended and puffed them until we could let off a good rush, and yet leave them tight.

Behaviour of Tyres.

Most days, however, we rode in the early morning and late afternoon, enjoying a much needed mid-day rest where we could. Jæger-clad, *cap à pie*, I was as independent as could be of changing temperature, though at night it grew piercing cold in contrast to the heat of the day. And once, having failed to overtake our man with his load, when taking refuge in an Arab tent, alongside of a calf and chicken, we were fain, in the dark, to roll ourselves on the ground in a native blanket, so filthy that when day broke we could not look at it.

THE AUTHOR PATCHING A TYRE.

Photograph by Dr. Rudduck.

The Culinary Department.

When we got our tent up, and could cook our own supper, everything went well, but when we had to rely on what we could get, we needed all the appetite the day had given us. The most sumptuous fare in the country was a musty flavoured preparation of barley, interspersed with chunks of mutton or chicken, and eggs *ad lib.* Milk could only be obtained when we arrived at the moment of milking, before the new was mixed with the old, though the resulting sour beverage was almost always to be had, and the Doctor liked it. Bread we had with us, and water we carried also. Once or twice we obtained oranges, and on several occasions we fell in with governors or other officials who invited us to join them at well-cooked and well-served repasts, with abundance of sweet green tea.

At last, after several days, between walking and riding, we reached Marrákesh, and one morning bowled up to the door of the Southern Morocco Mission, where we were most hospitably entertained. The already familiar bazaars of the city offered a never failing supply of artistic scenes and interesting studies, with their robed and shrouded figures, men in colours and women in white, an unending succession of picturesque types: its narrow, winding streets, lined with cupboard-like shops, and its extensive covered markets, were in turn invaded by the bicycle and camera, as witness these pages.

Consternation at the Capital.

Such consternation was caused, that rumours of it even reached the ears of the late Wazeer Regent, who sent a message to us requesting us not to ride within the walls, and giving notice that such things did not belong to Morocco. But we had had our ride, and still continued to enjoy ourselves, although the doctor had determined never again to cycle in Barbary.

I take occasion to correct here one or two slips in the previous description of Marrákesh, discovered after going to press. The main water supply, El Bashîah, which turns the corn mills, comes from the Ghegháya River, and a special supply of red water for irrigation from Tasultant; the Ṣaḥrîj el Baḳar (p. 291) is only about 400 *feet* square. The Melláḥ drinking place has been repaired since I saw it. Báb 'Aïlán (p. 296) is commonly known as Báb 'Aïlál, and Báb Kûs (p. 310) should read Báb Kûsh.

CHAPTER THE TWENTY-FOURTH

IN SEARCH OF "MILTSIN"

IN case there may be some among my readers who acknowledge doubt as to the whereabouts of "Miltsin," let me give them consolation by confessing equal ignorance. This may seem strange in one who offers to describe the Land of the Moors, but in this belated empire things are often unexpectedly reversed, and no such mountain is known in Morocco. With memories of school books, which asserted that the highest peak of the Atlas was "Miltsin, 11,400 feet above the sea;" with maps before me clearly marking this same peak in various positions to the south of Marrákesh, the city wherein I write, one day in May I started with two friends for the forbidden goal. Forbidden, as all mountains are in this country, whether to the Government or foreigners, by primitive Berber tribes whose ancient home they are, tribes which have never known subjugation.

A "Geography" Mountain.

On this account the visitors who have found access to them may be reckoned on one's fingers. Twice determined attempts have been made by English parties under Government escort; Hooker, Ball and Maw in the seventies, Joseph Thomson and Crichton-Browne in the eighties; while once or twice European hunting parties have gone up in search of áûdád. Of the two parties mentioned, the latter was by far the more successful, but neither reached

Previous Searches.

"Miltsin," so the highest peak yet remains to be ascended and its height recorded.*

Our Route.

Striking the mountains five and a half hours—say twenty miles—from here, at Tahanaût, we followed the route of Hooker and Thomson to Asni, a mud-built village at the head of the winding

ASCENDING THE GHEGHAYA VALLEY.

Photograph by Dr. Rudduck.

gorge of the Ghegháya, where that river is formed by the junction of the Iminán and the Aït Mîzán, from left and right respectively. So far the track lay along the river bed among the shingle, which we forded and re-forded at every turn, but from this point the gorges grew too narrow and rugged for that, and it was necessary to climb up and down the hill-sides, rounding, descending and mounting by the barest of tracks, often

* Mr. W. B. Harris suggests the Jebel Ayáshi, half-way between Fez and Tafîlált, may ultimately prove to be the highest peak in the whole range.[1]

[1] *Tafilet*, p. 88.

not more than six inches wide, along a precipice. As the only means of approach to the districts beyond, these paths are perforce kept practicable here and there by repairs, but they are only safe for mountain mules.*

Hooker's party had followed the Aït Mîzán gorge to where it ended beyond the village of Arromd at Ikhf n-T'fîlit (Fîli Head), in a pass across the Atlas to Tifnût, but they had been allowed to ascend no mountain. Thomson had therefore chosen the Iminán gorge, reaching thereby a similar pass beyond the village of Tashdîrt, to the right of which, on the afternoon of the day on which he had ridden in five hours from Asni, he made his highest ascent, Mount Likimt, 13,150 ft. This still remains the record, though from its summit, to use his own words, he was struck by the unexpected sight of "a magnificently rugged peak towering above the surrounding heights to an elevation of quite 2000 feet above our point of view This we were informed was the Tizi-n-Tamjurt... The highest elevation in the Atlas—certainly not less than 15,000 feet, and possibly more." In the name, however, Thomson was mistaken, for he saw before him the Tizi-n (Peak of) Tagharat, undoubtedly the veritable "Miltsin," with a sharp lower side peak, its distinguishing feature when viewed from here, called Borj Tishki or Tûbkál. Whence the name "Miltsin" has been culled I cannot divine, and no inquiries on the spot elicited the slightest information, in whatever way it was pronounced. I can only hazard the conjecture that Washington (1829) who seems to be responsible for it,[1] on enquiring the name of the snowy peak which overtops the scene to the south of Marrá-

Thomson's Achievement.

The Veritable "Miltsin."

* See illustration of one by my companion on p. 51 of *The Moorish Empire*: also p. 37 of this volume.

[1] R. G. S. *Proceedings*, Vol. I.

kesh, was informed that it was "Mûl' et-T'zin" or "Lord of the Peaks," the first word being Arabic, the last one Berber, a not uncommon combination where the two tongues overlap, one being used to amplify the other. The contraction to "Multzin" or "Miltsin" is just what one would expect.

Mt. Tagharát, "Lord of the Peaks."

Mount Tagharat or Tinzár lies to the right (W.) and Mount Imserdan to the left (E.) of the head of the Aït Mîzán glen, by no means so rugged and bleak as that of Iminán, and the ascent is made from the shrine of Sidi Shimhárôsh, a reputed king of the genii whose name has to me a decidedly Hebraic sound. To the left of this is the road across

A GORGE OF THE GREAT ATLAS BEYOND ASNI.
Photograph by Dr. Rudduck.

the pass to the lake of Ifni, which gives its name to the district of Tifnût, a lake in which large fish are said to be shot, though no European has ever been there. This is reached in a long day from Arromd, the last Aït Mîzán village, at which we stopped, some three miles over heavy roads from Shimhárôsh. Thence the Wád N'fís may be reached in another day, and the Gindáfi fortress—Tagundáft—in two and a half, past the Tizi n-Záût. This is the tempting round I would recommend to my successors, as we were reluctantly compelled to give it up.

Our Plans Balked.

An intelligent Tifnût Jew whom we found at Arromd engaged as a gun-smith, offered to guide us for a dollar a day, but was frightened into retraction by the villagers, who said that if we passed out of their district into that of their foes beyond, we would certainly be attacked, and the blame would be laid at their doors by the Sultan. At Asni we had been informed by the ex-Sheïkh—the one whom Thomson had found in prison—that the Aït Mîzán was up in arms, and that at Tashdîrt there had been fatal fighting that very day. Being out of office now, he was unable to prevent our running the risk, though two of the three Jewish guides we had engaged failed to put in an appearance in spite of heavy pay contracted for. The one, Makhlûf el Ḳabli el Kharráz of Asni, who did come, proved a most excellent fellow, though utterly cowed before natives. He and others served at a peseta (8d.) a day and their food, with a *favor* at parting, according to merit.

Scenery in the Atlas.

Arriving at Aṛromd during the afternoon of a splendid day, which we had richly enjoyed as we wound along the valley through successive regions of vegetation, we were thankful to find a decent room without trouble.* Soon after we had

* The entrance to our lodging is seen in the lower portion of the illustration on p. 25 of *The Moorish Empire*, where my second companion, Mr. Paton of the Southern Morocco Mission, is seen ascending the "stairs" to the high road passing level with our roof—behind the group of natives seated on the parapet. The standing figure in white is the Jew who had promised to take us to Tifnût.

quitted Asni we left behind us the olive and almond, and passing through the belt of prickly oak, gum-cistus and arbutus, reached the juniper and 'arár; and then the walnut region, beyond which the hill-sides are bare save for tufts of a horny scrub and grass which afford

NEARING THE SUMMIT.
Photograph by Dr. Rudduck.

subsistence for scattered herds of goats, sheep and cows. Not a horse or mule did we see, and very few donkeys. But on it all the sun shone, and the snow-streaked peaks before us, gleaming, glorious, fed sparkling rivulets which human hands diverted for the watering of narrow cultivated terraces wherever the valley widened. As for geological surroundings, Thomson felt assured that here is to be found the oldest part of the range, the nucleus of elevation, with its metamorphic and igneous rocks, and sedimentary formations east and west. The most abundant rocks, far more so here than in the valley of the Iminán, were porphyries and diorites in wonderful variety.

Troublesome Episodes.

Next morning, having engaged three guides with the promise of a dollar apiece if we reached the top of Tûbkál, we set off on our mules for Shimhárôsh, where those who mean to reach the summit should pitch their camp, if not as far as possible up the valley to the right; but this feat should not be attempted before midsummer, unless made over the snow. As we left the village we were stopped by an armed crowd demanding money. Riding ahead and inducing our men to follow, we hoped we were free, but as we dismounted at Shimhàrôsh seven of the men appeared with demands for a dollar apiece as guards and guides. This I flatly refused, declaring that if they turned us back they would have to suffer, but not another coin would I pay, and took the precaution of leaving cash and watch with a trusted servant in charge of the mules and provisions. Thrice on the way up they stopped us and tried their game without success, at one point demanding the cost of a sheep to sacrifice to the local saint. At last we attained Timlilt—a shoulder never before reached by Europeans, from which we saw that it would be impossible to make the summit that day, especially as clouds were falling and wind was rising: before we had finished a lunch assisted by mouthfuls of snow, it grew piercingly cold, so we regretfully turned. Straight up the valley before us stood Mount Wagan, also tempting untrodden ground.

Diplomacy Invoked.

Now came the time for diplomacy. While eating our meal near the shrine we were surrounded by a steadily increasing group of natives, armed with flint-locks and daggers, who surlily watched and commented on every movement, disappointed of their expected plunder. Seeing what must come, I engaged in friendly conversation with the few who spoke Arabic, one of whom kept the others informed by interpretation.

"Yes," I said, "they do malign you mountaineers on the plain: they describe you as cut-throats and thieves, inhospitable savages, but we were so convinced that this was only jealousy, that, as you see, we came among you unarmed,* and without even guards, relying on your good nature and unrivalled hospitality, and you will not, I am sure, allow any evil-disposed among you to prove the plainsmen right. All we have a fancy to do is to taste of yonder snows, and revel in the colder air which recalls our own northern homes, but of course the country is yours: we are but your guests, and if you refuse to admit us we cannot complain, though when you come to our land you shall go where you please."

Thus, with soft words, they were appeased, such exclamations as "Indeed, he is right!" "Certainly, certainly!" greeted any compliments paid. After things had smoothed down, we prepared to start. But while remounting, some of the by-standers, exasperated, came to blows with our men, and we were compelled to divide amongst them all apparently available cash, to the sum of two dollars, which, though paid into the hands of an

* It is never my practice to carry arms on my travels, relying rather on encountering good nature when prepared to show it, and I have not been disappointed. Of course I always carried little of value with me, and took care to make this known.

authorized guide, was speedily shared by all. Then we rode back disgusted. Only the appearance that evening of Ḥasan idd Manṣûr, the leading pro-government man—who had also been Hooker's guide—prevented our being further fleeced, and with his escort we were glad enough to retreat down the valley next day.

COUNCIL OF WAR BELOW ARROMD.

Photograph by Dr. Rudduck.

That night, however, our head man got lost on the hill-side, and although we put up for the night as soon as we missed him, we got no trace of him till the following morning, when we heard that he had passed down from Asni to Mulai Ibráhîm, a favourite shrine. Thence we subsequently learned that he had walked to Marrákesh, having been fairly scared by the mountains and mountaineers, thus earning the name by which we now know him, "the Jewess." Meanwhile, we made Tamgîst, the village before Tashdîrt in the Iminán valley, opposite Tizi-n-

Effect on a Moor.

Tamsûlt, the highest peak of the mass of which Likimt forms the southern end.

This time keeping our plans to ourselves, we engaged two guides besides our Jew, at a peseta each, at the moment of starting. After a four-and-a-half hours' climb those who led were stopped by a chasm, across which the summit is not to be reached without appliances, although it should be practicable from the south. Before descending, I cut out a huge chunk of snow, or rather conglomeration of hail, which I paid my guide to bring down in the hood of his cloak. What then was my disgust to see an hour later that he had taken it out because they all declared the wool kept it warm, and having pierced it, had slung it on a string in the sun! It took all my threats of no pay to get it wrapped up again, but as if for revenge, I found it after lunch in a bowl by the fire. Next day its ghost alone remained for our lemonade on the plains, and all we succeeded in bringing into Marrákesh was a piece the size of a walnut, a trophy of our attempt to climb "Miltsin."

Disappointed Again.

APPENDIX

"THE ACCOUNT OF THE VOYAGE ('PERIPLUS') OF HANNO, COMMANDER OF THE CARTHAGINIANS, ROUND THE PARTS OF LIBYA BEYOND THE PILLARS OF HERCULES, WHICH HE DEPOSITED IN THE TEMPLE OF SATURN AT CARTHAGE." *

IT was decreed by the Carthaginians about 500 B.C. that Hanno should undertake a voyage beyond the Pillars of Hercules to found there Liby-phœnician colonies. He sailed accordingly with sixty ships of fifty oars each, and a body of men and women to the number of 30,000, with provisions and other necessaries.

"When we had passed the Pillars on our way," recorded Hanno, "and had sailed beyond them for two days, we founded the first city, which we named Thymiatherion. Below it lay an extensive plain. Proceeding thence towards the west, we came to Soloeis, a promontory of Libya, a place thickly covered with trees, where we erected a temple to Neptune, and again proceeded for the space of half-a-day towards the east, until we arrived at a lake lying not far from the sea, filled with abundance of large reeds. Here elephants and a great number of other wild beasts were feeding. Having passed the lake about a day's sail, we founded cities near the sea, called Karikôn-Teikhos, Gytta, Akra, Melitta and Arambys. Thence we came to the great river Lixus, which flows from Libya. On its banks the Lixitæ, a shepherd tribe, were feeding flocks, amongst whom we continued some time on friendly terms. Beyond the Lixitæ dwelt the inhospitable Ethiopians, who pasture a wild country intersected by large mountains, from which they say the river Lixus flows. In the neighbourhood of the mountains lived the Troglodytæ, men of various appearances, whom the Lixitæ described as swifter than horses in running. Having procured interpreters from them, we coasted for two days along a desert country towards the south. Thence we proceeded towards the east the course of a day. Here we found in the recess of a certain bay a small island containing a circle of 5 stadia, where we settled a colony and called it Kernë. We judged from our voyage that this place lay in a direct line with Carthage; for the length of our voyage from Carthage to the Pillars was equal to that from the Pillars to Kernë.

* Revised from "*The Voyage of Hanno Translated, and accompanied with the Greek Text, explained from the accounts of Modern Travellers; Defended against the objections of Mr. Dodwell and other writers, and illustrated by maps from Ptolemy, D'Anville and Bougainville*, by THOMAS FALCONER, A.M., Fellow of C.C.C., Oxford. London MDCCXCVII."

"We then came to a lake which we reached by sailing up a large river called Khretes. This lake had three islands, larger then Kernë, from which proceeding a day's sail, we came to the extremity of the lake, that was overhung by large mountains, inhabited by savage men clothed in skins of wild beasts, who drove us away by throwing stones, and hindered us from landing. Sailing thence, we came to another river, that was large and broad, and full of crocodiles and river horses; whence turning back we came again to Kernë. Thence we sailed towards the south twelve days, coasting the shore, the whole of which is inhabited by Ethiopians, who would not await our approach, but fled from us. Their language was not intelligible even to the Lixitæ who were with us. Towards the last day we approached some large mountains covered with trees, the wood of which was sweet-scented and variegated. Having sailed by these mountains for two days, we came to an immense opening of the sea, on each side of which towards the continent was a plain; from which we saw by night fire arising at intervals in all directions, either more or less.

"Having taken in water there, we sailed forwards five days near the land, until we came to a large bay, which our interpreters informed us was called the Western Horn. In this was a large island, and in the island a salt-water lake, and in this another island, where, when we had landed, we could discover nothing in the day-time except trees, but in the night we saw many fires burning, and heard the sound of pipes, cymbals, drums, and confused shouts. We were then afraid, and our diviners ordered us to abandon the island. Sailing quickly away, we passed a country burning with fires and perfumes; and streams of fire supplied from it fell into the sea. The country was impassable because of the heat.

"We sailed quickly thence, being much terrified; and passing on for four days, we discovered at night a country full of fire. In the middle was a lofty fire, larger than the rest, which seemed to touch the stars. When day came we discovered it to be a large hill called the Chariot of the Gods. On the third day after our departure thence, having sailed by those streams of fire, we arrived at a bay called the Southern Horn, at the bottom of which lay an island like the former, having a lake, and in this another island full of savage people, the greater part of whom were women, whose bodies were hairy, and whom our interpreters called gorillas. Though we pursued the men, we could not seize any of them, but all fled from us, escaping over the precipices, and defending themselves with stones. Three women were, however, taken; but they attacked their conductors with their teeth and hands, and could not be prevailed on to accompany us. Having killed them, we flayed them, and brought their skins with us to Carthage. We did not sail farther on, our provisions failing us."

Thus far the famous narrative, a fragment which, brief as it is, has become the subject of volumes. It has been translated into many languages, and several times into English. The following comments, extracted from some of these, represent the views of various schools, and certainly add to its interest.*

"THE PERIPLUS OF HANNO, KING OF THE KARCHEDONIANS, CONCERNING THE LYBIAN PARTS OF THE EARTH BEYOND THE PILLARS OF HERAKLES, WHICH HE DEDICATED TO KRONOS, THE GREATEST GOD, AND TO ALL THE GODS DWELLING WITH HIM."†

"Some of the modern critics contend without any proof that the Periplus which has come down to us is a work, not of the Karchedonian Hannon, King of Karchedon, but of some other person. Others again, of different opinion, accept and affirm with ancient proof that this work is the genuine production of Hannon, which is indeed true. For Aristoteles of Kyrene also mentions it in the book 'About remarkable relations', speaking thus, 'It is said that all the parts beyond the Heracleian Straits burn, some constantly, some only during the night, as the Periplus of Hannon affirms.'"

From *Ancient Fragments of the Phœnician, Chaldean, Egyptian, Tyrian, Carthagenian, Indian, Persian, and other writers*,
By ISAAC PRESTON CORRY, Esq., Fellow of Caius, Cambridge.‡

"The Periplus of Hanno is an account of the earliest voyage of discovery extant... With respect to its age, Falconer agrees with Bougainville in referring it to the sixth century before the Christian Era... It may be sufficient, however, to remark that Thymiatherion the first of the colonies planted by Hanno, occupies a position very nearly, perhaps precisely the same with that of the present commercial city of Mogadore. The promontory of Soloeis corresponds with Cape Bojador nearly opposite to the Canaries. Karikón-Teikhos, Gytta, Akra, Melitta and Arambys are placed between Cape Bojador and the Rio D'Ouro which is supposed to be the Lixus. Kernë is laid down as the island of Arguin under the southern Cape Blanco; the river Khretes is perhaps the St. John, and the next large river mentioned is the Senegal. Cape Palmas and Cape Three Points are supposed to correspond respectively with the Western and Southern Horns, and some island in the Bight of Benin with that of Gorillae. Vossius, however, supposes the Western Horn to be Cape Verde, and the Southern Cape Palmas, in which case Sierra Leone will answer to the Okherma Theon, the Chariot of the Gods."

* See also Appendix to *The Moorish Empire*.

† London, Trübner, 1864: *Extract from Prolegomena*, p. 145.

‡ London, 1832. Introductory Dissertation, pp. xxvii—xxix.

From the *Foreign Quarterly Review*—July, 1834.

"Hanno drew up an account of his voyage, which was hung up in the temple of Saturn (Moloch) at Carthage; it was translated by some Greek, and this translation or abridgment has come down to us, and may be seen in the *Geographi Minores* of Hudson. It is quite manifest from it that Hanno sailed a long way along the coast of the negro country, but where his voyage terminated is a question that will perhaps never be adequately solved. Rennell thinks the utmost limit of it was Sherborough Sound; while Professor Lelewel, who follows Gosselin, calculates that it could not have been beyond Cape Bojador. Heeren agrees with Rennell, and so does Mr. Cooley, and we have no doubt but that they are right; for Herodotus (iv. 196) accurately describes the mode in which the Carthaginians traded for gold with a people on the coast of Africa, which is precisely the manner in which, at this very day, the caravans from Morocco carry on the *dumb trade* with the people of Guinea for gold dust and other articles."

From *The Phenix—a collection of Old and Rare Fragments*. New York, 1835. (From *The Spirit of Laws*, by the BARON DE MONTESQUIEU.)

"The relation of Hanno's voyage is a fine fragment of antiquity. It was written by the very man that performed it. His recital is not mingled with ostentation. Great commanders write their actions with simplicity because they receive more glory from facts than from words.

"The style is agreeable to the subject; he deals not in the marvellous; all he says of the climate, the soil, the behaviour, the manners of the inhabitants, correspond with what is every day seen on the coast of Africa; one would imagine it the journal of a modern sailor...

"This narration is so much the more valuable, as it is a monument of Punic antiquity, and from hence alone it has been regarded as fabulous; for the Romans retained their hatred of the Carthaginians even after they had destroyed them...

"Some moderns have imbibed these prejudices. 'What is become,' say they, 'of the cities described by Hanno, of which even in Pliny's time there remained no vestiges?' But it would have been a wonder indeed if any such vestiges remained. Was it a Corinth or Athens that Hanno built on these coasts? He left Carthaginian families in such places as were most commodious for trade, and secured them as well as his hurry would permit against savages and wild beasts. The calamities of the Carthaginians put an end to the navigation of Africa; these families must necessarily, then, either perish or become savages... We find, however, in Scylax and Polybius, that the Carthaginians had considerable settlements on this coast. These are the vestiges of the cities of Hanno: there are no other for the same reason that there are no other of Carthage itself."

INDEX OF PLACES

INDEX OF PERSONS

CPSIA information can be obtained
at www.ICGtesting.com
Printed in the USA
LVHW020835050522
717833LV00003B/58

9 781375 578721